PROJECT
FINANCING

WILEY FRONTIERS IN FINANCE

PROJECT FINANCING
Asset-Based Financial Engineering

John D. Finnerty, Ph.D.

JOHN WILEY & SONS, INC.

New York • Chichester • Brisbane • Toronto • Singapore • Weinheim

Copyright © 1996 by John D. Finnerty.
Published by John Wiley & Sons, Inc.

Library of Congress Cataloging-in-Publication Data:

Finnerty, John D.
    Project financing : asset-based financial engineering / John D.
    Finnerty.
        p.   cm. — (Wiley frontiers in finance)
    Includes bibliographical references and index.
    ISBN 0-471-14631-5 (cloth : alk. paper)
    1. Capital investments.   2. Capital investments—Case studies.
    3. Corporations—Finance—Case studies.   4. Financial engineering.
    I. Title.   II. Series.
    HG4028.C4F488   1996
    658.15—dc20   96-26913

Printed in the United States of America

10 9 8 7 6 5 4 3 2 1

To my son,
William Patrick Taylor Finnerty

Preface

project finance has intrigued me ever since I was introduced to it as an associate at Morgan Stanley & Co. Many years, and several other books, got in the way of writing this one. But my experience in project finance, both as an investment banker, currently at Houlihan Lokey Howard & Zukin, and as a professor of finance at Fordham University, has given me ample opportunity to crystallize my thinking on the subject.

Project financing is a well-established technique for large capital intensive projects. Its origins can be traced to the thirteenth century when the English Crown negotiated a loan from the Frescobaldi, one of the leading merchant bankers of the period, to develop the Devon silver mines. They crafted a loan arrangement much like what we would call a production payment loan today.

A great variety of investments have since been project financed, including pipelines, refineries, electric power generating facilities, hydroelectric projects, dock facilities, mines, mineral processing facilities, and many others. Indeed project finance experienced a resurgence in the 1980s when it was used frequently to finance cogeneration and other forms of power production. Project finance holds great promise, which is just beginning to be realized in the 1990s, as a means of financing projects designed to help meet the enormous infrastructure needs that exist in the developed countries and especially in the emerging markets.

I wrote this book with both practitioners and students of finance in mind. For practitioners, project financing can provide a cost-effective means of raising funds. Sponsors should carefully consider using it whenever a project is capable of standing on its own as a separate economic entity. In this book, I describe the types of capital investments for which project financing is suitable and explain how to engineer the financing arrangements that support it. Because of project financing's enormous practical value, students of finance would be wise to learn about it so they can include it in their financing skill set.

The audience for this book includes:

- Financial managers who are responsible for arranging financing for their companies' projects.
- Government officials who are wondering how to finance their wish lists of infrastructure projects.
- Investment bankers and commercial bankers who assist companies in raising funds for large capital intensive projects.
- Accountants, consultants, lawyers, and other professionals who work in the corporate finance area and wish to keep up-to-date.
- Investors who are considering committing funds to limited-purpose companies or to mutual funds that have been set up to invest in infrastructure projects in the emerging markets.
- MBA students and executive MBA students studying corporate finance.
- Students of finance who wish to be fully knowledgeable concerning the techniques modern financiers are using to finance large-scale projects.

The first two chapters describe project financing and the circumstances in which it is most likely to be advantageous. Project financing involves financing projects on a stand-alone basis, so particular attention must be paid to who bears the risks and who reaps the rewards. Chapter 3 explains how to identify the various risks associated with a project and Chapter 4 describes how to craft contractual arrangements to allocate these risks and the project's economic rewards among the interested parties. Chapter 5 discusses the legal, tax, and other issues that must be considered when selecting the legal structure for a project. Chapters 6 through 9 deal with financial issues: preparing a financing plan, performing discounted cash flow analysis, using the techniques of discounted cash flow analysis to evaluate a project's profitability, and raising the funds to invest in a project. Chapter 10 reviews the issues a host government faces when private entities will finance the project. This material is particularly relevant to infrastructure projects in emerging markets because the capital requirements are often well beyond the capacity of the local government to meet them on its own. Chapters 11 through 14 contain case studies that illustrate how the concepts discussed in the earlier chapters have been put into practice in four prominent projects. Finally, Chapter 15 provides some concluding thoughts on the direction in which project financing seems to be headed.

ACKNOWLEDGMENTS

I would like to express my gratitude to those who helped me with the preparation of this book. Thanks to my former colleagues at Morgan Stanley & Co. and Lazard Frères & Co. and my current colleagues at Houlihan Lokey Howard & Zukin for many informative discussions concerning project finance and about "what really makes it work." I am also grateful for the insights I have gained through numerous discussions with Zoltan Merszei, President of Thyssen Henschel America and former Chairman, President, and CEO of Dow Chemical Company, concerning the application of project financing to infrastructure investment, such as high-speed rail projects.

Special thanks go to Myles C. Thompson, Executive Editor in the Professional & Trade Division of John Wiley & Sons, who encouraged me to write the book; Jacque Urinyi, Associate Editor, who expertly managed the development process; Mary Daniello, Associate Managing Editor, and Nancy Marcus Land of Publications Development Company, who turned the final manuscript into a finished product.

I am also grateful to Lawrence A. Darby, III, Esq., and Stephen B. Land, Esq., partners of Howard, Darby & Levin. Larry is an experienced hand at project finance and provided many helpful suggestions, and Steve made sure I got the tax discussion right. Thanks too to my most recent graduate assistants at Fordham's Graduate School of Business, Ezra Y. Rosensaft and Barie-Lynne Dolby. (They are engaged. If nothing else, this book appears to have stimulated at least one romance!) Also, I would like to thank Cecilia Rueda, who cheerfully typed and proofread several drafts of the manuscript.

Finally, thanks to my wife, Louise for her patience and understanding while I took time away from our family to write. I hope that she and William are pleased with the result.

JOHN D. FINNERTY

New York, New York
August 1996

Contents

1

Introduction

Project financing can be arranged when a particular facility or a related set of assets is capable of functioning profitably as an independent economic unit. The sponsor(s) of such a unit may find it advantageous to form a new legal entity to construct, own, and operate the project. If sufficient profit is predicted, the project company can finance construction of the project on a *project basis*, which involves the issuance of equity securities (generally to the sponsors of the project) and of debt securities that are designed to be self-liquidating from the revenues derived from project operations.

Although project financings have certain common features, financing on a project basis necessarily involves tailoring the financing package to the circumstances of a particular project. Expert financial engineering is often just as critical to the success of a large project as are the traditional forms of engineering.

Project financing is a well-established financing technique. Chen, Kensinger, and Martin (1989) documented more than $23 billion worth of project financings between the first quarter of 1987 and the third quarter of 1989. They identified 168 projects financed on this basis, including 102 involving cogeneration and other forms of power production. Looking forward, the United States and many other countries face enormous infrastructure financing requirements (*Financing the Future*, 1993; Chrisney, 1995). Project financing is a technique that could be applied to many of these projects (Forrester, Kravitt, and Rosenberg, 1994).

WHAT IS PROJECT FINANCING?

Project financing may be defined as the raising of funds to finance an economically separable capital investment project in which the providers of the funds look primarily to the cash flow from the project as the source of funds to service their loans and provide the return of and a return on their equity invested in the project.[1] The terms of the debt and equity securities are tailored to the cash flow characteristics of the project. For their security, the project debt securities depend, at least partly, on the profitability of the project and on the collateral value of the project's assets. Assets that have been financed on a project basis include pipelines, refineries, electric generating facilities, hydroelectric projects, dock facilities, mines, and mineral processing facilities.

Project financings typically include the following basic features:

1. An agreement by financially responsible parties to complete the project and, toward that end, to make available to the project all funds necessary to achieve completion.
2. An agreement by financially responsible parties (typically taking the form of a contract for the purchase of project output) that, when project completion occurs and operations commence, the project will have available sufficient cash to enable it to meet all its operating expenses and debt service requirements, even if the project fails to perform on account of force majeure or for any other reason.
3. Assurances by financially responsible parties that, in the event a disruption in operation occurs and funds are required to restore the project to operating condition, the necessary funds will be made available through insurance recoveries, advances against future deliveries, or some other means.

Project financing should be distinguished from conventional direct financing, or what may be termed financing on a firm's general credit. In connection with a conventional direct financing, lenders to the firm look to the firm's entire asset portfolio to generate the cash flow to service their loans. The assets and their financing are integrated into the firm's asset and liability portfolios. Often, such loans are not secured by any pledge of collateral. The critical distinguishing feature of a project financing is that the project is a distinct legal entity; project assets, project-related contracts, and project cash flow are segregated to a substantial degree from the sponsoring entity. The financing structure is designed to allocate financial returns and risks more efficiently than a conventional financing structure. In a project financing, the sponsors provide, at most, limited recourse to cash flows from their other assets that are not part of the project. Also, they typically pledge the project assets, but none of their other assets, to secure the project loans.

The term *project financing* is widely misused and perhaps even more widely misunderstood. To clarify the definition, it is important to appreciate what the term does *not* mean. Project financing is *not* a means of raising funds to finance a project that is so weak economically that it may not be able to service its debt or provide an acceptable rate of return to equity investors. In other words, it is *not* a means of financing a project that cannot be financed on a conventional basis.

A project financing requires careful financial engineering to allocate the risks and rewards among the involved parties in a manner that is mutually acceptable. Figure 1.1 illustrates the basic elements in a capital investment that is financed on a project basis.

At the center is a discrete asset, a separate facility, or a related set of assets that has a specific purpose. Often, this purpose is related to

FIGURE 1.1　The Basic Elements of a Project Financing

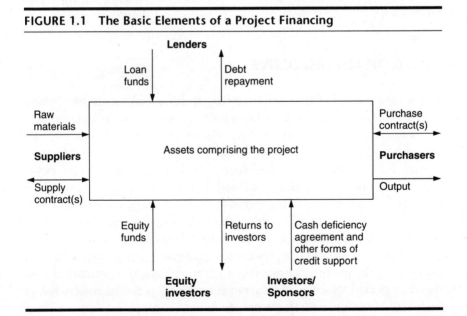

raw materials acquisition, production, processing, or delivery. More recently, this asset is a power-generating station, toll road, or some other item of infrastructure. As already noted, this facility or group of assets must be capable of standing alone as an independent economic unit. The operations, supported by a variety of contractual arrangements, must be organized so that the project has the unquestioned ability to generate sufficient cash flow to repay its debts.

A project must include all the facilities that are necessary to constitute an economically independent, viable operating entity. For example, a project cannot be an integral part of another facility. If the project will rely on any assets owned by others for any stage in its operating cycle, the project's unconditional access to these facilities must be assured at all times, regardless of events.

Project financing can be beneficial to a company with a proposed project when (1) the project's output would be in such strong demand that purchasers would be willing to enter into long-term purchase contracts and (2) the contracts would have strong enough provisions that banks would be willing to advance funds to finance construction on the basis of the contracts. For example, project financing can be advantageous to a developing country when it has a valuable resource deposit, other responsible parties would like to develop the deposit, and the host country lacks the financial resources to proceed with the project on its own.

A HISTORICAL PERSPECTIVE

Project financing is not a new financing technique. Venture-by-venture financing of finite-life projects has a long history; it was, in fact, the rule in commerce until the 17th century. For example, in 1299—nearly 700 years ago—the English Crown negotiated a loan from the Frescobaldi (a leading Italian merchant bank of that period) to develop the Devon silver mines.[2] The loan contract provided that the lender would be entitled to control the operation of the mines for one year. The lender could take as much unrefined ore as it could extract during that year, but it had to pay all costs of operating the mines. There was no provision for interest.[3] The English Crown did not provide any guarantees (nor did anyone else) concerning the quantity or quality of silver that could be extracted during that period. Such a loan arrangement was a forebear of what is known today as a *production payment loan*.[4]

Recent Uses of Project Financing

Project financing has long been used to fund large-scale natural resource projects. (Appendix B provides thumbnail sketches of several noteworthy project financings, including a variety of natural resource projects.) One of the more notable of these projects is the Trans Alaska Pipeline System (TAPS) Project, which was developed between 1969 and 1977. TAPS was a joint venture of eight of the world's largest oil companies. It involved the construction of an 800-mile pipeline, at a cost of $7.7 billion, to transport crude oil and natural gas liquids from the North Slope of Alaska to the port of Valdez in southern Alaska. TAPS involved a greater capital commitment than all the other pipelines previously built in the continental United States combined. Phillips, Groth, and Richards (1979) describe Sohio's experience in arranging financing to cover its share of the capital cost of TAPS.

More recently, in 1988, five major oil and gas companies formed Hibernia Oil Field Partners to develop a major oil field off the coast of Newfoundland. The projected capital cost was originally $4.1 billion. Production of 110,000 barrels of oil per day was initially projected to start in 1995. It is currently expected to commence in 1997. Production is expected to last between 16 and 20 years. The Hibernia Oil Field Project is a good example of public sector–private sector cooperation to finance a large project. (Public–private partnerships are discussed in Chapter 10.)

The Impact of PURPA

Project financing in the United States was given a boost in 1978 with passage of the Public Utility Regulatory Policy Act ("PURPA"). Under PURPA, local electric utility companies are required to purchase all the electric output of qualified independent power producers under long-term contracts. The purchase price for the electricity must equal the electric utility's "avoided cost"—that is, its marginal cost—of generating electricity. This provision of PURPA established a foundation for long-term contractual obligations sufficiently strong to support nonrecourse project financing to fund construction costs. The growth of the independent power industry in the United States can be attributed directly to passage of PURPA. For example, roughly half of all power production that came into commercial operation during 1990 came from projects developed under the PURPA regulations.

Innovations in Project Financing

Project financing for manufacturing facilities is another area in which project financing has recently begun to develop. In 1988, General Electric Capital Corporation (GECC) announced that it would expand its project finance group to specialize in financing the construction and operation of industrial facilities. It initiated this effort by providing $105 million of limited-recourse project financing for Bev-Pak Inc. to build a beverage container plant in Monticello, Indiana.[5] The plant was owned independently; no beverage producers held ownership stakes. Upon completion, the plant had two state-of-the-art production lines with a combined capacity of 3,200 steel beverage cans per minute. A third production line, added in October 1989, expanded Bev-Pak's capacity to 2 billion cans per year. This output represented about 40 percent of the total steel beverage can output in the United States. Bev-Pak arranged contracts with Coca-Cola and PepsiCo to supply as much as 20 percent of their can requirements. It also arranged a contract with Miller Brewing Company. Bev-Pak enjoyed a competitive advantage: its state-of-the-art automation enabled it to sell its tin-plated steel cans at a lower price than aluminum cans.[6] Moreover, to reduce its economic risk, Bev-Pak retained the flexibility to switch to aluminum can production if the price of aluminum cans were to drop.

Financing a large, highly automated plant involves uncertainty about whether the plant will be able to operate at full capacity. Independent ownership enables the plant to enter into arm's-length agreements to supply competing beverage makers. It thus diversifies its operating risk; it is not dependent on any single brand's success. Moreover, because of economies of scale, entering into a long-term purchase agreement for a portion of the output from a large-scale plant is more cost-effective than building a smaller plant in house. Finally, long-term contracts with creditworthy entities furnish the credit strength that supports project financing.

Infrastructure is another area ripe for innovation. Chapter 10 discusses the formation of public–private "partnerships" to finance generating stations, transportation facilities, and other infrastructure projects. Governments and multilateral agencies have recognized the need to attract private financing for such projects (see Chrisney, 1995; Ferreira, 1995). Chapter 12 describes how private financing was arranged for two toll roads in Mexico. In the past, projects of this type have been financed by the public sector.

REQUIREMENTS FOR PROJECT FINANCING

A project has no operating history at the time of the initial debt financing. Consequently, its creditworthiness depends on the project's anticipated profitability and on the indirect credit support provided by third parties through various contractual arrangements. As a result, lenders require assurances that (1) the project will be placed into service, and (2) once operations begin, the project will constitute an economically viable undertaking. The availability of funds to a project will depend on the sponsor's ability to convince providers of funds that the project is technically feasible and economically viable.

Technical Feasibility

Lenders must be satisfied that the technological processes to be used in the project are feasible for commercial application on the scale contemplated. In brief, providers of funds need assurance that the project will generate output at its design capacity. The technical feasibility of conventional facilities, such as pipelines and electric power generating plants, is generally accepted. But technical feasibility has been a significant concern in such projects as Arctic pipelines, large-scale natural gas liquefaction and transportation facilities, and coal gasification plants. Lenders generally require verifying opinions from independent engineering consultants, particularly if the project will involve unproven technology, unusual environmental conditions, or very large scale.

Economic Viability

The ability of a project to operate successfully and generate a cash flow is of paramount concern to prospective lenders. These providers of funds must be satisfied that the project will generate sufficient cash flow to service project debt *and* pay an acceptable rate of return to equity investors. There must be a clear, long-term need for the project's output, and the project must be able to deliver its products (or services) to the marketplace profitably. Therefore, the project must be able to produce at a cost-to-market price that will generate funds sufficient to cover all operating costs and debt service while still providing an acceptable return on the equity invested in the project. Project economics must be sufficiently robust to keep the project profitable in the face of adverse developments, such as escalation in construction cost; delays in construction or in the start-up of operations; increases in interest rates; or fluctuations in production levels, prices, and operating costs.

Availability of Raw Materials and Capable Management

Natural resources, raw materials, and the other factors of production that are required for successful operation must be available in the quantities needed for the project to operate at its design capacity over its entire life. To satisfy lenders, (1) the quantities of raw materials dedicated to the project must enable it to produce and sell an amount of output that ensures servicing of the project debt in a timely manner; (2) unless the project entity directly owns its raw materials supply, adequate supplies of these inputs must be dedicated to the project under long-term contracts; and (3) the term of the contracts with suppliers cannot be shorter than the term of the project debt. The useful economic life of a project is often constrained by the quantity of natural resources available to it. For example, the economic life of a pipeline serving a single oil field cannot exceed the economic life of the field, regardless of the physical life of the pipeline.

The project entity must have capable and experienced management. Many project sponsors enter into management contracts with engineering firms to ensure that skilled operating personnel are available. The sponsors of the Indiantown Cogeneration Project, discussed in Chapter 11, negotiated a management services agreement with an experienced operator of electric power generating plants.

APPROPRIATENESS OF PROJECT FINANCING

The ideal candidates for project financing are capital investment projects that (1) are capable of functioning as independent economic units, (2) can be completed without undue uncertainty, and (3) when completed, will be worth demonstrably more than they cost to complete.

In determining whether project financing might be an appropriate method of raising funds for a particular project, at least five factors should be considered:

1. The credit requirements of the lenders in light of both the expected profitability of the project and the indirect credit support to be provided by third parties;

2. The tax implications of the proposed allocation of the project tax benefits among the parties involved;
3. The impact of the project on the covenants contained in the agreements governing the sponsors' existing debt obligations;
4. The legal or regulatory requirements the project must satisfy;
5. The accounting treatment of project liabilities and contractual agreements.

These factors are discussed later in the book.

Risk Sharing

Often, the risks associated with a project are so great that it would not be prudent for a single party to bear them alone. Project financing permits the sharing of operating and financial risks among the various interested parties, and it does so in a more flexible manner than financing on the sponsors' general credit. Risk sharing is advantageous when economic, technical, environmental, or regulatory risks are of such magnitude that it would be impractical or imprudent for a single party to undertake them. A financing structure that facilitates multiple ownership and risk sharing is particularly attractive for projects such as electric power generating plants, where significant economies of scale are possible and the project will provide benefits to several parties.

Chapter 3 discusses the various risks involved in a project financing. Chapter 4 explains how contractual arrangements can be designed to allocate those risks among the parties involved with the project.

Expansion of the Sponsors' Debt Capacity

Financing on a project basis can expand the debt capacity of the project sponsors. First, it is often possible to structure a project so that the project debt is not a direct obligation of the sponsors and does not appear on the face of the sponsors' balance sheets. (Footnote disclosure is normally required if a sponsor's project-related debt obligations are material in relation to its overall financial position.) In addition, the sponsors' contractual obligations with respect to the project may not come within the definition of indebtedness for the purpose of debt limitations contained in the sponsors' bond indentures or note agreements.

Second, because of the contractual arrangements that provide credit support for project borrowings, the project company may be able to achieve significantly higher financial leverage than the sponsor would feel comfortable with if it financed the project entirely on its own balance sheet. The amount of leverage a project can achieve depends on the project's profitability, the nature and magnitude of project risks, the strength of the project's security arrangements, and the creditworthiness of the parties committed under those security arrangements.

AN EXAMPLE

A hypothetical cogeneration project (hereafter referred to as the Cogeneration Project) can be used to illustrate the basic elements of a project financing. In recent years, project financing has been used to finance many cogeneration facilities. Chen, Kensinger, and Martin (1989) estimate that more than $9 billion of project financings for cogeneration projects were announced between January 1, 1987, and October 13, 1989, making them by far the largest single category of project financings during this period. Such companies as Boise Cascade, DuPont, Exxon, and Southern California Edison have been involved in cogeneration projects.

Cogeneration involves the production of steam, which is used sequentially to generate electricity and to provide heat. In this sense, the two forms of energy, electricity and heat, are *cogenerated*. The owners of the cogeneration facility may use some of the electricity themselves; they can sell the rest to the local electric utility company. The leftover heat from the steam has a number of possible commercial uses, such as process steam for a chemical plant, for enhanced oil recovery, or for heating buildings. The Indiantown Cogeneration Project, discussed in Chapter 11, sells its leftover steam to a wholesale citrus juice processor.

As noted earlier, passage of PURPA gave cogeneration a boost. PURPA requires regulated electric utility companies to purchase the electric power produced by qualified independent power producers, which include cogeneration facilities. It also requires the electric utility companies to supply backup electricity to the cogeneration facilities (e.g., during periods when the cogeneration facilities are closed for maintenance) at nondiscriminatory prices (see Chen, Kensinger, and Martin, 1989). PURPA also exempts a qualified cogeneration project from rate-of-return regulation as a "public utility,"[7] thereby enabling sponsors of cogeneration facilities to benefit from the cost savings that cogeneration achieves. The profitability of these projects and the valuable credit support provided by the contractual arrangements with local electric utility companies have made it possible to finance many of these cogeneration projects independently, regardless of their sponsors' creditworthiness.

The Project

Engineering Firm has proposed to Chemical Company that it design and build a Cogeneration Project at Chemical Company's plant in New Jersey.

The Project Sponsor

Engineering Firm has considerable experience in designing and managing the construction of energy facilities. The market for engineering services is very competitive. Engineering Firm has found that its willingness to make an equity investment, to assist in arranging the balance of the financing, and to assume some of the responsibility for operating the project following completion of construction, can enhance its chances of winning the mandate to design and oversee construction of a cogeneration project. Nevertheless, Engineering Firm's basic business is engineering, and its capital resources are limited. Accordingly, it is anxious to keep its investments "small," and it is unwilling to accept any credit exposure. However, it is willing to commit to construction of the facility under a fixed-price turnkey contract, which would be backed up by a performance bond to ensure completion according to specifications.

The Industrial User

Chemical Company's plant began commercial operation in 1954. Two aged, gas-fired steam boilers produce the process steam used in the chemical manufacturing process at the plant. Local Utility currently supplies the plant's electricity.

Engineering Firm has suggested building a Cogeneration Project to replace the two boilers. The new facility would consist of new gas-fired boilers and turbine-generator equipment to produce electricity. The Cogeneration Project would use the steam produced by the gas-fired boilers to generate electricity. It would sell to Local Utility whatever electricity the plant did not need. It would sell all the waste steam to Chemical Company for use as process steam and would charge a price significantly below Chemical Company's current cost of producing process steam at the plant.

Chemical Company is willing to enter into a steam purchase agreement. But it will not agree to a term exceeding 15 years, nor will it invest any of its own funds or take any responsibility for arranging financing for the facility. Chemical Company is insistent that the steam purchase contract must obligate it to purchase only the steam that is actually supplied to its plant.[8]

The Local Utility

Local Utility is an investor-owned utility company. It provides both gas and electricity to its customers, including Chemical Company. Local Utility has stated publicly that it is willing to enter into long-term electric power purchase agreements and long-term gas supply agreements with qualified cogenerators. It has also formed an unregulated subsidiary for the express purpose of making equity investments in PURPA-qualified independent power projects. Its regulators have authorized it to make such investments, provided Local Utility owns no more than 50 percent of any single project.

Local Utility has informed Engineering Firm that it is in support of the Cogeneration Project. It is willing to enter into a 15-year electric power purchase agreement and a 15-year gas supply agreement. Local Utility has committed to accepting a provision in the gas supply agreement that would tie the price of gas to the price of electricity: The price of gas will escalate (or de-escalate) annually at the same rate as the price Local Utility pays for electricity from the Cogeneration Project. Local Utility is willing to invest up to 50 percent of the project entity's equity and to serve as the operator of the facility. However, it is not willing to bear any direct responsibility for repaying project debt. Local Utility would include the facility's electricity output in its base load generating capability. A 15-year inflation-indexed (but otherwise fixed-price) operating contract is acceptable to Local Utility. The contract would specify the operating charges for the first full year of operations. The operating charges would increase thereafter to match changes in the producer price index (PPI). These charges would represent only a relatively small percentage of the Cogeneration Project's total operating costs. Because such facilities are simple to operate, the completed Cogeneration Project will require only a dozen full-time personnel to operate and maintain it.

Outside Financing Sources

The balance of the equity and all of the long-term debt for the project will have to be arranged from passive sources, principally institutional equity investors and institutional lenders. The equity funds will have to be invested before the long-term lenders will fund their loans. The passive equity investors will undoubtedly expect Local Utility to invest its equity before they invest their funds. The strength of the electric power purchase and gas supply agreements will determine how much debt the Cogeneration Project will be capable of supporting. The availability of the tax benefits of ownership, as well as the anticipated profitability of the project, will determine how much outside equity can be raised for the project.

Use of the Example

In subsequent chapters, I will develop the basic concepts that pertain to project financing. I will then apply them to the Cogeneration Project, which will serve as an ongoing illustration.

CONCLUSION

Project financing involves raising funds to finance an economically separable capital investment project by issuing securities (or incurring bank borrowings) that are designed to be serviced and redeemed exclusively out of project cash flow. The terms of the debt and equity securities are tailored to the characteristics of the project. For their security, the project debt securities depend, at least partly, on the profitability of the project and on the collateral value of the project's assets. Depending on the project's profitability and on the proportion of debt financing desired, additional sources of credit support may be required (as described later in this book). A project financing requires careful financial engineering to achieve a mutually acceptable allocation of the risks and rewards among the various parties involved in a project.

2

The Rationale for Project Financing

S everal studies have explored the rationale for project financing.[1] These studies have generally analyzed the issue from the following perspective. When a firm is contemplating a capital investment project, three interrelated questions arise:

1. Should the firm undertake the project as part of its overall asset portfolio and finance the project on its general credit, or should the firm form a separate legal entity to undertake the project?[2]
2. What amount of debt should the separate legal entity incur?
3. How should the debt contract be structured—that is, what degree of recourse to the project sponsors should lenders be permitted?

PRIOR STUDIES' EXPLANATIONS

The finance literature on the subject of project financing is still in its formative stages. Careful analyses of the true benefits of project financing have only recently begun to appear. Shah and Thakor (1987) were among the first to provide a carefully thought-out analysis of the rationale for project financing. They explained why project financing seems most appropriate for very large, high-risk projects. Unfortunately, their analysis was based on only two projects.[3] Chen, Kensinger, and Martin (1989) observed that project financing is widely used for medium-size, low-risk projects, such as cogeneration facilities. They documented that project financing has become the dominant method of financing independent electric power generating facilities, including cogeneration projects developed for several Fortune 500 companies. At best, then, Shah and Thakor's theory appears incomplete.

Mao (1982) noted that in order for a project to secure financing as a separate economic entity, the relationships among the participants must be spelled out in detailed contracts.[4] Worenklein (1981) addressed the project's requirement for "sources of credit support" in the form of contracts to purchase output from the project and/or to supply the necessary inputs at controlled cost. The project's sponsors typically do not guarantee repayment of the project's debt, so creditworthy parties must provide credit support through such contractual undertakings.

THE NEED FOR CONTRACTS

One theme is clear. Project financing arrangements invariably involve strong contractual relationships among multiple parties. Project financing can only work for those projects that can establish such relationships and maintain them at a tolerable cost. To arrange a project financing, there must be a genuine "community of interest" among the parties involved in the project. Only if it is in each party's best interest for the project financing to succeed will all parties do everything they can to make sure that it does. For experienced practitioners, the acid test of soundness for a proposed project financing is whether all parties can reasonably expect to benefit under the proposed financing arrangement. To achieve a successful project financing arrangement, therefore, the financial engineer must design a financing structure—and embody that structure in a set of contracts—that will enable each of the parties to gain from the arrangement.

It seems unlikely that a single theory is capable of fully explaining the rationale for every project financing. Nevertheless, a brief review of the various explanations of the rationale for project financing can provide valuable insights. This review will also serve as a useful backdrop for our discussion of project financing in the remainder of the book.

THE ADVANTAGES OF SEPARATE INCORPORATION

Chemmanur and John (1992) have developed a rationale for project financing based on the benefits of corporate control. In their analysis, a firm's manager/owners derive, from being in control, benefits that they cannot contract away to other security holders. When the firm undertakes multiple projects its organizational structure and its financial structure both affect the owners' ability to remain in control. *Control benefits* include the owners' discretion to reinvest free cash flow in projects of their own choosing, their ability to pay themselves high salaries and perquisites, and their freedom to make other corporate decisions that might benefit their self-interest at the expense of lenders or shareholders. Chemmanur and John's model of the interrelationships among corporate ownership structure, organizational structure, and financial structure leads to interesting implications concerning (1) conditions under which it is optimal to incorporate a project as a separate legal entity; (2) the optimal amount of debt financing for a project, how to structure the debt contract (i.e., straight debt or limited-recourse debt), and how to allocate debt across a portfolio of projects; and (3) conditions under which limited-recourse project financing is the optimal financing technique for a project.

Special Form of Organization

Choosing project financing over conventional direct financing involves choosing an organizational form that differs from the traditional corporation in two fundamental respects:

1. The project has a finite-life. Therefore, so does the legal entity that owns it. That entity's identity is defined by the project. In contrast, a traditional corporation does not have a limited life.
2. The project entity distributes the cash flows from the project directly to project lenders and to project equity investors. In a traditional corporation, corporate managers can retain the free cash flow from profitable projects and reinvest it in other projects of management's own choosing. In a true project financing, equity investors get the free cash flow and make the reinvestment decision themselves.

Main Results

Chemmanur and John's main results can be summarized as follows. First, if management can maintain control of all the projects it has under consideration when they are entirely equity-financed, it will not issue any debt. This enables managers to avoid having lenders who will monitor (and restrict) their activities. If management has comparable abilities (relative to potential rivals) in managing all the projects, then forming a single corporation to own all the projects will be the predominating tactic. If, on the other hand, management's relative abilities differ significantly across the projects, then it will be better to incorporate at least some of the projects separately and hire separate management to run them.

Second, if management cannot retain control of all the projects if they all are entirely equity-financed (i.e., due to limited internal cash), then it will finance the projects by issuing a combination of debt and equity. If management's relative abilities are comparable across the projects, and the structure of the control benefits is also similar, the projects will be owned by a single corporation and partly financed with corporate debt. If, on the other hand, management's control benefits differ significantly from one project to another (while its relative abilities to manage the projects remain similar), limited-recourse project financing will be optimal. Management will operate all the projects but use limited-recourse financing to limit its liability.

Third, when a firm must issue debt to maintain control, and management's relative abilities differ significantly across the various projects, it will be optimal to spin off one or more of the separate firms.[5] Shareholders will benefit if better managers take over a spun-off firm that was poorly managed.

Fourth, the optimal allocation of limited-recourse project debt across different projects depends on the structure of management's control benefits. In general, a project with smaller control benefits per dollar of total project value will have a higher proportion of debt financing. Managers have less to lose if the higher proportion of debt leads to tighter restrictions on their activities.

Fifth, when some of the projects are spun off, the optimal debt allocation is also affected by management's relative abilities across projects. Less well-managed firms are less able to support leverage.

COUNTERING THE UNDERINVESTMENT PROBLEM

The *underinvestment problem* arises when a firm has a highly leveraged capital structure. A firm with risky debt outstanding may have an incentive to forgo a capital investment project that would increase its total market value. If the business risk does not change, the firm's shareholders would have to share any increase in total market value with the firm's debtholders. The underinvestment problem involves a bias against low-risk projects. (See Emery and Finnerty, 1991, pp. 229–230.)

The Underinvestment Incentive

John and John (1991) have developed a model in which outstanding debt gives rise to an underinvestment incentive. They analyze how project financing arrangements can reduce this incentive, and they identify circumstances in which project financing is the optimal financing structure for a project. Their model builds on the prior work of Myers (1977), who argued that outstanding debt tends to distort a firm's capital investment choices. Risky (i.e., *not* free of default risk) debt can cause corporate managers to pass up positive-net-present-value projects in situations where the projects would operate to the benefit of debtholders but to the detriment of shareholders. For example, suppose that, without the project, the firm could not fully repay its debt under all possible scenarios. However, the project is sufficiently profitable that if the firm undertakes it, the debtholders are assured of being repaid in full. The debtholders would clearly benefit. But the firm's managers will only undertake the project if the firm's shareholders can expect to realize a positive net present value on their equity investment in the project—excluding whatever benefit the debtholders realize. Thus, a project might involve a positive net present value from the standpoint of the firm as a whole (i.e., debtholders and shareholders taken together) but a negative net present value from the narrower perspective of its shareholders. In that case, the firm's managers, who presumably operate the firm for the benefit of its shareholders, would decide not to invest in the project.

Passing up positive-net-present-value projects is not costless to the shareholders, however. Prospective lenders will demand a higher rate of return for their loans if they find the firm engaging in such behavior. The higher rate of return represents an agency cost. *Agency costs* arise out of the competing claims of shareholders and debtholders to corporate assets and cash flow. They occur because security holdings in large corporations are widely dispersed, and monitoring tends to be costly and therefore incomplete. For example, lenders can observe the firm's overall investment level but they generally do not have access to full information regarding specific capital investment projects. Project financing can alter that situation by enabling lenders to make their lending decisions on a project-by-project basis.

How Project Financing Can Counter This Bias

In John and John's model, each project can be financed separately. All debt is nonrecourse (although the conclusions would be equally valid if the debt were only limited-recourse). The economic interests of debtholders and shareholders become better aligned when financing is accomplished on a project basis. Debt is allocated between the project sponsor and the project entity in a value-maximizing manner. John and John compare project financing to straight debt financing entirely on the sponsor's balance sheet. Project financing increases value (1) by reducing agency costs (the underinvestment incentive is countered) and (2) by increasing the value of interest tax shields. Because more projects are financed, more debt is issued, and therefore more interest tax shields are created. Both factors enhance shareholder value.

REALLOCATING FREE CASH FLOW

In the traditional corporate form of organization, the board of directors determines how the free cash flow is allocated between distributions to investors and reinvestment. *Free cash flow* is what is left over after a company has paid all its costs of production, has paid its lenders, and has made any capital expenditures required to keep its production facilities in good working order. Generally, when a corporation decides to invest in a new project, cash flow from the existing portfolio of projects will fund the investment in the new one. Management has the option to roll over the existing portfolio's free cash flow into still newer ventures within the company later on—without necessarily exposing its decisions to the discipline of the capital market.[6] This discretion gives corporate management considerable power in determining the direction of the corporation. Whether this discretion is misapplied has become an important issue in the debate over shareholder rights.[7]

Free Cash Flow and Project Financing

Project financing can give investors control over free cash flow from the project. Typically, all free cash flow is distributed to the project's equity investors. As noted, because a project financing is specific to a particular pool of assets, the entity created to own and operate it has a finite life. Moreover, the project financing documents that govern the terms of the equity investments in the project typically spell out in writing the project entity's "dividend policy" over the life of the project.

Why Project Financing Can Be Beneficial

Jensen (1986a) developed the concept of the agency cost of free cash flow. Managers, when left to their own devices, may not be sufficiently demanding when comparing projects that can be financed internally with other projects that must be financed externally. Giving managers (or boards of directors, which are often dominated or controlled by the managers of the corporation) the discretion to reinvest free cash flow can result in a loss of shareholder value. Forcing the free cash flow to be dispersed exposes the managers of the corporation to the discipline of the capital market because investors control the uses to which the free cash flow will be put. Such a shift in control should enhance shareholder value.[8]

Project financing can be beneficial because direct ownership of assets places investors in control when the time comes to make reinvestment decisions. Giving investors control resolves potential conflicts of interest that can arise when management has discretion over reinvestment. With project financing, funding for the new project is negotiated with outside investors. As the project evolves, the capital is returned to the investors, who decide for themselves how to reinvest it.

REDUCING ASYMMETRIC INFORMATION AND SIGNALING COSTS

The form of security a firm chooses to issue when it decides to raise capital externally can have important signaling effects (Smith, 1986). Consider, for example, a decision to issue debt rather than equity. Debt requires fixed charges in the form of interest and principal payments. These payments are contractual obligations. In contrast, dividends are not contractual obligations. Issuing debt, rather than common stock, signals that the firm expects to generate sufficient cash flow to service the additional debt in a timely manner.

Shah and Thakor (1987) have argued that project financing reduces the signaling costs associated with raising capital under asymmetric information, particularly in the case of large-scale, high-risk projects. *Asymmetric information* occurs when managers have valuable information about a new project that they cannot communicate unambiguously to the capital market. When a company announces a new project and how it intends to finance it, the best investors can do is try to interpret what the announcement really signifies (e.g., whether the method of financing indicates how profitable the firm expects the project to be). If the information is technical and complex in nature, communicating it to the market would be costly. Processing this information would also be costly to prospective investors.[9]

There is a second potential barrier to communication. Valuable information about what makes an opportunity potentially profitable must be kept from competitors in order to maintain a competitive advantage. When managers have information that is not publicly available, raising funds for new investment opportunities may be difficult unless this information is revealed to the public.[10]

How Project Financing Can Solve the Communication Problem

Project financing provides a potential solution. Managers can reveal sufficient information about the project to a small group of investors and negotiate a fair price for the project entity's securities. In this way, the managers can obtain financing at a fair price without having to reveal proprietary information to the public. The danger of an information leak is small because the investors have a financial stake in maintaining confidentiality.

According to Shah and Thakor (1987), project financing is useful for projects that entail high informational asymmetry costs (e.g., large mineral exploration projects are often project financed). As Chen, Kensinger, and Martin (1989) note, Shah and Thakor's argument *does not explain* the use of project financing for low-risk projects that do not require the sponsor to hold back proprietary information.

Preserving Financial Flexibility

Chen, Kensinger, and Martin (1989) point out that corporate managers choose project financing for projects that entail low informational asymmetry costs (so-called *transparent projects*). By doing so, they preserve their flexibility to use internally generated funds to finance projects that are available to the firm but cannot be fully disclosed to the public without disclosing valuable proprietary information to competitors.[11]

Chen, Kensinger, and Martin's hypothesis is developed along the following lines. Suppose that a firm has (1) an opportunity to invest in a transparent project and (2) other investment opportunities about which management has important information that it is unwilling to make available to competitors or the general public. It would be advisable for the firm to reserve its internally generated cash flow to fund these opportunities (see Myers and Majluf, 1984). All forms of external financing are subject to informational asymmetry costs, which has led to the "pecking order" theory of capital structure choice (see Myers and Majluf, 1984). According to this theory, internally generated cash flow is preferable for financing information-sensitive projects. Internally generated cash flow is followed, in descending order of preference, by secured debt, unsecured debt, hybrid securities, and external common equity (least desirable).

The firm's internal cash flows, together with its unused borrowing capacity (as determined principally by the senior debt rating it would like to maintain), represent a limited financial resource. This resource can be used to take advantage of opportunities that would otherwise impose significant informational asymmetry costs. The firm can avoid incurring these costs by taking advantage of opportunities to sell transparent projects when it can obtain a fair price for the project securities. Choosing project financing in situations that entail low informational asymmetry costs thus preserves the firm's financial flexibility by conserving the firm's internal financing capacity to fund future projects that have potentially high informational asymmetry costs. The implication for the firm is: Sell projects that entail low informational asymmetry costs in order to preserve internal capital for those projects that have high informational asymmetry costs.

Why Project Financing Can Enhance Shareholder Value

The added financial flexibility that project financing affords enhances shareholder value by giving the firm the opportunity to pursue, in the near future, growth opportunities about which management will want to withhold proprietary information in order to maximize project value. Thus, firms with the most attractive information-sensitive investment projects will be most likely to utilize project financing for their transparent projects. Management's decision to resort to project financing can thus be interpreted as a positive signal regarding the attractiveness of the firm's proprietary investment projects.

MORE EFFICIENT STRUCTURING OF DEBT CONTRACTS

The inherent conflicts of interest between shareholders and lenders give rise to a variety of agency costs (see Jensen and Meckling, 1976). Lenders deal with these agency costs by negotiating covenant structures that are contained in loan agreements. Covenants facilitate monitoring the borrower's financial performance. In addition, there are debt repayment provisions, such as sinking funds, that are designed to limit management's discretion to use cash flow that might otherwise be used to repay debt for other purposes.

Project financing can reduce these agency costs. A project has a finite life. Even the equity investors demand the distribution of free cash flow to the providers of capital. Management's discretion to reinvest cash flow net of operating expenses—to the possible detriment of outside equity investors as well as lenders—is thus restricted contractually. Lenders have the senior claim on cash flow net of operating expenses. It is therefore generally easier to design a debt contract for a specific project rather than for the entire firm. This factor protects lenders against the asset substitution problem.[12] For example, debt covenants can be tailored to suit the project's expected profitability and cash flow. If the targets are not met, violation of the covenants will trigger some form of contract renegotiation. Also, the sinking fund can be contingent on project cash flow. If the project performs better than anticipated, lenders will be repaid sooner, rather than having the cash flow invested by management in other projects, possibly to their detriment.

MORE EFFECTIVE CORPORATE ORGANIZATION AND MANAGEMENT COMPENSATION

Project financing can enhance the effectiveness with which assets are managed. Brickley, Lease, and Smith (1988) and Schipper and Smith (1986) have explored the link between the ownership structure of the firm and firm value. They note the benefits that can result from giving managers a direct ownership stake in the firm. The purpose of such compensation programs is to align more closely the objectives of the firm's professional managers and its equity investors.

Project financing lends itself nicely to management incentive schemes. Management compensation can be tied directly to the performance of the project. Profit-sharing programs are but one example.

When managers have a direct share in the profits of the project, they can be strongly motivated to make decisions that enhance its profitability.

PROJECT FINANCING VERSUS DIRECT FINANCING

Project financing should be compared to direct financing on the sponsor's general credit, when deciding how best to finance a project whose characteristics would make it suitable for project financing. Figure 2.1 compares direct financing by the sponsor and project financing, on the basis of several criteria. It is important to appreciate that just because project financing *might* be arranged does not mean that the project *should* be financed in this manner. The relative advantages and disadvantages of these alternative means of financing (discussed in the next sections) should be carefully weighed to determine which technique will be more advantageous to the project sponsor's shareholders.

ADVANTAGES OF PROJECT FINANCING

Project financing should be pursued when it will achieve a lower after-tax cost of capital than conventional financing. In an extreme case, the sponsors' credit may be so weak that it is unable to obtain sufficient funds to finance a project at a reasonable cost on its own. Project financing may then offer the only practical means available for financing the project.

Capturing an Economic Rent

A natural resource deposit has scarcity value when the content is in short supply (for example, a deposit of low-sulphur coal at a time of heightened demand because of tighter environmental regulation) or can be mined at a relatively low cost (for example, an ore body in which the ore is highly concentrated). The legal entity that controls such a natural resource deposit may be able to arrange long-term purchase contracts that are capable of supporting project financing and offer supernormal rates of return on investment. Economists refer to the portion of the total return that represents excess return as an *economic rent*. The project sponsors can monetize the economic rent by entering into long-term purchase contracts. These contracts, provided they are

FIGURE 2.1   A Comparison of Direct Financing and Project Financing

Criterion	Direct Financing	Project Financing
Organization	• Large businesses are usually organized in corporate form. • Cash flows from different assets and businesses are commingled.	• The project can be organized as a partnership or limited liability company to utilize more efficiently the tax benefits of ownership. • Project-related assets and cash flows are segregated from the sponsor's other activities.
Control and monitoring	• Control is vested primarily in management. • Board of directors monitors corporate performance on behalf of the shareholders. • Limited direct monitoring is done by investors.	• Management remains in control but is subject to closer monitoring than in a typical corporation. • Segregation of assets and cash flows facilitates greater accountability to investors. • Contractual arrangements governing the debt and equity investments contain covenants and other provisions that facilitate monitoring.
Allocation of risk	• Creditors have full recourse to the project sponsor. • Risks are diversified across the sponsor's portfolio of assets. • Certain risks can be transferred to others by purchasing insurance, engaging in hedging activities, and so on.	• Creditors typically have limited recourse—and in some cases, no recourse—to the project sponsors. • Creditors' financial exposure is project-specific, although supplemental credit support arrangements can at least partially offset this risk exposure.

(Continued)

FIGURE 2.1   (Continued)

Criterion	Direct Financing	Project Financing
		• Contractual arrangements redistribute project-related risks. • Project risks can be allocated among the parties who are best able to bear them.
Financial flexibility	• Financing can typically be arranged quickly. • Internally generated funds can be used to finance other projects, bypassing the discipline of the capital market.	• Higher information, contracting, and transaction costs are involved. • Financing arrangements are highly structured and very time-consuming. • Internally generated cash flow can be reserved for proprietary projects.
Free cash flow	• Managers have broad discretion regarding the allocation of free cash flow between dividends and reinvestment. • Cash flows are commingled and then allocated in accordance with corporate policy.	• Managers have limited discretion. • By contract, free cash flow must be distributed to equity investors.
Agency costs	• Equity investors are exposed to the agency costs of free cash flow. • Making management incentives project-specific is more difficult. • Agency costs are greater than for project financing.	• The agency costs of free cash flow are reduced. • Management incentives can be tied to project performance. • Closer monitoring by investors is facilitated. • The underinvestment problem can be mitigated. • Agency costs are lower than for internal financing.

FIGURE 2.1 *(Continued)*

Criterion	Direct Financing	Project Financing
Structure of debt contracts	• Creditors look to the sponsor's entire asset portfolio for their debt service. • Typically, debt is unsecured (when the borrower is a large corporation).	• Creditors look to a specific asset or pool of assets for their debt service. • Typically, debt is secured. • Debt contracts are tailored to the specific characteristics of the project.
Debt capacity	• Debt financing uses part of the sponsor's debt capacity.	• Credit support from other sources, such as purchasers of project output, can be channeled to support project borrowings. • The sponsor's debt capacity can be effectively expanded. • Higher leverage (which provides valuable interest tax shields) than the sponsor would feel comfortable with if it financed the project directly can be achieved.
Bankruptcy	• Costly and time-consuming financial distress can be avoided. • Lenders have the benefit of the sponsor's entire asset portfolio. • Difficulties in one key line of business could drain cash from "good" projects.	• The cost of resolving financial distress is lower. • The project can be insulated from the sponsor's possible bankruptcy. • Lenders' chances of recovering principal are more limited; the debt is generally not repayable from the proceeds of other unrelated projects.

properly drafted, can be used to secure project borrowings to finance the development of the ore body. They will also generate the cash flow to service project debt and provide equity investors the return of and a return on their investment.

Achieving Economies of Scale

Two or more producers can benefit from joining together to build a single facility when there are economies of scale in production. For example, two aluminum producers might decide to build a single aluminum processing plant near a location where each has a large supply of bauxite. Or, the firms in a densely industrialized area might decide to cooperate in a single cogeneration facility, with each firm agreeing to buy steam to meet its own needs for heat and the group selling all the excess electricity to the local electric utility.

Risk Sharing

A joint venture permits the sponsors to share a project's risks. If a project's capital cost is large in relation to the sponsor's capitalization, a decision to undertake the project alone might jeopardize the sponsor's future. Similarly, a project may be too large for the host country to finance prudently from its treasury. To reduce its own risk exposure, the sponsor or host country can enlist one or more joint-venture partners.

Expanded Debt Capacity

Project financing enables a project sponsor to finance the project on someone else's credit. Often, that someone else is the purchaser(s) of the project's output. A project can raise funds on the basis of contractual commitments when (1) the purchasers enter into long-term contracts to buy the project output and (2) the contract provisions are tight enough to ensure adequate cash flow to the project, enabling it to service its debt fully under all reasonably foreseeable circumstances. If there are contingencies in which cash flow might be inadequate, supplemental credit support arrangements will be required to cover these contingencies. Nevertheless, the contractual purchase commitments form the foundation that supports the project financing.

The project company may be able to finance with significantly greater leverage than would be normal in the sponsor's capitalization. A broad range of projects have been financed with capitalizations consisting of 70 percent or more debt. However, the degree of leverage that a project can achieve depends on the strength of the security arrangements, the risks borne by creditworthy participants, the type of project, and its profitability.

Lower Overall Cost of Funds

If the output purchaser's credit standing is higher than that of the project sponsors, the project will be able to borrow funds more cheaply than the project sponsors could on their own. Also, to the extent the project entity can achieve a higher degree of leverage than the sponsors can comfortably maintain on their own, the project's cost of capital will benefit from the substitution of lower-cost debt for equity.

Release of Free Cash Flow

The project entity typically has a finite life. Its "dividend policy" is usually specified contractually at the time any outside equity financing is arranged. Cash flow not needed to cover operating expenses, pay debt service, or make capital improvements—so-called free cash flow—must normally be distributed to the project's equity investors. Thus, the equity investors, rather than professional managers, get to decide how the project's free cash flow will be reinvested.

When a project is financed on a company's general credit, the project's assets become part of the company's asset portfolio. Free cash flow from the project augments the company's internal cash resources. This free cash flow is retained or distributed to the company's shareholders at the discretion of the company's board of directors.

Project financing eliminates this element of discretion. Investors may prefer to have the project company distribute the free cash flow, allowing them to invest it as they choose. Reducing the risk that the free cash flow might be retained and invested without the project's equity investors' approval should reduce the cost of equity capital to the project.[13]

Note that the sponsor is not necessarily placed at a disadvantage under this arrangement. If the sponsor is considering additional projects that it believes are profitable, it can negotiate funding for these projects with outside equity investors. If they agree to fund any of these additional investments within the project entity, the dividend requirement can be waived by mutual agreement and the funds invested accordingly.

Reduced Cost of Resolving Financial Distress

The structure of a project's liabilities will normally be less complex than the structure of each sponsor's liabilities. A project entity's capital structure typically has just one class of debt, and the number of other potential claimants is likely to be small.

As a general rule, the time and cost required to resolve financial distress increase with the number of claimants and with the complexity of the debtor's capital structure. Over time, a corporation will tend to accumulate a large number of claims, including pension claims, that may be difficult to handle in the event of insolvency or debt default. An independent entity with one principal class of debt, particularly if the debt is held privately by a small number of sophisticated financial institutions, tends to emerge from financial distress more easily.

Project financing does, however, limit the lenders' opportunity for recovering principal in the event of financial distress. Loans directly to the sponsor would be backed by the sponsor's entire portfolio of assets; if one line of business failed, lenders could still be repaid using cash flow from the sponsor's other lines of business. In a project financing, the project assets are normally segregated from the sponsor's other assets. Access to those assets (and the related cash flows) is limited by the degree of recourse to the sponsor that is granted to lenders in the project loan agreement. On the other hand, segregating the project assets from the sponsor's other assets insulates lenders to a project from the risk that the sponsor might go bankrupt, provided that the sponsor's lenders do not have recourse to the project corporation.[14]

Reduced Legal or Regulatory Costs

Certain types of projects, such as cogeneration projects, involve legal or regulatory costs that an experienced project sponsor can bear more cheaply than an inexperienced operator can.[15] For example, a chemical company or an oil company that undertakes a cogeneration project on its own would face significant costs because of an unfamiliar technology and legal and regulatory requirements. A general contracting firm that specializes in cogeneration projects understands the technology involved and is experienced in dealing with regulatory bodies (which must approve the terms on which the electric utility company purchases the cogeneration project's excess electricity). For this type of firm, a cogeneration project is a normal business undertaking to which it can apply the knowledge and experience it has gained in earlier cogeneration projects.

When managed expertly, project financing can lead to economies of scale in controlling legal and regulatory costs. The continued economic viability of the project might depend on continued cooperation with several outside organizations (such as the local utility that buys the electricity) over which the industrial firm has no direct control. At some point, it might be necessary to enforce one or more agreements, thereby incurring legal fees and running the risk of regulatory interference. Using an experienced developer who has successfully completed similar projects can also reduce operating costs. The project's independent status, coupled with the developer's willingness to make a long-term commitment to make the project profitable, can reduce the risks the industrial firm would face if it financed the cogeneration project internally.

A Questionable Advantage

Practitioners often argue that project financing is beneficial when it keeps project debt off each sponsor's balance sheet. It is important to recognize that financial risk does not disappear simply because project-related debt is not recorded on the face of the balance sheet. The accounting profession, in the United States at least, has tightened footnote disclosure requirements in recent years. In a reasonably *efficient market*—one in which investors and the rating agencies process all available financial information intelligently—the benefits of off-balance-sheet treatment are likely to prove illusory. The investors and the rating agencies in such a market environment can translate the footnote information into an assessment of the sponsor's credit risk exposure related to the project financing. The rating agencies factor such assessments into their bond rating decisions, and investors can incorporate their assessments (and the debt rating) into the prices they are willing to pay for each sponsor's outstanding securities.

DISADVANTAGES OF PROJECT FINANCING

Project financing will not necessarily lead to a lower cost of capital in all circumstances. Project financings are costly to arrange, and these costs may outweigh the advantages enumerated above.

Complexity of Project Financings

Project financing is structured around a set of contracts that must be negotiated by *all* the parties to a project. They can be quite complex and therefore costly to arrange. They normally take more time to arrange than a conventional financing. Project financings typically also require a greater investment of management's time than a conventional financing.

Indirect Credit Support

For any particular (ultimate) obligor of the project's debt and any given degree of leverage in the capital structure, the cost of debt is typically higher in a project financing than in a comparable conventional financing because of the indirect nature of the credit support. The credit support for a project financing is provided through contractual commitments rather than through a *direct* promise to pay. Lenders to a project will naturally be concerned that the contractual commitments might somehow fail to provide an uninterrupted flow of debt service in some unforeseen contingency. As a result, they typically require a yield premium to compensate for this risk. This premium is generally between 50 and 100 basis points, depending on the type of purchase contract negotiated. The *hell-or-high-water contract*, described in Chapter 4, provides the greatest degree of credit support and therefore requires a yield premium that is at the low end of this range.

Higher Transaction Costs

Because of their greater complexity, project financings involve higher transaction costs than comparable conventional financings. These higher transaction costs reflect the legal expense involved in designing the project structure, researching and dealing with project-related tax and legal issues, and preparing the necessary project ownership, loan documentation, and other contracts.

CONCLUSION

Project financing represents an alternative to conventional direct financing. Choosing project financing over direct financing involves choosing an alternative organizational form that is different from the traditional corporation in two fundamental respects: (1) the project financing entity has a finite life, and (2) the cash flows from the project are paid directly to the project investors, rather than reinvested by the sponsor. Project financing can:

- Reduce the agency costs of free cash flow by giving investors the right to control reinvestment of the project's free cash flow;
- Mitigate the underinvestment problem that arises when firms have risky debt outstanding;
- Enhance a company's financial flexibility by giving it the ability to husband internally generated cash flow for investment in projects that involve proprietary information that it does not wish to disclose to investors at large;
- Facilitate the design of less costly debt contracts, which can be tailored to the cash flow characteristics of the project.

Because of the higher transaction costs and the yield premium that is required, when both financing alternatives are available, project financing will usually be more cost-effective than conventional direct financing when (1) project financing permits a higher degree of leverage than the sponsors could achieve on their own and (2) the increase in leverage produces tax shield benefits sufficient to offset the higher cost of debt funds, resulting in a lower overall cost of capital for the project.

3

Analysis of Project Viability

Obtaining the financing needed to fund the construction cost of a project requires satisfying prospective long-term lenders (and prospective outside equity investors, if any) of the project's technical feasibility, economic viability, and creditworthiness. Investors are concerned about all the risks a project involves, who will bear each of them, and whether their returns will be adequate to compensate them for the risks they are being asked to bear. Both the sponsors and their financial adviser must be thoroughly familiar with the technical aspects of the project and the risks involved, and they must independently evaluate the project's economics and its ability to service project-related borrowings. This chapter discusses the factors that are relevant to such an assessment.

TECHNICAL FEASIBILITY

Prior to the start of construction, the project sponsor(s) must undertake extensive engineering work to verify the technological processes and design of the proposed facility. If the project requires new or unproven technology, test facilities or a pilot plant will normally have to be constructed to test the feasibility of the processes involved and to optimize the design of the full-scale facilities. Even if the technology is proven, the scale envisioned for the project may be significantly larger than existing facilities that utilize the same technology. A well-executed design will accommodate future expansion of the project; often, expansion beyond the initial operating capacity is planned at the outset. The related capital cost and the impact of project expansion on operating efficiency are then reflected in the original design specifications and financial projections.

The design, and ultimately the technical feasibility, of a project may be influenced by environmental factors that may affect construction or operation. Arctic pipelines and North Sea oil production facilities illustrate the impact that extreme environmental conditions can have on the construction and operation of production facilities. Although large-scale oil pipelines and offshore drilling and production platforms had a history of successful operation, the environmental conditions present in the Alaskan Arctic and in the North Sea necessitated significant design modifications.

Project sponsors often retain outside engineering consultants to assist with design work and to provide an independent opinion concerning the project's technological feasibility. It is not unusual for long-term lenders to require confirming opinions from independent experts that (1) the project facilities can be constructed within the time schedule proposed; (2) upon completion of construction, the facilities will be capable of operating as planned; and (3) the construction cost estimates, together with appropriate contingencies for cost escalation, will prove adequate for completion of the project. The project's financial adviser must be apprised fully of any technological uncertainties and their potential impact on the project's financing requirements, operational characteristics, and profitability.

Project Construction Cost

The detailed engineering and design work provides the basis for estimating the construction costs for the project. Construction cost estimates should include the cost of all facilities necessary for the project's operation as a free-standing entity. If the project is to be located in a remote area or if it will require additional infrastructure, such as roads, electricity, schools, or housing, the project sponsors must determine whether the cost of the necessary infrastructure will be borne by the project or by others (such as the host government, perhaps with some form of international financial assistance). If the project must bear these costs, they might substantially increase the projected overall construction cost (especially for projects with a lengthy construction period). Consequently, appropriate escalation factors should be applied to the relevant cost components. Construction cost estimates should also include a contingency factor adequate to cover possible design errors or unforeseen costs. The size of this factor depends on uncertainties that may affect construction but, in most major projects, a 10 percent contingency factor (i.e., 10 percent of direct costs) is normally viewed as sufficient if the design of the project facilities has been finalized. Larger contingency factors will be necessary if the project is still in the design phase; the more preliminary the design, the larger the contingency factor that will be appropriate. Finally, the aggregate capital cost estimates must adequately provide for the project's working capital requirements as well as for interest payable during construction.

Project sponsors or their advisers generally prepare a time schedule detailing the activities that must be accomplished before and during the construction period. A quarterly breakdown of capital expenditures normally accompanies the time schedule. The time schedule should specify (1) the time expected to be required to obtain regulatory or environmental approvals and permits for construction, (2) the procurement lead time anticipated for major pieces of equipment, and (3) the time expected to be required for preconstruction activities—performing detailed design work (which typically must conform to permit stipulations), ordering the equipment and building materials, preparing the site, and hiring the necessary manpower. The project sponsor should examine the critical path of the construction schedule to determine where the risk of delay is greatest and then assess the potential financial impact of any projected delay.

ECONOMIC VIABILITY

The critical issue concerning economic viability is whether the project's expected net present value is positive. It will be positive only if the expected present value of the future free cash flows exceeds the expected present value of the project's construction costs. All the factors that can affect project cash flows are important in making this determination.

Assuming that the project is completed on schedule and within budget, its economic viability will depend primarily on the marketability of the project's output (price *and* volume). To evaluate marketability, the sponsors arrange for a study of projected supply and demand conditions over the expected life of the project. The marketing study is designed to confirm that, under a reasonable set of economic assumptions, demand will be sufficient to absorb the planned output of the project at a price that will cover the full cost of production, enable the project to service its debt, and provide an acceptable rate of return to equity investors. The marketing study generally includes (1) a review of competitive products and their relative cost of production; (2) an analysis of the expected life cycle for project output, expected sales volume, and projected prices; and (3) an analysis of the potential impact of technological obsolescence. The study is usually performed by an independent firm of experts. If the project will operate within a regulated industry, the potential impact of regulatory decisions on production levels and prices—-and, ultimately, on the profitability of the project—must also be considered.

The cost of production will affect the pricing of the project output. Projections of operating costs are prepared after project design work has been completed. Each cost element, such as raw materials, labor, overhead, taxes, royalties, and maintenance expense, must be identified and quantified. Typically, this estimation is accomplished by dividing the cost element into fixed and variable cost components and estimating each category separately. Each operating cost element should be escalated over the term of the projections at a rate that reflects the anticipated rate of inflation. From a financing standpoint, it is important to assess the reasonableness of the cost estimates and the extent to which the pricing, and hence the marketability, of the project output is likely to be affected by estimated cost inflation rates.

In addition to operating costs, the project's cost of capital must be determined. The financial adviser typically is responsible for this task. The financial adviser develops and tests various financing plans for the project in order to arrive at an optimal financing plan that is consistent with the business objectives of the project sponsor(s). Those objectives typically include producing a competitively priced product while at the same time realizing the highest possible rate of return on the sponsors' equity investment.

The project financial adviser develops a base case financial plan, as described in Chapter 6, and then assesses the sensitivity of the profitability of the project and the projected return on the sponsors' equity investment to various contingencies. Analysis of these factors almost always requires computer modeling and extensive sensitivity analysis, for which the project financial adviser is responsible. Computer modeling is used to analyze the effects of cost overruns, delays in completion, interruptions of project operations, fluctuations in product price, changes in operating costs, and other significant factors. The projected price in relation to the project's "breakeven price"—calculated by dividing total cash costs of production by the number of units produced—associated with various output levels is often used to gauge the project's operating margin of safety.

Adequacy of Raw Material Supplies

Lenders will insist, at a minimum, that the project have access to sufficient supplies of raw materials to enable it to operate at design capacity over the term of the debt. For natural resource projects, lenders generally insist that the project sponsors engage independent geologists or engineering consultants to evaluate the quantity, grade, and rate of extraction that the mineral reserves available to the project are capable of supporting. The accuracy of the reserve estimates is subject to a margin of error; its range depends on the nature of the engineers' examination. This uncertainty is typically taken into account by dividing the reserve estimates into proven, probable, and possible. Lenders may also ask the sponsors to employ independent experts to analyze the extraction and production technologies and determine whether they are appropriate in light of the particular characteristics of the reserves. In addition to demonstrating that adequate reserves are available, the project sponsors will have to establish the project's ability to access these reserves. Proof of such access might be evidenced by direct ownership, lease, purchase agreement, or some other form of contractual undertaking that affords the project, at a minimum, an unconditional legal right to secure specified quantities over the term of the debt.

CREDITWORTHINESS

A project has no operating history at the time of its initial debt financing (unless its construction was financed on an equity basis and the project debt financing funds out some portion of the construction financing). Consequently, the amount of debt the project can raise is a function of the project's expected capacity to service debt from project cash flow— or, more simply, its credit strength. In general, a project's credit strength derives from (1) the inherent value of the assets included in the project, (2) the expected profitability of the project, (3) the amount of equity project sponsors have at risk (after the debt financing is completed), and, indirectly, (4) the pledges of creditworthy third parties or sponsors involved in the project.

Credit Derived from the Inherent Value of Project Assets

In a production payment financing, which is often used in connection with the development of resource properties, the loans are secured by proven resource reserves and are repaid from funds generated from the production and sale of the resource. This type of indebtedness is incurred by the owner of a working interest in proven reserves, where possible, on a nonrecourse basis. The purchaser of a production payment is entitled to a percentage of production revenues as reserves are recovered during the specified production period. Such financing, often employed in the oil and gas industry, has also been used to finance the development of other types of mineral reserves. Requirements for securing this type of financing include (1) adequate proven reserves, (2) a proven technology to recover these resources, and (3) an assured market for the product.

Expected Profitability of the Project

The expected profitability of a project represents the principal source of funds to service project debt and provide an adequate rate of return to the project's equity investors. Lenders generally look for two sources of repayment for their loans: (1) the credit strength of the entity to which they are loaning funds and (2) the collateral value of any assets the borrower pledges to secure the loans. In a project financing, there is a third source: the credit support derived indirectly from pledges of third parties.

Amount of Equity Project Sponsors Have at Risk

Debt ranks senior to equity. In the event a business fails, debt holders have a prior claim on the assets of the business. Given the value of project assets, the greater the amount of equity, the lower the ratio of debt to equity. Therefore, the lower the degree of risk lenders face.

Credit Support Derived Indirectly from Pledges by Third Parties

Although lenders look principally to the revenues generated from the operations of a project to determine its viability and creditworthiness, supplemental credit support for a project may have to be provided by the sponsors or other creditworthy parties benefiting from the project. The contractual agreements among the operator/borrower, the sponsors, other third parties, and the lender(s), which are designed to ensure debt repayment and servicing, as well as the credit standing of these guarantors, are necessary to provide adequate security to support the project's financing arrangements.

CONCLUSION AS TO VIABILITY

To arrange financing for a stand-alone project, prospective lenders (and prospective outside equity investors, if any) must be convinced that the project is technically feasible and economically viable and that the project will be sufficiently creditworthy if financed on the basis the project sponsors propose. Establishing technical feasibility requires demonstrating, to lenders' satisfaction, that construction can be completed on schedule and within budget and that the project will be able to operate at its design capacity following completion. Establishing economic viability requires demonstrating that the project will be able to generate sufficient cash flow so as to cover its overall cost of capital. Establishing creditworthiness requires demonstrating that even under reasonably pessimistic circumstances, the project will be able to generate sufficient revenue both to cover all operating costs and to service project debt in a timely manner. The loan terms—in particular, the debt amortization schedule lenders require—will have a significant impact on how much debt the project can incur and still remain creditworthy.

ASSESSING PROJECT RISKS

As a rule, lenders will not agree to provide funds to a project unless they are convinced that it will be a viable going concern. A project cannot have an established credit record prior to completion—in fact, it cannot have such a record prior to having operated successfully for a long enough period to establish its viability beyond any reasonable doubt. Consequently, lenders to a project will require that they be protected against certain basic risks. Lending to a project prior to the start-up of construction, without protection against the various business and financial risks, would expose project lenders to equity risks. But lenders, who are often fiduciaries, find it imprudent to assume technological, commercial, or other business risks. Therefore, they require assurances that creditworthy parties are committed to provide sufficient credit support to the project to compensate fully for these contingencies.

Legal investment requirements will also affect the ability of certain institutional lenders to extend funds to a project. The major life insurance companies have historically supplied the largest portion of the long-term fixed-rate debt funds for major projects. The statutory provisions governing their permissible reserve investments therefore represent a significant constraint on the design of security arrangements. The legal investment requirements imposed on life insurance companies doing business in the State of New York (the location of most major life insurance companies) are among the most restrictive in the United States. They consequently serve as the guideline most often followed in structuring project security arrangements. (Appendix C contains the relevant sections of the New York State Insurance Law.)

In light of the business and financial risks associated with a project, lenders will require security arrangements designed to transfer these risks to financially capable parties and to protect prospective lenders. The various risks are characterized here as: completion, technological, raw material supply, economic, financial, currency, political, environmental, and force majeure risks. Each is discussed in the sections that follow.

COMPLETION RISK

Completion risk entails the risk that the project might not be completed. Lenders to projects are particularly sensitive to becoming creditors of a "dead horse." They will therefore insist on being taken out of their investment if completion fails to occur.

Completion risk has a monetary aspect and a technical aspect. The monetary element of completion risk concerns the risk either (1) that a higher-than-anticipated rate of inflation, shortages of critical supplies, unexpected delays that slow down construction schedules, or merely an underestimation of construction costs might cause such an increase in the capital expenditures required to get the project operational that the project would no longer be profitable; or (2) that a lower-than-expected price for the project's output or a higher-than-expected cost for a critical input might reduce the expected rate of return to such an extent that the sponsors no longer find the project profitable. For a major project, a cost overrun of even 25 percent, which in recent years would have been considered a modest overrun for a large construction project, may well equal or exceed the sponsors' total equity contribution.

The other element of completion risk relates to the technical processes incorporated in the project. In spite of all the expert assurances provided to the lenders prior to the financing, the project may prove to be technically infeasible or environmentally objectionable. Alternatively, it may require such large expenditures, in order to become technically feasible, that the project becomes uneconomic to complete. For example, a large petrochemical project was abandoned when it was discovered that the production processes did not operate properly. A small pilot plant had worked well. But the scaled-up project never performed as designed because the chemicals involved did not react properly in large quantities.

An Example

Completion risk is a serious concern, particularly when a facility will incorporate a new technology or a significant scale-up of an existing technology. For example, Cominco Ltd., a Canadian lead and zinc producer, announced in April 1993 that it had abandoned any hope of restarting its new lead smelter, which had been shuttered for three years because of production problems.[1] It also announced that it was considering converting the smelter to a "more promising" smelting process, which would cost an estimated $100 million Canadian, and that it might seek compensation from the manufacturer of the smelter.

TECHNOLOGICAL RISK

Technological risk exists when the technology, on the scale proposed for the project, will not perform according to specifications or will become prematurely obsolete. If the technological deficiency causes the project to fail its completion test, the risk element properly belongs in the category of completion risk. However, the project may meet its completion requirement but nevertheless not perform to its technical specifications. Such failures impair equity returns.

The risk of technical obsolescence following completion becomes particularly important when a project involves a state-of-the-art technology in an industry whose technology is rapidly evolving.

Normally, such technical risks would preclude project financing. However, lenders might be willing to fund the project in spite of these risks, if creditworthy parties (such as output purchasers) are willing to protect lenders from these risks.

RAW MATERIAL SUPPLY RISK

Particularly in connection with natural resource projects, there is a risk that the natural resources, raw materials, or other factors of production necessary for successful operation may become depleted or unavailable during the life of the project. As a general rule of thumb, minable reserves should be expected to last at least twice as long as the reserves that will be mined during the project loan servicing period. Prospective lenders to a project will almost always require an independent reserve study to establish the adequacy of mineral reserves for a natural resource project.

ECONOMIC RISK

Even when the project is technologically sound and is completed and operating satisfactorily (at or near capacity), there is a risk that demand for the project's products or services will not be sufficient to generate the revenue needed to cover the project's operating costs and debt service and provide a fair rate of return to equity investors. Such a development might result, for example, from a decline in the price of the project's output or from an increase in the cost of an important raw material. Depending on the economics of a particular project, there might be very little margin for a price change to occur before any return to equity is eliminated and the project's ability to service its debt becomes impaired. Project lenders are often willing to permit a mine to close down—and defer repayment of principal—if cash revenue from the mine falls short of the cash operating cost. Repayments resume when the mine becomes capable of generating positive net cash flow.

An important element of economic risk is the efficiency with which the project's facilities will be operated. Lenders will insist that the project sponsors arrange for a competent operator/manager.

A project has no inherent creditworthiness before operations commence. Lenders have no past operating history that they can study to evaluate the project's economic risks. They will therefore require undertakings from creditworthy parties sufficient to ensure that project debt service requirements will be met. These undertakings take the form of security arrangements, which are described in Chapter 4.

Hedging with Forwards and Futures

A *forward contract* obligates the contract seller to deliver to the contract buyer (1) a specified quantity (2) of a particular commodity, currency, or some other item (3) on a specified future date (4) at a stated price that is agreed to at the time the two parties enter into the contract. A *futures contract* is similar to a forward contract except that (1) a futures contract is traded on an organized exchange (whereas forwards are traded over-the-counter) and (2) a futures contract is standardized (whereas forward contracts are customized as to the item involved or the time of delivery).

Forwards and futures enable project sponsors to sell their output for future delivery. They are, at least, guaranteed quantity and price for items that can be sold on this basis. Forwards and futures are available for most commodities and all major currencies. The market for natural gas futures has exploded within the past five years. A market for electricity futures is developing. Other markets will develop if there is a demand for them.[2]

Gold Loans

Among the other strategies for transferring risks to others through the financial markets,[3] the gold loan is worth noting. A sponsor of a gold mining project can borrow gold (i.e., the physical commodity) and sell the gold to raise cash to finance construction. The gold loan is repaid out of production from the mine. For example, Inmet Mining arranged a 180,000-ounce 8½-year gold loan to finance part of the cost of its Troilus Gold Project. The project involved development of a gold mine in Quebec, Canada, with annual production of 150,000 ounces.

FINANCIAL RISK

If a significant portion of the debt financing for a project consists of floating-rate debt, there is a risk that rising interest rates could jeopardize the project's ability to service its debt. However, during the

1980s, various new financial instruments were developed that would enable a project's sponsors to eliminate the project's interest rate risk exposure. The traditional method of eliminating (or at least controlling) such risk exposure involved arranging fixed-rate debt for the project. However, floating-rate lenders, typically commercial banks, are often more willing to assume greater completion or other business risks than fixed-rate lenders, such as life insurance companies and pension funds. The availability of interest rate risk hedging vehicles enables project sponsors to eliminate interest rate risk without having to accept a trade-off involving other risk exposures.

Interest Rate Cap Contract

An *interest rate cap contract* obligates the writer of the contract to pay the purchaser of the contract the difference between the market interest rate and the specified cap rate whenever the market interest rate exceeds the cap rate. For example, a 3-month LIBOR cap contract that specifies a cap rate of 6 percent would pay the holder whenever 3-month LIBOR rises above 6 percent. LIBOR is the London Interbank Offer Rate at which banks lend each other dollar deposits in the London money market. It is a widely used benchmark for pricing dollar loans. Suppose the loan agreement specifies an interest rate of LIBOR +1.25 percent with quarterly resets. If LIBOR is, say, 8 percent on the interest rate reset date, the borrower will have to pay the lender 9.25 percent interest for that interest period but will receive 2 percent (8 percent − 6 percent) interest under the cap contract. The borrower's true interest cost can never rise above 7.25 percent, the cap rate plus 1.25 percent.[4]

Interest Rate Swap Agreement

An *interest rate swap agreement* involves an agreement to exchange interest rate payment obligations based on some specified notional principal amount. A project that borrows funds from a commercial bank on a floating-rate basis can enter into an agreement with a financial institution under which it agrees to pay a fixed rate of interest and receive a floating rate of interest. The floating-rate receivable under the swap agreement is designed to cancel out the floating-rate payable under the bank loan agreement.

Figure 3.1 illustrates how an interest rate swap agreement can convert a floating-rate obligation into a (net) fixed-rate obligation. The

FIGURE 3.1   An Interest Rate Swap

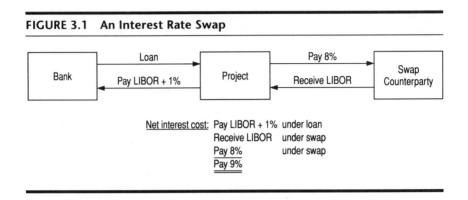

project borrows funds from a bank at an interest rate of LIBOR + 1 percent. It agrees to pay 8 percent and receive LIBOR under the swap agreement. Its (net) interest cost is 9 percent (fixed rate).

CURRENCY RISK

Currency risk arises when the project's revenue stream or its cost stream is denominated in more than one currency, or when the two streams are denominated in different currencies. In such cases, a change in the exchange rate(s) between the currencies involved will affect the availability of cash flow to service project debt. For example, if the project's revenues are denominated in U.S. dollars and its costs must be paid in a currency other than U.S. dollars, there is foreign currency risk exposure. If the U.S. dollar depreciates relative to the other currency without any changes in dollar price per unit of output, and if project debt is denominated in the same nondollar currency as the project's operating costs, the depreciation in value will increase the risk that the project will not be able to service its debt in a timely manner.

This risk can be managed by (1) borrowing an appropriate portion of project debt funds in U.S. dollars, (2) hedging using currency forwards or futures, or (3) arranging one or more currency swaps.[5] Figure 3.2 illustrates how a currency swap agreement can convert a loan obligation from one currency to another. Converting the loan into one that is denominated in U.S. dollars reduces the project's currency risk because the U.S. dollar revenues can be used to meet the project's U.S.-dollar swap obligation, and the local currency payments under the swap agreement can be used to meet the debt service obligations under the loan agreement.[6]

FIGURE 3.2   A Currency Swap

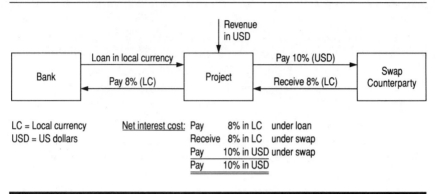

LC = Local currency   Net interest cost: Pay   8% in LC   under loan
USD = US dollars   Receive   8% in LC   under swap
                                             Pay   10% in USD under swap
                                             Pay   10% in USD

POLITICAL RISK

Political risk involves the possibility that political authorities in the host political jurisdiction might interfere with the timely development and/or long-term economic viability of the project. For example, they might impose burdensome taxes or onerous legal restrictions once the project commences operation. In the extreme case, there is a risk of expropriation. Political risk can be ameliorated by borrowing funds for the project from local banks (which would suffer financially if the project is unable to repay project debt because its assets were expropriated). It can also be mitigated by borrowing funds for the project from the World Bank, the Inter-American Development Bank, or some other multilateral financing agency, if the host country is relying on such agencies to fund public expenditures (expropriation would jeopardize such funding). In addition, project sponsors can often arrange political risk insurance to cover a wide range of political risks (see Chapter 9).

Often, the project sponsors must devote considerable time and effort to obtaining the appropriate legislative and regulatory approvals to allow a project to proceed. The existence of such hurdles can have a significant impact on the sponsors' decision on where to build the project. Making the appropriate arrangements with the host country government can reduce substantially, or even eliminate, this element of political risk.

Example

Enron Corporation's recent experience with the Dabhol Power Project in India illustrates how political risk can affect a project.[7] Enron, with backing from Bechtel Enterprises Inc. and General Electric Capital Corporation, was building a 2,015-megawatt power project at a cost of $2.8 billion in the Indian state of Maharashtra. The national government had given the project its blessing and had recognized Enron as a "show-case investor." Upon completion, the project would have been the largest foreign investment in India. Three thousand workers were at the site, and the foundations for two of the three enormous generators had already been laid. The sponsors had spent $600 million by the time the project was 23 percent complete. Nevertheless, a newly elected state government announced, in August 1995, that its cabinet had canceled the second half of the two-stage project and repudiated the power contract for the first phase because of concerns that: the project had not been awarded through competitive bidding, the power tariffs in the power purchase contract were too high, and the project was environmentally risky. On the third issue, the environmental lawsuits previously filed against the project's developers had been dismissed by Indian courts. Press reports noted that "the project got caught in a political swamp" when the Congress Party lost control of the Maharashtra state government in the March 1995 elections.[8]

Political Risk in the United States

Some people think that political risk exists only in the emerging markets. This is not so. Political risk is not even limited to foreign countries: it also exists in the United States. The federal government and state governments have a troubling tendency to make changes in law retroactively. Environmental laws are an example. Many project finance professionals believe the United States has perhaps the highest level of political risk of any developed country.

Consider the Tenaska Power Project in Tacoma, Washington. The Bonneville Power Administration (BPA), an agency of the U.S. Government, entered into an agreement to purchase the electric output from a new plant. Chase Manhattan Bank lent more than $100 million to finance construction. BPA broke the contract because it had lost customers to other independent power producers.[9] As of October 1995, the plant was still about half a year from completion. But construction had been halted, and both the project sponsors and the Chase Manhattan Bank had sued the BPA.

The Tenaska Power Project illustrates what may be the beginning of a trend. Because of falling oil and gas prices during the 1990s, power production costs have come down. The pending broad deregulation of the utility industry will cause competition to increase. As a result of both factors, utilities have stepped up pressure on independent power suppliers to cut their electricity charges or cancel new projects. Deregulation, in particular, reflects political risk because it requires the government's authorization.

How Other Risks Can Turn into Political Risk

Other risks, such as economic risk or currency risk, can be transformed into political risk. For example, suppose an electric power project in an emerging market borrows funds in U.S. dollars. It charges electricity tariffs in the local currency, but the tariff is indexed to the local currency/U.S. dollar exchange rate. If the local currency depreciates, the tariff goes up. But will the project company be able to charge the full tariff if the local currency devalues sharply (as happened in Mexico in 1995), or will the government step in and block the tariff increase?

ENVIRONMENTAL RISK

Environmental risk is present when the environmental effects of a project might cause a delay in the project's development or necessitate a costly redesign. For example, in connection with a mining project, disposal of tailings is often a very sensitive environmental issue that can add significantly to the cost of operations. Interestingly, the frequent changes in environmental regulations in the United States (at both the state and federal levels), and, often, the aggressive lobbying activities and legal challenges mounted by environmental groups, have given rise to significant environmental risks for environmentally sensitive projects in the United States. To the extent environmental objections are voiced through the political process, they give rise to political risk.

FORCE MAJEURE RISK

This category concerns the risk that some discrete event might impair, or prevent altogether, the operation of the project for a prolonged period of time after the project has been completed and placed in operation. Such an event might be specific to the project, such as a catastrophic technical failure, a strike, or a fire. Alternatively, it might be an externally imposed interruption, such as an earthquake that damages the project's facilities or an insurrection that hampers the project's operation.

Lenders normally insist on being protected from loss caused by force majeure.[10] Certain events of force majeure, such as fires or earthquakes, can be insured against. Lenders will require assurances from financially capable parties that the project's debt service requirements will be met in the event force majeure occurs. If force majeure results in abandonment of the project, lenders typically require repayment of project debt on an accelerated basis. In the case of events covered by insurance, lenders will require the project sponsors to pledge the right to receive insurance payments as part of the security for project loans. Project sponsors will have to rebuild or repair the project—or else repay project debt—out of the insurance proceeds, if one of these insured events occurs.

Most of the aforementioned risks represent business risks (as opposed to credit risks). Business risks are not normally accepted knowingly by lenders. However, by means of guarantees, contractual arrangements, and other supplemental credit support arrangements, the project's business risks can be allocated among the various parties involved in the project (i.e., project owners, purchasers of the project's output, suppliers of raw materials, governmental agencies), thus providing the indirect credit support the project needs to attract financing.

IMPLICATIONS FOR PROJECT FINANCING

The magnitude of certain project-related risks may exceed the financial capacity of the project's sponsors and/or the purchasers of its output to bear them. In that event, project lenders will insist that some third party cover those risks in order for the project to proceed. For example, public utilities that operate in a highly regulated environment generally have limited financial resources. They therefore seek to pass a portion of project risks on to the ultimate consumer by having the regulatory authorities agree to set prices at a level that will cover project operating costs and debt service. Alternatively, a host government might agree to provide credit support to the project or to lend funds at a subsidized interest rate. The former could take the form of a guarantee of project debt. As a third alternative, such financial support might consist of an undertaking to advance funds to the project during certain events that the sponsors do not have the financial strength to backstop. However, the host government will agree to provide such financial support only if it believes that the social benefits it will derive from the project justify the cost implicit in providing this support.

THE COGENERATION PROJECT

The Cogeneration Project is a relatively low-risk project as compared to project financings generally. The project's technology is proven: many projects utilizing this particular technology are operating successfully in the United States. Engineering Firm, which has built several such facilities, will build the cogeneration facility under a fixed-price turnkey contract and will guarantee that the cogeneration facility will operate according to its design specifications. Engineering Firm has designed and built several such plants recently. Its performance will be backed by a performance bond. Technological risk during operations will be minimal; cogeneration facilities similar in design and size have demonstrated their capability to operate successfully.

Local Utility will supply gas to the cogeneration facility under a 15-year gas supply agreement. This contract will insulate the Cogeneration Project from raw material supply risk. Natural gas represents the largest component of the facility's operating cost. The gas supply agreement links the price the Cogeneration Project will pay Local Utility for gas to the price Local Utility will pay Cogeneration Company for electricity. This linking mitigates the risk that a divergence of gas and electricity prices could harm the project's profitability.

Local Utility will purchase electricity under a 15-year electric power purchase agreement. Chemical Company will purchase steam under a 15-year steam purchase agreement. Both companies are strong creditworthy entities. They will be obligated contractually to take all of the Cogeneration Project's output that is offered to them, except for a very limited right to refuse deliveries during exceptional periods (e.g., when the chemical plant is not operating, to allow scheduled maintenance). Local Utility will enter into a 15-year agreement to operate the plant. The operating charges will be linked to changes in the producer price index (PPI), but these charges represent only a relatively small percentage of the cogeneration facility's operating costs. Also, the steam purchase agreement provides that the price of steam will escalate with changes in the PPI, which will at least partially offset inflation in the operating charges. The nexus of contracts is designed to minimize the Cogeneration Project's exposure to economic risk as well as raw material supply risk.

The Cogeneration Project's financial risk is largely a function of the chosen capital structure. Financial projections, which are discussed in Chapter 8, must be made in order to address this issue. (The Cogeneration Project's financial risk will be examined in Chapter 8.)

The Cogeneration Project involves no currency risk. The provisions of PURPA make the political risk, or regulatory risk, minimal. However, it is important for Chemical Company to purchase sufficient steam to qualify the Cogeneration Project under PURPA. The steam purchase agreement accomplishes this requirement. Environmental risk will be handled by making sure the Cogeneration Project receives all necessary environmental permits prior to the start of construction.

Force majeure risk is of two principal types: (1) force majeure asserted by one of the parties contractually obligated to Cogeneration Company to supply inputs or purchase output and (2) force majeure asserted by Cogeneration Company due to a natural calamity, such as an earthquake, or a catastrophic event, such as a fire. Cogeneration Company can purchase insurance to cover these risks. The insurance proceeds will be pledged to the Cogeneration Project's lenders, to help secure the loans.

CONCLUSION

Lenders will generally not lend funds to a project if their loans would be exposed to business or economic risks. Lenders are typically willing to bear some financial risk but they will insist on being compensated for bearing such risk. A critical aspect of financial engineering for a large project involves identifying all significant project risks and then crafting contractual arrangements to allocate those risks (among the parties who are willing to bear them) at the lowest ultimate cost to the project. Recent innovations in finance, including currency futures, interest rate swaps and caps, and currency swaps, have provided project sponsors with new vehicles for managing certain types of project-related risks cost-effectively.

4

Security Arrangements

Passive investors typically provide the bulk of the capital for a project. Generally, these investors, which include passive equity investors as well as lenders, are only interested in receiving a return on their financial investment. They are usually prepared to bear certain credit risks but extremely reluctant to bear significant operating risks or other risks not premised on the ability of the project entity to meet its financial obligations. Consequently, project financing entails developing a network of security arrangements to insulate the passive investors from all the noncredit risks associated with the project.

In a project financing, lenders require the sponsors or other creditworthy parties involved with the project to provide assurances, generally through contractual obligations, that (1) the project will be completed even if costs exceed those originally projected (or, if the project is not completed, its debt will be repaid in full); (2) the project, when completed, will generate cash sufficient to meet all of its debt service obligations; and (3) if for any reason, including force majeure, the project's operations are interrupted, suspended, or terminated, the project will continue to service (and fully repay on schedule) its debt obligations.

The credit supporting a project financing comes in the first instance from the project itself. Such credit strength often needs to be supplemented by a set of security arrangements between the project and its sponsors or other creditworthy parties. The benefit of these arrangements is assigned to project lenders. The security arrangements provide that creditworthy entities will undertake to advance funds to the project if needed to ensure completion. They also usually provide for some sort of undertaking on the part of creditworthy entities to supplement the project's cash flow after completion, to the extent required to enable the project entity to meet its debt service requirements. The precise form of these commitments varies, depending on the nature and projected economics of the project and on the prevailing political and capital market environments.

Several identifiable parties will normally have an interest in a project. Interested parties may include the sponsors, the suppliers of raw materials, the purchasers of project output, and the host political jurisdiction's government. The interests of these parties may diverge. Often, a particular party may have more than one area of interest. For example, a purchaser of the project's output may also be an equity investor in the project. Broadly speaking, a sponsor seeks to earn a rate of return on his or her equity investment that is commensurate with the project-related risks the sponsor assumes. A purchaser of the project's output is interested in obtaining a long-term source of supply at the lowest possible price. A government may regulate the price of the project's output or support the project for reasons of national interest, such as promoting employment. The willingness and ability of the various parties to assume risks associated with the project depend on the benefits each expects to derive from the project, the financial strength and business objectives of each party, and the perceived likelihood that those bearing project risks will be compensated fully for doing so.

PURPOSE OF SECURITY ARRANGEMENTS

Arranging sufficient credit support for project debt securities is a necessary precondition to arranging debt financing for any project. Lenders to a project will require that security arrangements be put in place to protect them from various risks. The contractual security arrangements apportion the risks among the project sponsors, the purchasers of the project output, and the other parties involved in the project. They represent a means of conveying the credit strength of going-concern entities to support project debt.

These contractual arrangements, whether in the form of a "hell-or-high-water" contract, a tariff, a financial support agreement, or some other form of contract, serve as the means by which the requisite credit support is conveyed to the project. The nature and extent of these contractual arrangements will depend on the type and magnitude of project risks, the financial strength of the parties at interest relative to those risks, and the profitability of the project.

Contractual undertakings that provide legal recourse to the credit strength of third parties normally form the nucleus of the security arrangements of a project. In most circumstances, these obligations will be several; each obligor's liability will be limited to a defined proportion of the total liability. The adequacy of such security depends on the creditworthiness of the parties so obligated, as well as on the extent of their respective obligations. The lenders' assessment of the adequacy of any security that is offered is likely to be strongly influenced by the economics of the project. If the economics of the project are sufficiently compelling so as to make many of the normal business risks appear highly remote, lenders may be willing to assume certain types of risks that they would otherwise eschew. The discussion below, concerning the security arrangements utilized in various gas pipeline financings, illustrates this point.

Project debt is normally secured by the direct assignment to lenders of the project's right to receive payments under various contracts, such as a completion agreement, a purchase and sale contract, or a financial support agreement. In addition, the indenture under which project debt is issued usually grants lenders a first mortgage lien on the project's assets. It will also contain certain covenants restricting activities of the project company. These covenants typically include limitations on (1) permitted investments, (2) funded indebtedness, (3) dividends to equity investors, (4) additional liens or other encumbrances, (5) expansion of the project, or (6) sales and leasebacks of project assets. In certain instances, lenders may also require the sponsors to agree to covenants designed to prevent any dissipation of their credit strength until the project is completed. Although all of the above items are relatively standard components of the lenders' security package, they are of varying practical value. For example, the degree of credit support a purchase and sale contract furnishes depends on the creditworthiness of the purchaser.

DIRECT SECURITY INTEREST IN PROJECT FACILITIES

Lenders will also require a direct security interest in project facilities, usually in the form of a first mortgage lien on all project facilities. This security interest is often of limited value prior to project completion. A half-completed petrochemical plant may be worth substantially less than what it has cost to build thus far, particularly if there are concerns about its ability to perform. In the extreme, a plant that has been constructed but fails to pass its completion test may be worth only its scrap value (which is why lenders normally insist that the project debt must be repaid immediately if a project fails to satisfy its completion test).

Following completion of the project, the first lien provides added security for project loans. The lien gives lenders the ability to seize the project assets and sell them (or hire someone to operate them on the lenders' behalf) if the project defaults on its debt obligations. It thus affords a second possible source of debt repayment (the first source is project cash flow). However, lenders would much prefer to have the project entity service its debt in a timely manner out of its cash flow. So, although the collateral value of a project's assets can affect the amount of funds prospective lenders would be willing to lend to a project, the adequacy of project cash flow is the primary criterion that lenders apply.

SECURITY ARRANGEMENTS COVERING COMPLETION

The security arrangements covering completion typically involve an obligation to bring the project to completion or else repay all project debt. Lenders normally require that the sponsors or other creditworthy parties provide an unconditional undertaking to furnish any funds needed to complete the project in accordance with the design specifications and place it into service by a specified date. The specified completion date normally allows for reasonable delays. If the project is not completed by the specified date, or if the project is abandoned prior to completion for any reason, the completion agreement typically requires the sponsors or other designated parties to repay all project debt. The obligations of the parties providing the completion undertaking terminate when completion of the project is achieved. (Appendix A compares the terms of three completion agreements.)

Completion is usually defined in terms of commercial completion. *Commercial completion* occurs when the construction of substantially all elements of the project is finished and an engineer's certificate is obtained as proof that (1) the sponsors of the project have accepted the work performed under the construction contract and agreed to make the payments called for under the contract and (2) the project has sustained a certain specified level of operations over a specified period of time (i.e., as defined in the completion agreement).

A completion undertaking requires that the sponsors (or other designated obligors) stand by to provide whatever additional funds are needed to complete the project in the event a cost overrun occurs. The strength of this obligation, which the lenders will require, will depend on a number of factors, including the amount of equity the project sponsors have contributed (and will commit to contribute) and the perceived risk of noncompletion. The completion undertaking typically represents an open-ended liability (although this is not always the case). Depending on the size of the project, the potential liability could be so great that the sponsors would be unable to discharge it on their own. Lenders will then require other creditworthy entities to stand behind the sponsors and shore up the completion undertaking. Lenders must be satisfied that the sponsors and any other designated obligors have adequate credit capacity, severally and in the aggregate, to advance funds to the extent necessary to complete the project or else repay project debt.

SECURITY ARRANGEMENTS COVERING DEBT SERVICE

After the project commences operations, contracts for the purchase and sale of the project's output or utilization of the project's services normally constitute the principal security arrangements for project debt. Broadly speaking, such contracts are intended to ensure that the project will receive revenues that are sufficient to cover operating costs fully and meet debt service obligations in a timely manner. Lenders almost always insist that these contractual obligations be in place, valid, and binding (governmental or regulatory approval may be required) before any portion of their loans can be drawn down.

The nature of the project's operating risks and the extent to which the purchase and sale contract protects lenders from these risks will determine whether the lenders will accept the purchase contract alone as security for their project loans. If the contract fails to cover certain contingencies that might call into question the project's ability to service its debt, and if prospective lenders view these adverse contingencies as significant, then other supplemental credit support arrangements will have to be added. For example, such arrangements might take the form of a cash deficiency agreement, which assures lenders that the project will always have adequate cash available to service its debt.

Examples

In the 1950s and 1960s, a number of so-called "promotional pipelines" were financed on the basis of take-or-pay contracts, which freed the gas purchasers from their obligations to pay in certain events of force majeure. The pipelines were built to transport gas from the newly discovered gas fields in West Texas and Oklahoma to the rapidly expanding markets in California and the Midwest. Laying a gas pipeline in the southwestern part of the United States was not deemed difficult or risky by lenders. Also, the operating experience of gas pipelines provided comfort that any outage would last no longer than a few days. The economics of these projects were compelling. A seemingly inexhaustible supply of natural gas could be obtained at prices (set by the Federal Power Commission) substantially below the cost of alternative fuels, and the markets for this product were expanding rapidly. Overall, lenders perceived the technical and operating risks as insignificant once the pipeline was placed into service. The combination of compelling economics and minimal business risks was sufficient to convince lenders to accept the take-or-pay obligations as a principal element of the security for their loans.

In contrast, the financing plan proposed for the Canadian Arctic Gas Pipeline envisioned that every element of project risk would be adequately covered by the security agreements. The project would have involved a number of unusual risks, including (1) dependence on a single petroleum reservoir, (2) use of a relatively new technology with respect to pipe diameter and pressurization, (3) extreme environmental conditions, (4) a large magnitude of projected capital costs relative to the financial capacity of the sponsors, and (5) a delivered cost of gas that made the project only marginally profitable. In addition, the large cost overruns the Trans Alaska Pipeline System experienced under similar environmental conditions caused concern, among prospective lenders to the Canadian Arctic Gas Pipeline, regarding completion risk. As a result, the project's financial advisers concluded that creditworthy parties had to agree to complete the project or else repay all project debt, and to provide revenues sufficient to cover operating costs and debt service costs in *all events,* including force majeure.

TYPES OF PURCHASE AND SALE CONTRACTS

Lenders typically require that creditworthy parties either directly guarantee the project debt or else provide assurances contractually that the debt will be fully serviced out of project revenues. In many circumstances, the purchase and sale contract does not have to be treated as indebtedness by the sponsors for financial reporting purposes. Off-balance-sheet treatment is possible when such contracts are considered to be commercial obligations that relate to operating expenditures rather than direct financial obligations. However, payments under such contracts must typically be disclosed in the footnotes to the purchaser's financial statements (unless they are not material), and they may constitute fixed charges for the purpose of calculating a sponsor's fixed charge coverage ratio.

The factors that determine what type of purchase and sale contract is most appropriate in connection with any particular project financing include (1) the type of facilities involved, (2) the nature of the purchase transaction, (3) the parties to the contract, and (4) the project's inherent risks. Figure 4.1 summarizes the most widely used types of purchase and sale contracts and characterizes their degree of credit support. A discussion of each type follows. (For examples of terms of three actual purchase and sale contracts, see Appendix A.)

Take-if-Offered Contract

A take-if-offered contract obligates the purchaser of the project's output or services to accept delivery and pay for the output and services that the project is able to deliver. The contract does not require the purchaser to pay if the project is unable to deliver the product or perform the services. Therefore, the contract protects lenders only if the project is operating at a level that enables it to service its debt. Consequently, if a project's performance might be subject to serious risk of prolonged curtailment or interruption, lenders will normally require that the credit support furnished by the take-if-offered contracts be supplemented with other security arrangements in order to provide adequate protection against events of force majeure.

Take-or-Pay Contract

A take-or-pay contract is similar to the take-if-offered contact. It obligates the purchaser of the project's output or services to pay for the output or services whether or not the purchaser takes delivery. It gives the buyer the option to make a cash payment in lieu of taking delivery, whereas the take-if-offered contract requires the buyer to accept deliveries. Cash payments are usually credited against charges for future deliveries. Like the take-if-offered contract, a take-or-pay contract usually does not require the purchaser to pay if the project is unable to

FIGURE 4.1   Types of Purchase and Sale Contracts

Type of Contract	Degree of Credit Support Provided
Take-if-Offered Contract	The contract obligates the purchaser of the project's output or services to take delivery and pay for the output or services only if the project is able to deliver them. No payment is required unless the project is able to make deliveries.
Take-or-Pay Contract	The contract obligates the purchaser of the project's output or services to pay for the output or services, regardless of whether the purchaser takes delivery. Cash payments are usually credited against charges for future deliveries.
Hell-or-High-Water Contract	There are no "outs," even in adverse circumstances beyond the control of the purchaser; the purchaser must pay in all events, even if no output is delivered.
Throughput Agreement	During a specified period of time, the shippers (e.g., oil companies or gas producers) ship through the pipeline enough product to provide the pipeline with sufficient cash revenues to pay all of its operating expenses and meet all of its debt service obligations.
Cost-of-Service Contract	The contract requires each obligor to pay its proportionate share of project costs as actually incurred, in return for a contracted share of the project's output or of the project's available services.
Tolling Agreement	The project company levies tolling charges for processing a raw material that is usually owned and delivered by the project sponsors.

deliver the product or perform the services. Therefore, the contract protects lenders only if the project is operating at a level that enables it to service its debt. Consequently, if a project's performance might be subject to serious risk of prolonged curtailment or interruption, lenders will normally require supplemental credit support to provide adequate force majeure protection.

Hell-or-High-Water Contract

A hell-or-high-water contract is similar to a take-or-pay contract except that there are no "outs," even when adverse circumstances are beyond the control of the purchaser. The purchaser must pay in all events, regardless of whether any output is delivered. This type of obligation therefore provides lenders with tighter security than either a take-if-offered contract or a take-or-pay contract because it protects against events of force majeure.

Throughput Agreement

A throughput agreement, typically employed in connection with an oil or petroleum product pipeline financing, requires that, during a specified period of time, the shippers (e.g., oil companies or gas producers) will ship through the pipeline enough product to provide the pipeline with sufficient cash revenues to pay all of its operating expenses and meet all of its debt service obligations. The throughput requirement is normally supplemented by a cash deficiency agreement, also called a "keep well" agreement. It obligates the shipping companies to advance funds to the pipeline if, for any reason, the pipeline does not have sufficient cash to discharge its obligations as they come due. Such cash payments are usually credited as advance payments for transportation services under the throughput agreement.

Cost-of-Service Contract

A cost-of-service contract requires each obligor to pay its proportionate share of project costs as actually incurred, in return for a contracted share of the project's output (e.g., electricity) or of the project's available services (e.g., space in a gas pipeline). Such a contract typically requires payments to be made whether or not any product or service is delivered. A limited form of cost-of-service obligation would cover (1) only the fixed charges that relate to providing the project's capacity or (2) only the variable costs that relate to furnishing the commodity or service. A full cost-of-service contract would cover operating, administrative, and maintenance expenses; depreciation and amortization; interest; return on equity capital; and income and other taxes (including any deferred taxes). This type of contract, therefore, entails a hell-or-high-water obligation. It protects the project's lenders against escalation in operating expenses, changes in tax laws, and other factors.

The full cost-of-service concept has been advanced by many public utilities as the basis for the proposed tariffs in connection with gas pipelines and liquefied natural gas projects. Protection against escalation in operating costs is particularly important in such projects because of the regulatory lag inherent in the rate-making process. Without this feature, the degree of leverage that might be achieved for these projects would be lower, which could adversely affect the rate of return available to the project's sponsors.

When the purchasers of the project company's output or services are public utilities, the cost-of-service tariff needs to be supported by assurances from the cognizant regulatory authorities that the purchasers of the project's output will be able to recover their share of the project's costs through the rates charged to their customers. Public utilities are normally allowed to earn a specified permitted maximum rate of return on their equity investment. The permitted rate of return is only sufficient to compensate them for bearing limited risks. As a result, they have neither the financial incentive nor the credit capacity to assume full responsibility for their share of a project's cost-of-service charges in all events. The regulatory assurances are designed to allocate the project risks to the purchasers' customers by recovering all costs of producing the particular good or providing the particular service. Although such cost recovery assurances would, in theory, compensate for most deficiencies in the public utility purchaser's creditworthiness, lenders tend to be skeptical of the permanence of any regulatory arrangement that provides security for a long-term contract. Unfortunately, regulatory authorities have displayed a distressing tendency to reverse themselves at a later date, based on new developments (and probably also hindsight).

Tolling Agreement

Under a tolling agreement, the project company levies tolling charges for processing a raw material that is usually owned and delivered by the project sponsors. The tolling charge payable by each participant is generally equal to its proportionate share of the total expenses incurred by the project. At a minimum, the tolling charge will be equal to the amount of operating costs and fixed charges, including debt service.

Step-Up Provisions

The strength of these various agreements can be enhanced in situations where there are multiple purchasers of the output (or multiple users of the facility). A step-up provision is often included in the purchase and sale contracts. It obligates all the other purchasers to increase their respective participations, thereby taking up the slack, in case one of the purchasers goes into default. Each of the purchasers coinsures the obligations of the others.

RAW MATERIAL SUPPLY AGREEMENTS

Purchase and sale contracts obligate the purchasers of the project's output or services to lend credit support to the project. Raw material supply agreements obligate the providers of the project's inputs to lend credit support. A raw material supply agreement represents a contract to fulfill the project's raw material requirements. The contract specifies certain remedies when deliveries are not made. Often, both purchase contracts and supply agreements are arranged to provide the credit support for a project.

A "supply-or-pay" contract obligates the raw material supplier to furnish the requisite amounts of the raw material specified in the contract or else make payments to the project entity that are sufficient to cover the project's debt service. For example, under a "supply-or-pay" contract in connection with a cogeneration project, a utility might undertake to supply the natural gas needed by the project. If the gas is not supplied for any reason, the utility would be obligated to pay all the project's costs. This obligation would not operate during periods of normal maintenance. Often, there is also a limited volume of deliveries that can be curtailed each year without triggering the supply-or-pay obligation under the contract.

SUPPLEMENTAL CREDIT SUPPORT

Depending on the structure of a project's completion agreement and the purchase and sale contract(s), it may be necessary to provide supplemental credit support through additional security arrangements. These arrangements will operate in the event the completion undertaking or the purchase and sale contracts fail to provide the cash to enable the project entity to meet its debt service obligations. Such mechanisms, also referred to as "ultimate backstops," might take the form of a financial support agreement, a cash deficiency agreement, a capital subscription agreement, a clawback agreement, or an escrow fund. All of these agreements are designed to accomplish the same purpose: They provide a commitment from one or more creditworthy parties to supply any cash that may be necessary for the project to meet its cash obligations. The way in which the cash payment is treated, however, may differ, depending on the form of the backstop arrangement.

Financial Support Agreement

A financial support agreement can take the form of a letter of credit or similar guarantee provided by the project sponsors. Payments made under the letter of credit or guarantee are typically treated as subordinated loans to the project company. In some cases, it is advantageous to purchase the guarantee of a financially able party (such as a bank, an insurance company, or a credit insurer) to provide credit support for the obligations of the project company. Such forms of credit support are frequently used in connection with tax-exempt financings and commercial paper financings.

Cash Deficiency Agreement

A cash deficiency agreement, as the name implies, is designed to cover any cash shortfalls that would impair the project company's ability to meet its debt service requirements. The obligor makes a cash payment sufficient to cover the cash deficiency. Payments made under a cash deficiency agreement, as discussed in connection with throughput agreements, are usually credited as cash advances toward payment for future services or product from the project.

Capital Subscription Agreement

A capital subscription agreement obligates one or more creditworthy parties to purchase, for cash, securities issued by the project entity, to the extent required to enable the project entity to cover any cash shortfall. A payment under a capital subscription agreement is typically structured as a cash purchase of junior securities, such as common stock or subordinated debt.

Clawback Agreement

A clawback agreement represents an undertaking to contribute cash to the project to the extent the project sponsors (1) received any cash dividends from the project company or (2) realized any project-related tax benefits on account of their investments in the project. If they received tax benefits, the potential cash contribution obligation is limited to the cash value of the project-related tax benefits. Payments made under a clawback agreement can be structured by the project sponsors as either an equity investment or a subordinated loan.

Escrow Fund

In certain instances, lenders may require the project to establish an escrow fund that typically contains between 12 and 18 months' debt service. A trustee can draw moneys from the escrow fund if the project's cash flow from operations proves insufficient to cover the project's debt service obligations.

INSURANCE

Lenders typically require that insurance be taken out to protect against certain risks of force majeure. The insurance will provide funds to restore the project in the event of force majeure, thereby ensuring that the project remains a viable operating entity. Insurance protection is especially important when the ability of the obligated parties to repay project debt on an accelerated basis is questionable. To the extent available, the project sponsors normally purchase commercial insurance to cover the cost of damage caused by natural disasters. They may also secure business interruption insurance to cover certain other risks. In addition, lenders may require the sponsors to agree contractually to provide additional funds to the project to the extent insurance proceeds are insufficient to restore operations.

As noted earlier, project financing has enjoyed wide application in funding the development of independent power projects. One subclass of independent power projects consists of hydropower facilities, and a principal risk inherent in such projects is uncertainty about the future water level of the river on which the facility is located. Insurers have been willing to write policies to protect lenders against the risk of low water. The insurer pays on the policy during periods when the facility is not able to generate (and sell) sufficient electricity to enable the project to make its scheduled debt service payments (see Kensinger and Martin, 1988, p. 73).

THE COGENERATION PROJECT

The contractual arrangements specific to any particular project can be designed so as to allocate the project risks among the various parties to the project according to their respective risk tolerances. In complex projects that involve several parties, a number of contracts may be interwoven to provide the security arrangements. Figure 4.2 shows the principal contractual arrangements that support the financing for the Cogeneration Project. The nexus of contracts is designed, ultimately, to allocate the economic benefits of the project in a manner commensurate with the allocation of project risks. These contractual arrangements

FIGURE 4.2 Contractual Arrangements That Support the Financing for the Cogeneration Project

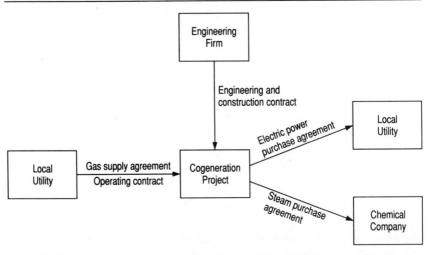

furnish the credit support network necessary to arrange debt financing and passive equity financing.[1]

Engineering and Construction Contract

Engineering Firm is willing to enter into a fixed-price turnkey contract to design and construct the cogeneration facility. The specified fixed price is $100 million. Engineering Firm estimates that design, construction, and preoperation testing will take two years. Engineering Firm will guarantee that the cogeneration facility will operate at its design capacity, consisting of 250 megawatts of electricity and 150,000 pounds per hour of steam.

Engineering Firm will arrange with subcontractors to warrant their work. The licensor of the technology for the Cogeneration Project will have to warrant that it will work. Because the technology is not only proven but also operational in many plants in the United States, the technology licensor should be willing to provide this warranty.

Gas Supply Agreement

Local Utility and Cogeneration Project will enter into a 15-year gas supply agreement. Local Utility will supply all the natural gas the project will need—1,950 million BTUs (British thermal units) per hour, at capacity operation. During the first year of operations, the gas charge will be $3.00 per million BTUs. Thereafter, the gas price will change in line with the change in the price Cogeneration Project receives for the electricity it sells to Local Utility. The gas supply agreement eliminates the risk that the project's operations might be interrupted because Cogeneration Project is unable to obtain sufficient fuel at an acceptable price.

Operating Contract

Local Utility and Cogeneration Project will enter into an operating contract in which Local Utility will assume full responsibility for operating and maintaining the cogeneration facility. Local Utility has agreed to furnish these services for $6 million per year, including management fees, during the initial year of operations. It has also agreed to escalate its charges for these services in subsequent years at the rate of increase in the PPI. Having an experienced operator with a sound track record and an incentive to keep the facility operating should satisfy lenders that the cogeneration facility's operations are unlikely to be interrupted because of operator errors.[2] The specified lump-sum operator charges and the specified escalation rate are designed to control economic risk.

Electric Power Purchase Agreement

Local Utility and Cogeneration Project will enter into a 15-year electric power purchase agreement. Local Utility will be obligated contractually to purchase all of the electricity Cogeneration Project offers to Local Utility. The purchase price will be $40.00 per megawatt-hour during the first year of operations. The agreement provides that Local Utility will purchase part of the electricity according to a schedule of fixed prices and the balance at prices that will vary according to the price Local Utility receives when it sells the electricity to industrial users. The net effect is that Cogeneration Project expects the price it will realize from the sale of electricity to Local Utility to escalate at the rate of 6 percent per annum over the life of the contract.

The electric power purchase agreement is a take-if-offered contract, not a take-or-pay contract. Local Utility must accept delivery of all the electric power the Cogeneration Project offers to sell it, except for its very limited right under the contract to refuse a small amount of deliveries. Local Utility is obligated to pay only for electric power that Cogeneration Project delivers to Local Utility. Consequently, Engineering Firm's guarantee of the cogeneration facility's ability to perform and Local Utility's ability to operate and maintain the facility properly are important to ensure that adequate quantities of electricity will be available for regular delivery to Local Utility.

Steam Purchase Agreement

Chemical Company and Cogeneration Project will enter into a 15-year take-if-offered steam purchase agreement. Cogeneration Project agrees contractually to supply a minimum of 1,182.6 million pounds of steam per year (representing 90 percent of capacity) to Chemical Company. The steam will have to satisfy various quality standards that the contract will specify. The steam price will be $4.00 per thousand pounds during the initial year of operations. Thereafter, the steam price will escalate with the PPI.

In addition to these contractual arrangements, Cogeneration Project will arrange appropriate insurance coverage via property and casualty, workers' compensation, personal liability, and business interruption insurance policies.

CONCLUSION

Security arrangements are designed to fortify the credit strength of a project. In effect, they increase the proportion of a project's construction cost that can be funded with project borrowings. Security arrangements fall into two general categories: (1) those that ensure project completion (or else repayment of project debt in full) and (2) those that ensure timely payment of debt service following project completion. The security arrangements for a project are crafted to suit the economic characteristics of the project and the risk-return preferences of the various parties associated with the project. They take the form of contractual undertakings, which allocate project risks as well as financial returns.

5

Legal Structure

One of the most critical questions project sponsors need to address is whether a legally distinct "project financing entity" should be employed, and if so, how it should be organized. The appropriate legal structure for a project depends on a variety of business, legal, accounting, tax, and regulatory factors, including: (1) the number of participants and the business objectives of each; (2) the project's capital cost and the anticipated earnings pattern of the project; (3) the requirements of regulatory bodies; (4) the existing debt instruments and the tax positions of the participants; and (5) the political jurisdiction(s) in which the project will operate.[1] This chapter analyzes these factors as they relate to the undivided joint interest, corporate, partnership, and limited liability company forms of organization. Figure 5.1 summarizes the principal considerations associated with selecting the appropriate form of organization for a project.

UNDIVIDED JOINT INTEREST

Projects are often owned directly by the participants as tenants in common. Under the undivided joint interest ownership structure, each participant (1) owns an undivided interest in the real and personal property constituting the project and (2) shares in the benefits and risks of the project in direct proportion to the ownership percentage. The ownership interests relate to the entire assets of the project; no participant is entitled to any particular portion of the property.

When the project is organized, the participants choose someone in their ranks to serve as the project operator. This arrangement is particularly suitable when one of the owners already has operations in the same industry that are of a similar nature, or otherwise has qualified employees available. The duties of the operator and the obligations of all other parties are specified in an operating agreement. The agreement is an attempt to provide for all possible situations that might arise in the relationships among the various parties. The operator is responsible for maintaining a record of capital expenditures and operating expenses and for making the day-to-day operating decisions that determine the profitability of the project.

The operating agreement normally provides that the sponsors will bear the liabilities arising out of the project *severally,* in proportion to their respective ownership percentages. However, there is no dollar limit to the potential liability each sponsor may face. As a matter of law, the project sponsors are severally liable for all the obligations relating to the co-tenancy. But suppose that, for business or other reasons, they prefer not to accept a new co-owner who has acquired the interest of a defaulting sponsor. To avoid this situation, the remaining sponsors may elect to assume the obligations of the defaulting sponsor. In that case, the nature of each sponsor's liability is, in practical terms, joint and several rather than merely several. To lay off the attendant risks, the project sponsors normally purchase extensive commercial insurance covering general business liabilities.

In general, the joint venture agreement will require each participant to assume responsibility for raising its share of the project's external financing requirements. Each sponsor will be free to do so by whatever means are most appropriate to its circumstances. Thus, for example, if a sponsor owns 25 percent of the project, it will be required to provide, from its own resources, 25 percent of the funds necessary to construct the project. The project entity could not issue debt securities on its own because it does not have the legal standing to enter into a contract to repay the obligation.

There are often financing advantages to the undivided joint interest structure. The project sponsors are the financing entities. Each sponsor normally has established an earnings record and has an equity base and outstanding debt instruments. Accordingly, it has established banking relationships and experience in issuing new securities.

The undivided joint interest structure has particular appeal when firms of widely differing credit strength are sponsoring the project. By financing independently, the higher-rated credits can borrow at a cost that is lower than the cost at which the project entity can borrow,

FIGURE 5.1 Comparison of Alternative Forms of Organization for a Project

	Undivided Joint Interest	Corporation
Ownership of Project Assets	All property constituting the project is owned directly by the participants as tenants in common. Ownership interests therefore relate collectively to all property.	Project assets are owned by the corporation.
Operating Characteristics:		
—Management	Co-owners appoint an operator (usually a co-owner) to manage the project. Approval by a steering committee containing representatives of all the co-owners is often required for major decisions.	The project corporation operates the project. Employees of the project corporation manage the project. The equity owners are represented on the project corporation's board of directors.
—Sharing of project costs and benefits	Project costs and benefits are usually allocated in the same proportion as project ownership. Co-owners enter into an operating agreement, which specifies their rights and obligations.	Allocation is determined by the contracts between the project corporation and the other parties at interest. Such contracts normally cover completion, purchase of project output, and supplemental arrangements to cover the project's debt service obligations.
Participants' Liability for Project Obligations:		
—Nature of liability	Operating agreement normally provides that any liabilities relating to the co-tenancy will be borne severally by the project's co-owners in proportion to their respective ownership percentages.	Equity owners have no direct liability for project obligations except as specifically defined in contractual undertakings.
—Dollar amount of exposure	Unlimited liability.	Liability limited to equity invested except as otherwise agreed.
Financing:		
—General structure	Each co-owner is responsible for providing its pro rata share of the capital cost of the project from its own financial resources.	Equity funds are contributed by sponsors. The project corporation issues debt secured by a lien on project assets and by the project corporation's right to receive payments under various contracts.

Partnership	Limited Liability Company
Project assets are owned by the partnership.	Project assets are owned by the company.
The project partnership operates the project. One of the general partners is usually designated the manager of partnership operations. The partnership agreement specifies who exercises operating and management authority.	The project company operates the project. Employees of the project company manage the project. The equity owners are represented on the project company's board of directors.
The partners enter into a partnership agreement, which specifies their rights and obligations. Project costs and benefits are typically allocated in proportion to project ownership.	Allocation is determined by the contracts between the project company and the other parties at interest. Such contracts normally cover completion, purchase of project output, and supplemental arrangements to cover the project's debt service obligations.
Under local law, general partners are jointly and severally liable for all obligations of the partnership as well as for certain liabilities incurred by any general partner. However, partnership agreement and contractual undertakings generally provide for several liability. Limited partners have no liability for partnership obligations except obligations they specifically undertake.	Equity owners have no direct liability for project obligations except as specifically defined in contractual undertakings.
Liability unlimited for general partners. Liability limited to equity invested for limited partners except as otherwise agreed.	Liability limited to equity invested except as otherwise agreed.
Sponsors provide equity in the form of partners' capital contributions. The partnership issues debt secured by a lien on project assets and the project company's right to receive payments under various contracts.	Equity funds are contributed by sponsors. The project company issues debt secured by a lien on project assets and by the project company's right to receive payments under various contracts.

(Continued)

FIGURE 5.1 *(Continued)*

	Undivided Joint Interest	*Corporation*
Financing: *(continued)*		
—Financing vehicle	Corporate subsidiary of each co-owner.	Project corporation or a special-purpose corporate subsidiary.
Participants' Accounting Treatment for Equity Investment		
—Less than 20% ownership and no effective control	Proportional consolidation of project assets, revenues, and expenses.	Equity investment accounted for under the "cost method." Income recognized only to the extent dividends are received. Project assets and liabilities are not reflected on equity holder's balance sheet.
—Greater than 20% and not over 50% ownership; no control	Proportional consolidation of project assets, revenues, and expenses.	Equity investment accounted for under the "equity method." Pro rata share of project income or loss is recognized by sponsor. Project assets and liabilities are not reflected on sponsor's balance sheet. If investment is material, summary financial statements of project would be disclosed in footnote to sponsor's financial statements. Sponsor may elect proportional consolidation of project income statement and balance sheet on a line-by-line basis if certain conditions are met.
—Greater than 50% ownership	Proportional consolidation of project assets, revenues, and expenses.	Full consolidation is normally required.
Income Tax Treatment[a]		
—Taxable entity	Co-owners.	Project corporation.
—Election of tax accounting methods	Separate election by each co-owner.	Single election by project corporation.

Partnership	Limited Liability Company
Special-purpose corporate subsidiary of the general partnership.	Project company or a special-purpose corporate subsidiary.
Equity investment accounted for under the "cost method." Income recognized only to the extent dividends are received. Project assets and liabilities are not reflected on equity holder's balance sheet.	Equity investment accounted for under the "cost method." Income recognized only to the extent dividends are received. Project assets and liabilities are not reflected on equity holder's balance sheet.
Equity investment accounted for under the "equity method." Pro rata share of project income or loss is recognized by sponsor. Project assets and liabilities are not reflected on sponsor's balance sheet. If investment is material, summary financial statements of project would be disclosed in footnote to sponsor's financial statements. Sponsor may elect proportional consolidation of project income statement and balance sheet on a line-by-line basis if certain conditions are met.	Equity investment accounted for under the "equity method." Pro rata share of project income or loss is recognized by sponsor. Project assets and liabilities are not reflected on sponsor's balance sheet. If investment is material, summary financial statements of project would be disclosed in footnote to sponsor's financial statements. Sponsor may elect proportional consolidation of project income statement and balance sheet on a line-by-line basis if certain conditions are met.
Full consolidation is normally required.	Full consolidation is normally required.
Partners.	Shareholders in the company, which is treated as a partnership for federal income tax purposes.
Most elections are made by the partnership; binding on all partners.[a]	Most elections are made by the company; binding on the shareholders.[a]

(Continued)

FIGURE 5.1 *(Continued)*

	Undivided Joint Interest	*Corporation*
Income Tax Treatment *(continued)*		
—Availability of project depreciation, interest expense, and investment tax credit (ITC) to sponsors	All tax consequences of project flow through directly to the co-owners.	Project affects taxable income of equity holders only to the extent of dividends received from the project unless one equity holder owns (1) at least 80% of voting stock and (2) at least 80% of all nonvoting stock other than nonvoting preferred of the project corporation, in which case the project corporation may be consolidated with the 80% owner for tax purposes.
—Limitation on project deductions taken by participants	No limitations.	Project deductions may not be taken by equity holders unless consolidation is permitted. No limitation if tax consolidation occurs.
—Taxation of project income	Project income is taxed at co-owner level only.	Project income is taxed at project corporation level. Dividends are also taxable to equity holders after 70% dividends received deduction.[b]

[a] If a partnership qualifies under Section 761 of the Internal Revenue Code for exclusion from partnership tax treatment, the tax treatment of the partners will be the same as that of co-owners specified in the Undivided Joint Interest column. In order to qualify for the Section 761 election, the partners must (1) own the project assets as co-owners, (2) reserve the right separately to take their respective shares of any property produced or extracted, and (3) not jointly sell services or the property produced or extracted.

based on its composite credit. Depending on the sponsors' ability to take immediate advantage of the tax benefits of ownership arising out of the project, direct co-ownership may also provide the project sponsors with immediate cash flow to fund their equity investments.

In certain situations, economic and financial considerations may suggest that it would be preferable to create a separate project entity that can arrange the financing for the project. If the project's construction cost is large relative to each sponsor's total capitalization, the project-related financing obligation of each sponsor, together with the normal financing requirements of its ongoing business, might

Partnership	Limited Liability Company
Tax benefits normally flow through to partners in same proportion as ownership percentages. Disproportionate allocation of iTC is virtually impossible. Disproportionate allocation of other items is substantially restricted.[a]	Tax benefits normally flow through to shareholders in same proportion as ownership percentages. Disproportionate allocation of ITC is virtually impossible. Disproportionate allocation of other items is substantially restricted.[a]
Deductions (except ITC) are normally limited to the tax basis of each partner's investment. Calculation of basis generally excludes nonrecourse liabilities.[a]	Deductions (except ITC) are normally limited to the tax basis of each shareholder's investment. Calculation of basis generally excludes nonrecourse liabilities.[a]
Project income is taxed at partner level only.	Project income is taxed at shareholder level only.

[b] An unaffiliated corporation can deduct 70% of the dividends it receives from the project corporation. The deduction percentage is 80% when the sponsoring corporation owns at least 20% but less than 80% of the project corporation. The deduction percentage is 100% when the sponsoring corporation owns at least 80% of the project corporation (because full tax consolidation is then possible).

exceed the debt limits imposed by its existing debt agreements. The additional debt load might cause the sponsors' debt-to-equity ratios and interest coverage ratios to suffer. Serious deterioration in these ratios might even result in lower bond ratings and therefore higher interest costs. The problem becomes more serious when there is a lengthy construction period during which the project has no earnings. It is also important to note that the ratio of indebtedness to capitalization required by the indentures of some going concerns is considerably lower than the debt ratios that lenders have permitted some new projects to achieve.

Accounting Considerations

An undivided joint interest is not recognized as a separate entity for accounting purposes. Each participant reflects its proportionate share of project assets, revenues, and operating expenses in its own financial statements. Any direct liabilities incurred by a co-owner in order to fund its share of the project's construction cost would appear on its own balance sheet.

Tax Considerations

The Internal Revenue Service (IRS) has taken the position that the expense-sharing arrangement embodied in a manufacturing or processing facility that is organized as an undivided joint interest should be treated for tax purposes as a partnership.[2] However, Section 761 of the Internal Revenue Code permits the sponsors to make an election to exclude the project from the rules pertaining to the taxation of partnerships. In general, the project sponsors can make a Section 761 election if they (1) own the property as co-owners, (2) reserve the right separately to take in kind or dispose of their respective shares of project output, and (3) do not jointly sell project output. Each project sponsor may delegate authority to sell its share of project output for a period of time, which cannot exceed one year. Exclusion from partnership tax treatment permits each sponsor to make its own tax elections as best suit its own tax situation. For example, the project sponsors would not all be required to use the same method to depreciate project assets. If the sponsors make a Section 761 election, the amount of tax deductions arising out of the project that a corporate co-owner can claim on its tax return becomes less restricted. But if the project is treated as a partnership for tax purposes, corporate partners, in some cases, will not be able to deduct amounts in excess of the tax basis in their respective partnership interests. (For a more complete discussion, see the Partnership section on tax considerations, later in this chapter.) Whether the undivided joint interest is taxed as a co-tenancy or as a partnership, project tax deductions arising from interest, depreciation, and investment tax credit, if any, flow through directly to the co-owners; "double taxation" of project income is avoided.

   In some instances, the IRS has deemed an undivided joint interest to be an "association," which is treated as a corporation for tax purposes.

Because of the disadvantages that arise from being taxed as a corporation, it is important to draft the operating agreement in a manner that avoids certain "indicia" of corporate status. At least two of the following conditions must be satisfied: (1) there is joint decision making by the sponsors rather than centralized management; (2) ownership interests are not transferable without the consent of the other sponsors; (3) at least one of the sponsors must have direct exposure to project liabilities (and that sponsor cannot simply be a shell without substantial assets); or (4) the joint venture terminates upon the bankruptcy, resignation, or expulsion of any sponsor. Before committing funds to the project, lenders normally require a ruling from the IRS or, at a minimum, an opinion of counsel, as to the tax treatment that will apply.

CORPORATION

The form of organization most frequently chosen for a project is the corporation. A new corporation is formed to construct, own, and operate the project. This corporation, which is typically owned by the project sponsors, raises funds through the sponsors' equity contributions and through the sale of senior debt securities issued by the corporation. The senior debt securities typically take the form of either first mortgage bonds or debentures containing a negative pledge covenant that protects their senior status. The negative pledge prohibits the project corporation from granting a lien on project assets in favor of other lenders unless the debentures are secured ratably. The corporate form permits creation of other types of securities, such as junior debt (second mortgage, unsecured, or subordinated debt), preferred stock, or convertible securities.

The corporate form of organization offers the advantages of limited liability and an issuing vehicle. Nevertheless, the corporate form has disadvantages that must be considered. The sponsors usually do not receive immediate tax benefits from any investment tax credit (ITC) the project entity can claim or from construction period losses of the project (see "Tax Considerations" below). Also, the ability of a sponsor to invest in the project corporation may be limited by provisions contained in the sponsor's bond indentures or loan agreements. In particular, the provisions restricting "investments" either by amount or by type may impose such limitations.

Accounting Considerations

Accounting Research Bulletin No. 51 (ARB 51) and Accounting Principles Board Opinion No. 18 (APB 18) embody the generally accepted accounting principles governing consolidation for financial reporting purposes. ARB 51 requires an entity that controls another entity to consolidate the controlled entity's financial results with its own on a line-by-line basis. Control normally means ownership of more than a 50 percent voting interest. However, control may also be exercised by other means, such as an agreement that vests control irrespective of the distribution of voting rights. APB 18 calls for equity accounting in noncontrol situations where there is a significant ownership interest.

The impact a project has on the financial statements of a project sponsor depends principally on the sponsor's percentage ownership of the project corporation. If a single sponsor owns more than 50 percent of project equity, full consolidation is generally required. In that case, the sponsor must consolidate the project's financial statements on a line-by-line basis and report a minority interest to reflect the equity interest owned by others. The "equity method" is normally employed by project sponsors that have an equity ownership interest of between 20 percent and 50 percent. Under equity accounting, a sponsor carries its ownership interest in the project on its balance sheet as an investment, and reports its proportionate share of project income or loss. Project assets and liabilities in that case are not included on the sponsor's balance sheet. On the other hand, a sponsor may be able to consolidate its proportionate share of project financial statements on a line-by-line basis ("proportional consolidation") if the project is in a line of business that is related to one of the sponsor's principal lines of business and certain other conditions are met. If a sponsor owns less than 20 percent of project equity, it will normally account for its investment under the "cost method": The equity contribution is carried as an investment at original cost, and the sponsor reports income only to the extent it receives dividends from the project corporation. Project assets and liabilities are not included on the sponsor's balance sheet.

Regardless of the manner in which a sponsor accounts for its equity investment in the project, the sponsor would normally have to disclose in a footnote (1) any material contingent liability with respect to the project, and (2) summary financial statements for the project if the investment is material with respect to the sponsor's overall operations. The nature of the footnote disclosure for contingent liabilities depends principally on two factors: (1) the extent to which it can quantify the potential dollar amount of the liability and (2) the materiality of this amount in the context of the sponsor's overall operations. Figure 5.2 is an example of a footnote disclosure of contingent payment liabilities relating to pipeline transportation services.

Tax Considerations

A project corporation is a separate taxable entity. Section 1501 of the Internal Revenue Code permits an affiliated group of corporations to file a consolidated federal income tax return. Section 1504(a), as amended, permits a corporation to be included in an affiliated group only if other members of the group hold (1) 80 percent or more of the total voting power of the corporation's stock (common and preferred) and (2) 80 percent or more of each nonvoting class of stock other than nonvoting preferred stock. Assuming that no single participant owns sufficient equity to consolidate the project entity for tax purposes, the tax benefits of ownership arising out of the project, such as investment tax credit, depreciation deductions, and interest deductions, including deductions for interest paid during the construction period, are available only to the project corporation; they can be claimed only to the extent the project generates adequate taxable income once it starts operations. Such tax benefits would have to be deferred if the project corporation has operating losses. The tax benefits would be lost forever if carryforward periods are exceeded.

FIGURE 5.2   Footnote Disclosure of Minimum Payment Obligation

Trunkline has contracts for transportation services which provide for minimum monthly charges determined by those companies' effective rates, as approved by FERC [the Federal Energy Regulatory Commission]. Trunkline's payments under such contracts in 1992, 1991, and 1990 were $13.6 million, $16.3 million, and $17.2 million, respectively. These amounts included payments to an affiliate in 1991 and 1990 of $5.3 million and $10.6 million, respectively. Minimum annual payments under the above agreements are $12.5 million for 1993, $11.6 million in 1994, $3.0 million in 1995, 1996, and 1997, and $1.3 million in 1998.

Source: Panhandle Eastern Corporation, Annual Report, 1992, p. 47. (Trunkline Gas Company (Trunkline) is a wholly owned subsidiary of Panhandle Eastern Corporation.)

Under certain circumstances, a corporate structure with a capitalization that consists of disproportionate dollar amounts of voting and nonvoting securities can enable a project sponsor to realize the flow-through of the tax benefits of ownership, as happens with a partnership. For example, if the equity of the project corporation were comprised of $1,000 of nonvoting preferred stock and $10 of voting common stock, a sponsor who owns 80 percent of the voting stock would normally be able to consolidate the project entity for tax purposes. Tax consolidation would enable it to receive a direct flow-through of the project-related tax benefits of ownership.

Because the project corporation is a taxable entity, absent consolidation, the project's income is exposed to two levels of taxation. If the project corporation declares any dividends, the dividend income would be subject to income taxes at each sponsor's applicable income tax rate (which is reduced by the intercorporate dividends received deduction[3]). To this extent, "double taxation" of project earnings occurs.

PARTNERSHIP

The partnership form of organization is frequently used in structuring joint venture projects. Each project sponsor, either directly or through a subsidiary, becomes a partner in a partnership that is formed to own and operate the project. The partnership issues securities (either directly or through a corporate borrowing vehicle) to finance construction. Under the terms of a partnership agreement, the partnership hires its own operating personnel and provides for a management structure and a decision-making process.

A partnership is particularly attractive for so-called "cost companies"; a profit is not realized at the project level but instead is earned further downstream in the sale of the project's output. The Internal Revenue Code generally precludes the utilization of a cost company in the corporate form of organization because, in the absence of consolidation, the tax benefits of ownership cannot flow through to any of the project sponsors.

The Uniform Partnership Act imposes joint and several liability on all the general partners for all obligations of the partnership. They are also jointly and severally liable for certain other project-related obligations any of the general partners incurs in the ordinary course of business or within the scope of a general partner's apparent authority. In theory, the extent of a general partner's potential liability could exceed its reported balance sheet liabilities if one of the general partners were to act improperly. A partnership can also have any number of limited partners. They are not exposed to unlimited liability. However, there must be at least one general partner who does have such exposure. The exposure of the project sponsors to project liabilities can be reduced in two ways. First, a wholly owned corporate subsidiary (called a "buffer subsidiary") can be created to act as a general partner in the project. Figure 5.3 exhibits such a structure. However, there is necessarily some risk that a court might, in the future, "pierce

FIGURE 5.3 Ownership Structure When a Project Is Organized as a Partnership

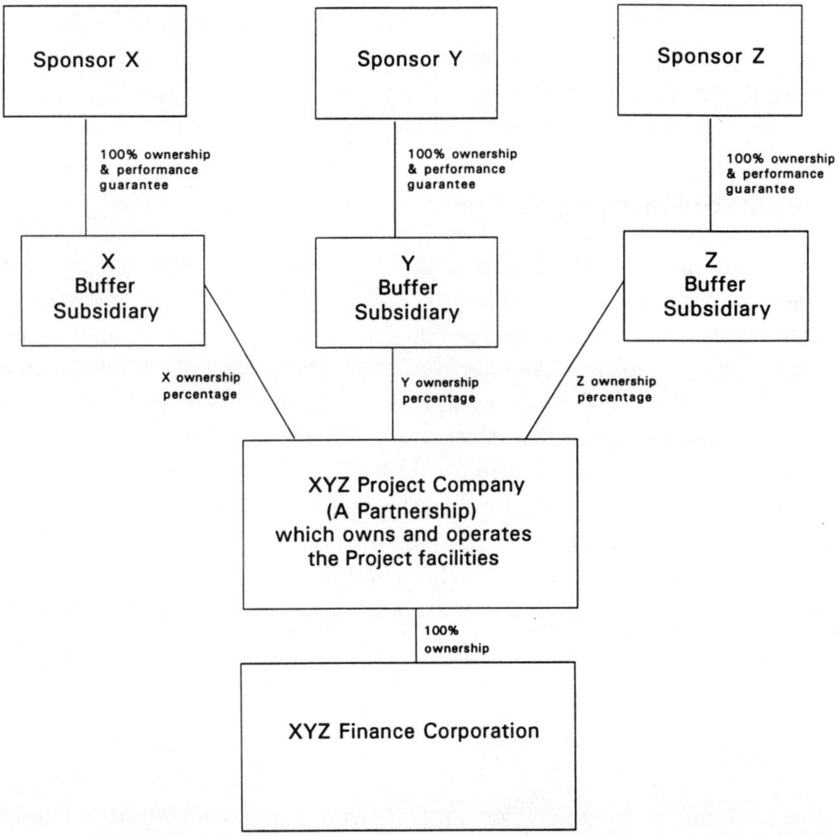

the corporate veil" and impose liability on the parent unless the court is satisfied that the corporate subsidiary has a valid business purpose. Second, and more importantly, the partnership can provide in its loan agreements and other contracts that recourse under these contracts is limited to partnership assets.

Each project sponsor must determine whether any provisions contained in its corporate charter would limit its ability to act as a general partner, and whether any bond indenture or loan agreement covenants exist that might prevent it from acting in that capacity. It must also check whether any of these debt agreements would include in the general partner's outstanding "indebtedness" for covenant compliance test purposes any portion of the partnership's debt. Similarly, indentures and loan agreements must be analyzed to determine whether any such restrictions would also apply to a buffer subsidiary, if one is used. Even if using a buffer subsidiary would avoid potentially troublesome charter or indenture restrictions, it might create other indenture problems. For example, indenture provisions governing permitted investments might prevent the use of a buffer subsidiary even in cases where they would not prevent a direct investment in the general partnership.

Corporate Financing Vehicle

A partnership typically borrows through a special-purpose corporate financing vehicle that is owned by the partnership. Legal investment regulations or investment policy considerations that limit certain major lenders' ability to purchase noncorporate obligations often necessitate the use of a corporate borrowing vehicle. In that borrowing structure, notes issued by the partnership would secure the debt obligations of the corporate borrowing vehicle. The terms of the partnership notes would be substantially identical to the terms of the notes issued by the corporate financing vehicle. The terms of the partnership notes would normally preclude recourse to the general credit of the partners. Accordingly, project lenders would have to look solely to the project cash flow for the payment of interest and for repayment of the principal on project debt.

Example

The Indiantown Cogeneration Project, which is the subject of Chapter 11, utilizes a corporate borrowing vehicle. The organizational structure is a limited partnership, Indiantown Cogeneration, L.P. The partnership set up Indiantown Cogeneration Funding Corporation to serve as a co-issuer of the debt incurred to finance construction of the project. The corporate vehicle has nominal assets and will not conduct any operations of its own; it was set up for the sole purpose of allowing certain institutional investors that might be limited as a matter of law or policy from investing in securities issued by partnerships to purchase first mortgage bonds issued by the partnership.[4]

Accounting Considerations

An equity interest in a partnership is generally accounted for by each partner in the same manner as an equity investment in a corporation, provided that recourse for partnership liabilities is limited to partnership assets. If a partner owns no more than 50 percent (but at least 20 percent) of partnership equity and does not exercise effective control, the partner would normally account for its equity investment under the equity method. Accordingly, the partner would recognize in its income statement its pro rata share of project income or loss. However, the partner would not reflect project assets and liabilities on its balance sheet. If a partner owns more than 50 percent of partnership equity, full consolidation is normally required.

A partner's contingent liabilities with respect to the partnership are accounted for in the same manner as discussed in connection with the corporate form. In addition, each partner is normally required to disclose summary financial statements of the partnership in a footnote to its own financial statements, if the partner's investment is material in relation to its overall financial condition.

Tax Considerations

A partnership is a separate entity for tax purposes. Unlike a corporation, the net income or loss of the partnership will be passed through to the partners. The partnership itself does not incur any income tax liability. Each partner includes in its own tax return its proportionate share of partnership income or loss. Each partner benefits from investment tax credits, if any, arising from qualifying capital investment projects. The use of a buffer subsidiary to serve as one of the general partners does not impair the sponsor's ability to claim these tax deductions so long as the subsidiary is consolidated for income tax purposes.

However, a partner may deduct partnership losses only to the extent of its tax basis in its investment in the partnership. A general partner's tax basis includes the sum of (1) its original investment in the partnership, (2) a pro rata share of partnership liabilities, and (3) a pro rata share of the partnership's undistributed income reduced by a pro rata share of the partnership's losses and distributions to the general partner.[5] A limited partner's tax basis is determined in the same manner as a general partner's, except that it excludes partnership liabilities for which only the general partners are liable. The Internal Revenue Code provides that most elections affecting the partners' taxable income must be made at the partnership level, in which case they apply uniformly to all partners.

As in the case of an undivided joint interest, the partners to a project can make a Section 761 election in order to avoid partnership tax treatment, even though the project is legally constituted as a partnership. Such an election permits each partner to account for its investment in the project by utilizing, for tax purposes, the method most appropriate to its own tax situation. It also enables a partner to deduct its share of losses from the partnership in excess of its tax basis in its partnership investment. However, the Section 761 election is only available if the partners (1) own the project assets as co-owners and (2) reserve the right to take their separate shares of any output that is produced or extracted. This election will generally not be available if the project is structured as a partnership under applicable partnership law (see the discussion of tax considerations for an undivided joint interest, earlier in this chapter).

If the partnership structure is chosen, care must be taken to ensure that the partnership does not have too many corporate characteristics. The Internal Revenue Code provides that a partnership will be characterized as an association—which is taxed as a corporation—if its fundamental characteristics more closely resemble those of a corporation rather than a partnership. The Code identifies four basic indicia of corporate status: (1) continuity (or unlimited life), (2) centralization of management, (3) free transferability of ownership interests (i.e., shares), and (4) limited liability for all owners. To avoid characterization as an association, the project entity must qualify as a partnership under applicable state law (or, in the case of foreign projects, under applicable foreign law) and fail at least two of the tests of corporate status by having two of these characteristics: (1) the partnership has a limited life; (2) the general partner must act independently of any limited partners, who may not participate actively in the management of the partnership;

(3) the partnership interests are not freely transferable; and (4) at least one general partner has unlimited liability for the obligations of the partnership, and the general partners are adequately capitalized.[6] Most partnerships have been structured so as to fail the free transferability of ownership interests and limited liability tests.

Chen, Kensinger, and Martin (1989) note that project financing is part of a trend toward increasing direct investment in natural resources and capital equipment. Under the Internal Revenue Code, the traditional corporate form of organization is usually not the most tax-efficient form of organization for such activities; the partnership form is more advantageous from a tax standpoint.

Master Limited Partnerships

Publicly traded limited partnerships, often referred to as master limited partnerships (MLPs), became popular in the United States in the 1980s. MLPs were free of double taxation, just like any other partnership, but could be publicly traded. Partnership units were listed on a major stock exchange, just like shares of common stock of a corporation. The Revenue Act of 1987 eliminated the tax advantage of most MLPs by requiring that they be taxed as corporations. However, there is an important exception. MLPs engaged in the natural resource extraction and oil and gas pipeline industries, and some other kinds of partnerships with essentially passive income, are still taxed as partnerships.[7] The master limited partnership vehicle should be considered as an alternative to the corporate form when the project sponsors hope to have the project company's equity interests publicly traded eventually (e.g., after several years of successful operation) *and* the project involves the exploration, development, production, processing, refining, transportation (including an oil or gas pipeline), or marketing of any mineral or natural resource (including timber or geothermal energy).[8]

LIMITED LIABILITY COMPANY

Virtually every state in the United States, including Delaware, has enacted a statute authorizing limited liability companies.[9] A limited liability company is treated as a corporation for legal liability purposes. In 1988, the Internal Revenue Service ruled that a Wyoming limited liability company should be treated as a partnership for federal income tax purposes. A project company wishing to organize as a limited liability company must comply with the particular limited liability company requirements under the laws of the state in which the company will be organized and must also meet the other requirements for partnership tax treatment under the Internal Revenue Code.

A limited liability company is a distinct legal entity. It has three advantages relative to alternative forms of organization:

1. The owners enjoy limited liability (as they do in a corporation or a limited partnership[10]); they are not liable for the limited liability company's obligations beyond their capital contributions to the company.
2. The limited liability company can qualify for partnership tax treatment (which is similar to the flow-through treatment accorded to a Subchapter S corporation); income flows through to the owners of the company without income taxation at the company level.
3. In contrast to an S corporation, there are no limitations on the number or type of owners; in contrast to limited partnerships, all the owners may participate actively in the management of the company without risking loss of their limited liability.

The IRS has previously ruled that a limited liability company can qualify as a partnership for federal income tax purposes only if the limited liability company possesses no more than two of the basic features of a corporation. The basic corporate features—continuity of life, centralization of management, free transferability of ownership interests, and limited liability—were discussed in the section on partnerships. As noted there, most entities organized as partnerships are structured so as to fail the free transferability of ownership interests and limited liability tests. Master limited partnerships, which permit free transferability, have been structured to fail the continuity of life test. Limited liability companies, which provide limited liability to all owners, have generally been organized to fail the free transferability of ownership interests and continuity of life tests.

A limited liability company can be organized in almost any state. However, some states do not recognize the limitation on liability for a limited liability company formed in another state. As of year-end 1995, the IRS had approved the limited liability company statutes of 18 states for partnership tax treatment. The limited liability company form of organization may be suitable for a joint venture planned for a state that has adopted the required legislation and has managed to secure IRS approval.

THE COGENERATION PROJECT

Engineering Firm and Local Utility, the two active equity investors in the Cogeneration Project, immediately dismissed the undivided joint interest structure from consideration. Neither company wanted project-related debt on its balance sheet. They agreed that a separate

FIGURE 5.4   Ownership Structure for the Cogeneration Project

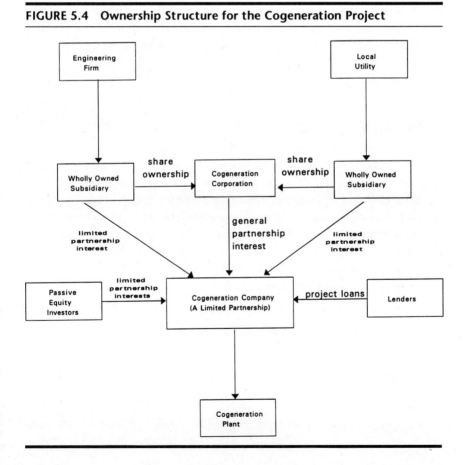

legal entity would be established to construct and own the cogeneration facility.

Engineering Firm and Local Utility wanted to shield themselves from project liability, which the corporate form of organization would achieve. However, neither company would be able to consolidate the project company because neither one would own an 80 percent voting interest. The corporate form of organization would bottle up the losses for tax purposes during the planned 24-month construction period and the early years of operations (because of the accelerated depreciation provisions of the Internal Revenue Code and the large interest deductions).

The partnership form of organization would flow through the losses for tax purposes. However, both Engineering Firm and Local Utility wanted the flexibility to market equity interests in the project entity to outside investors. Passive equity investors do not want to be general partners because a general partner is exposed to operating risks and other noncredit risks. They therefore decided to employ a limited partnership structure by forming a special-purpose corporation to serve as the general partner. Figure 5.4 illustrates the ownership structure selected for the Cogeneration Project.

CONCLUSION

The choice of legal structure can have important tax implications. It can also affect the availability of funds to a project and the cost of raising project financing. Project financing requires that the economic rewards be allocated in a manner commensurate with the project risks. The choice of a project's legal structure affects both allocations. Project sponsors need to work closely with the project's financial and legal advisers to evaluate alternative legal structures and determine the structure that is most advantageous.

6

Preparing the Financing Plan

esigning the optimal financing plan for a project generally involves meeting six principal objectives: (1) ensuring the availability of sufficient financial resources to complete the project; (2) securing the necessary funds at the lowest practicable cost; (3) minimizing the project sponsors' credit exposure to the project; (4) establishing a dividend policy that maximizes the rate of return on the project sponsors' equity subject to the constraints imposed by lenders and the cash flow generated by the project; (5) maximizing the value of the tax benefits of ownership to which the project will give rise; and (6) achieving the most beneficial regulatory treatment. These objectives may not be perfectly compatible, in which case trade-offs will have to be made. In general, the lowest cost of capital will be achieved in a project financing when (1) debt is maximized as a percentage of total capitalization and (2) the amortization schedule for the project debt is matched, as closely as the capital market will permit, to the cash flows of the project.

GENERAL CONSIDERATIONS

A financing plan for a project includes arrangements for both construction financing and permanent financing. The development of a specific financing plan requires a careful analysis of the potential sources of funds in relation to the project's year-to-year funds requirements, available cash flow, and availability of credit support mechanisms to support project debt. The following considerations are important in the design of the financing plan for a project.

Amount of External Funds Required

The formulation of a financing plan begins with an estimate of the total external funds requirements. The amount of external funds required equals the sum of (1) the total cash cost of facilities required for basic completion plus (2) interest that must be paid on project debt during the construction period and the fees and other out-of-pocket expenses that are incurred in connection with arranging the project financing plus (3) the initial investment in working capital plus (4) the cash to cover salaries and other operating expenses prior to project completion. The amount of funds required is reduced to the extent that any cash revenues are generated by the partial operation of the project during the construction period. Such revenues can be realized when the project will be completed in phases and will commence operations before the final phase has been completed.

Sufficient funds must be arranged to provide a margin of safety beyond this estimated total. The margin of safety is necessary to finance possible cost overruns (or to cover shortfalls in internally generated funds, if any are expected). The magnitude of this required safety margin will depend on the contingency factors included in the project construction cost estimates, and lenders' confidence in the feasibility of the construction plan and the accuracy of the cost estimates.

A related consideration concerns how the funds a particular institution provides to a project might reduce its willingness to lend funds to one or more sponsors for other projects. Where legal lending limits might be reached, the financing plan should provide for alternative sources of funds.

Precommitments of Funds

Commitments from lenders and equity investors to provide funds must be coordinated with the project sponsors' commitments to contractors for initial construction expenditures. The two considerations are interrelated. The amount of funds to be raised will depend on the expected cost of construction. Construction cannot commence until the sponsors have obtained commitments covering the total amount of funds necessary to complete the project. Because various classes of funds providers differ with respect to their willingness to enter into forward commitments, project sponsors must tailor the financing plan accordingly.

Securing financing commitments entails, with respect to equity funds, obtaining contractual undertakings by financially capable investors to provide the required amount of equity. With respect to the debt portion of the planned capitalization, commitments must be obtained from institutional lenders or banks for the full amount required, unless adequate assurances can be obtained from credible financial institutions that the necessary debt funds can be raised in the public or private capital market under all circumstances. Seldom can such assurances be obtained in advance of the commencement of construction. Delays or cost overruns that would adversely affect project economics could jeopardize the project entity's ability to arrange subsequent financings. Thus, any planned public offering during construction must be backstopped by firm commitments from credible financial institutions. Such commitments are usually in the form of standby loan facilities from banks. The commitments obligate the banks to provide funds if the public offerings are not consummated as planned.

Maximum Feasible Debt/Equity Ratio

The appropriate project debt/equity ratio depends on (1) the expected profitability and operating risks of the project, (2) the adequacy of the project's security arrangements, and (3) the creditworthiness of the parties obligated under such arrangements. Of particular importance is whether the purchaser(s) of the project's output or services is willing to lend direct or indirect credit support by entering into sufficiently strong long-term purchase commitments. The weaker these commitments, the less the degree of credit support they provide, and the lower will be the maximum feasible debt/equity ratio. Lenders will make their own assessments of these factors, and they will limit project leverage accordingly. In the past, a broad range of projects has been financed with capitalizations that included 70 percent or more debt.

Depending on the maximum feasible debt/equity ratio and the sponsors' ability to contribute equity to the project, it may be necessary to arrange for outside equity investors. The financing plan must address the requirement for, desirability of, and potential identity of outside equity investors for the project. The requirement for or desirability of outside equity investors will depend on many factors. The potential attractiveness of proposals for outside equity investment in a project by a variety

2222222222222222

of prospective providers of debt and equity capital—and the extent to which these potential funds sources would wish to participate in operational aspects of the project—will affect the sponsors' willingness to arrange for outside equity investors. It is sometimes advantageous to the project sponsors to make a portion of the equity in the project available to certain lenders or other participants. For example, financial institutions might be induced to lend more—or to lend on superior terms and conditions—to the project if an "equity kicker" is provided (see p. 98). As a second example, purchasers of the project's output might view an equity participation as sufficient inducement to enter into long-term purchase contracts that would provide meaningful credit support to the project.

Timing of Drawdowns

Once construction begins, a number of factors affect the timing of debt and equity drawdowns. In general, the pattern of drawdowns of long-term funds should match the schedule of construction expenditures. Matching will minimize the warehousing of excess funds and/or the need for short-term bridge financing.

Lenders normally require that the sponsors (or outside equity investors) invest a certain amount of equity in the project prior to the initial drawdown of any debt funds. Lenders that do not insist on equity funds being invested first will require, at a minimum, that debt and equity be drawn down in some specified proportion. These requirements assure lenders that the project's equity investors have a substantial financial commitment to the project from its earliest stages.

The maximum forward commitment that long-term lenders are willing to provide imposes another restriction on the pattern of drawdowns. The maximum commitment period varies according to prevailing market conditions and lending practices of the particular institutions that are asked to provide funds to the project. Life insurance companies, for example, are normally willing to enter into longer forward commitments than most other types of financial institutions.

Expected Project Cash Flow Profile

The project's expected pattern of cash generation constrains the amounts and types of securities utilized in the financing plan. In particular, the expected pattern of project cash flow will determine what debt repayment schedules are feasible. The cash flow will, therefore, have an important effect on the mix of bank loans and long-term fixed-rate debt.

As a general rule, a project's financing plan should seek to match the maturities of the funds raised with the project's ability to generate cash to repay those funds. Matching will tend to minimize the project's exposure to refinancing risk. Also, by coordinating the currency and repayment schedule of project debt with projected revenues arising under sales contracts, the project's exposure to foreign exchange risk can be controlled.

Currency Profile of Project Revenues and Costs

When certain revenues will be received, or certain costs paid, in different currencies, project borrowings can be tailored to hedge the project's foreign exchange risk. For example, if a project will have revenues denominated in U.S. dollars but its operating costs will be paid in Australian dollars, a significant proportion of the project's borrowings should be arranged in U.S. dollars. The balance, including a working capital facility for the project, would be arranged in Australian dollars. Typically, project sponsors arrange a consolidated multicurrency loan facility that provides for maximum specified funds availability in each of two or more currencies.

Expected Useful Economic Life of the Project

The maturity of project debt cannot exceed the expected useful economic life of the project as of the date project financing is arranged. For natural resource projects, conditional acceleration of project debt—faster repayment—may be triggered if, during project operations, the expected life of natural resource reserves (at normal production levels) associated with the project falls below the remaining term of the debt.

Sources of Supply for the Equipment for the Project

If export financing is available in certain countries at concessionary rates, purchasing equipment for the project from suppliers located in one of those countries can reduce the project's cost of funds. Often, a trade-off must be made involving the quality of the equipment procured and the cost of financing. The concessionary rate must provide a subsidy that is large enough to compensate for any differences in quality if the equipment that is available for export financing is not the most attractive from an engineering standpoint.

CONSTRUCTION FINANCING

Bank Loan Facility

One alternative for construction financing is to have the project company or a special-purpose finance corporation issue short-term promissory notes or borrow short-term funds for construction directly from commercial banks.[1] If a special-purpose finance corporation is used, the project company would borrow the money raised by the special-purpose finance corporation under terms substantially identical to those under which the finance corporation borrowed the money. Under this alternative for construction financing, security for the lending institutions will consist of the same completion undertaking and other contractual arrangements that long-term lenders will rely on for security in connection with the permanent financing. Typically, long-term lending commitments are arranged by the time the construction financing is put in place. The long-term lenders agree to "take out" the construction lenders, provided the project meets all its completion tests.

Syndication Risk

When arranging bank financing, it is desirable to avoid syndication risk—the risk that the lead banks will not be able to enlist a sufficient number of additional banks to provide the needed funds. Project sponsors avoid this risk by asking the prospective lead banks to submit fully underwritten (as opposed to best-effort) financing proposals. An underwritten loan commitment obligates the lead banks to provide the full loan facility whether or not they can enlist any other banks to participate in the credit facility.

A typical loan syndication works in the following manner. The project sponsors contact a small number of banks that possess the necessary in-house project financing expertise and ask them to submit competing proposals. After evaluating the proposals, the sponsors request selected banks to form a group and submit a fully underwritten proposal. This bank group serves as the "lead managers." The lead managers then syndicate the project loan by inviting co-managers, participants, and others as needed.

Direct Loans by the Sponsors to the Project Company

A second alternative is to have each of the sponsors borrow its share of the required construction financing directly, on a short-term basis, from commercial banks, and then lend such funds to the project company. Following project completion, the project company arranges long-term financing on the basis of the long-term contractual commitments for the sale of project output, use of project processing facilities, and so on. The project company then repays its borrowings from the project sponsors out of the proceeds of the long-term financing. This second alternative makes the project sponsors directly responsible for all the completion risk—unless they can arrange turnkey construction contracts to transfer this risk to the firms responsible for project construction.

LONG-TERM FINANCING

Investors are generally reluctant to commit funds more than two years in advance of takedown. Thus, for projects with lengthy construction periods, there will be some uncertainty as to whether permanent financing can be arranged before construction commences. In addition, especially for large projects that involve unproven technology, investors are often unwilling to commit to permanent financing without assurances that all the needed funding commitments have been obtained. In these circumstances, commitments covering all the funds requirements will have to be arranged at the same time, rather than having the project company conduct a series of financings during the construction period. However, when a project has a proven technology and a relatively modest capital cost, it is usually possible to finance a significant portion (or possibly all) of its cost at the beginning of construction, if the project sponsors so desire. Securing such financing commitments would require, at a minimum, that the project sponsors enter into a firm completion agreement. When separate construction financing is not appropriate, permanent financing must be arranged prior to the start of construction. Such loan facilities typically provide for quarterly delayed-delivery takedowns for the amounts to be spent during the construction period. Lenders normally require a commitment fee of approximately ½ percent per annum on the committed but undrawn amounts. The loan agreement should give the project company the flexibility to select alternative borrowing bases, such as prime rate and LIBOR. Bank loans carry floating interest rates. When they are used in long-term financing, the sponsors usually arrange interest rate swaps or interest rate caps to limit the project entity's interest rate risk exposure.

Private Placements

Long-term fixed-rate project debt is normally placed privately with sophisticated financial institutions, such as life insurance companies and pension funds. Direct placement avoids the cumbersome securities registration process that is required to effect a public offering. A private placement memorandum is prepared to describe the project and the security arrangements. It also provides a business description and a set of financial statements for each of the project sponsors.

The maturity of the project debt depends on prevailing market conditions. The debt would have to provide for annual sinking fund payments (to the full extent project economics and cash flow will allow). The sinking fund would probably have to begin the first year after completion of the project. The debt would probably have to be nonrefundable for 10 years, through borrowings at a lower cost of money. The debt would probably also provide for a contingent sinking fund. For example, the amortization schedule could be structured so as to provide for specified repayment amounts subject to a maximum amount and a minimum amount in each period. To the extent project cash flow is stronger than what the parties to the project anticipated at the time the project loans were entered into, the contingent sinking fund ensures that the bulk of the excess cash flow, and perhaps even all of it, will be dedicated to repaying project debt. If available cash flow exceeds the specified maximum, the project sponsors would receive cash flow benefits from the project (in the early years) before retirement of the bank debt.

Equity Kickers

The inclusion of an equity kicker in a privately placed financing can broaden the market for the project's debt, lower the front-end fixed cost components of the financing, and induce lenders to accept less restrictive covenants and less demanding credit support. In effect, lenders receive an equity incentive to assume additional risk. Alternative forms of equity kickers include a direct equity participation, net or gross revenue royalty payments (perhaps only of a limited duration), or one-time or multiyear contingent payments. The equity kicker feature is designed to raise the lenders' expected rate of return commensurate with the incremental risk they are being asked to bear.

WITHHOLDING TAX CONSIDERATIONS

The existence of withholding taxes can influence the design of the financing plan for a project. Countries typically apply a withholding tax to dividend payments, interest payments, management fees, and royalty payments made to foreign entities. Often, the withholding tax rate is governed by a tax treaty; the foreign recipient may not even be subject to withholding tax. Where tax treaties grant favorable withholding tax treatment to recipients in certain specified foreign jurisdictions, the project will have a tax incentive to raise funds in those jurisdictions (if funds need to be raised outside the host country).

To the extent that certain types of cash payments are subject to withholding tax but others are not, the project sponsors have a tax incentive to design the project's capital structure so as to minimize the tax liability. For example, principal repayments generally are not subject to withholding tax (because they represent a return of principal), but dividends typically are subject to withholding tax. Project sponsors therefore often have a tax incentive to advance at least a portion of their investment in the form of a subordinated loan. The project company can repay subordinated advances (before paying dividends) in order to minimize the withholding tax on distributions to the foreign sponsor(s).

ESTIMATING THE BORROWING CAPACITY OF A PROJECT

The borrowing capacity of a project is defined as the amount of debt the project can fully service during the loan repayment period. This period is determined by such factors as the bank lenders' general lending policies, the risk characteristics of the project, and the state of the market for bank loans, as well as other considerations.

Bank lenders to a project typically estimate the borrowing capacity of a project in two ways: (1) they employ a discounted cash flow methodology, and (2) they test the ability of the project entity to meet its debt service payment obligations year by year.

This chapter estimates the amount that can be borrowed based on the financial characteristics of the project and the loan parameters established by the lender. In particular, project lenders are generally willing to lend an amount that does not exceed some specified multiple of the present value of the stream of cash flow expected to be available for debt service during the loan repayment period. They also establish certain coverage benchmarks that must be satisfied. Both tests of a project's borrowing capacity will be discussed.

LOAN REPAYMENT PARAMETERS

Bank lenders to discrete, stand-alone projects are seldom willing to lend for periods that exceed 10 years from the date the project is completed. Exceptions to this policy do exist; for example, lenders to infrastructure projects, which are typically long-lived, will lend for longer periods. Sponsors of infrastructure projects have been able at times to arrange bank loan facilities that provide for a scheduled final loan repayment 12 years from completion of construction.

As a general rule, project financings are structured so that the project borrowing entity's leverage is consistent with Baa/BBB credit quality. The differential between the interest rate required on Baa/BBB-rated long-term debt and long-term Treasury debt varies, based on the general level of interest rates. For the interest rates that prevailed on November 30, 1994, the interest rate required on project debt was estimated to average approximately the 30-year U.S. Treasury rate plus 100 basis points, or 9 percent per annum. To be conservative, and to allow for the possibility that interest rates might increase before financing could be arranged, it might be appropriate to add a safety margin—say, 100 basis points. That would suggest using an interest rate of 10 percent in the borrowing capacity analysis.

BORROWING CAPACITY, ASSUMING FULL DRAWDOWN IMMEDIATELY PRIOR TO PROJECT COMPLETION

The borrowing capacity model determines, for a given set of project and loan parameters, the maximum amount of debt the project's cash flow stream will support. The amount the banks will lend equals a fraction of the present value (PV) of the available cash flow stream. Stated equivalently, the present value of the available cash flows must not be less than some specified multiple of the maximum loan amount. Let $PV = \alpha D^{\circ}$, where PV denotes the present value of the cash flow stream that is available to service project debt, α is the target cash flow coverage ratio, and D° is the maximum loan amount. Then the maximum loan amount is:

$$D^{\circ} = PV/\alpha. \qquad (6.1)$$

PV is calculated from the cash flow projections for the project. Often, sponsors desire a rough estimate of a project's borrowing capacity before a detailed set of projections is available. So long as the sponsors can estimate (1) the revenues and expenses during the first full year of project operations and (2) the rate(s) at which revenues and expenses are likely to grow during the period when project debt is outstanding, the following model can be used to estimate the project's borrowing capacity.

First, the variables are defined as:

R = cash revenues during the first full year;
E = cash expenses during the first full year;
C = noncash expenses deductible for tax purposes each year;
T = income tax rate;
g_R = annual growth rate of cash revenues;
g_E = annual growth rate of cash expenses;
K = total capital cost;
i = interest rate on the debt;
N = life of the loan measured from the date of project completion.

The amount of revenue realized in year t is $R(1 + g_R)^{t-1}$. The amount of cash expenses incurred in year t is $E(1 + g_E)^{t-1}$. The amount of annual noncash expenses is assumed to be C each year. Consequently, the amount of cash flow available for debt service in year t is:

$$(1 - T)[R(1 + g_R)^{t-1} - E(1 + g_E)^{t-1} - C] + C =$$

$$(1 - T)[R(1 + g_R)^{t-1} - E(1 + g_E)^{t-1}] + TC.$$

The present value of the cash flow stream that is available during the N-year period between project completion and final loan repayment is:

$$PV = \sum_{t=1}^{N} \frac{(1 - T)[R(1 + g_R)^{t-1} - E(1 + g_E)^{t-1}] + TC}{[1 + i]^t}. \qquad (6.2)$$

Equation (6.2) can be rewritten by evaluating the various terms within the summation to obtain:

$$PV = \sum_{t=1}^{N} \frac{(1 - T)R(1 + g_R)^{t-1}}{(1 + i)^t} - \sum_{t=1}^{N} \frac{(1 - T)E(1 + g_E)^{t-1}}{(1 + i)^t}$$

$$+ \sum_{t=1}^{N} \frac{TC}{(1 + i)^t} = \frac{(1 - T)R}{i - g_R}\left[1 - \left(\frac{1 + g_R}{1 + i}\right)^N\right]$$

$$- \frac{(1 - T)E}{i - g_E}\left[1 - \left(\frac{1 + g_E}{1 + i}\right)^N\right] + \frac{TC}{i}\left[1 - \left(\frac{1}{1 + i}\right)^N\right]. \qquad (6.3)$$

The maximum loan amount D^* is obtained by substituting α and the present value (PV) amount calculated from equation (6.3) into equation (6.1).

The approach just described calculates the amount of debt D^* for given values of revenue R and the other parameters defined above. Some project sponsors have a target, or desired, capital structure and an estimate of the total capital cost of the project. Multiplying the two together gives a target, or desired, debt level. Denote this amount D. Given the desired loan amount D, we can use equation (6.3) to determine how large the first full year's revenue R must be in order for $PV = \alpha D$ to hold. The resulting expression for R is:

$$R = \frac{\alpha D + \dfrac{(1 - T)E}{i - g_E}\left[1 - \left(\dfrac{1 + g_E}{1 + i}\right)^N\right] - \dfrac{TC}{i}\left[1 - \left(\dfrac{1}{1 + i}\right)^N\right]}{\dfrac{(1 - T)}{i - g_R}\left[1 - \left(\dfrac{1 + g_R}{1 + i}\right)^N\right]}. \qquad (6.4)$$

Equation (6.4) assumes that either the loan is fully drawn down immediately prior to completion (or upon completion, as, for example, to refinance construction borrowings) or the borrowing capacity formula is applied as of the project completion date without regard to when the loan drawdowns actually take place.

Example 1

Assume the following parameter values:

R = $150 million	E = $26 million	g_R = 5 percent p.a.
α = 1.50	C = 0	i = 10 percent
T = 40 percent	g_E = 5 percent p.a.	N = 12 years

When $g_E = g_R$ and $C = 0$, equation (6.3) simplifies to:

$$PV = \frac{(1 - T)(R - E)}{i - g_R}\left[1 - \left(\frac{1 + g_R}{1 + i}\right)^N\right]. \tag{6.5}$$

Substituting the parameter values into equation (6.5) implies:

PV = <u>$636.54 million.</u>

Substituting this value for PV and 1.50 for α in Equation (6.1), we find that:

$$D° = PV/\alpha = \$636.54/1.50 = \$424.36$$

The project is capable of supporting $424.36 million of debt bearing a 10 percent interest rate and amortizing over 12 years.

Example 2

Assume the same parameter values as in Example 1 with one exception. Suppose the sponsors would like to know how much revenue the project would have to generate during the first full year of operations if the debt level is D = $350 million.

When $g_E = g_R$ and $C = 0$, equation (6.4) simplifies to:

$$R = \frac{\alpha D(i - g_R)}{(1 - T)\left[1 - \left(\frac{1 + g_R}{1 + i}\right)^N\right]} + E. \tag{6.6}$$

Substituting the given parameter values into equation (6.6) implies:

R = $102.271 + 26.0 = <u>$128.3 million.</u>

The lower debt level, $350 million versus $424.36 million, requires less revenue than the initial year's revenue assumed in Example 1.

Example 3

Assume the same parameter values as in Example 1 with one exception. Suppose the expected long-run growth rate of revenue is 3 percent rather than 5 percent per annum. Substituting into equation (6.4) gives:

$$R = \frac{(1.50)(350) + 133.469}{4.678} = \$140.8 \text{ million.}$$

The higher growth rate of operating expenses necessitates a higher initial level of revenue in order to maintain the target debt coverage ratio of 1.50.

BORROWING CAPACITY, ASSUMING PERIODIC LOAN DRAWDOWNS

Suppose the revenues and operating expenses do not begin for M years, on average, from the date the loan is initially drawn down. This situation occurs when the loan is drawn down during the construction period, a time when the project is normally not generating any revenue. In that case:

$$PV^\circ = PV \div (1 + i)^M$$

where PV is given by equation (6.3). Also, as before, a target debt coverage ratio of α must be maintained:

$$PV^\circ = \alpha D^\circ$$

and so

$$PV = (1 + i)^M \alpha D^\circ. \tag{6.7}$$

Given any particular present value amount PV, the period of deferral reduces the amount that can be borrowed, given any particular desired target debt coverage ratio α.

The maximum loan amount D° in this case is:

$$D^\circ = PV/[\alpha(1 + i)^M] \tag{6.8}$$

where PV is given by equation (6.3). Equation (6.8) provides the maximum borrowing capacity as of the date of the initial loan drawdown.

Substituting $(1 + i)^M \alpha D$ for αD in equation (6.4) gives the following expression for the amount of revenue the project must realize during the first full year of operations in order to meet the cash flow coverage ratio test:

$$R = \frac{(1 + i)^M \alpha D + \dfrac{(1 - T)E}{i - g_E}\left[1 - \left(\dfrac{1 + g_E}{1 + i}\right)^N\right] - \dfrac{TC}{i}\left[1 - \left(\dfrac{1}{1 + i}\right)^N\right]}{\dfrac{(1 - T)}{i - g_R}\left[1 - \left(\dfrac{1 + g_R}{1 + i}\right)^N\right]}. \tag{6.9}$$

Example 4

Assume the same parameter values as in Example 1. Assume, in addition, that the deferral period is 2 years. Applying equation (6.8), the maximum loan amount is:

$D^\circ = 636.54/[1.50(1.1)^2] = \underline{\$350.71 \text{ million.}}$

Example 5

Assume the same parameter values as in Example 3. Assume, in addition, that the deferral period is $M = 3$ years. Applying equation (6.9), the amount of revenue required during the first full year of operations is:

$$R = \frac{(1.1)^3(1.50)(350) + 133.469}{4.678} = \underline{\$177.9 \text{ million.}}$$

APPLICATION TO A HYPOTHETICAL HIGH-SPEED RAIL PROJECT

Consider a hypothetical high-speed rail project that will require substantial funding from the U.S. government and from the government of the state in which it will be located. Private sources of funds, including bank loans, will provide the balance of the funds required.

The borrowing capacity of the project will depend on the timing of the loan drawdowns. The equity funds and the governmental funding will probably have to be contributed to the project prior to the drawdown of the private bank loans. Under that assumption, the average

TABLE 6.1   Average Life of Loan Drawdown Schedule (Dollar
Amounts in Millions)

Year	Percent of Capital Cost Incurred	Elapsed Time to Completion[a]	Portion of Capital Cost Borrowed	Fraction of Loan Drawn	Life of Drawdown[b]	Average Life Calculation[c]
1	10%	4.5 years	—	—	—	—
2	25	3.5	—	—	—	—
3	25	2.5	$ 30	.086	2.5 years	0.215 years
4	25	1.5	200	.571	1.5	0.857
5	15	0.5	120	.343	0.5	0.172
Total			$350		Average life	1.244 years

[a] Assumes loans drawn down evenly throughout the year.
[b] Equals elapsed time to completion.
[c] Equals fraction of loan drawn multiplied by life of drawdown.

life of the bank loans prior to the completion of construction is calculated as shown in Table 6.1.

Example 6

Assume the following parameter values:

D = $350 million E = $26 million g_R = 5 percent p.a. M = 1.244 years
α = 1.50 C = 0 i = 8 percent
T = 40 percent g_E = 5 percent p.a. N = 12 years

When $g_E = g_R$ and $C = 0$, equation (6.9) simplifies to:

$$R = \frac{(1+i)^M \alpha D(i - g_R)}{(1-T)\left[1 - \left(\frac{1 + g_R}{1 + i}\right)^N\right]} + E. \tag{6.10}$$

Substituting the given parameters into equation (6.10) implies:

R = $67.528 + 26.0 = $93.5 million.

Example 7

Suppose instead that revenues are expected to grow at only a 3 percent
annual rate. In that case, applying equation (6.9), the required first full
year's revenues increase to R = $139.6 million. The slower growth in

revenues increases the amount of revenues that is required during the first full year of operations to meet the target cash flow coverage ratio.

Example 8

Suppose that there is concern about the possibility of sharply rising interest rates. To allow for this concern, let $i = 10$ percent. If it is assumed that both revenues and operating expenses grow at a 5 percent annual rate, then:

$R = \$115.145 + 26.0 = \underline{\$141.1 \text{ million.}}$

If it is assumed that revenues grow at a 3 percent annual rate while operating expenses grow at a 5 percent annual rate, then:

$R = \underline{\$154.9 \text{ million.}}$

ANNUAL COVERAGE TESTS

Three financial ratios are widely used to measure a project's ability to service its debt: (1) the interest coverage ratio, (2) the fixed charge coverage ratio, and (3) the debt service coverage ratio.

The *interest coverage ratio*, expressed as:

Interest coverage = EBIT/Interest   (6.11)

measures the project's ability to cover interest charges. It equals earnings before interest and taxes (EBIT), or the amount of funds available to pay interest, divided by interest charges. Interest charges represent interest that must be paid in cash, whether or not it is capitalized for accounting purposes.

An interest coverage ratio below 1.00 would indicate that a project cannot cover its interest charges fully out of operating income. An interest coverage ratio below 1.00 for the first few years of project operations would indicate that the project was incapable of supporting the level of borrowings planned for it. Because of uncertainty regarding future income and cash flow, lenders typically set a threshold greater than 1.00. For example, they might require that projected interest coverage never fall below 1.25.

There may be rental agreements that do not appear on the project company's balance sheet. Rent includes an interest component. The Securities and Exchange Commission (SEC) permits companies to treat one-third of rental payments as the interest component. The *fixed charge coverage ratio* takes into account these other "interest charges":

$$\text{Fixed charge coverage} = (\text{EBIT} + \tfrac{1}{3}\text{ rentals})/(\text{Interest} + \tfrac{1}{3}\text{ rentals}) \quad (6.12)$$

where ⅓ rentals denotes one-third of annual rental expense.

The fixed charge coverage ratio is interpreted similarly to the interest coverage ratio. A value below 1.00 serves as a warning that the level of debt (including rental arrangements) planned for the project is too high. When the project entity will rent a substantial portion of the equipment it will need to operate the project, it is important to calculate projected fixed charge coverage as well as projected interest coverage in order to assess properly the project's ability to borrow.

Debt service includes principal as well as interest. Unlike interest and rental payments, principal payments are not tax-deductible. Also, if one-third of rental expense consists of an interest charge, the other two-thirds represents a principal component (which is tax-deductible when it is part of a rental payment). To allow properly for the non-tax-deductibility of principal repayments on loans, notes, and debentures, those payments are divided by 1.00 minus the income tax rate; the payments are made out of after-tax dollars. In addition, depreciation and amortization (DA) expenses represent noncash charges; these amounts are available to repay principal. The *debt service coverage ratio* accounts for all debt service payment obligations:

$$\text{Debt service coverage} = \frac{\text{EBITDA} + \text{Rentals}}{\text{Interest} + \text{Rentals} + \dfrac{\text{Principal repayments}}{1 - \text{Tax rate}}} \quad (6.13)$$

where EBITDA denotes earnings before interest, taxes, depreciation, and amortization.

The debt service coverage ratio is interpreted similarly to the other two coverage measures. It is the most comprehensive measure of the three. When debt service coverage falls below 1.00, the project cannot fully service its debt out of project cash flow and will have to borrow funds or seek equity contributions to obtain funds to cover the shortfall. The debt service coverage ratio is particularly useful in designing the amortization schedule for project debt. For example, requiring the debt service coverage ratio never to fall below, say, 1.10 would indicate how much cash flow would be available after making required interest (and rental) payments to pay down principal.

CONCLUSION

The sponsors of a project will choose to have it financed on a project basis, rather than on their general credit, when project financing represents the lower-cost alternative. Whether project financing turns out to be the lower-cost alternative will depend, to a large extent, on how well the financing plan for the project is designed and how effectively it is executed. In preparing the project's financing plan, project sponsors and their financial advisers need to consider carefully all potential sources of funds in order to determine the financing package that affords the lowest cost of capital consistent with regulatory or any other project-specific constraints.

Lenders use the interest coverage ratio, fixed charge coverage ratio, and debt service coverage ratio to gauge the capacity of a project to support debt on a year-by-year basis. These annual measures can be used in conjunction with the discounted cash flow debt capacity model developed in this chapter to determine how much debt a project is capable of supporting and how the repayment schedule for the debt should be designed. Lenders' risk tolerances and loan preferences change over time. The debt capacity model is sufficiently general to accommodate any particular set of lender-imposed constraints by altering the parameters of the model appropriately.

7

Discounted Cash Flow Analysis

Projects typically involve the purchase of *capital assets*—long-lived tangible assets such as land, plant, and machinery. When considering a proposed project that would involve investing in capital assets, the sponsors should evaluate the expected future cash flows in relation to the amount of the initial investment.

Discounted cash flow techniques are available to facilitate the evaluation process. The objective is to find projects that are worth more to the sponsors than they cost—projects that have a positive net present value (NPV).

A sponsor's evaluation of a proposed project is not unlike an individual's investment decision. The steps are the same:

1. Estimate the expected future cash flows from the project. This is like estimating the coupon payments for a bond or the dividend stream for a stock, and a maturity value or terminal sale price.
2. Assess the risk and determine a required rate of return (cost of capital) for discounting the expected future cash flows.
3. Compute the present value of the expected future cash flows.
4. Determine the cost of the project and compare it to what the project is worth. If the project is worth more than it costs—if it has a positive NPV—it is worth undertaking.

This chapter is based on Douglas R. Emery and John D. Finnerty, *Corporate Financial Management* (Prentice Hall, 1997), chapters 7, 10, and 11.

In this chapter, we develop a discounted cash flow framework for assessing the profitability of a proposed project. The chapter explains and illustrates sound methods of evaluating capital investments, which can be applied to any capital investment, whether or not it is a discrete project.

INCREMENTAL AFTER-TAX CASH FLOWS

The initial step in measuring the value of a capital investment project is estimating the expected incremental after-tax cash flows. Three important concepts are involved. First, as with any investment, the costs and benefits associated with a project should be measured in terms of *cash flow* rather than earnings. This distinction is critical. Earnings calculations also reflect certain noncash items. But ultimately, cash, not earnings, is required to meet the firm's financial obligations. Failure to raise enough cash can cause a firm to pay penalty fees or can even bring bankruptcy to an otherwise healthy firm. And, only cash flow can be paid to the sponsors, either immediately or through reinvestment and later disbursement. The *timing* of a cash flow affects its value, because of the time value of money. Finally, including indirect noncash benefits leads to ambiguity and subjective (nonfinancial) choices that can greatly confuse the analysis.[1]

The second important concept is that the cash flows must be measured on an *incremental* basis. They are the difference between the sponsor's cash flows with and without the project. So, if a cash flow will occur regardless of whether the project is undertaken, it is not relevant. Funds that have already been expended—for example, for preliminary work—are *sunk costs*. They are irrelevant to the analysis. Only *future* expenditures and revenues are relevant to the decision of whether to proceed with the project.

Third, the expected future cash flows should be measured on an after-tax basis. A project sponsor is concerned with after-tax cash flows in the same way that an individual is interested in take-home pay: ultimately, that's the amount available to spend for other purposes. Because taxes represent one of the costs of doing business, they must be subtracted from the pretax operating cash flows.

Finally, by convention, cash flows are assumed to occur at the end of each time period unless their occurrence is explicitly stated otherwise. This is done for convenience in making computations.

Tax Considerations

Although some sections of the Internal Revenue Code are complex and are changed periodically, we can make some generalized statements about tax effects. Three things affect a firm's taxes: (1) revenues, (2) expenses, and (3) how and when those revenues and expenses are declared for tax purposes. Just as the timing of any cash flow affects its value, *when* a cash flow is recognized for tax purposes affects the present value of the taxes paid.

One very important tax effect occurs whenever there is a discrepancy between cash flow timing and recognition of the cash flow for tax purposes. The present value of taxes paid is less on a revenue item, the further into the future that tax payment actually occurs. For example, suppose a firm takes in a cash advance of $1,000 on goods that are yet to be manufactured but are promised for delivery one year from today. If the tax will be $100, the firm will earn $900. But if the tax need not be paid until the goods are delivered, the present value of the tax is only $92.59 at an 8 percent discount rate (= $100/1.08). With that result, the firm actually earns $907.41 ($1,000 − $92.59) rather than $900.

Similarly, the present value of taxes saved is greater on an expense item, the sooner the reduction in taxes paid actually occurs. The most frequent discrepancy between cash flow timing and tax recognition occurs with respect to depreciation.

Depreciation plays an important role in the determination of cash flow. Over time, machines wear out. The accounting treatment of depreciation expense, whereby it is deducted in each reporting period, reflects this wear.

For capital budgeting decisions, depreciation has an important impact on the timing of the firm's tax payments. Depreciation is a non-cash expense. Cash was expended to acquire the asset. *Depreciation* is simply the recognition of the expense as the asset is used over time. Because depreciation is deducted from revenue when calculating taxable income, it affects the timing of the firm's tax payments. Similarly, *depletion expense* is recognized as natural resource reserves (e.g., a coal deposit or a natural gas reserve) are used up, and *amortization expense* is recorded as the remaining value of intangible assets (e.g., a patent) dissipates.

Depreciation (as well as depletion and amortization) arises when assets are *capitalized*—when the cost of the asset is allocated to two or more time periods. The entire cost is not an immediately recognized expense. Instead, the expenditure is recognized as a prespecified series of expenses at various times in the future. By contrast, cash expenditures for items that are not required to be capitalized can be expensed immediately. Cash expenditures that are *expensed* are recognized for tax purposes entirely at the time of expenditure. Therefore, expensed items do not have any *subsequent* tax consequences, because they do not involve the process of depreciation. To contrast these two different tax treatments, consider the following example.

Example

Suppose General Mining Corporation is going to purchase an asset that costs $1 million. Suppose further that General's marginal tax rate is 40 percent. How does the pattern of expenses recognized for tax purposes differ between (1) capitalizing the asset on a straight-line basis over 4 years and (2) expensing the $1 million now?

The pattern of expenses recognized over time for expensing versus capitalizing the expenditure for the asset is (in $ millions):

Time (years):	0	1	2	3	4	Total
Expensed:	1.0	0	0	0	0	1.0
Capitalized:	0	.25	.25	.25	.25	1.0

Note that the *total* amount of expenses claimed in both cases is $1 million. The only difference is the time at which the expense is claimed. Because of the time value of money, General is clearly better off if it can expense the asset rather than having to capitalize it.

The Internal Revenue Code *requires* that certain assets be capitalized. The preceding example suggests that a project sponsor is generally best off when it uses, for each asset, the most accelerated depreciation method available under the Code.

Incremental Cash Flows

The cash flows associated with a capital investment project fall into four basic categories:

1. Net initial investment outlay.
2. Future net operating cash flow benefits to be realized from operating the asset.

3. Nonoperating cash flows required to support the initial investment outlay, such as those necessary for a major overhaul.
4. Net salvage value, which is the after-tax total amount of cash received and/or spent upon termination of the project.

Note that financing charges are *not* included in the incremental cash flow computation because the cost of capital implies a financing cost. Therefore, only extraordinary financing costs, such as special transaction costs explicitly tied to the project, are included in the incremental cash flow computations. Such costs will most often be included in the net initial investment outlay.

    1. *Net initial investment outlay.* The net initial investment outlay can be broken down into cash expenditures, changes in net working capital, net cash flow from the sale of old equipment, and investment tax credits.

As already noted, capitalized expenditures do not affect taxes at the start of the project, whereas expensed items have an immediate tax effect. If we denote the net expenditure to be capitalized as I_0, the net expenditure to be expensed immediately as E_0, and the company's marginal income tax rate as τ, then the first component of the initial outlay is:

$$\text{Cash expenditure} = -I_0 - E_0 + \tau E_0 = -I_0 - (1 - \tau)E_0. \qquad (7.1)$$

The negative signs indicate cash outflows. As of year-end 1995, the federal statutory corporate income tax rate was 35 percent. To allow also for state income taxes, many financial analysts use $\tau = 0.40$.

Changes in net working capital at the start of an investment project are also part of the initial outlay for the project. For example, additional cash may be needed to open up an expansion outlet. Additional inventory and accounts receivable may be required to process a greater level of production and sales. The additional net working capital requires funding. Similarly, if the project reduces the firm's net working capital, those funds are freed up to be invested elsewhere.

The third component of the initial outlay is the net cash flow from the sale of old equipment. When an asset is sold, there is revenue and maybe an expense, but there may also be a tax effect. A tax effect will occur if the asset is sold for a net sale price that is different from the tax basis of the asset at the time of its sale (i.e., its net, or depreciated, book value). For example, suppose an asset was purchased 5 years ago for $2,000, and $300 of depreciation expense has been claimed for tax purposes for each of the past 5 years. The net book value of that asset is currently $500 ($2,000 − 5($300)). If the asset is sold today for more than $500, then "too much" depreciation was claimed and the government will "recapture" the excess depreciation by taxing the amount above the net book value. Likewise, if the asset is sold today for less than $500, "too little" depreciation was claimed and the firm can now claim the rest of the depreciation. The firm gets a tax credit by claiming the amount below the net book value as an expense. If we denote the net sale price (revenues minus expenses) S_0 and the net book value B_0, then the after-tax cash flow for selling the old equipment is:[2]

Net cash flow from
the sale of old equipment $= S_0 - \tau(S_0 - B_0) = S_0(1 - \tau) + \tau B_0.$ $\qquad$ (7.2)

Finally, the purchase of certain capitalized assets may give rise to an investment tax credit. This aspect of the tax law has changed fairly often, so we include it only as a reminder to check the Code at the time the project is to be undertaken. Denoting the investment tax credit I_c and the change in net working capital ΔW, then the net initial outlay, C_0, can be expressed as:

$$C_0 = -I_0 - \Delta W - (1 - \tau)E_0 + (1 - \tau)S_0 + \tau B_0 + I_c. \qquad (7.3)$$

2. *Net operating cash flow.* Let ΔR and ΔE denote, respectively, the changes in revenue and expense connected with undertaking the project in each period. Therefore, the net operating cash flow, CFAT (cash flow after tax), can be expressed as the pretax cash flow $\Delta R - \Delta E$, less the tax liability on this amount:

Net operating cash flow = CFAT = $\Delta R - \Delta E$ − tax liability. $\qquad$ (7.4)

The tax liability depends in part on the incremental change in depreciation. For simplicity, we assume that all depreciation is recognized on a straight-line basis. Therefore, the change in depreciation expense is identical each period. Denoting the depreciation change ΔD, the tax liability will be $\tau(\Delta R - \Delta E - \Delta D)$, and

$$\text{CFAT} = \Delta R - \Delta E - \tau(\Delta R - \Delta E - \Delta D). \qquad (7.5)$$

Rearranging gives

$$\text{CFAT} = (1 - \tau)(\Delta R - \Delta E) + \tau \Delta D. \tag{7.6}$$

In this form, CFAT is represented as the after-tax revenue minus expenses plus the "tax shield" from the depreciation expense. Equivalently, we can rearrange the expression:

$$\text{CFAT} = (1 - \tau)(\Delta R - \Delta E - \Delta D) + \Delta D. \tag{7.7}$$

In this alternative form, CFAT can be thought of as net income plus depreciation. This is because $(1 - \tau)(\Delta R - \Delta E - \Delta D)$ would be the net income from the project if the firm were entirely equity-financed.

3. *Nonoperating cash flows.* The treatment of nonoperating cash flows parallels that of cash expenditures for the initial investment outlay. Nonoperating cash flows are either required to be capitalized or allowed to be expensed immediately. Therefore, their effect on net cash flow is like initial cash expenditures. The expensed nonoperating cash flows are multiplied by $(1 - \tau)$ to adjust for taxes. Capitalized nonoperating cash flows involve an initial cash outflow when they occur, and they give rise to a series of depreciation expenses that follow.

4. *Net salvage value.* The net salvage value is the after-tax net cash flow for terminating the project. It can be broken into: sale of assets, cleanup and removal expenses, and release of net working capital.

The adjustment for the sale of assets was described earlier, in our discussion of the net initial investment outlay. Dropping the zero subscripts from equation (7.2), the adjustment is $[(1 - \tau)S + \tau B]$. Cleanup and removal expenses are generally expensed immediately. Therefore, they are multiplied by $(1 - \tau)$ to adjust for taxes. The release of net working capital is unaffected by tax considerations. Tax law treats it as an internal transfer of funds, such as exchanging inventory and accounts receivable for cash. Therefore, the release of net working capital is simply an added cash flow. With cleanup and removal expenses denoted REX, net salvage value is:

$$\text{Net salvage value} = (1 - \tau)S + \tau B - (1 - \tau)\text{REX} + \Delta W. \tag{7.8}$$

The term *salvage value* typically refers to the before-tax difference between the sale price (S) and the cleanup and removal expense (REX). That is, salvage value = $S -$ REX.

An Example of Incremental Cash Flow Analysis

Rocky Mountain Mining Corporation is thinking of investing in a mining project that would involve purchasing equipment costing $55 million. The new equipment would be depreciated over a 10-year period on a straight-line basis to a net book value of $5 million. The mining project would produce pretax cash flow of $15 million per year for 10 years.

Rocky Mountain estimates that the project would involve additional start-up costs amounting to $6 million. Of this amount, $5 million would be capitalized in the same way as the equipment, and the remaining $1 million would be expensed immediately. The project would also require an investment in net working capital of $3 million. Finally, it is expected that, at the end of 10 years, the project will require $500,000 of removal and cleanup costs. Rocky Mountain estimates a marginal tax rate of 40 percent for the project.

The cash expenditures for the initial outlay in this case are: the $55 million purchase price, the $5 million capitalized installation cost, and the $1 million expensed installation cost; therefore, $I_0 = \$60$ million, and $E_0 = \$1$ million. The increase in net working capital is $\Delta W = \$3$ million. No investment tax credit has been specified. The net initial investment outlay can now be computed, using equation (7.3):

$$C_0 = -I_0 - \Delta W - (1 - \tau)E_0 + (1 - \tau)S_0 + \tau B_0 + I_c$$
$$= -60,000,000 - 3,000,000 - .6(1,000,000) + 0 + 0 + 0 = -63,600,000.$$

Note that care must be taken to treat correctly sunk costs that have been incurred more recently. Dollars that have already been spent— for example, on feasibility studies, prior research and development, and site preparation—are irrelevant for purposes of capital investment analysis. They are sunk costs; whether or not Rocky Mountain proceeds with the project, the timing and levels of prior capital expenditures cannot change because these expenditures have already been incurred.

The net operating cash flows resulting from investing in the project can be calculated using either equation (7.6) or equation (7.7). The change in revenue minus expenses, $\Delta R - \Delta E$, is $15 million. Depreciation will amount to $5 million per year (($55 million − $5 million)/10) for the next 10 years. Therefore, ΔD is $5 million for years 1 through 10. Using equation (7.6):

$$\text{CFAT} = (1 - \tau)(\Delta R - \Delta E) + \tau\Delta D$$

$$\text{CFAT (1 through 10)} = (1 - .4)(15,000,000) + (.4)(5,000,000) = \$11,000,000.$$

Because no nonoperating cash flows are anticipated over the life of this project, no additional adjustments are necessary.

The equipment is expected to have a market value of $5 million at the end of the project's life. A removal and cleanup expenditure of $500,000 is expected. From equation (7.8), the net salvage value is:

$$\text{Net salvage value} = (1 - \tau)S + \tau B - (1 - \tau)\text{REX} + \Delta W$$

$$= .6(5,000,000) + .4(5,000,000) - .6(500,000) + 3,000,000$$

$$= \$7,700,000.$$

The incremental cash flows for this project are then (in $ millions):

Year:	0	1	2	3	4	5	6	7	8	9	10
Cash flow:	−63.6	11.0	11.0	11.0	11.0	11.0	11.0	11.0	11.0	11.0	18.7

THE HURDLE RATE

How high a rate of return do investors require, to compensate for a particular degree of risk? A required rate of return can be thought of as an opportunity cost. Investors will require a rate of return at least as great as the percentage return they could earn in the most nearly comparable investment opportunity. But suppose there's no comparable opportunity from which to estimate a required rate of return? What factors determine a required rate of return? In other words, how does the market determine a required rate of return?

The Weighted Average Cost of Capital

The weighted average cost of capital (WACC) serves as the hurdle rate for a project. It can be described in terms of financing rates. More importantly, it can *always* be represented as the weighted average cost of the components of *any* financing package that will allow the project to be undertaken. For example, such a financing package could be 20 percent debt plus 80 percent equity; 55 percent debt plus 45 percent equity; and so on. Or, it could be 30 percent 30-year debt, 10 percent 180-day debt, 10 percent preferred stock, 15 percent 20-year convertible debt, and 35 percent common stock. The cost of capital is the rate of return required by a group of investors to take on the risk of the project.

Before proceeding, we need to specify exactly what is meant by the components of a financing package. For simplicity, we will restrict the analysis to the proportions of financing provided by debt and equity. Let θ denote the ratio of debt financing to total investment value. For example, suppose a capital investment project has a total present value of $10,000, and $4,000 of debt will be used to finance the project. Then $\theta = .4$. It is important to note that θ does not depend on the initial cost of the investment project; θ depends on the total value of the project.

Suppose our example project has an initial cost of $8,000 and an NPV of $2,000, making its present value $10,000. Then the sponsors of this project will be putting up $4,000 and getting $6,000, because they get the NPV. The sponsors then own 60 percent of the value, even though they will be putting up only 50 percent of the initial cost ($4,000 of the $8,000). The project is referred to as *40 percent debt-financed and 60 percent equity-financed* because those proportions reflect the distribution of the *market* value of the project among the claimants. The proportions of the initial cost are not relevant because they would disregard the project's NPV.

The required rate of return to the sponsors depends on the degree of leverage in the project's financial structure. The debt holders' required rate of return also depends on the degree of leverage. When default is possible, the required rate of return to the debt holders must increase to reflect the risk that debt holders might not receive full payment.

A Cost of Capital Formula

The weighted average cost of capital (WACC) can be expressed as the weighted average of the required rate of return for equity, r_e, and the required rate of return for debt, r_d:

$$\text{WACC} = (1 - \theta)r_e + \theta(1 - \tau)r_d \tag{7.9}$$

where τ represents the marginal income tax rate on the project's income. Equation (7.9) reduces the task of estimating the WACC to a calculation of the cost of debt and the cost of equity and an appropriate weighting of these component costs.

Note that the WACC is expressed as an after-tax rate of return. Because the returns to equity investors are paid after corporate taxes, r_e is also an after-corporate-tax rate of return (to equity). The return to debt, r_d, is a pretax rate of return; it must be multiplied by $(1 - \tau)$ to convert it to an after-tax basis.

Estimating the Cost of Debt

The pretax cost of debt can be calculated by solving the following equation for r_d:

$$\text{NP} = \frac{C_1}{(1 + r_d)} + \frac{C_2}{(1 + r_d)^2} + \frac{C_3}{(1 + r_d)^3} + \ldots + \frac{C_T}{(1 + r_d)^T}, \quad (7.10)$$

where NP represents the net proceeds from the debt issue (i.e., gross proceeds minus flotation expenses, such as underwriting fees, legal fees, and so on), and C_i represents the pretax *cash* debt service requirement payable in period i (i.e., interest plus principal). Typically, project debt must be repaid in installments. When this is so, C_i includes the portion of principal that must be repaid in period i.

The after-tax cost of debt can be calculated in either of two ways. The after-tax payment obligations, rather than the pretax amounts, can be used in equation (7.10). This procedure requires adjusting interest payments for taxes—because interest is a tax-deductible expense—as well as allowing for the amortization of new issue expenses. The amortization of new issue expenses is treated in the same manner as the depreciation of capital assets, which was discussed earlier in this chapter.

Alternatively, the after-tax cost of debt can be approximated as:

$$\text{After-tax cost of debt} \cong (1 - \tau)r_d, \quad (7.11)$$

which appears in equation (7.9). Equation (7.11) will usually produce a very close approximation to the true after-tax cost of debt. Differences occur when a project entity cannot utilize the interest tax deductions on a current basis—for example, when a project entity is organized as a corporation and construction extends over several periods during which there is no income to offset the interest deductions for income tax purposes.

Estimating the Cost of Equity:
The Capital-Asset-Pricing Model

Debt involves contractual payment obligations; equity does not. Thus, the procedure for estimating the cost of equity differs from the procedure for estimating the cost of debt. The capital-asset-pricing model is useful for estimating the cost of equity for a project.

An investor will purchase a risky asset only if he or she expects to get a rate of return that makes it worthwhile to take on the risk. The greater the risk, the higher the required rate of return. The capital-asset-pricing model (CAPM) expresses the required rate of return as the risk-free rate plus a risk premium. It has the following form:

$$\begin{matrix} \text{Required rate} \\ \text{of return} \end{matrix} = \begin{matrix} \text{Risk-free} \\ \text{rate} \end{matrix} + \text{Beta}$$

$$\times \left(\begin{matrix} \text{Expected return on} \\ \text{market portfolio} \end{matrix} - \begin{matrix} \text{Risk-free} \\ \text{rate} \end{matrix} \right). \tag{7.12}$$

The risk premium is a function of two variables. Beta measures the asset's incremental contribution to the riskiness of a diversified portfolio. As a measure of the asset's riskiness, beta reflects the correlation between an asset's returns and those of the market portfolio. The difference (the expected return on market portfolio minus the risk-free rate), called the *market risk premium,* can be thought of as the additional return investors require to compensate for bearing each additional unit of risk. This very simple structure for the risk premium is what distinguishes the CAPM from other models.

How individual stock returns vary with respect to the market portfolio's return can be estimated by applying a statistical method called *linear regression.* We can express the actual historical rate of return on a stock r_j as a linear function of the actual historical excess rate of return on the market portfolio $(r_M - r_f)$, so that:

$$r_j = r_f + \beta_j (r_M - r_f). \tag{7.13}$$

We can then apply the technique of linear regression to estimate β_j from historical data. That procedure involves collecting a sample of simultaneous observations of r_j, r_M, and r_f, and fitting Equation (7.13) to the historical data to estimate the value of the regression coefficient β_j.

Because of equation (7.13), the correlation coefficient between a common stock's rate of return and the excess rate of return on the market portfolio has come to be called the common stock's *beta*. Beta plays a particularly important role in asset pricing. It is a *linear measure* of how much an individual asset contributes to the standard deviation of the market portfolio. So the beta of an asset is a simple, well-behaved measure of the risk of the individual asset.

Beta indicates the sensitivity of a security's returns to changes in the returns on the market portfolio. If a security's beta is 1.0, its returns tend to track the market portfolio. If the market portfolio increases or decreases by 10 percent, the stock also tends to move up or down by 10 percent. If a stock has a beta less than 1.0, it will rise or fall less than the market. For example, suppose a stock has a beta of 0.5. If the market portfolio increases or decreases by 10 percent, the stock will tend to move up or down only 5 percent. A stock with a beta greater than 1.0 will rise or fall more than the market. For example, a stock with a beta of 1.5 will tend to rise or fall by 15 percent when the market portfolio increases or decreases 10 percent. Values of beta for most common stocks fall within the range from 0.75 to 1.50.

Sample Cost of Capital Calculation

Rocky Mountain Mining Corporation's mining project will utilize only long-term debt and common equity financing. Rocky Mountain has identified similar securities that are traded regularly in active markets. What is the WACC for Rocky Mountain's proposed project?

To begin, Rocky Mountain gathered the following information:

Risk-free interest rate	6 percent
Common equity beta	1.25
Expected excess return on the market portfolio	8.4 percent
Expected cost of debt (pretax)	10 percent
Proportion of debt financing	60 percent
Project's marginal income tax rate	40 percent

Based on this information, we can use the capital-asset-pricing model to estimate r_e:

$$r_e = 6.0 + 1.25(8.4) = 16.5 \text{ percent.}$$

The proportion of debt financing, θ, is .60. From equation (7.9), the WACC for Rocky Mountain's project is:

$$\text{WACC} = (1 - \theta)r_e + \theta(1 - \tau)r_d = (.4)(.165) + (.6)(.6)(.10)$$

$$= .102, \text{ or } 10.2 \text{ percent.}$$

Adjusting for Financial Risk

If a project is *all*-equity-financed (no money owed at any time, no matter what), then the project involves no financial risk. Note that such a project would not have even one creditor. All of the risk of this hypothetical project would be its operating risk because the project never owes anyone anything. Note also that, in such a case, default is not a possibility or an option. In effect, the shareholders' limited liability has no effect on value. Such a project could fail. But, although the sponsors could lose everything they invested in the project, no wealth can be transferred because no loss can ever be inflicted on anyone other than the project sponsors. So, although the sponsors still cannot lose more than they have invested in the project, they also cannot benefit from limited liability and the default option.

Because financial risk depends on (financial) leverage, adjustment for the impact of financial risk must be done on the basis of whatever unit has responsibility for that financial obligation. In a project financing—and in contrast to a conventional debt financing—the financial obligation is specific to the project. In evaluating a prospective project financing, the financing considerations should be accounted for on a project-by-project basis. By way of contrast, in connection with projects financed on a conventional basis, the financial obligations are at the level of the firm. The impact of leverage on required rates of return is determined in such situations by the capital structure of the whole firm.

Impact of Project Financing

When a firm employs project financing and thereby limits its liability with respect to project debt, the capital structure of the project becomes the relevant consideration for calculating the required returns and the cost of capital. Therefore, if a firm is considering financing something on a project basis, which would achieve limited liability for the firm, the cost of capital for the project should reflect the capital structure of the project.

ESTIMATING THE COST OF CAPITAL FOR A PROJECT

This section explains how to estimate the cost of capital for a project. Two alternatives are considered. In the first, the project has the same operating risk profile and the same capital structure as the sponsor. In the second, either the operating risk profile is different or the capital structure is different (or both are different).

Lone Star Mining Corporation, which has worldwide mining operations, is planning to finance a copper mine on a project basis. The mine would cost $100 million, which would be 60 percent debt-financed and 40 percent equity-financed.

When the Sponsor's WACC Can Be Used

Suppose Lone Star believes the mining project will be of "average risk" when compared to all of the projects Lone Star is operating. Suppose also that Lone Star is 60 percent debt-financed and that Lone Star's common stock is publicly traded. Thus, the proposed project has the same operating risk profile and the same capital structure (and hence, the same financial risk profile) as Lone Star. Therefore, Lone Star's WACC can be used to evaluate the project. Lone Star's common stock beta is 1.25. Lone Star can issue additional long-term debt at a pretax yield of 10 percent. Lone Star's marginal income tax rate is 40 percent. Finally, r_f and r_M are 6 percent and 14 percent, respectively. Therefore, based on equations (7.9) and (7.13), Lone Star should use a cost of capital for the proposed project of about 10.0 percent:

$$r_e = r_f + \beta(r_M - r_f) = .06 + 1.25(.14 - .06) = .16$$
$$\text{WACC} = (1 - \theta)r_e + \theta(1 - \tau)r_d = (.4)(.16) + (.6)(.6)(.1)$$
$$= .10, \text{ or } 10 \text{ percent.}$$

When the Sponsor's WACC Should Not Be Used

Suppose now that Lone Star is a diversified mining company that is one-third debt-financed. Lone Star's WACC is not a good estimate of the project's cost of capital because (1) the copper mining project may have an operating risk profile different from Lone Star's other assets, and (2) the project will be more highly leveraged and therefore involve greater financial risk.

The steps for estimating the beta for this project are:

1. Obtain estimates of common stock betas for a sample of firms whose primary business is copper mining. These "pure plays" should have operating risk profiles similar to the proposed project because they are all in the same business.
2. Estimate the unleveraged β for each of these firms by applying the equation:

$$\beta_U = (1 - \theta)\beta_L, \tag{7.14}$$

where θ and β_L are the respective debt ratios and leveraged betas. This step is necessary because the pure plays will typically have different capital structures. The unleveraged betas reflect operating risk only.
3. The average of all of the firms' unleveraged betas serves as an estimate of the unleveraged beta for the project. Table 7.1, which illustrates the above procedure, estimates the appropriate unleveraged beta to be 1.14.
4. Adjust the unleveraged beta to reflect the riskiness of the project by applying the equation:

$$\beta_L = \beta_U/(1 - \theta), \tag{7.15}$$

where β_U denotes the average unleveraged beta for the pure plays, and θ denotes the debt ratio for the project.

TABLE 7.1   Estimating Beta for Lone Star's Copper Mining Project

Sample Firm	β_L	θ	$\beta_U = (1 - \theta)\beta_L$
A	1.70	.29	1.21
B	1.85	.45	1.02
C	1.95	.37	1.23
D	1.90	.43	1.08
E	2.00	.42	1.16
F	1.60	.35	1.04
G	1.65	.26	1.22
H	1.80	.34	1.19
			Average beta = 1.14

For the proposed copper mining project, $\beta_U = 1.14$ and $\theta = 0.6$, so:

$\beta_L = 1.14/0.6 = 1.90.$

The riskless rate is 6 percent, and r_M is 14 percent. The cost of capital for the project is:

$$r_e = r_f + \beta(r_M - r_f) = .06 + 1.9(.14 - .06) = 0.212.$$
$$\text{WACC} = (1 - \theta)r_e + \theta(1 - \tau)r_d = (.4)(.212) + (.6)(.6)(.1)$$
$$= .1208, \text{ or } 12.08 \text{ percent.}$$

Choice of Operating Method

Operating risk affects the beta of an investment project. The cost of capital calculation method outlined above requires one additional consideration when there is a choice of operating method. If there are significant differences in operating risk among potential production methods, the sample of representative firms must be restricted to firms that are using a set of assets and production methods that are approximately equivalent to those in the proposed investment project.

NET PRESENT VALUE ANALYSIS

The net present value (NPV) of a project is the difference between what the project costs and what it is worth. The best we can do in advance is *estimate* a project's NPV. We will not know its true market value, or what it is *really* worth, until the project is completed and the returns are collected.

The Procedure

The NPV of a capital investment project is the present value of *all* of the after-tax cash flows (CF) connected with the project—all its costs and revenues, now and in the future:

$$\text{NPV} = \text{CF}_0 + \frac{\text{CF}_1}{(1 + r)} + \frac{\text{CF}_2}{(1 + r)^2} + \ldots + \frac{\text{CF}_n}{(1 + r)^n}$$
$$= \sum_{t=0}^{n} \frac{\text{CF}_t}{(1 + r)^t}.$$

$$(7.16)$$

The decision rule to follow when applying NPV is: Undertake the capital investment project if the NPV is positive.

We estimate the value of a project by using *discounted cash flow (DCF) analysis* and computing the present value of all the cash flows connected with ownership. This procedure is similar to discounting the interest payments on a bond or dividends on a stock, and it is the essence of the net present value method.

An Example

To illustrate, let's continue our earlier example of Rocky Mountain Mining Corporation's mining project. Previously, we found that the project's cost of capital is 10.2 percent. What is the project's NPV?

Applying equation (7.16) to the project's annual incremental cash flows, we have:

$$NPV = \sum_{t=0}^{n} \frac{CF_t}{(1 + r)^t}$$

$$= -63.6 + \sum_{t=1}^{9} \frac{11.0}{(1.102)^t} + \frac{18.7}{(1.102)^{10}}$$

$$= \$6.3 \text{ million.}$$

The project should be accepted because its NPV is positive.

Table 7.2 illustrates a format that can be used to lay out the periodic cash flows for an NPV analysis.

INTERNAL RATE OF RETURN ANALYSIS

Another method of evaluating a proposed project is called the internal rate of return method. The internal rate of return (IRR) is the capital investment project's expected rate of return. If the cost of capital (required rate of return) equals the IRR (expected rate of return), the NPV would equal zero. But because of the uncertainty connected with risky cash flows, the realized rate of return will almost surely be different from the IRR. Earlier in this chapter, we showed how to find the expected rate of return for a bond—the pretax cost of debt. Here, we apply those same time-value-of-money techniques to compute IRRs, the expected internal rates of return for capital investment projects.

TABLE 7.2 NPV Analysis of Rocky Mountain Mining's Proposed Project (Dollar Amounts in Millions)

Item	Time (Years)											Total by Item	
	0	1	2	3	4	5	6	7	8	9	10		
Capitalized installation and equipment cost	-60.0											-60.0	t = 0
Expensed installation cost	-0.6											-0.6	t = 0
Change in net working capital	-3.0											-3.0	t = 0
Sale of old equipment	—												t = 0
Investment tax credit	—												t = 0
Lost depreciation from sale of old equipment													t = 0
Depreciation		2.0	2.0	2.0	2.0	2.0	2.0	2.0	2.0	2.0	2.0	2.0/yr	t = 1–10
Change in revenues minus expenses		9.0	9.0	9.0	9.0	9.0	9.0	9.0	9.0	9.0	9.0	9.0/yr	t = 1–10
Sale of equipment											5.0	5.0	t = 10
Removal expense											-0.3	-0.3	t = 10
Return of net working capital											3.0	3.0	t = 10
Total by year	-63.6	11.0	11.0	11.0	11.0	11.0	11.0	11.0	11.0	11.0	18.7		

The IRR for a project is the discount rate that makes the NPV zero:

$$0 = \sum_{t=0}^{n} \frac{CF_t}{(1 + IRR)^t} = CF_0 + \sum_{t=1}^{n} \frac{CF_t}{(1 + IRR)^t}.$$ (7.17)

Most financial calculators will calculate the IRR of a cash flow stream.

The decision rule to apply when using the internal rate of return method is: Undertake the capital investment project if the IRR exceeds r, the project's cost of capital.

In its simplest form, the IRR rule is intuitively appealing. In essence, it says: Does the expected rate of return on the investment exceed the required rate of return? In other words, will it create value? At first glance, this seems to be saying the same thing the NPV rule says. As we shall see, this is generally but not always true. The intuitive appeal, however, probably does account for the widespread use (and in some cases, even the preference) for the IRR method in practice.

Example

The mining project Rocky Mountain Mining Corporation has under consideration has a cost of capital of 10.2 percent. What is the IRR of the project, and should Rocky Mountain undertake it?

The IRR solves the equation:

$$0 = -63.6 + \sum_{t=1}^{9} \frac{11.0}{(1 + IRR)^t} + \frac{18.7}{(1 + IRR)^{10}}.$$

IRR = 12.4 percent > 10.2 percent.

Because the IRR exceeds the project's cost of capital, Rocky Mountain should undertake the project.

COMPARING IRR AND NPV ANALYSES

In the Rocky Mountain example, the IRR and NPV methods agree. This will happen whenever the projects are both independent and conventional. An *independent project* is one that can be chosen independently of other projects; that is, undertaking it neither requires nor precludes any other investment. A project that requires other investments is simply part of a larger project and must be evaluated together with all of its parts. When undertaking one project prevents investing in another project, and vice versa, the projects are said to be *mutually exclusive.*

A *conventional project* is a project with an initial cash outflow that is followed by one or more expected future cash inflows; that is, after making the investment, the total cash flow in each future year is expected to be positive. A purchase of a stock or bond is a simple example of a conventional project. An investor buys the security (a negative cash flow), and the terminal sale price and any dividends or interest payments received while the investor owns it will be positive (recall that liability is limited).

NPV Profile

Another way to look at NPV is to graph it as a function of the discount rate. This graph, called an *NPV profile,* includes both NPV and IRR. It also shows the value of the project at different possible costs of capital. Therefore, if sponsors are unsure about a project's cost of capital, the NPV profile would identify costs of capital at which the project would and would not add value.

Figure 7.1 shows an NPV profile for the Rocky Mountain Mining Project. To construct this profile, vary the discount rate in equation (7.16). When $r = 0$, the NPV is just the sum of the cash flows:

NPV = $-63.6 + 11(9) + 18.7 = \$54.1$ million.

When $r = 12.4$ percent, NPV = 0 because IRR = 12.4 percent. We also calculated what the NPV would be at discount rates of 5 percent, 10 percent, and 20 percent, and then drew the curve through these points.

The NPV profile in Figure 7.1 shows the general relationship between IRR and NPV for independent, conventional projects. If the IRR exceeds the cost of capital, the NPV is positive. If the IRR is less than the cost of capital, the NPV is negative. The vertical distance from the x-axis to the NPV line is the NPV of the project at each cost of capital, r.

When IRR and NPV Can Differ: Mutually Exclusive Projects

So far, we've only looked at the question of whether to undertake an independent project. Often, in practice, we have to choose from a set of

FIGURE 7.1   NPV Profile for Rocky Mountain Mining Project

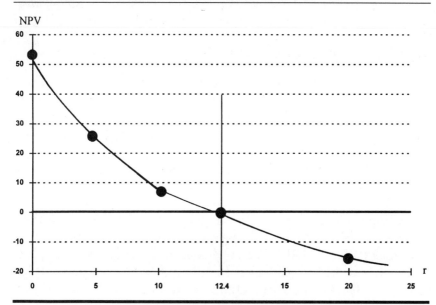

mutually exclusive projects. If we undertake one, we can't undertake any of the others.

For example, a firm that plans to build a new processing plant might have three possible locations and four possible plant configurations. But the firm only needs *one plant*. Therefore, it has to choose one configuration in one location, and the alternatives are mutually exclusive. In such situations, we can get conflicting recommendations from the IRR and NPV methods because of a difference in (1) the *size* of the projects, or (2) the *cash flow timing*. An example of the latter is when cash flows from one project come in mainly in the beginning, and cash flows from another project come in later. We'll look at each of these differences in turn.

Size Differences

When one project is larger than another, the smaller project often has a larger IRR but a smaller NPV. For example, let's say project A has an IRR of 30 percent and an NPV of $100, and project B has an IRR of 20 percent and an NPV of $200. The choice between these two projects—and therefore the resolution of such conflicts—is fairly straightforward.

Take the project that will add the most wealth, the one with the greater NPV. In general, the NPV decision rule is the better rule to follow when there is a size difference between mutually exclusive projects.

Cash Flow Timing Differences

The problem of cash flow timing can arise because of *reinvestment rate assumptions.* The question is: What will the cash inflows from the project earn when they are subsequently reinvested in other projects? The IRR method assumes that the future cash inflows will earn the IRR. The NPV method assumes they will earn the cost of capital.

The following example illustrates the reinvestment rate assumption conflict that results from a difference in cash flow timing. Suppose a company can invest in only one of two projects, A and B. The cost of capital is 10 percent, and the projects have the expected future cash flows shown in Table 7.3. Which is the better project?

Project A has an IRR of 22.08 percent, and project B has an IRR of 20.01 percent. But project A has an NPV of $76.29, and project B has an NPV of $94.08. The IRR method tells us to choose A, but the NPV method says to choose B.

A look at Figure 7.2 indicates that project A will have a higher NPV than project B whenever the cost of capital is higher than 15.40 percent, the crossover point.[3] Both projects would have an NPV of $37.86 if the cost of capital were 15.40 percent. Project B has a steeper NPV profile than project A because the present values of cash flows further in the future are more sensitive to the discount rate. A similar profile occurs for bond market values; the market value of a long-term bond changes more than that of a short-term bond in response to a given interest rate change.

Which method makes the more reasonable assumption about the rate of return the reinvested cash flows will earn? If the cost of capital is computed correctly, it's the required rate of return for the capital investment project. Over time, competitive forces will ensure that the

TABLE 7.3 Cash Flow Streams for Two Projects

Project	0	1	2	3	4	5	6	IRR (%)	NPV ($)
				Year					
A	−250	100	100	75	75	50	25	22.08	76.29
B	−250	50	50	75	100	100	125	20.01	94.08

FIGURE 7.2   IRR vs. NPV

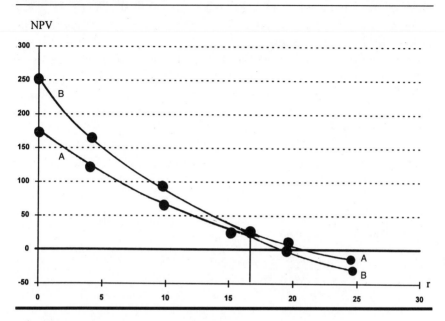

required rate of return equals the expected rate of return. In the long run, then, reinvested cash flows can earn the cost of capital, but not the extra—positive—NPV. The NPV method's assumption that the reinvestment rate will equal the cost of capital is the better assumption. Again, the NPV decision rule is superior to the IRR decision rule.

CONCLUSION

This chapter has described the basics of discounted cash flow analysis. Projects typically require substantial investments in long-lived assets, so an analysis of the profitability of a proposed project before committing funds to it is very important.

Discounted cash flow analysis involves estimating the amount of the initial investment, projecting the incremental after-tax cash flows, estimating the cost of capital, and then using the NPV method or the IRR method to determine whether the project is worth more than it will cost. The cost of capital depends on the risk of the capital investment project, not on the firm that undertakes the project. The value of the project is based on its ability to generate future cash flows, just as the value of a share of stock is based on its expected future cash dividends. If, compared to other firms, a particular firm can generate higher expected future cash flows using the project's assets, the project will add more value to that firm than to the other firms. However, the risk of the asset is the same, regardless of which firm owns it. Therefore, the project's cost of capital must be the same for all firms; differences in the value of a project among firms are reflected in the expected cash flows, not in the cost of capital.

In practice, we might be tempted to "add a few points" to a cost of capital "just for insurance." Ad hoc adjustments for "judgmental" factors should be avoided. This is not to belittle the valuable role that specialized judgment can play in a firm's choice of assets. But there are better methods of incorporating those important "other" factors into the decision-making process.

8

Financial Modeling and Project Evaluation

F inancial modeling plays an important role in project evaluation. Lenders are concerned about the timeliness of project debt service payments, and equity investors are concerned about the adequacy of their returns. Cash flow modeling is used to address both sets of concerns.

For a project financing to be viable, the project's cash flow must be adequate both to service project debt in a timely manner and to provide an acceptable rate of return to equity investors. The expected rate of return on investment must be commensurate with project risk. Equity investors require a higher expected rate of return than lenders, and active equity investors expect a higher rate of return than passive equity investors.

PREPARING CASH FLOW PROJECTIONS

The economic viability of a project depends on the adequacy of the cash flows generated as compared to the cash flows that must be expended. The timing of the cash inflows and outflows is a contributing factor. Thus, discounted cash flow analysis is crucial in determining the economic viability of a proposed project and the adequacy of the rates of return that providers of capital to the project can expect to realize.

Projecting the cash outflows and inflows is a critical part of this analysis. The cash outflows are typically easier to predict. They occur primarily in the earlier years of the project. The more distant operating cash inflows are inherently more difficult to predict. The discount rate chosen to calculate the net present value of the cash flows—or to evaluate the adequacy of the internal rate of return—should take into account this riskiness.

Estimating the Project's Total Cost

First, the project's total cost must be determined. Total cost includes (1) all direct costs, such as engineering, labor, and materials; and (2) all indirect costs, such as financing-related charges (including interest and commitment fees) and the cost of financial guarantees or other credit support mechanisms.

In the case of the Cogeneration Project, Engineering Firm and Local Utility, the two owners of Cogeneration Corporation, have agreed to pay various preconstruction costs—mainly, the fees for securing the many permits the Cogeneration Project will need to have before lenders will advance any construction funds. Preconstruction costs amount to $3 million. Engineering Firm and Local Utility contributed these permits to the project in return for equity in Cogeneration Company.[1]

The principal engineering firm usually supplies a construction drawdown schedule. The construction period allows time for preliminary engineering and licensing in addition to the actual construction. For the Cogeneration Project, funds needed during the construction period will be supplied by a commercial bank. Bank debt will fund 100 percent of the cost during the construction period. Engineering Firm and Local Utility have arranged a $120 million construction loan facility. They have agreed to pay the bank a 1 percent loan facility fee on behalf of Cogeneration Company; the bank received $1.2 million at closing. In addition, Engineering Firm and Local Utility committed to the bank that they would arrange permanent financing for Cogeneration Company.[2] They estimate that Cogeneration Company will incur approximately $2 million of fees in connection with arranging the permanent financing. Construction-period loans are generally made on a floating-rate basis.

Contingency for Cost Overruns

The construction loan should have sufficient capacity to provide funds for contingencies and for fluctuations in interest rates. Because the construction loan entails loan fees that depend on the size of the loan commitment, it is important not to oversize the construction loan.

Capital Cost

Table 8.1 indicates the total project cost of the Cogeneration Project, given a 24-month construction drawdown schedule and an interest rate of 10 percent. Interest is paid on funds that are drawn down, and a commitment fee is charged on the unused balance of the commitment. The loan commitment is designed to accommodate higher interest rates during the construction period and higher construction costs (for example, to cover design changes).

Construction is expected to cost $100 million. Commitment fees and interest will add $7.308 million, bringing the total construction cost to $107.308 million. The unused balance of $12.692 million shown in Table 8.1 is available to cover cost overruns or higher interest charges. Including the $3 million of preconstruction costs and $3.2 million cost of arranging financing, total expected project cost is $113.508 million.

The total project cost is sensitive to the interest rate applicable during the construction period. If the interest rate is higher than expected, project cost increases accordingly. The higher project cost requires a larger amount of permanent financing. As discussed in Chapter 3, the sponsors of a project can eliminate their interest rate risk exposure by arranging interest rate swaps. The bank would receive a fee for arranging the swap transaction, which would have to be added to the project cost.

Ownership Arrangements

The Cogeneration Project's target capital structure is 25 percent equity and 75 percent debt. The proportions of equity and debt were determined by analyzing the profitability of the project. The greater the level of operating income that can be contractually assured, the greater the amount of debt a project can support. Cogeneration Company's debt will be nonrecourse to the equity investors. Long-term lenders must look solely to the project's cash flow for their repayment. The equity investors will receive their returns in the form of tax benefits, dividends paid out of excess cash flow from the project (i.e., after payment of debt service), and any residual value of the cogeneration plant.

TABLE 8.1 Cogeneration Project: Total Project Cost and Construction Loan Drawdown Schedule (Millions of Dollars)

Total direct costs	$100 million
Commitment amount	$120 million
Commitment fees	.5 percent per annum
Interest rate	10 percent per annum

End of Month	Construction Drawdown	Commitment Fees[a]	Interest[b]	Total Financing Costs	Total Construction and Financing	Cumulative Funds Used	Unused Balance of Commitment
0	—	—	—	—	—	—	$120.000
1	$ 0.250	$0.050	—	$0.050	$ 0.300	$ 0.300	119.700
2	0.250	0.050	$0.003	0.053	0.303	0.603	119.397
3	0.375	0.050	0.005	0.055	0.430	1.033	118.967
4	0.375	0.050	0.009	0.059	0.434	1.467	118.533
5	0.500	0.049	0.012	0.061	0.561	2.028	117.972
6	0.500	0.049	0.017	0.066	0.566	2.594	117.406
7	1.000	0.049	0.022	0.071	1.071	3.665	116.335
8	1.500	0.048	0.031	0.079	1.579	5.244	114.756
9	2.000	0.048	0.044	0.092	2.092	7.336	112.664
10	2.000	0.047	0.061	0.108	2.108	9.444	110.556
11	3.000	0.046	0.079	0.125	3.125	12.569	107.431
12	4.000	0.045	0.105	0.150	4.150	16.719	103.281
13	5.000	0.043	0.139	0.182	5.182	21.901	98.099
14	6.000	0.041	0.183	0.224	6.224	28.125	91.875
15	7.000	0.038	0.234	0.272	7.272	35.397	84.603
16	8.000	0.035	0.295	0.330	8.330	43.727	76.273
17	10.000	0.032	0.364	0.396	10.396	54.123	65.877
18	11.000	0.027	0.451	0.478	11.478	65.601	54.399
19	10.000	0.023	0.547	0.570	10.570	76.171	43.829
20	8.750	0.018	0.635	0.653	9.403	85.574	34.426
21	7.000	0.014	0.713	0.727	7.727	93.301	26.699
22	6.000	0.011	0.778	0.789	6.789	100.090	19.910
23	3.500	0.008	0.834	0.842	4.342	104.432	15.568
24	2.000	0.006	0.870	0.876	2.876	107.308	12.692
Total	$100.000	$0.877	$6.431	$7.308	$107.308		

[a] Calculated on the unused balance of commitment. [b] Calculated on cumulative funds used.

Figure 8.1 indicates the initial capitalization of Cogeneration Company following completion of construction. Total capitalization equals $113.508 million, divided between long-term debt and equity:

	Amount	Percent
Long-term debt	$ 85.131 million	75.0
Equity:		
General partner	2.838	2.5
Limited partners	25.539	22.5
Total equity	28.377	25.0
Total capitalization	$113.508 million	100.0

Engineering Firm and Local Utility each own half of the general partner, Cogeneration Corporation. Each will invest 25 percent of total project equity, and the passive equity investors will invest the other half of the equity. Engineering Firm and Local Utility invest just enough funds in Cogeneration Corporation to capitalize the general partner adequately for federal income tax purposes.

Initially, the general partner will receive 10 percent of the partnership's income, losses, and cash distributions, and the limited partners will receive the remaining 90 percent. Once the limited partners have received cumulative cash distributions equal to their original investment of $25.539 million, the 10/90 split will change to 50/50.[3] The initial split is in proportion to the equity investors' respective investments in the Cogeneration Project. Following reversion, the general partner shares equally with the limited partners with respect to partnership income, losses, tax credits, and cash distributions. This shift in distribution arrangements is designed to reward the general partner if the partnership performs well.

Project Economics

The Cogeneration Project's principal sources of revenue are from the sale of electricity under the 15-year electric power purchase agreement with Local Utility and from the sale of steam under the 15-year steam purchase agreement with Chemical Company. Electricity revenues can be predicted with a high degree of certainty because (1) the electric power purchase agreement defines contractually the price for each megawatt-hour of electricity delivered to Local Utility each year for 15 years, and (2) the capacity of the cogeneration facility to generate

FIGURE 8.1 Sources of Long-Term Financing and the Allocation of Income, Losses, and Cash Distributions for the Cogeneration Project

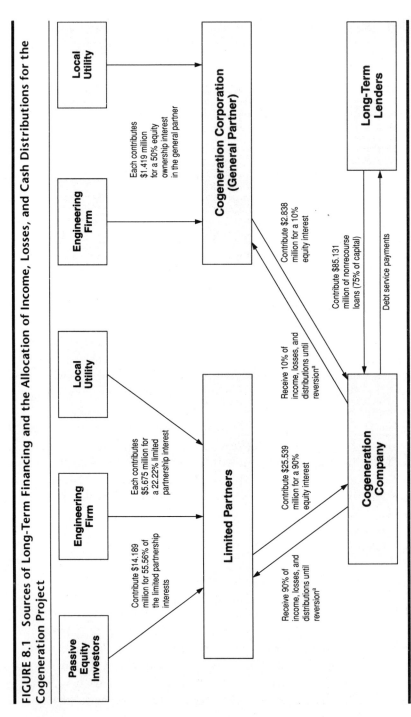

[a] Reversion occurs when the limited partners have received cumulative cash distributions equal to their original investment of $25.539 million. Thereafter, the general partner (Cogeneration Corporation) is entitled to receive 50 percent of all partnership income, losses, and cash distributions.

electricity is known and the operating reliability of similar plants has been well-documented. The steam purchase agreement establishes minimum purchase quantities, specifies the price per thousand pounds of steam, and provides that this price will increase during the 15-year term of the contract, based on annual changes in the U.S. producer price index (PPI).

The Cogeneration Project's operating costs are largely contractually determined. Local Utility will supply gas under a 15-year gas supply agreement. The contract specifies a gas price that will prevail during the initial year of the contract. The gas price will change in subsequent years, in line with changes in the price Cogeneration Company receives for the electricity it sells to Local Utility. Local Utility will operate Cogeneration Company. Its management fees will be a specified fixed amount for the initial year; they will escalate thereafter in line with changes in the PPI. Local Utility has agreed to maintain and repair the cogeneration facility in accordance with an agreed-on fee schedule. Engineering Firm has guaranteed that the cogeneration facility will operate at its design capacity for at least 15 years.

Cash Flow Projections

The cash flow projection assumptions for the Cogeneration Project are shown in Table 8.2. The contract volumes of electricity (as specified in the electric power purchase agreement) and steam (as specified in the steam purchase agreement) establish the base output levels for 15 years. The electric power purchase agreement specifies electricity prices. The steam purchase agreement provides a base steam sales price, which can be escalated using a forecast of future changes in the PPI. (Such forecasts are available from economic forecasting services.) The projected volumes and prices can be used to forecast annual revenue amounts.

The design of the cogeneration facility will determine the annual levels of gas usage. The gas supply agreement escalates the gas price to match future increases in electricity prices, which were used to prepare the revenue projections. Management fees and other operating expenses will also increase with the PPI, as provided for in the 15-year operating contract entered into with Local Utility. Management fees are included in "Operating and other cash expenses" in Table 8.2.

Table 8.3 contains the projected operating cash flows. They are based on the assumptions provided in Table 8.2. When preparing a set of cash flow projections for a prospective project, it is important to give all the critical details. Prospective lenders and equity investors

---

TABLE 8.2   Cogeneration Project: Assumptions for the Cash Flow Projections[a]

1. Capacity utilization: 90 percent
2. Prices at the time the plant is placed in service, and contracted escalation factors:
   Electricity $40.00/megawatt-hour; 6% annually
   Steam $4.00/thousand pounds; PPI[b]
   Natural gas $3.00/million BTU; 6% annually
3. Predicted volumes:

	At Capacity	Maximum Annual	At 90 Percent Utilization
Electricity production	250 MW	2,190,000 MWH	1,971,000 MWH
Steam production	150,000 PPH	1,314 M P	1,182.6 M P
Gas usage	1,950 M BTU/hour	17,082 B BTU	15,373.8 B BTU

4. Operating and other cash expenses[c]:
   First Year = $8 million/year; escalation factor = PPI.
5. Tax rate: 40 percent.

---

[a] MW = megawatts; MWH = megawatt-hours; PPH = pounds per hour; M P = million pounds; BTU = British thermal unit; M BTU = million BTUs; B BTU = billion BTUs.
[b] The producer price index, which is assumed to escalate at the rate of 5 percent per annum.
[c] Includes operating costs, maintenance expenditures, and management fees amounting to $6 million, and insurance and local taxes amounting to $2 million.

---

are particularly interested in the assumptions because the projections are meaningful only to the extent the assumptions have a sound basis.

Constant Dollars Versus Current Dollars

An error frequently committed when making cash flow projections involves escalating revenue items at one rate and cost items at another rate, without any real justification for doing so. When these escalation rates differ, it is important to furnish an explanation along with the projections. Escalating revenues at a higher rate than costs will introduce a basis in favor of proceeding with the project. An economically unprofitable project may then appear to be profitable.

Some financial economists recommend preparing the projections for a project on the basis of dollars of constant purchasing power (or, more simply, constant dollars). Constant dollars differ from so-called current dollars, which is the unit of measurement employed for the Cogeneration Project, in that constant dollars have the effect of general inflation removed. Many companies have found it useful to prepare cash flow projections in constant dollars when evaluating a project that would be developed in a high-inflation economy and

TABLE 8.3 Cogeneration Project: Projected Operating Cash Flows (Millions of Dollars)

Year	Revenues		Cash Expenses		Noncash Expenses[a]	Income from Operations[b]		Cash Flow from Operations[b]
	Electricity	Steam	Natural Gas	Operating & Other		Pretax	After-Tax	
1	$ 78.84	$4.73	$ 46.12	$ 8.00	$11.35	$18.10	$10.86	$22.21
2	83.57	4.97	48.89	8.40	11.35	19.90	11.94	23.29
3	88.58	5.22	51.82	8.82	11.35	21.81	13.08	24.44
4	93.90	5.48	54.93	9.26	11.35	23.83	14.30	25.65
5	99.53	5.75	58.23	9.72	11.35	25.98	15.59	26.94
6	105.51	6.04	61.72	10.21	11.35	28.26	16.96	28.31
7	111.84	6.34	65.42	10.72	11.35	30.68	18.41	29.76
8	118.55	6.66	69.35	11.26	11.35	33.25	19.95	31.30
9	125.66	6.99	73.51	11.82	11.35	35.97	21.58	32.93
10	133.20	7.34	77.92	12.41	11.35	38.85	23.31	34.66
11	141.19	7.71	82.60	13.03	—	53.27	31.96	31.96
12	149.66	8.09	87.55	13.68	—	56.52	33.91	33.91
13	158.64	8.50	92.81	14.37	—	59.96	35.98	35.98
14	168.16	8.92	98.37	15.09	—	63.62	38.17	38.17
15	178.25	9.37	104.28	15.84	—	67.50	40.50	40.50

[a] Deductible for tax purposes. Assumes the total project cost of $113.508 million can be deducted on a straight-line basis over 10 years.
[b] Before interest charges but after deduction of the equity investors' tax liabilities on their partnership income.

would have certain critical revenue or cost items received or paid, respectively, in the local currency.

When a project's revenues and costs are all denominated in a single freely tradable currency, and the inflation rate in the country that issued the currency is comparatively low (no more than a single-digit rate), the extra work required to prepare the projections on a constant-dollar basis is seldom justified. A better analytical approach is to specify the inflation assumptions, as in Table 8.2, and then show the effects of different inflation assumptions in a separate sensitivity analysis.

PREPARING PROJECTED FINANCIAL STATEMENTS

A project's initial capitalization table shows the financial condition of the project. The cash flow projections will indicate how profitable the project is expected to be, how much cash flow it is expected to generate, and how that cash flow will be allocated among the various providers of capital. These projections can also be used to predict how the project's financial condition is expected to change over the life of the project. Consequently, the initial capitalization table can be used in conjunction with the information underlying the cash flow projections to prepare a set of projected financial statements—income statement, balance sheet, and statement of cash flows—for each year in the project's life.

EVALUATING A PROJECT'S DEBT CAPACITY

The amount of debt a project can support depends on the amount of cash flow that is available to make debt service payments, the extent of supplemental credit support mechanisms, and the loan parameters—the interest rate, the maturity date, the loan amortization requirements, and the lenders' coverage requirements.

Borrowing Capacity

Chapter 6 presented various models for gauging a project's borrowing capacity. The cash flow information contained in Table 8.3 can be used together with equations (6.1) and (6.3) to determine the borrowing capacity of the Cogeneration Project. The present value of the projected cash flows for years 1 through 10, calculated at a 10 percent discount rate, is $165.22 million. Suppose that long-term lenders require a cash flow coverage ratio of $\alpha = 1.75$. Then the maximum borrowing capacity is $94.41 million, which exceeds by a comfortable margin the $85.131 million initial debt level planned for the Cogeneration Project.

Annual Coverage Tests

Chapter 6 discussed three coverage tests that lenders apply to measure a project's capacity to pay debt service year by year. The interest coverage, fixed charge coverage, and debt service coverage ratios have been presented in equations (6.11), (6.12), and (6.13), respectively. Table 8.4 provides the annual interest coverage and debt service coverage ratios for the Cogeneration Project. Cogeneration Company does

TABLE 8.4   Cogeneration Project: Annual Interest and Debt Service Coverage Ratios

Assumptions:

1. Principal amount: $85.131 million.
2. Term: 10 years.
3. Interest rate: 10 percent per annum
4. Principal repayment: years 1–3 = 5 percent
                         years 4–7 = 10 percent
                         years 8–10 = 15 percent

Calculations (millions of dollars):

Year	EBIT[a]	EBITDA[b]	Debt Service Interest	Debt Service Principal	Tax-Adjusted Principal[c]	Interest Coverage Ratio	Debt Service Coverage Ratio
1	$18.10	$29.45	$8.51	$ 4.26	$ 7.09	2.13	1.89
2	19.90	31.25	8.09	4.26	7.09	2.46	2.06
3	21.81	33.16	7.66	4.26	7.09	2.85	2.25
4	23.83	35.18	7.24	8.51	14.19	3.29	1.64
5	25.98	37.33	6.38	8.51	14.19	4.07	1.81
6	28.26	39.61	5.53	8.51	14.19	5.11	2.01
7	30.68	42.03	4.68	8.51	14.19	6.55	2.23
8	33.25	44.60	3.83	12.77	21.28	8.68	1.78
9	35.97	47.32	2.55	12.77	21.28	14.08	1.99
10	38.85	50.21	1.28	12.77	21.28	30.43	2.23

[a] Earnings before interest and taxes.
[b] Earnings before interest, taxes, depreciation, and amortization.
[c] Principal repayments divided by (1 − tax rate).

not plan to rent any equipment, so the fixed charge coverage ratio would be identical to the interest coverage ratio. If, however, Cogeneration Company did decide to rent significant amounts of equipment or real estate, then the fixed charge coverage ratio would have to be calculated for each year.

The interest coverage ratio increases steadily as the project loan is repaid. The debt service coverage ratio decreases in those years when the principal repayment increases. Lenders are most concerned with the values of these ratios during the early years of a project's life. For Cogeneration Project, the interest coverage ratio is 2.13 in year 1 and exceeds 3.00 in year 4. The debt service coverage ratio is 1.89 in year 1 and never falls below 1.64. In view of the strength of the Cogeneration Project's contractual arrangements, coverages of the magnitudes just calculated would suggest that Cogeneration Company should be able to service its debt in a timely manner.

Interest Rate Risk

If the debt incurred for a project bears a floating rate of interest, rising interest rates can impair the project's coverage ratios. A different form of interest rate risk also exists. At the time a project is initially financed, floating-rate bank debt is often arranged to cover construction costs; the expectation is that it will be refunded with fixed-rate debt following completion. But if interest rates rise during the construction period, the fixed-rate long-term debt will prove to be more expensive than anticipated.

A number of strategies are available for handling these risks. First, the construction loan can be arranged so that the portion that is not repaid with the proceeds from the equity financing turns into a term loan. The term loan can be refunded if interest rates decrease. But interest rates might not decrease for several years; hence, this strategy really does not reduce the project's interest rate risk exposure.

Alternatively, the interest rate risk can be hedged. Selling financial futures contracts short during the construction period is one hedging strategy. If interest rates rise during the construction period, and if the hedges have been structured properly, the profit realized on closing out the financial futures positions will offset the impact of the higher interest rates on the project's cost of debt. Figlewski (1986) and Tucker (1991) contain detailed discussions of hedging strategies and how to implement them. An alternative hedging strategy that is useful for locking-in a future fixed rate of interest utilizes a deferred interest rate swap agreement. The project company could obtain protection against a possible increase in interest rates by entering into a deferred swap contract under which (1) the project company would agree to swap interest payment obligations with the counterparty to the contract beginning as of the completion of project construction, and (2) the project company's obligation would be calculated at a specified fixed interest rate and the counterparty's obligation would be calculated based on a specified floating interest rate. That is, a deferred swap contract establishes the terms of the interest rate swap as of the date the contract is entered into, but the start of the swap period is delayed for some agreed-on period (see Kapner and Marshall, 1990, p. 279).[4]

MEASURING EXPECTED RATES OF RETURN

The projected operating cash flows in Table 8.3 form the basis for measuring the expected rates of return to Engineering Firm, Local Utility, and the passive equity investors. Engineering Firm and Local Utility invest identical amounts. Each has the same expected rate of return; I refer to it as the "return to sponsor equity." I refer to the expected rate of return to the passive equity investors as the "return to limited partnership equity." The latter is the easier of the two to calculate, so I consider it first.

Return to Limited Partnership Equity

The passive equity investors, as limited partners, are junior to the lenders; they receive cash distributions out of what is left over after Cogeneration Company pays debt service for the year. The size of the cash distributions is not specified contractually; it depends on the profitability of the Cogeneration Project. The passive equity investors also receive their share of the tax benefits associated with project ownership plus a share of the Cogeneration Project's residual value. To realize these benefits, the passive equity investors had to commit to the construction lenders to invest a stated percentage of the project's equity capital (55.56 percent of limited partnership capital and 50 percent of total equity capital), once the Cogeneration Project passes its completion tests.

As illustrated in Figure 8.1, the limited partners (including Engineering Firm and Local Utility, to the extent of their limited partnership interests) are entitled to 90 percent of income, losses, and cash distributions from the Cogeneration Project prior to reversion, and 50

TABLE 8.5 Annual After-Tax Cash Flow to Cogeneration Project's Passive Equity Investors[a] (Millions of Dollars)

Year	Investment	Cash Flow from Operations	Less Debt Service	Cash Available for Distribution	Cash Distributed to Limited Partners Percent	Amount
Construction						
−2	—	—	—	—	—	—
−1	—	—	—	—	—	—
0	($14.19)	—	—	—	—	—
Operation						
1	—	$29.45	$12.77	$16.68	50.00	$ 8.34
2	—	31.25	12.34	18.90	50.00	9.45
3	—	33.16	11.92	21.24	27.78	5.90
4	—	35.18	15.75	19.43	27.78	5.40
5	—	37.33	14.90	22.43	27.78	6.23
6	—	39.61	14.05	25.57	27.78	7.10
7	—	42.03	13.20	28.84	27.78	8.01
8	—	44.60	16.60	28.00	27.78	7.78
9	—	47.32	15.32	31.99	27.78	8.89
10	—	50.21	14.05	36.16	27.78	10.04
11	—	53.27	—	53.27	27.78	14.80
12	—	56.52	—	56.52	27.78	15.70
13	—	59.96	—	59.96	27.78	16.66
14	—	63.62	—	63.62	27.78	17.67
15	—	67.50	—	67.50	27.78	18.75

[a] The cash flows occur throughout the year, and the timing of the cash flows does affect the investors' rate of return. However, for simplicity, it is assumed that cash flows occur discretely at the end of each year.

[b] The residual value is calculated in the following manner:

Five times after-tax cash flow = 5 × 40.5	= $202.5	Gross proceeds =	$202.5
Original tax basis	100.0	Taxes =	73.825
Capital gain	$102.5	After-tax proceeds =	128.675
Depreciation recapture tax liability = .40 × 100.0 = $ 40.0		Passive investors' share =	× .2778
Capital gain tax liability = .33 × 102.5 =	33.825	Residual value to passive investors =	$ 35.75
Total tax liability =	$ 73.825		

| Partnership Tax Items | | | Allocation of Taxes Paid (Saved) | | | | |
| Depreciation & | | | Allocation to Passive Equity Investors | | | | |
Amortization Deduction	Interest Deduction	Taxable Income	Percent	Taxable Income	Taxes Paid	Residual Value	After-Tax Cash Flow
—	—	—	—	—	—		—
—	—	—	—	—	—		—
—	—	—	—	—	—		($14.19)
$11.35	$8.51	$ 9.59	50.00	$ 4.79	$1.92		6.42
11.35	8.09	11.81	50.00	5.91	2.36		7.09
11.35	7.66	14.15	27.78	3.93	1.57		4.33
11.35	7.24	16.60	27.78	4.61	1.84		3.55
11.35	6.38	19.60	27.78	5.44	2.18		4.05
11.35	5.53	22.73	27.78	6.31	2.53		4.58
11.35	4.68	26.00	27.78	7.22	2.89		5.12
11.35	3.83	29.41	27.78	8.17	3.27		4.51
11.35	2.55	33.41	27.78	9.28	3.71		5.18
11.35	1.28	37.58	27.78	10.44	4.18		5.87
—	—	53.27	27.78	14.80	5.92		8.88
—	—	56.52	27.78	15.70	6.28		9.42
—	—	59.96	27.78	16.66	6.66		9.99
—	—	63.62	27.78	17.67	7.07		10.60
—	—	67.50	27.78	18.75	7.50	$35.75[b]	47.00

percent of these amounts thereafter. The passive equity investors are entitled to 55.56 percent of these amounts—both before and after reversion. Thus, prior to reversion, the passive equity investors will receive 50 percent of income, loss, and cash flow; after reversion, they will receive 27.78 percent (i.e., 55.56 percent of the limited partners' 50 percent share).

Table 8.5 shows the details of the calculation of annual after-tax returns to the passive equity investors. The expected rate of return is calculated as the internal rate of return of the after-tax cash flow stream. This calculation assumes that the passive equity investors' share of the Cogeneration Project's residual value, net of related taxes, is $35.75 million.[5] In particular, it is assumed that Cogeneration Company can be sold at the end of the fifteenth year for a price equal to five times the year-15 after-tax cash flow.

The expected rate of return for the passive equity investors in the Cogeneration Project, based on the after-tax cash flow stream in Table 8.5, is 40.09 percent. They will agree to invest in the Cogeneration Project only if this expected rate of return is no less than the rates of return they could expect to realize by investing in projects of comparable risk.

The timing of the equity investment affects the investors' expected rate of return. The passive equity investors in the Cogeneration Project will have to commit to invest their equity prior to the start of construction. Table 8.5 treats the equity investment as occurring at the time these equity commitments are funded, that is, just prior to the start of operations. It can be argued, however, that the equity investment really occurs at the time the commitment is made. The truly correct approach is not entirely clear because the passive equity investors will not have to fund their commitments unless and until the Cogeneration Project passes its completion tests. If the expected rate of return is calculated based on when the commitments are entered into, the passive equity investors' expected rate of return is 25.72 percent.[6]

Passive equity investors often perform a third expected rate of return calculation in which they assume that their equity investments are made as construction proceeds and represent the percentage of the total project cost that they have effectively agreed to fund. Equity will represent 25 percent of Cogeneration Company's capital structure. The passive equity investors will provide half of this amount. The passive equity investors, under this conservative approach to measuring their expected rate of return, would treat their equity investments as taking place as construction and related costs occur in an amount equal to 12.5 percent of these costs (i.e., 50 percent of the 25 percent project equity).

Under this approach, $2.865 million of the passive equity investment occurs at construction year − 2 and $11.324 million occurs at construction year − 1.[7] This investment pattern leads to an expected rate of return of 29.45 percent.

Table 8.6 summarizes the expected rate of return analysis for the passive equity investors. Depending on how the passive equity investors view the timing of their equity investments, their expected rate of return falls between 25.72 percent and 40.09 percent. If their required rate of return is 15 percent, their expected net present value falls between $13.11 million and $21.32 million. The net present value remains positive even when the required rate of return is 25 percent and the equity investment is treated as occurring coincident with the initial commitment to invest ($0.48 million NPV).

TABLE 8.6   Cogeneration Project: Analysis of the Expected Rate of Return to the Passive Equity Investors (Millions of Dollars)

Expected net present value:

		Conservative Approaches	
Discount Rate	Basic Approach	Phased Investment[a]	Initial Commitment[b]
15.0%	$21.32	$14.40	$13.11
17.5	16.31	9.92	8.48
20.0	12.47	6.62	5.04
22.5	9.48	4.15	2.45
25.0	7.14	2.29	0.48
Expected rate of return:	40.09 percent	29.45 percent	25.72 percent
Payback:	2.16 years	4.16 years	4.16 years

[a] Treating the equity investment as being phased: $2.865 million at construction year -2 and $11.324 million at construction year -1.

[b] Treating the entire equity investment as being made at the time the passive equity investors commit to invest in the Cogeneration Project.

Return to Sponsor Equity

Engineering Firm and Local Utility have equal ownership interests in Cogeneration Corporation, the general partner of Cogeneration Company. Cogeneration Corporation owns 10 percent of the equity in Cogeneration Company. It receives 10 percent of the income, loss, and cash distributions of Cogeneration Company until reversion occurs, and 50 percent thereafter. In addition, Engineering Firm and Local Utility each own 22.22 percent of the limited partnership interests in Cogeneration Company. For managing the business of Cogeneration Company, Local Utility will receive a management fee equal to 3 percent of project revenue. Local Utility estimates that this management fee will approximate its cost of managing Cogeneration Company, so no profit will be generated.

Like the passive equity investors, Engineering Firm and Local Utility will commit to fund their equity investments prior to the start of the construction period. Table 8.7 shows the annual after-tax cash flow to the sponsors, Engineering Firm and Local Utility. Table 8.8 summarizes the expected rate of return analysis for the sponsors. Note in Table 8.7 that the sponsors will receive 50 percent of profits, losses, and cash distributions prior to reversion, but they will receive 72.22

TABLE 8.7 Annual After-Tax Cash Flow to Cogeneration Project's Sponsors[a] (Millions of Dollars)

		Cash Distributed to All Partners				
Year	*Investment*	*Cash Flow from Operations*	*Less Debt Service*	*Cash Available for Distribution*	*Cash Distributed to Sponsors* *Percent*	*Amount*
Construction						
−2	($6.20)	—	—	—	—	—
−1	—	—	—	—	—	—
0	(7.99)	—	—	—	—	—
Operation						
1	—	$29.45	$12.77	$16.68	50.00	$8.34
2	—	31.25	12.34	18.90	50.00	9.45
3	—	33.16	11.92	21.24	72.22	15.34
4	—	35.18	15.75	19.43	72.22	14.04
5	—	37.33	14.90	22.43	72.22	16.20
6	—	39.61	14.05	25.57	72.22	18.46
7	—	42.03	13.20	28.84	72.22	20.82
8	—	44.60	16.60	28.00	72.22	20.22
9	—	47.32	15.32	31.99	72.22	23.11
10	—	50.21	14.05	36.16	72.22	26.11
11	—	53.27	—	53.27	72.22	38.47
12	—	56.52	—	56.52	72.22	40.82
13	—	59.96	—	59.96	72.22	43.31
14	—	63.62	—	63.62	72.22	45.95
15	—	67.50	—	67.50	72.22	48.75

[a] The cash flows occur throughout the year, and the timing of the cash flows does affect the sponsors' rate of return. However, for simplicity, it is assumed that cash flows occur discretely at the end of each year.

[b] The residual value is calculated in the following manner:

Five times after-tax cash flow = 5 × 40.5 =	$202.5	Gross proceeds =	$202.5
Original tax basis	100.0	Taxes =	73.825
Capital gain	$102.5	After-tax proceeds =	128.675
Depreciation recapture tax liability = .40 × 100.0 =	$ 40.0	Sponsors' share =	× .7222
Capital gain tax liability = .33 × 102.5 =	33.825	Residual value to sponsors =	$ 92.93
Total tax liability =	$ 73.825		

| Allocation of Taxes Paid (Saved) | | | | | | | |
| Partnership Tax Items | | | Allocation to Sponsors | | | | |
Depreciation & Amortization Deduction	Interest Deduction	Taxable Income	Percent	Taxable Income	Taxes Paid	Residual Value	After-Tax Cash Flow
—	—	—	—	—	—		($6.20)
—	—	—	—	—	—		—
—	—	—	—	—	—		(7.99)
$11.35	$8.51	$ 9.59	50.00	$4.79	$1.92		6.42
11.35	8.09	11.81	50.00	5.91	2.36		7.09
11.35	7.66	14.15	72.22	10.22	4.09		11.25
11.35	7.24	16.60	72.22	11.99	4.79		9.24
11.35	6.38	19.60	72.22	14.15	5.66		10.54
11.35	5.53	22.73	72.22	16.41	6.57		11.90
11.35	4.68	26.00	72.22	18.78	7.51		13.31
11.35	3.83	29.41	72.22	21.24	8.50		11.72
11.35	2.55	33.41	72.22	24.13	9.65		13.45
11.35	1.28	37.58	72.22	27.14	10.86		15.26
—	—	53.27	72.22	38.47	15.39		23.08
—	—	56.52	72.22	40.82	16.33		24.49
—	—	59.96	72.22	43.31	17.32		25.98
—	—	63.62	72.22	45.95	18.38		27.57
—	—	67.50	72.22	48.75	19.50	$92.93[b]	122.18

percent after reversion (i.e., the 50 percent general partner's share plus 44.44 percent of the limited partners' 50 percent share).

The sponsors' expected rate of return on equity exceeds the passive equity investors' expected rate of return. This is to be expected because of the sponsors' greater risk exposure.

SENSITIVITY ANALYSIS

Tables 8.2 through 8.8 contain results for the expected case. But results rarely turn out exactly as expected. For the Cogeneration Project, the residual value is uncertain. Also, unless some form of interest rate protection is arranged, the interest rate on the 10-year debt issue is uncertain. On the other hand, the construction contract eliminates

TABLE 8.8   Cogeneration Project: Analysis of the Expected Rate of Return to the Sponsors (Millions of Dollars)

Expected net present value:

Discount Rate	Basic Approach	Conservative Approach[a]
15.0%	$44.01	$37.06
17.5	32.79	25.99
20.0	24.55	17.89
22.5	18.41	11.89
25.0	13.79	7.40
Expected rate of return:	44.25 percent	31.66 percent
Payback:	4.06 years	4.06 years

[a] Treating the equity investment as being made at the time the sponsors commit to invest in the Cogeneration Project.

uncertainty with regard to the construction cost. Design changes could affect this cost, but the Cogeneration Project is unlikely to require significant design changes because it will utilize a plant design developed previously. The 15-year electric power purchase agreement and the 15-year steam purchase agreement mitigate output pricing risk. There is still a risk that revenues might fall short of expectations because of unplanned outages; however, this risk is small because the operating reliability of similar plants has been well-documented. The 15-year gas supply agreement eliminates gas price risk. If these contracts were not in place, then a sensitivity analysis would have to be performed for each of the factors mentioned—construction cost, electricity price, steam price, gas price, and the levels of electric power and steam output.

Figure 8.2 illustrates the sensitivity of the projected returns on equity to variation in the residual value. Residual value is shown both before and after taxes. Both calculations were based on the actual timing of the cash equity investments, as shown in Tables 8.5 and 8.7. Even if the residual value is zero, the projected rate of return to the passive equity investors is 39.41 percent, and the projected rate of return to the sponsors is 43.75 percent. The projected rates of return show very little sensitivity to the residual value.

Table 8.9 illustrates the sensitivity of the interest coverage ratio and the debt service coverage ratio, in years 1 through 4, to changes in the interest rate on the 10-year debt issue. Even if the interest rate on this debt should increase to 14 percent, the interest coverage ratio during the first four years never falls below 1.52, and the debt service coverage

FIGURE 8.2   Sensitivity of Returns on Equity to Variation in the Residual Value

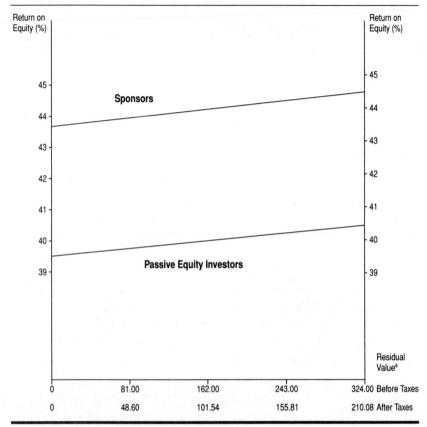

[a]Before allocation between the passive equity investors and the sponsors.

ratio during the same period never falls below 1.45. The Cogeneration Project appears financially feasible when financed on the basis contemplated, even if the interest cost of project debt should rise to 14 percent. Nevertheless, if interest rates were to rise above 14 percent, the coverage ratios would deteriorate further and would, at some point, jeopardize the sponsors' ability to raise the amount of debt financing contemplated. To eliminate this risk, the sponsors could prefinance or else purchase some form of interest rate protection.

If the electric power purchase, steam purchase, construction, and gas supply agreements were not in place, then additional sensitivity

**TABLE 8.9   Sensitivity of the Interest Coverage and Debt Service
Coverage Ratios to the Rate of Interest on Long-Term Debt**

	Interest Rate on Long-Term Debt								
Ratios	6%	7%	8%	9%	10%	11%	12%	13%	14%
Interest Coverage:									
Year 1	3.54	3.04	2.66	2.36	2.13	1.93	1.77	1.64	1.52
2	4.10	3.51	3.08	2.73	2.46	2.24	2.05	1.89	1.76
3	4.74	4.07	3.56	3.16	2.85	2.59	2.37	2.19	2.03
4	5.49	4.71	4.12	3.66	3.29	2.99	2.74	2.53	2.35
Debt Service Coverage:									
Year 1	2.41	2.26	2.12	2.00	1.89	1.79	1.70	1.62	1.55
2	2.62	2.45	2.30	2.17	2.06	1.95	1.86	1.77	1.70
3	2.84	2.66	2.51	2.37	2.25	2.14	2.04	1.94	1.86
4	1.90	1.83	1.76	1.70	1.64	1.59	1.54	1.49	1.45

analyses like those presented in Figure 8.2 and Table 8.9 would indicate how sensitive the equity rates of return and loan coverage parameters are to variation in these prices and quantities.

Chapters 11 through 14 contain other examples of sensitivity analyses for four large project financings.

CONCLUSION

Discounted cash flow analysis plays an important role in project financing. A project cannot be financed on a project basis—or on any other basis—unless it is expected to be profitable. Discounted cash flow analysis plays a crucial role in determining a project's expected profitability.

A financial model of the project is also useful in demonstrating the project's ability to service its debt obligations and provide an acceptable rate of return to the project's equity investors. Prospective lenders to a project, and its equity investors, will carefully review these projections before committing any funds.

9

Sources of Funds

The project sponsors typically provide the greatest proportion of initial project equity. Often, the purchasers of the project's output are also asked to make equity investments in the project. Outside equity investors, usually financial institutions, may be offered the opportunity to invest equity in a project.

Commercial banks and life insurance companies have traditionally been the principal sources of debt for large projects. In the typical financing structure, commercial banks would provide construction financing on a floating-rate basis, and life insurance companies would then provide "permanent financing" on a fixed-rate basis by refinancing the bank loans following project completion. The development of the interest rate swap market has given borrowers the flexibility to recharacterize floating-rate loans into fixed-rate obligations. Also, during the 1980s, commercial banks became willing to accept longer loan maturities. As a result of these developments, commercial bank loans were used to an increasing extent during the 1980s and became the principal source of long-term debt for project financing.

Stricter bank capital regulations instituted in 1989 forced many banks to cut back on their lending commitments, thereby reducing the availability of bank financing for large projects. However, investors in the public and quasi-public debt securities markets have been willing to invest in certain types of relatively-low-risk projects. The development of these markets for project debt securities only partially offset the effect of the reduction in bank lending.

In the 1990s, infrastructure projects have become a high priority. Commercial banks, having adjusted to the tighter capital standards, have expanded their role in project financing. They advise as well as lend. The public and quasi-public debt markets have become more receptive to project debt issues that are properly structured. Those that qualify for an investment-grade rating enjoy the widest market. Finally, multilateral agencies, such as the World Bank and the Inter-American Development Bank, have stepped up their efforts to combine public and private sources of capital to finance infrastructure projects. Perhaps more than ever before, the financing package for a project is likely to draw on several sources of funds in order to tailor it to the particular needs of investors and project sponsors.

This chapter provides an overview of these sources of financing.

EQUITY

In evaluating the attractiveness of an investment in a project, prospective equity investors will assess the benefits that are expected to be derived from the operation of the project. Such benefits include, at a minimum, earning an acceptable rate of return on funds invested. They may also include obtaining an assured source of supply by taking some portion of the output of the project, or securing an assured market for their own output by selling raw materials or providing services to the project. The expected benefits must be commensurate with the project risks to the equity investor, in order to justify the equity investor's commitment to invest funds in the project.

Several factors bear on who will be most likely to make an equity investment in a project. In addition to the usual business and financial risks that equity investors must typically endure, sponsors of a project are often contingently liable for additional assessments in the event cost overruns occur or the project fails. Project failure typically triggers debt repayment. If the project requires a long construction period, equity investors will have to accept delayed dividends. A project cannot pay dividends before operations commence, and lenders normally restrict the payment of dividends during the early years of operation, until the debt has been substantially repaid. They naturally prefer that all available free cash flow be applied first to repay project debt.

The equity investors in a project typically are those parties who will directly benefit from the operation of the project: the purchasers of the project's output, the owners of any natural resource reserves the project will utilize, and the suppliers of essential products and services to the project, including engineering firms. It is generally not possible to offer common shares to public investors at the inception of a project. After the project entity has demonstrated a record of profitability and the period of time until the commencement of cash dividends has been reduced to an acceptable length, common equity or other forms of junior securities may be sold to the public and to other passive investors.

Commercial banks and credit companies are typically sources of equity for tax-oriented transactions. They are also a frequent source of interim financing for a project, and they are often willing to take on more completion risk or greater regulatory risk than other types of prospective lenders.

Structuring the Equity Investments

Structuring the equity investments in a project involves four main areas of concern: (1) how to organize and capitalize the venture, (2) how to manage and control the venture, (3) how to resolve disputes among the sponsors/equity investors, and (4) how to terminate the venture. Organizational issues were covered in Chapter 5. Capitalization—in particular, determining how much debt a project can incur—was discussed in Chapter 6.

Management and control procedures, dispute resolution, and venture termination are issues that must be addressed in the contract to which the sponsors/equity investors are parties.[1] First, consider management and control. Critical decisions, such as altering the capital expenditure schedule or incurring additional debt, might require unanimous approval. Management arrangements become particularly sensitive when public–private partnerships are formed to finance infrastructure projects. (These partnerships are discussed in Chapter 10.[2])

Second, dispute resolution procedures must be put in place to handle disagreements. The sponsors may disagree about how to interpret various contract provisions. Arbitration may be needed to break the deadlock. However, differences that concern fundamental business issues, or alleged breaches of significant provisions of agreements between the parties, may not be suitable for arbitration. A buy–sell or a put–call arrangement may work better. Under a *buy–sell arrangement,* one party can offer to buy out the other's ownership interest. The offeree can accept the offer and sell, or buy out the offeror at the specified offer price. Under a *put–call arrangement,* a nondefaulting party has the right to sell its ownership interest to the defaulting party, or to buy the defaulting party's ownership interest. In either case, the original agreement between the parties should provide that the buy–sell price or put–call price is based on the *fair market value* of the ownership interest, as determined by independent experts.

Committed Investment Funds

Fund managers have formed *committed investment funds* to make equity investments in certain specified types of projects. The fund's sponsors make all the investment decisions. One example is the Scudder Latin American Power Fund ("Latin Power"), which was formed to make equity investments in independent power projects in Latin America and the Caribbean.[3] There are four lead investors; each has committed $25 million. They serve on the project review committee, which considers investing in projects that the fund's investment adviser (Scudder, Stevens & Clark) has analyzed and proposed.

Committed funds enable sophisticated investors to pool their resources. They reap the benefits of diversification, and they benefit from the investment adviser's experience and expertise in evaluating projects of a particular type. When more than one experienced sponsor/investor is involved, they realize economies from pooling information and sharing responsibility for monitoring their joint investments. These efficiencies make it cheaper for the sponsor/investors to invest jointly rather than separately. These benefits are likely to be greater in the emerging markets than in the developed markets because information tends to be more difficult and expensive to obtain in the emerging markets.

Pooled Equity Vehicles

A *pooled equity vehicle* is a separate company that is formed by an existing operating company to own and manage certain specified types of projects. One example is Enron Global Power & Pipelines L.L.C. (EGP&P).[4] EGP&P was structured as a limited liability company.[5] Enron Corporation owns 52 percent of EGP&P, which will own and manage Enron's natural gas pipelines and power plants outside the United States, Canada, and Western Europe. Initially, EGP&P's assets consisted of two power plants in the Philippines, one in Guatemala, and a 4,069-mile natural gas pipeline system in Argentina.

Enron granted EGP&P the right of first refusal to purchase all of Enron's ownership interests in any power plant or natural gas pipeline project Enron develops or acquires (outside the United States, Canada, and Western Europe) that commences commercial operation prior to 2005. Enron will manage all the projects.

Pooled equity vehicles provide investors with geographic diversity and the opportunity to invest in projects of a particular type alongside an experienced operator. EGP&P enables investors to benefit from Enron's experience in selecting power and pipeline projects for development and from Enron's expertise in operating them. Pooled equity vehicles can raise funds publicly (as EGP&P did), which enables them to tap the retail equity market. Pooled equity vehicles, like committed investment funds, reflect the growing role of intermediaries in project finance. Pooling investment funds represents an efficient means of investing in a targeted class of projects, particularly when the individual projects are relatively small and the costs of obtaining information, evaluating projects, and monitoring construction and performance are high.

LONG-TERM DEBT MARKET

There is an extensive market for long-term debt financing for projects in the capital markets in the United States, Europe, and Japan. Financial institutions such as life insurance companies and pension funds provide fixed-interest-rate financing, and commercial banks provide floating-interest-rate financing. For most project financings, commercial bank construction financing or precompletion private placements with institutional lenders constitute the initial phase of the financing plan. Three primary factors contribute to their predominance in the initial phase:

1. The size and term of the initial forward commitments required to ensure that sufficient funds are available to complete the project;
2. The degree of sophistication needed to understand the complex security arrangements typically involved in a project financing;
3. The difficulties and time delays involved in registering securities for project financings with the SEC, and the necessity of obtaining an investment-grade rating to ensure broad marketability among the purchasers of publicly offered debt securities.[6]

Several factors influence the breadth of the international long-term debt market for financing a project. They include:

1. *Profitability of the project.* As a general rule, lenders will not provide funds for a project unless the project is expected to be profitable in the sense that its expected rate of return on assets will be sufficient to cover its debt service requirements and provide an acceptable rate of return to the project's equity investors.

2. *Project leverage.* Lenders will be reluctant to lend to a project unless they are comfortable that the project can service its debt in a timely manner. Put somewhat differently, they will require that project sponsors commit sufficient equity to make the project creditworthy.

3. *Lenders' assessments of project risks.* Lenders will insist on being fully compensated for the risks they are being asked to bear. Their evaluation of the various types of risk associated with the project and their assessment of their exposure to each type of risk will therefore affect the rate of interest they are willing to accept before they advance funds to the project.

4. *Credit standing of the project entity.* The credit standing of the project's bonds is an important determinant of the amount of funds the project will be able to raise from all categories of lenders. Project leverage is a major contributing factor. The ability of certain investors to commit will be directly affected by the rating assigned the project's debt securities by the major rating agencies (Moody's and S&P). As a matter of statute or policy, many public pension funds insist on a rating of single-A or better, as a condition to purchasing a corporate bond.

5. *Interest rate on project debt.* The interest rate must be high enough to attract the substantial commitments required to complete the financing. In particular, it must be high enough to compensate lenders fully for the default risk and illiquidity risk they must bear.

6. *Liquidity of project debt securities.* The market for a project's initial long-term debt financing is typically restricted to institutional investors who are willing to purchase securities not registered with the SEC. The lack of liquidity inherent in purchasing privately placed securities significantly reduces the attractiveness of the investment for some investors and requires a higher

interest rate. Following project completion, however, many projects have been able to refinance bank debt or private placement financing by making public offerings of their bonds.

Other factors that may influence the availability of funds to a project include the degree of competition for capital from other projects being constructed and financed, the rate of inflation, and the general attitude among institutional investors toward investment in projects of the type and in the locale of the project being financed. Life insurance companies have historically been the most important source of debt funds for large industrial and utility projects. They are likely to continue to be an important source of project loans in the future.

Table 9.1 summarizes the relative sizes of the different segments of the long-term debt market as of June 30, 1995.

COMMERCIAL BANK LOANS

Commercial banks have played an active role in project finance since the 1930s, when a Dallas bank made a nonrecourse *production payment* loan to develop oil and gas properties (see Forrester, 1995). Commercial banks have demonstrated an ability to evaluate complex project credits and a willingness, at times, to bear completion and other noncredit risks that other types of lenders usually shy away from.

TABLE 9.1   Sources of Long-Term Funds[a]

Segment	Total Assets (in billions)	Holdings of Corporate and Foreign Bonds	
		Amount (in billions)	Percent of Total Assets
Life insurance companies	$1,992.4	$818.5	41.1%
Other insurance companies	704.4	104.2	14.8
Public pension funds	1,316.3	280.4	21.3
Private pension funds[b]	2,610.4	318.2	12.2
Commercial banks	4,339.2	103.7	2.4

[a] Data as of June 30, 1995.
[b] Includes the Federal Employees' Retirement System Thrift Savings Plan.
Source: Federal Reserve Board, *Flow of Funds Accounts: Quarterly Levels* (September 13, 1995).

Four alternative types of bank credit facilities may be arranged to finance a project:

1. *Revolving credit.* Commercial banks often provide construction financing in the form of a revolving credit facility. The sponsors can draw down on the facility as funds are needed, subject to a maximum funds availability.
2. *Term loan.* The project sponsors can draw down on a term loan during the construction period. The amount borrowed typically peaks at completion of the basic facilities. Term loans have an amortization schedule that is related to the anticipated cash flow from the project. The term typically does not exceed 10 years following completion of basic facilities, but longer repayment periods are achievable when project economics are sufficiently compelling or the project is very long-lived (e.g., an infrastructure project). If the cash flow from the project is insufficient to fully amortize the term loan during this period, the sponsors must bear the risks of refinancing the loan. The specific terms available in the future will depend on the economic and monetary climate then prevailing.
3. *Standby letter of credit.* A standby letter of credit facility provides borrowers with the flexibility to arrange letters of credit to support commercial paper issuance. Drawings under the letter of credit would pay commercial paper holders if the commercial paper issuer is unable to (e.g., because it is unable to roll over the maturing commercial paper into another commercial paper issue).
4. *Bridge loan.* A bridge loan covers any gap between the timing of expenditures and the scheduled drawdowns of long-term funds. Bridge loans are supported by firm take-out commitments from long-term lenders or equity investors. The cost of funds provided by a bridge loan reflects the risk that bridge loan providers must bear, which in turn reflects the credit standing of the long-term lenders or equity investors who provide the "takeout" commitments. In many cases, the structure of the bridge loan facility extended to projects has provided for a nonamortizing loan with a term of up to 4 years.

Credit facilities should, in each case, provide for alternative borrowing bases, including (1) U.S. prime rate, (2) LIBOR (one or more specified alternatives), and (3) the lender's CD rate (one or more specified alternatives).

Comprehensive Credit Facility

Instead of negotiating a separate loan commitment in each category, commercial banks may propose to arrange a comprehensive credit facility covering all of a project's loan requirements. This frequently involves a revolving credit facility during the construction period, some portion of which converts to a term loan upon completion. The revolving credit facility may also allow a portion of its availability to be used as a standby letter of credit facility. For large projects, the credit facility would be provided by a syndicate of banks. A comprehensive credit facility can often provide greater financial flexibility both to the bank(s) and to the project.

Legal Lending Limits

The constraints placed on individual banks with regard to loans to a single borrower can limit the availability of bank financing to a very large project. For national banks, the legal limit for investment in obligations of a single issuer is 10 percent of the bank's capital surplus and undivided profits. In addition to legal lending limits, banks normally have internal policy guidelines that restrict their ability to provide funds to a single borrower. These internal policy guidelines base the amount the bank can lend on (1) the credit strength of the borrower, (2) prevailing money market conditions, (3) the type(s) of facilities requested (shorter maturities are preferable to long-term loans), (4) the interest rate necessary in light of the project's financial leverage and its business and other risks, and (5) the expected overall profitability of the bank's relationship with the project's sponsors, which will depend on the fees and other revenues the bank expects to earn from loan, cash management, and other services it will provide to the sponsors and to the project entity.

Terms of Bank Loans

Project sponsors usually seek commitments from commercial banks for both construction financing and permanent financing. The construction commitment depends on the length of the construction period; a 2-year or 3-year commitment is typical for many projects. Permanent financing has a longer maturity. Maturities as long as 15 years from date of completion are often possible for infrastructure projects.[7] But the maturity of a natural resource project, for example, will be limited by the size of the resource deposit and how long it will take to exhaust it. Convincing banks to loan for periods exceeding half the expected life of the deposit is usually difficult because they want a significant margin of safety to protect against misestimation of the size of the deposit.

Bank loans are usually at floating interest rates, expressed as a *margin* over some specified benchmark, such as prime rate or one of the LIBOR rates. Loans for permanent financing usually specify increases in the margin every few years. These increases are designed to encourage project sponsors to refinance the bank debt prior to its scheduled maturity. Most sponsors will refinance the bank debt in one of the fixed-rate debt markets described later in this chapter.

International Commercial Banks

The large clearing banks in the United Kingdom; large commercial and universal banks in France, Germany, Japan, and Switzerland; and, to a lesser extent, the consortium banks based in London are likely candidates for providing funds to a major project. These banks may lend to a project through their participation in one or more syndicates of bank lenders to the project, or, in the case of the larger European or Japanese banks, they may facilitate the project financing by placing bonds with institutional investors. Table 9.2 lists the 10 leading arrangers of project bank loans in 1995, and Table 9.3 indicates the 20 largest syndicators of bank loans in 1995 (for project financing as well as other purposes).[8]

The international banking market has developed into one of the most dynamic financial markets in the world. Because it is not subject to national regulation, the market is free to intermediate on a flexible basis between depositors and borrowers from different countries. Virtually all the major banks in the United States, Canada, the United Kingdom, Continental Europe, and Japan actively participate. The U.S. dollar is the dominant currency. Other important currencies are the Deutsche mark and the Swiss franc. Substantial growth occurred in the 1970s, with the large inflow of deposits from the Middle East's oil-producing nations, and in the 1980s, when the United States continued to run enormous balance-of-payments deficits.

The tighter capital standards that were imposed on commercial banks beginning in 1989 made it more difficult to arrange large,

TABLE 9.2 Leading Arrangers of Project Bank Loans, 1995 (Dollar Amounts in Millions)

Rank	Bank	Amount
1	Chase Manhattan	$7,286
2	Bank of America	7,033
3	Citibank	6,102
4	Societe Generale	5,321
5	ABN AMRO	4,
6	Union Bank of Switzerland	4,499
7	Barclays Bank	3,959
8	Banque Paribas	3,949
9	Deutsche Bank	3,099
10	Industrial Bank of Japan	2,862

Source: *Project Finance International* (IFR Publishing).

TABLE 9.3 Largest Syndicators of Bank Loans, 1995 (Dollar Amounts in Millions)

Rank[a]	Bank	Number of Loans	Amount[b]
1	Chemical Banking	518	$389,781
2	J.P. Morgan	260	294,015
3	NationsBank	156	292,153
4	Bank of America	394	280,155
5	Citicorp	416	277,720
6	Societe Generale	150	173,806
7	First Chicago	229	171,299
8	CS First Boston	157	171,186
9	Bank of New York	148	163,333
10	Deutsche Bank	155	162,540
11	Chase Manhattan	297	156,594
12	Toronto-Dominion	139	143,768
13	Union Bank of Switzerland	97	142,615
14	Industrial Bank of Japan	161	138,206
15	ABN AMRO	145	132,019
16	Canadian Imperial	106	128,738
17	Bank of Nova Scotia	147	122,970
18	Credit Lyonnais	135	120,064
19	Royal Bank of Canada	110	119,312
20	NatWest	203	111,362

[a] Based on amount.
[b] Based on full credit to co-agent/co-arranger.
Source: *Investment Dealers' Digest* (January 15, 1996), p. 23.

syndicated bank loan facilities for major projects. Banks generally decreased the magnitude of the underwriting commitments they were willing to make. Interest-rate spreads widened, loan maturities were shortened, credit standards became more demanding, and bank fees were increased. Nevertheless, bank loan financing was available for projects that were fundamentally sound. In recent years, the situation in the bank loan market has improved as banks have adjusted to the new capital standards. Banks have expanded their role in project financing by becoming more active as advisers and as lenders.

FIXED-RATE DEBT MARKET

Historically, life insurance companies have been the principal source of long-term fixed-rate loans for major projects, and pension funds have served as an important source of debt and equity funds for corporations. Other financial institutions that provide long-term debt financing for projects include: open-end and closed-end investment trusts, university endowment funds, charitable foundations, property and casualty insurance companies, and professional investment advisers. Property and casualty insurance companies also lend to projects but are typically more tax-conscious than life insurance companies.

Compared to the public securities markets, the private placement market has generally been much more receptive to project debt financings. Historically, projects have been able to tap the public securities markets only after having completed at least a few years of profitable operations. The complexity of the security arrangements has usually made it difficult for the rating agencies to evaluate the true credit risk and assign debt ratings. This situation appears to be changing. The rating agencies have become more sophisticated in their credit analysis. Also, their recent experience in rating complex mortgage-backed and receivables-backed financings has enhanced their ability to rate complicated debt security structures.

Figure 9.1 illustrates the issuance of bonds in the public and private placement markets from 1975 to 1994. Note that the amount of debt placed privately exceeded the amount sold publicly in 1988 and 1989, but, from 1989 to 1993, the volumes of offerings in these two markets diverged. Public offerings skyrocketed to more than $187 billion in 1993; private placements fell dramatically to around $29 billion in 1994. During the period 1986–1994, the volume of bonds

FIGURE 9.1   Gross Issuance of Bonds by Domestic Nonfinancial
Corporations in the Public and Private Markets, 1975–1994

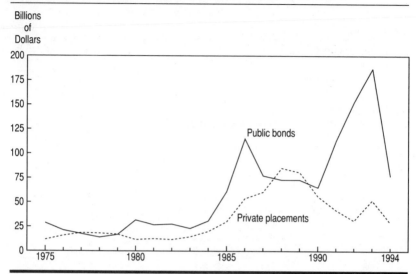

Source: Carey et. al. (1993), p. 1, subsequently updated for 1993 and 1994.

publicly offered by nonfinancial corporations averaged $105 billion
per year; the volume of bonds privately placed by nonfinancial corporations during the same period averaged $56 billion per year (Carey,
Prowse, Rea, & Udell, 1993b, as updated).

The private placement market is dominated by life insurance companies. Carey et al. (1993) examined a sample consisting of 351 private
placements during the period 1990–1992. Life insurance companies
purchased 83 percent of these issues, as measured by aggregate dollar
amount. Table 9.4 indicates the market shares of the other participants
in this market.

Figure 9.2 compares the characteristics of the bank loan, private
placement, and public bond markets. The bank loan market tends to prefer shorter-term floating-rate loans with relatively tight covenant restrictions. The public bond market is generally willing to accept longer
maturities and larger issues with relatively nonrestrictive covenants.
The private placement market falls in between the other two markets
with respect to average borrower and loan size, covenants, collateral requirements, and intensity of monitoring. However, lender reputation is
most important in the private placement market. Lenders in this market

TABLE 9.4   Lender Shares in the Traditional Market for Private Placements, 1990–1992

Type of Lender	Share of Dollar Volume
Life insurance companies	82.6%
Foreign banks	3.6
U.S. commercial banks	3.3
Pension, endowment, and trust funds	1.7
Finance companies	1.4
Property and casualty insurance companies	1.4
Mutual funds	.7
Thrifts	.7
Others	4.6
Total	100.0%

Source: Carey, Prowse, Rea, and Udell (1993b), p. 27.

FIGURE 9.2   Comparison of the Characteristics of the Bank Loan, Private Placement, and Public Bond Markets

Characteristic	Debt Markets		
	Bank Loan	Private Placement	Public Bond
Maturity	Short	Medium to long	Long
Interest rate	Floating	Fixed	Fixed
Severity of information problems posed by the average borrower	High	Moderate	Small
Average loan size	Small	Medium to large	Large
Average borrower size	Small	Medium to large	Large
Average observable risk level	High	Moderate	Lowest
Covenants	Many, tight	Fewer, looser	Fewest
Collateral	Frequent	Less frequent	Rare
Renegotiation	Frequent	Less frequent	Infrequent
Lender monitoring	Intense	Significant	Minimal
Liquidity of loan	Low	Low	High
Lenders	Intermediaries	Intermediaries	Various
Principal lender	Banks	Life insurance companies	Various
Importance of lender reputation	Somewhat important	Most important	Unimportant

Source: Carey, Prowse, Rea, and Udell (1993b), p. 33.

perceive that they have significant reputational capital at stake when they make a decision to loan money to a project. Consequently, the lending standards they apply tend to be rigorous.

Life Insurance Companies

The major life insurance companies possess a high degree of investment sophistication. Their analytical ability allows them to make judgments on their own as to the credit risk and other risks present in highly complex undertakings, such as a project financing. Smaller life insurance companies do not have this capability. Consequently, they have traditionally been influenced in their commitments by the participation of the major life insurance companies and by the debt rating(s), if any, assigned by the major rating agencies.

Because of the nature of their business, life insurance companies have a relatively assured annual cash flow, which they are willing to commit, under certain circumstances, for takedown up to several years in the future. Once they are satisfied with the creditworthiness of a project and the adequacy of the security for their loans, life insurance companies are influenced primarily in their investment decisions by the attractiveness of the rate of return offered by the project relative to the rates of return offered by competing investments. It is necessary to offer an acceptable commitment fee to lenders when asking them to commit their funds in advance of the takedown dates.

Project debt is typically sold to life insurance companies through private placements. Privately placed securities are not registered with the Securities and Exchange Commission (SEC). They generally have shorter maturities than comparable publicly traded debt securities. Twenty-year money is available from some institutions, but a 15-year term is preferable. The growth of the managed money/guaranteed investment contract business has made life insurance companies enthusiastic buyers of intermediate-term (i.e., 5- to 10-year) debt.

Security arrangements and restrictive covenants tend to be important issues in private placement negotiations. The public securities market generally accepts less onerous arrangements. Project loan agreements typically include limitations on indebtedness, on liens, and on cash distributions, and they impose liquidity/working capital tests.

It is sometimes advantageous to obtain a rating from one of the major rating agencies. The issue of a rating involves a trade-off between the more stringent security and credit arrangements required to obtain a favorable rating on the one hand, and access to a broader market on the other.

Life insurance companies are very sensitive to the creditworthiness of project debt securities. The National Association of Insurance Commissioners (NAIC) has instituted a rating system for private placements, and the reserves that life insurance companies are required to maintain against the loans they hold in their portfolios are dependent on the NAIC ratings. Because of these reserve requirements, life insurance companies have exhibited a strong preference for debt that is rated minimally as investment-grade (NAIC-2).[9] Figure 9.3 shows the distribution of credit ratings for privately placed debt held in the general accounts of life insurance companies at December 31, 1994.

Duff & Phelps and Standard & Poor's have both announced new private placement rating systems.[10] In general, private placement rating systems are more lenient than the respective public debt rating systems because the private placement ratings express a view concerning the likelihood of ultimate repayment. Public debt ratings also stress *timeliness* of payment.

FIGURE 9.3 Distribution of Credit Ratings of Privately Placed Debt Held in the General Accounts of Life Insurance Companies, December 31, 1994

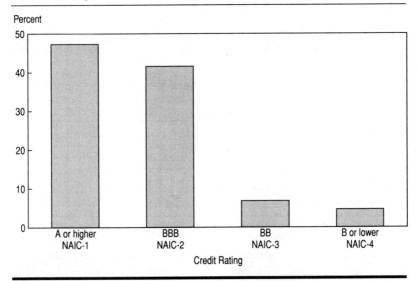

Source: ACLI Data. Compiled by R. Rubrich of Actuarial Research.

The life insurance industry is characterized by a concentration of investable funds in the largest companies. Table 9.5 lists the 25 largest buyers of private placements in the United States. From a borrower's perspective, such concentration can be important. Often, the need to approach only a few institutions in order to secure commitments for the full amount of the financing desired reduces the cost and time required to arrange the project financing.

Although it is not always at its most robust, the private market remains a substantial source of funds for complex project financings or for one portion of the overall project financing—for example, for equipment financings, production payments, or other specialized funding.

TABLE 9.5 Largest Buyers of Private Placements in the United States, 1993 (Dollar Amounts in Millions)

Rank	Company	Amount
1	Prudential Life Insurance	$5,000.0
2	Metropolitan Life Insurance	4,104.1
3	Teachers Insurance and Annuity	4,050.0
4	John Hancock Mutual Life	3,932.0
5	Principal Financial Group	3,462.3
6	CIGNA	3,200.0
7	New York Life	1,800.0
8	Travelers Insurance	1,455.0
9	Mass Mutual	1,300.0
10	Pacific Mutual Life	1,039.0
11	Northwestern Mutual Life	954.7
12	American General	850.0
13	Lincoln National Life	714.8
14	Great-West Life & Annuity	651.5
15	Hartford Insurance	650.0
16	Mutual of Omaha	625.0
17	Nationwide Life	625.0
18	Mimlic Asset Management	532.5
19	New England Mutual Life	437.3
20	Aegon USA	400.0
21	State of Wisconsin Investment Board	400.0
22	Provident Life & Accident	387.5
23	Lutheran Brotherhood	337.9
24	America United Life	242.7
25	Canada Life Assurance	241.9

Source: Private Placement Letter (September 19, 1994), p. 6.

Rule 144A Quasi-Public Market

In April 1990, the SEC adopted Rule 144A under the Securities Act of 1933. Rule 144A liberalized the restrictions that had existed on trading unregistered debt and equity securities. Prior to the adoption of Rule 144A, the U.S. securities laws imposed significant restrictions on the resale of unregistered securities. These restrictions rendered such securities illiquid, causing private placement buyers to demand an *illiquidity premium* (e.g., a higher interest rate). As a result of the SEC's adopting Rule 144A, large, sophisticated, qualified financial institutions ("qualified institutional buyers" or "QIBs") can trade unregistered debt and equity securities with each other without regard to the private placement restrictions that otherwise apply to unregistered securities.[11] Consequently, debt and equity securities issued under Rule 144A are considered "quasi-public" securities because of the absence of these restrictions.[12] The Rule 144A market came of age in 1992.

A Rule 144A private placement can be underwritten. The issuer can sell its securities to one or more investment banks (in reliance on a private placement exemption from registration under the 1933 Act). The investment banks then resell the securities to QIBs. This method of issuance is very similar to the sequence in an underwritten public offering, but without the extensive documentation being made publicly available as occurs in connection with a public offering.

Rule 144A issues can generally be arranged more quickly than public offerings because the securities do not have to be registered with the SEC. Covenants are normally less restrictive than private placement covenants. The absence of private placement trading restrictions makes Rule 144A issues more liquid than privately placed securities, and the greater liquidity makes possible a reduced interest rate.

The principal buyers of Rule 144A debt offerings are large life insurance companies. They are receptive to Rule 144A debt offerings that are rated investment-grade (e.g., Moody's Baa 3 or better, or Standard & Poor's BBB− or better). The major rating agencies apply the same rating criteria to Rule 144A debt issues that they do to public debt issues. These agencies have made it clear that only a select group of completed, successfully operating projects will merit an investment-grade rating. It would be rare indeed for a project to be rated investment-grade prior to construction (except possibly when there is an airtight completion undertaking from a strong investment-grade credit). The debt rating requirement essentially limits the Rule 144A debt market, as well as the public debt market, to the funding of construction loans for projects with clearly ascertainable and easily managed risks.

At least two large project financings have been arranged in the Rule 144A debt market:

1. COSO Funding Corporation, a special-purpose corporation formed by California Energy Company, Inc., raised $560.2 million in December 1992, on a nonrecourse (to California Energy) basis to refinance bank debt and fund additional capital expenditures for three geothermal electric power generating plants. The notes were rated Baa 3 by Moody's and BBB−by Standard & Poor's.
2. In January 1993, Sithe/Independence Funding Corporation raised $717.2 million to fund an independent power project.[13] The notes were also rated Baa 3 by Moody's and BBB−by Standard & Poor's.

The Rule 144A market has reached critical mass. Volume has increased, liquidity has improved, and yields have moved much closer to the yields available in the public debt market. The Rule 144A market has thus become relatively more attractive for project financing—particularly for infrastructure projects, for which long-term fixed-rate debt is desired.

Public Pension Funds

Public pension funds consist primarily of state and local government employee retirement funds. Because they generally maintain a high proportion of fixed-income securities in their portfolios, they represent an important potential source of long-term funds for a project financing.

The decision-making characteristics of public pension funds are different from those of life insurance companies. The flow of funds into state and municipal pension funds depends on current legislation, the salary levels of state and municipal employees, and, in some instances, the cash management requirements of the sponsoring state or municipality. Because of these uncertainties, as well as a reluctance to attempt to predict future market conditions, public pension funds, unlike life insurance companies, tend to be unwilling to commit to extend loans far in advance.

Most public pension funds are quality-sensitive buyers, either by preference or by statute or regulation. Many are required by statute or policy to invest in securities that are rated single-A or higher. Many are also prohibited from buying securities of foreign corporate obligors. Other legal investment requirements, such as a minimum length of corporate existence or a minimum coverage of fixed charges, may preclude certain public pension funds from purchasing the debt securities of a particular project.

Private Pension Funds

Private pension funds consist primarily of corporate pension funds. They have historically been an important supplier of capital to corporate borrowers. Prior to the mid-1960s, private pension funds invested primarily in fixed-income securities. With the increased emphasis on performance that began developing in the mid-1960s, these funds began to increase substantially their equity commitments; nevertheless, they continue to invest substantial portions of their available funds in fixed-income securities. Private pension funds can serve as an important source of funds to a major project if the rate of return offered is attractive to them. Liquidity is also an important consideration for these investors.

Many large corporations manage their own pension funds. However, most corporate pension funds are managed either by the trust departments of commercial banks or by private investment management firms. As with life insurance companies, a high percentage of the investable assets is managed by a relatively small number of institutions.

Private pension funds are normally not restricted as to the credit quality of the securities they may purchase. Therefore, the rating of a project's bonds is a less important consideration than it would be for a public pension fund. In addition, private pension funds normally face few, if any, restrictions—other than the requirements of ERISA—on their ability to purchase securities issued by foreign corporations.

Other Financial Institutions

Other classes of financial institutions, when considered class by class, tend to be relatively less important purchasers of a project's bonds. However, taken collectively, they may, in certain cases, turn out to be significant purchasers. These institutions have diverse investment policies, so it is difficult to generalize about the investment objectives of the group as a whole. Normally, they will look on a project's bonds as an alternative investment to corporate bonds and common stocks (just as private pension funds do). Accordingly, the rate of return offered on a project's securities is the most important factor in obtaining significant participation from these institutions.

Market Comparison

Table 9.6 compares the terms on which funds could be borrowed for project financing purposes in the U.S. debt market as of mid-1994. The loan terms that are available at any point in time within each market segment may change because of economic, regulatory, or other factors.

INTERNATIONAL CAPITAL MARKET

The international capital market, broadly defined, is the market for medium-term and long-term securities that functions outside the national capital markets of the world. Its existence reflects (1) the accumulation of dollar and foreign currency balances by foreign investors and (2) the willingness of those investors to purchase securities of issuers that are located outside the country that issued the currency. Such international markets are often referred to generically as the Euromarkets (e.g., the Eurodollar market, the Eurosterling market, and so on).

Credit Sensitivity

Although international investors are very conscious of security quality, historically they have not calibrated credit risks as finely as the U.S. debt market does. This situation is changing as credit ratings become more widely accepted in the Euromarkets. As a general rule, however, a borrower must be large and well-known. Commitments made by major U.S. institutional lenders also provide strong endorsements for borrowers in the international capital market.

A number of companies that were not going concerns at the time of their initial financing have been able to arrange financings in the international capital market. Accomplishing such a financing for a project would require, at a minimum, demonstrating the economic

TABLE 9.6 Comparative Analysis of Project Financing Borrowing Alternatives

Class of Borrower	Commercial Bank Market	Private Placement Market	Rule 144A Quasi-Public Market
Maturity	Up to 15 years.	Up to 20 years.	Up to 30 years.
Market breadth	Limited market for debt of large projects.	Limited market for debt of large projects.	Relatively large potential market for debt of large projects.
Interest rate	Floating rate. Interest rate risk can be eliminated through interest rate swap.	Fixed rate or floating rate.	Fixed rate or floating rate.
Prepayments	Permitted, subject to unwinding the interest rate swap, if any.	Requires compensation to make up for any lost future interest income (i.e., a "make-whole" provision).	Normally permits greater refunding flexibility than the commercial bank and private placement markets.
Covenants	Comprehensive set of financial covenants.	Comprehensive set of financial covenants.	Usually less restrictive covenants than in the commercial bank and private placement markets.
Time to arrange	15 to 25 weeks.	10 to 20 weeks.	10 to 15 weeks.
Rating requirements	None.	Generally requires at least an NAIC-2 rating.	Generally requires investment-grade ratings from at least two major rating agencies.

viability of the project beyond a reasonable doubt. It is equally important that entities that are well-known, established, and creditworthy provide sufficient supplemental credit support for the project requesting the financing.

Maturity Choice

Even under very favorable market conditions, investors in the international capital market generally are not willing to accept debt maturities as long as those available in the United States. The typical maturity for long-term debt in the international capital market does not exceed 10 years, although there have been longer-dated issues. Under weak market conditions, maturities of between 5 and 7 years become prevalent.

Currency Considerations

The flow of funds to the international capital market is volatile, for a number of reasons. Most investors in this market can also invest in their respective domestic capital markets, as well as in other national markets. Few investors commit funds on a regular basis exclusively to the international capital market. Instead, investors move their funds from one market to another—primarily on the basis of short-term considerations. The short-term outlook concerning the strength of the currency in which the investment is denominated is one of the principal investment considerations. Changes in currency expectations have led, from time to time, to costs of borrowing that are lower than those achievable in a particular national capital market. This situation often occurs when a currency is deemed particularly attractive. At the other extreme, diminished expectations have led to the virtual closing of one or more sectors within the international capital market when the currencies involved were deemed especially unattractive.

Inflation has a significant impact on the international capital market. In general, when one country has a rate of inflation that is high relative to other countries, its currency is less attractive to international lenders. At the very least, the rate of interest will have to be high enough to compensate for the higher inflation rate. When all countries are suffering from very high rates of inflation, investors tend to eschew long-term fixed-interest-rate debt obligations. In addition, the investors' view of world stability and the political and economic stability of their respective countries will influence the international capital market. Investing funds outside the domestic market on a medium-term or long-term basis requires that investors pay close attention to political events that might alter the value of their investments.

Types of Investors

Investors in the international capital market generally fall into two categories. Historically, the largest group, which accounts for a substantial proportion of the invested funds, consists of individuals buying for their own account through banks. The clients of Swiss banks and other banks where client anonymity is protected are prominent in this category. Not all of these accounts are discretionary; nevertheless, the attitudes of the banks involved can be crucial. The second group of investors, which has become larger than the first and continues to grow in relative importance, consists of institutions in several countries that purchase international issues for their own account. These institutional investors, which include banks, insurance companies, pension funds, investment trusts, and certain government agencies, buy private placements as well as public issues.

Investors judge the attractiveness of the expected rate of return for a given international security in relation to the expected rates of return for comparable domestic securities. Investors in the international capital market therefore usually require that interest payments be free of withholding tax. Withholding tax is levied on dividend payments and interest payments made to entities that reside outside the country in which the borrower is located. The tax is designed to compensate for the difficulty tax authorities face in trying to collect income taxes from nonresidents. In countries where there is a withholding tax, offshore finance subsidiaries have been created in non-withholding-tax (or at least in low-withholding-tax) jurisdictions to avoid having to collect withholding tax. Trust indentures normally provide that the issuer will gross-up interest payments sufficiently to allow holders to receive the originally stated rate of interest in the event of a future imposition (or an increase in the rate) of withholding tax.

SUPPLIER CREDITS

Project sponsors frequently arrange supplier credits to finance the purchase of equipment. These credits often serve as an attractive means of financing equipment that will not be part of the permanent structure of the project but is necessary during construction. Supplier credits covering equipment to be used in operating the project may extend as long as 7 to 10 years. The security arrangements for such supplier credits must be integrated into the corresponding security arrangements for the long-term financing for the project. Like bank loans, supplier credits generally require a commitment fee on the undrawn balance.

The structure and terms of supplier credits may vary, depending on the countries involved. Under certain circumstances, which depend principally on where the project is located, government export credits may be available on concessionary terms. Alternatively, insurance or direct guarantees may be procured. More frequently, however, project sponsors arrange for a syndicate of banks in a country to provide commercial credit for a large portion of the project's purchases of equipment in that country.

GOVERNMENTAL ASSISTANCE

A project may be eligible to receive some form of government support, or support from a supranational agency, for its financing. Included in the government support category are export credits and loan guarantees. In the second category are loans from the World Bank and from any of the regional development banks.

Export Credit Financing

Each of the major developed nations has established an export–import bank. Such institutions were set up to promote the export of equipment manufactured within that country. Export credit financing has been an important topic of debate among the industrialized countries in recent years. Generally, it appears that the trend is away from the degree of subsidization that applied in the past. The terms and conditions on which the export credit financing agencies advance credit are governed by the "Arrangements on Guidelines for Officially Supported Export Credits" (or, more cryptically, the "Consensus") negotiated by the Organization for Economic Cooperation and Development (OECD) countries. The Consensus is not legally binding. Often, significant differences in the terms and conditions available from different countries have developed, depending on specific circumstances.

Export credits can take the form of either "buyer credits" or "supplier credits." In general, the export credit agencies are reluctant to bear the credit risk associated with a start-up project without some form of identifiable credit support. As of mid-1995, the following standard loan terms were consistent with the "Consensus":

Maximum Percentage Financed	85 percent
Interest Rate	7 percent
Guarantee Fees	1 percent
Maturity	5 years
Repayment	Level debt semiannual

The U.S. Export-Import Bank ("Eximbank") is one example of a major export credit agency. Eximbank provides direct loan and loan guarantee programs to finance the purchase of products manufactured in the United States by projects located outside the United States. An Eximbank loan typically covers 30 percent to 55 percent of the cost of the equipment. Availability and amount of the loan vary, depending on the particular type of equipment and the availability of foreign financing for competing foreign-built equipment. Eximbank charges ½ percent per annum as a commitment fee on any undrawn balance. The maximum term for loans of this type is 10 to 12 years, depending on the country where the project is located.

Eximbank's recently formed project finance group has become proactive in promoting its services to project sponsors. It has also simplified Eximbank's application requirements and approval procedures.

Eximbank may guarantee an additional portion of the purchase price that is funded by commercial banks at a commercial bank rate of interest. The guaranteed amount, which may be borrowed outside the United States, is typically extended at a floating rate of interest. The fee for an Eximbank guarantee is between ¾ percent and 1½ percent per annum, depending on the country where the project is located. Eximbank cannot provide loans and guarantees that exceed 90 percent of the cost of any item of equipment. The balance of the equipment cost is considered the down payment on the transaction and is usually financed from non-U.S. sources.

In cases where the Eximbank does not extend a loan, it may guarantee up to 85 percent of the cost of the project's facilities. The fee on this type of guarantee is also between ¾ percent and 1½ percent of the outstanding balance. In addition, the Eximbank charges a commitment fee of ⅛ of 1 percent for its guarantee.

Eximbank was established to promote exports, but it will not assume imprudent credit risk. In special cases, Eximbank requires a guarantee from a creditworthy bank or from the host government. The guarantee increases the financing cost by the amount of the guarantee fee.

Direct Federal Agency Loans and Insurance

The Overseas Private Investment Corporation (OPIC) is a profit-making U.S. government agency that was established in 1971 to encourage long-term American private investment in emerging markets and developing nations. Its mission is threefold: (1) to further American competitiveness and domestic economic interests, (2) to promote the economic development of emerging nations, and (3) to advance foreign policy goals. OPIC financial support is available only to projects that take steps to protect the local environment and workers' rights. Like Eximbank, OPIC has recently formed a project finance group and increased its project financing efforts. It recently increased the level of support it can offer to an individual project to $400 million.

To American corporations or private investors who are considering investing in a foreign project, OPIC can give assistance in four principal ways. OPIC can: (1) extend direct loans to small projects; (2) provide loan guarantees of up to $200 million; (3) insure foreign investment projects against a wide range of political risks, including currency non-convertibility, expropriation, and political violence also up to $200 million; and (4) provide guidance regarding economic, business, and political conditions, as well as possible local business partners, in the political jurisdiction(s) the project sponsors are considering. All of OPIC's guarantee and insurance obligations are backed by the full faith and credit of the U.S. government. OPIC is active in more than 140 countries. In fiscal 1995, OPIC committed $1.8 billion in financing and $8.6 billion in political risk insurance coverage.

Loan Guarantees

Many other government guarantee programs are available, depending on the type of project. For example, the U.S. Maritime Administration (MARAD) offers financial assistance to projects involving the construction, reconstruction, or reconditioning of vessels built in U.S. shipyards. To be eligible, the ships must be owned and operated by citizens of the United States and must be registered in the United States.

The Title XI program is the best known of the MARAD programs. Under Title XI, bonds or notes guaranteed by the U.S. government may be issued to finance up to 75 percent of the cost of an eligible vessel. The portion guaranteed depends on several factors. One of the most important of these factors is whether a construction differential subsidy is involved in the transaction. In return for its guarantee, MARAD receives a mortgage on the vessel and an annual guarantee fee (at least ½ of 1 percent, but not more than 1 percent, of the amount of bonds guaranteed). Title XI bonds may also be issued to fund the long-term debt portion of a leveraged lease involving an eligible vessel.

Other U.S. government guarantee programs for projects include those sponsored by OPIC and those sponsored by the Energy Research and Development Association (ERDA). As already noted, OPIC was established to facilitate the participation of U.S. capital and skills in the economic and social development of less developed countries. ERDA assists sponsors in demonstrating the commercial feasibility of energy projects and promotes the development of such projects in other ways.

WORLD BANK LOANS

The World Bank Group ("World Bank") includes three institutions that play a role in international project finance:

1. International Bank for Reconstruction and Development (IBRD) extends market-rate loans amounting to more than $15 billion per year. It also provides training and technical assistance to help countries manage their development. IBRD loans typically represent only a portion of the financing for a project; often, other multinational agencies, such as the Asian Development Bank or the African Development Bank, co-finance a project along with the IBRD. IBRD loans are intended to promote economic development rather than commercial development. IBRD loans might be arranged to finance part of the cost of developing infrastructure for a project in a less-developed country.
2. International Finance Corporation (IFC) helps mobilize capital for promising commercial ventures that lack sufficient financing. In 1991, IFC approved direct loans and equity investments totaling $2.9 billion. These investments attracted additional financing sufficient to fund total investments of $10.7 billion.

IFC seeks to stimulate economic growth within developing countries by promoting private sector investment. It extends loans, makes equity investments, and arranges additional third-party financing. Its loans are generally floating rate, based on its own cost of borrowing.[14] Loans are available in virtually any major currency. IFC also provides an array of advisory services. Functioning as an international-scale merchant bank, IFC has provided more than $9 billion of direct financing to more than 1,000 companies in over 100 developing countries.

3. Multilateral Investment Guarantee Agency (MIGA) was created recently to ensure capital investments in developing countries against political risks, such as breach of contract, civil disturbance, expropriation, or war.

IBRD, IFC, and MIGA often cooperate in putting together a financing package for a project. According to the World Bank, roughly two of every three projects the World Bank finances include some support for private-sector development.[15] Many others involve the public financing of investments in infrastructure or other projects that are critical to private-sector development.

IFC has created an infrastructure department. It has also sponsored and invested in several infrastructure funds. The IFC has syndicated many of its loans, in imitation of the large commercial bank loan syndicators.

INTER-AMERICAN DEVELOPMENT BANK

The Inter-American Development Bank (IDB) is a multilateral agency that promotes development in Latin America and the Caribbean. The IDB's board of governors recently authorized IDB to expand its financing for privately owned and operated infrastructure projects in those regions. For example, in September 1995, IDB agreed to lend $10 million for the renovation, modernization, and operation of a major port terminal in Buenos Aires.[16] This loan will fund approximately 20 percent of the project's total cost.

IDB has also developed a new policy of lending directly to the private sector.[17] Loans to support private sector infrastructure projects will be limited to 5 percent of IDB's total loan portfolio. IDB's participation in any single project cannot exceed the lesser of (1) 25 percent of total project cost and (2) $75 million. IDB will try to attract additional funding from other sources for the infrastructure projects in which it participates.

IDB, like the World Bank and a variety of other multilateral and government agencies, represents an attractive source of long-term funds for infrastructure projects.

LOCAL SOURCES OF CAPITAL

Borrowing funds or raising equity in the local capital market is often a good way to reduce political risk. Any event that harms the profitability of the project will affect local lenders and investors. This prospect tends to furnish a disincentive for the local government to take adverse actions. The strength of the disincentive depends on how much local investors and lenders have at stake in the project.

The capital markets in the developed countries are good potential sources of funding. The capital markets in the emerging countries are less desirable. Funds availability is limited and maturities are short. As of year-end 1995, Brazil, Ecuador, India, Indonesia, Malaysia, Mexico, South Korea, Thailand, and Trinidad and Tobago all had viable corporate debt markets. But in Brazil, the market consisted mainly of leasing company bonds maturing within 18 months from the date of issue. In Mexico, the longest maturity available for corporate debt was 7 years, but only about half had an original maturity exceeding 1 year. South Korea had the deepest corporate debt market of the countries mentioned above, but original debt maturities could not exceed 5 years. A notable exception to the short-maturity limitation was Trinidad and Tobago. Maturities of up to 25 years and 15 years were possible in the government bond market and the corporate bond market, respectively.

As the economies within the emerging markets develop, so will the local capital markets. Where such markets exist, project sponsors should carefully consider raising at least a portion of the funds they need in those markets.

CONCLUSION

This chapter has reviewed the main sources of funds with which to finance projects. It is important to keep in mind that the world capital markets have become more closely integrated over the past two decades. Also, the Euromarkets represent a truly international capital market.

At different times, different capital markets may provide funds on the most attractive terms. Also, new financial instruments, such as interest rate swaps and currency swaps, increase the array of financing alternatives available to a project. A project can borrow in one capital market, use these instruments to transform the characteristics of the loan, and possibly achieve a lower all-in cost of funds than the project could obtain from one of the traditional sources of project-type loans. These new instruments offer opportunities to recharacterize a debt obligation's interest rate or currency characteristics. Consequently, they have expanded the menu of financing alternatives available to a project.

Multilateral agencies, such as the World Bank and IDB, and various government agencies, such as Eximbank and OPIC, have stepped up their funding of private infrastructure projects. Local capital markets are a useful source of funds in many emerging markets. Raising funds locally can reduce a project's political risk exposure. Project financial engineering requires examining all likely possible sources of debt and equity—not just the traditional ones—to determine which markets can provide the needed funds on acceptable terms at the lowest possible cost.

10

Issues for the Host Government

A decision to proceed with a project involves a number of critical issues for the host government. In brief, a host government should proceed with a project—or provide financial or other support to it—only if the expected social *benefit* to be derived from the project exceeds the expected social *cost* (in each case, expressed on a present-value basis). This chapter reviews some of these critical issues.

CONTRIBUTION TO THE HOST JURISDICTION'S ECONOMIC DEVELOPMENT

The project must have a positive net economic value to the host jurisdiction; the aggregate social benefit of the project should exceed the project's social cost. Social benefits might include: (1) the construction of infrastructure (e.g., roads, dock facilities, or an airport) for which the financing is by third parties and the cost is repaid entirely out of project cash flows; (2) the education and training of a local workforce; (3) the construction of public facilities (e.g., schools, housing, or fire stations) financed by the project's sponsors; (4) the establishment or expansion of an industrial base (which will attract further investment and can lead to the development of various service companies and other "spin-off" effects); (5) the generation of incremental tax revenue, which can be used to finance public projects; and (6) the "multiplier" impact that typically accompanies any major capital investment project. International projects have two additional potential benefits; (7) the generation of incremental hard currency, which will be valuable to the extent that the host country's shortage of hard currency is inhibiting its economic development; and (8) the development of a local capital market.

HOST JURISDICTION'S EXPECTED ECONOMIC RETURN

A country's resources should, ideally, be put to their most profitable uses in order to maximize the public welfare. A host jurisdiction, particularly if it is a developing country, has limited resources. The possible alternative uses for any resources that would have to be committed to a project must be carefully considered. Besides the economic return that may emanate from direct participation in the project, as already noted, there may be additional benefits: investments in the infrastructure that the project sponsors finance; development of a trained workforce; and generation of additional tax revenue, and hard currency. These benefits must be weighed against any project-related costs, especially if the host government is asked to provide certain investment incentives.

Investment Incentives

A host government that hopes to attract foreign investment must provide a conducive investment environment. When a project could be located in any of two or more jurisdictions, the governments competing for the project will have to offer investment incentives. Typically, these incentives include: (1) a tax "holiday," which exempts the project entity from income taxation for a specified number of years; (2) a grant of land free of charge or at a nominal rent or price; (3) assurances as to the availability of raw materials, feedstocks, or power at prices no higher than competitive world rates; (4) provision of certain items of infrastructure at no cost to the project (or at a subsidized cost); (5) cash subsidies; (6) support in arranging part of the financing for the project at concessionary interest rates (e.g., for infrastructure or for production equipment), possibly including loan guarantees; or (7) assurances as to the availability of hard currency to make project debt service payments or to repatriate profits from the project for a specified number of years. The greater the incentives the host government provides, the less its expected economic return from the project.

Structuring government assistance often requires some financial engineering. Government entities are typically unwilling to make funds available to a private project at a below-market cost if they believe that the implicit subsidy will result in the private sponsors' realizing above-market rates of return. The project's sponsors in such situations must be prepared to demonstrate to the host government that their expected returns are commensurate with the investment risks they are taking by investing their own equity in the project.

Tax Revenues

When deciding whether to approve a proposed project, a host government should consider the stream of future tax revenues the project is likely to generate. Tax revenues are particularly beneficial to a developing country if they are paid in hard currency. The tax revenues will be realized, of course, only after any tax holiday granted to the project's sponsors has expired. The future tax revenues must therefore be present-valued in order to determine their worth.

Project Participation

Host countries typically require a project's sponsors to provide them with a carried ownership interest in the project. A *carried ownership interest* is an equity ownership interest that is provided to the host government, free of charge, as consideration for granting the project's sponsors the right to proceed with the project. The magnitude of the carried ownership interest that is agreeable to the project's sponsors will depend, among other factors, on their expected returns net of the carried ownership interest. Thus, for example, an arbitrary government rule that *all* projects must award the host government, say, a 50 percent equity ownership interest will tend to discourage prospective project sponsors from pursuing potentially high-risk-high-return projects. Instead, they will pursue projects for which the expected carried ownership interest is as small as possible.

A fixed, high-amount, required carried interest imposes a counterproductive incentive: It discourages investment. A variable incentive structure, which bases the percentage of the carried interest on the risk–return characteristics of the project, is likely to work much better.

IMPACT ON THE AVAILABILITY OF HARD CURRENCY

The allocation of hard currency is a potentially contentious issue for projects located in developing countries. The co-sponsors of a project will normally require assurances that sufficient hard currency will be available from the project to service project debt and to enable them to realize an acceptable rate of return on their investments. Lenders will want to ensure that sufficient hard currency is available to service project debt in a timely manner. The host country will want to maximize its receipt of hard currency in order to further its development objectives.

Usually, a compromise is reached. When the output of international projects is sold overseas, generating hard currency, the project financing arrangements often include an overseas escrow account maintained by a reputable financial institution. Hard currency is applied first to operating costs (by remitting sufficient funds back to the project entity), then to servicing project debt (by remitting funds directly to project lenders), and finally to the sponsors/equity investors. Foreign equity investors would, of course, like to have the hard currency remitted directly to them, rather than processed back through the project entity, where it might get trapped by foreign exchange controls. The host country would like to see the hard currency remitted to the project entity so that it might be able to obtain at least part of it for other purposes. Contractual undertakings are necessary to reconcile these competing interests.

EXPOSURE OF THE HOST GOVERNMENT TO THE PROJECT'S OBLIGATION TO REPAY PROJECT DEBT

A developing country has, almost by definition, limited credit capacity and therefore limited ability to provide credit support for project debt. The expected economic rewards must justify the financial risk. As a general rule, projects in less developed countries have to be structured so as not to depend on the host country government for any degree of credit support for project debt.

For a project located in a developed country, a government guarantee (or a partial guarantee) can sometimes mean the difference between a project's going ahead or its being abandoned. As a general rule, if a project is so unprofitable that it cannot be financed without a full and direct government guarantee of all project debt, the project is not really being financed on a project basis. Instead, the project is being financed by the government on the government's own general credit.

In a more normal situation, a project may be marginally profitable, and the host government may be willing to provide financial support in the form of a (limited) guarantee in order to ensure that the project can be financed. The guarantee effectively subsidizes the project's cost of funds. The host country then needs to satisfy itself that the project will produce sufficient public benefit to justify the social cost implicit in the subsidy. Given a particular senior debt rating for the host country's debt, the guarantee will consume part of the host country's debt capacity; it will reduce the amount of additional debt the host country can issue for other purposes before its senior debt rating decreases and its cost of debt consequently increases.

DESIRABILITY OF PRECEDENTS

The host government will understandably be concerned as to whether the project, and the manner in which it is structured and financed, establishes any undesirable precedents that might adversely affect negotiations with prospective co-sponsors of future projects. Particularly important in this regard are the tax arrangements, including any tax holidays or withholding tax provisions; any development incentives, such as subsidized land, guaranteed feedstocks or power, and so on; and the arrangements governing the allocation of the hard currency generated by the project.

Example

In connection with the Paiton Energy Project, certain key features of which are summarized in Appendix B, bank lenders asked the Indonesian government to guarantee the state-owned power utility's obligation to purchase electricity under the 30-year electricity purchase agreement that formed the principal source of credit support for the project financing. The Indonesian government refused, even though, in the past, it had provided similar guarantees for much smaller projects. The size of the Paiton Energy Project was a concern. Developers of other large projects would undoubtedly seek guarantees if the Indonesian government provided one for the Paiton Energy Project, and guaranteeing several large purchase obligations could have an adverse effect on Indonesia's credit rating. Thus, the Indonesian government was unwilling to set what might eventually become a costly precedent.

HIBERNIA OIL FIELD PROJECT

The Hibernia Oil Field Project illustrates how public–private cooperation can further the development of a project when mutual self-interests
are served. Hibernia Oil Field Partners was formed in 1988 to develop
a major oil field off the coast of Newfoundland, 195 miles southeast of
St. John's. Mobil Oil of Canada will serve as the managing general partner of Hibernia Oil Field Partners and as the project operator. The
other four partners are Chevron Oil (through a Canadian affiliate), Columbia Gas System (through a Canadian affiliate), Gulf Canada Resources, and Petro-Canada. The oil field will cost approximately US$4.1
billion to develop. It is expected to produce 110,000 barrels of oil per
day beginning in 1997 and to reach a plateau level of production of
135,000 barrels per day. Reserves total roughly 615 million barrels, giving the field an expected life of between 16 and 20 years.

The Hibernia Oil Field Project will provide the region with economic benefits long before the first drop of oil flows and the first royalty check arrives. The region near the field is severely depressed. The
project will provide construction jobs and economic stimuli through
the multiplier effect. Moreover, the project can create other opportunities. Developing the Hibernia Oil Field will create an environment
conducive to the development of nearby fields.

Because of the public benefits that are expected to flow from the
project, the Canadian Federal Government will provide C$2.7 billion
(equivalent to roughly US$2.23 billion) in grants and loan guarantees.
It will pay 25 percent of the construction cost, up to a maximum of
C$1.04 billion. It will also guarantee up to C$1.66 billion of nonrecourse project loans. In return, it will get 10 percent of the project's
profits after all project loans have been repaid. The Newfoundland
Provincial Government will forgo most sales tax that would otherwise
be payable on the purchase of the project's output, and it will accept
royalties from production at a reduced rate.[1]

Why was the Hibernia Oil Field Project financed in this manner?
First, the project is probably too large and too risky for any one partner
to pursue on its own. Second, it is possible that none of the individual
participants, acting alone, could capture enough economic benefit to
make the project worthwhile. Columbia Gas, for example, had been
seeking a buyer for its Canadian transmission unit. That entity will
have the contract for transporting the natural gas from the Hibernia
field. The project clearly improves Columbia's long-term prospects and

enhances the transmission unit's value to a prospective acquirer. Columbia can benefit from its participation in the project but probably would not wish to undertake it alone.

Communities and companies in the surrounding area will benefit significantly from the project. They would undoubtedly have been delighted to get a free ride. But it took government financial support, effectively trading off enhanced future tax revenues and other public benefits for a package of financial incentives, to make the Hibernia Oil Field Project sufficiently attractive to the private partners to justify their undertaking it.

PUBLIC–PRIVATE INFRASTRUCTURE PARTNERSHIPS

In recent years, transportation and other infrastructure needs in the United States have grown more rapidly than the available funding.[2] Many states have passed legislation designed to encourage private-sector participation in the development, financing, operation, and ownership of transportation facilities, such as toll roads. Because private-sector entities require a financial rate of return that is commensurate with what they could earn on alternative projects of comparable risk, public–private partnership structures must be designed so as to provide competitive rates of return.[3]

Outside the United States, particularly in the emerging markets, there is an enormous need for infrastructure investment, which cannot be met locally (see Chrisney, 1995). Projects have typically been developed using public funds supplemented by World Bank, IDB, and other multilateral agency loans. As discussed in Chapter 9, the World Bank, IDB, and other bodies have launched efforts to attract private capital to infrastructure projects.

Public–private partnerships are joint ventures in which business and government cooperate, each applying its particular strengths, to develop a project more quickly and more efficiently than the government could accomplish on its own. Public–private partnership arrangements vary from full private ownership subject to government approval and oversight to public projects in which the private partner serves as a financial contributor to the government-sponsored project.

Private-sector involvement is increasing in many areas of public-use infrastructure. Transportation projects seem particularly well-suited to private participation. For example, toll roads and bridges, airports, and rail systems can often generate enough revenue from user fees and neighboring commercial real estate development to attract private capital. In general, if a transportation project can collect user fees (or attract commercial development), it is a candidate for a public–private partnership to finance its development.

It is important to appreciate that these public–private partnerships are not unregulated monopolies. They are governed by negotiated agreements that specify public and private responsibilities, impose public regulation of safety, require quality of service, and often restrict user fees (or profitability). These projects also pay substantial new taxes to federal, state, and local treasuries, which would not be the case if they were entirely publicly funded. For example, the Toll Road Corporation of Virginia's $250 million toll road project in Loudon County, Virginia, is expected to pay approximately $450 million of federal and state income taxes over its 40-year taxable life, as well as $96 million in property taxes to the Loudon County government.[4]

In addition to tax revenue, state and local governments often receive profit-sharing payments through ground leases (for example, by leasing government-owned land to a private project in return for a percentage of revenues) or through a contractual requirement that "excess" project profits be paid to the state.[5]

PUBLIC–PRIVATE FINANCING STRUCTURES

A variety of public–private financing structures have been suggested for transportation infrastructure projects. These structures differ in the manner in which the public-sector and private-sector entities share the responsibilities, risks, and rewards associated with the projects. This section briefly describes some possible public–private financing structures.[6]

For each project, a judgment as to the most appropriate partnership structure depends on the answers to the following questions:

- Who will be responsible for the design and construction of the project?
- Who will provide the construction funds?
- Who will arrange the financing?
- Who will hold legal title to the project's assets, and for how long?
- Who will operate the project facility, and for how long?
- Who will be responsible for each source of project revenue?

For a fully private facility, the answer to all of these questions would be: the private developer. But a transportation project may have a mixture of public and private responsibilities. For example, a private firm might be responsible for designing, constructing, financing, and operating the entire project. The host government would not provide any capital or take any responsibility for generating revenue but would nevertheless take title to the project assets immediately upon completion and would take over the project's operation, say, 40 years later.

There are at least ten models for public–private transportation partnerships.[7] Each is discussed briefly here. Eight involve significant private-partner responsibilities for planning, financing, and operations. The models are presented in descending order according to the private partner's share of project responsibilities. The list of models is not exhaustive but it includes the principal structures.

Perpetual Franchise Model

Private entities finance and operate the project under a perpetual franchise from the host government. These entities retain title to the assets. Within this model, all the financial support for project-related borrowings is provided by private entities. The government regulates safety, quality of service, and, possibly, user charges or profits.

The perpetual franchise model is the most flexible of the models discussed in this section. It can accommodate financing in the public securities markets. However, in view of the innovative nature of many projects and the attendant economic risks, the public securities markets, both for debt and for equity, will usually be available only after a project has operated successfully for a few years and has established an acceptable record of profitability.

Build-Operate-Transfer (BOT) Model

Private entities receive a franchise to finance, build, and operate the project for a fixed period of time, after which ownership would revert to the host government (or some local or regional public authority administered by the host government).[8] Ownership reversion would be planned to occur only after the private-sector entities had received the return of, and a satisfactory return on, the capital they had invested in the project. In return for the ownership reversion, the host government might be asked to furnish some (limited) credit support for project borrowings.

The BOT structure is attractive to host governments because of the ownership reversion feature. It is becoming commonplace for transportation infrastructure, energy, and environmental projects.

Build-Transfer-Operate (BTO) Model

Private entities design, finance, and build the project. They transfer legal title to the host government (or some local or regional public authority) immediately after the project facility passes its completion tests.[9] The private entities then lease the project facility back from the public authority for a fixed term. A long-term lease agreement gives the private entities the right to operate the project facility and to collect revenues for its own account during the term of the lease. At the end of the lease term, the public authority operates the project facility itself or hires someone else (possibly the private entities originally involved) to operate it.

Under this model, the host government or public authority has, at most, only a very limited responsibility for the project's financial obligations; the project company has principal responsibility.

Buy-Build-Operate (BBO) Model

A private firm buys an existing facility from the host government (taking legal title), modernizes or expands it, and operates it as a regulated profit-making public-use facility. Underdeveloped, deteriorating, or congested roadways, bridges, and airports are good candidates for this type of financing structure. The BBO model may prove to be popular in coming years because of the many existing public facilities that require repair or expansion.

Lease-Develop-Operate (LDO) Model

A private firm leases an existing publicly owned facility and surrounding land from the host government. It then expands, develops, and operates the facility under a revenue-sharing contract with the host government for a fixed term. The host government holds legal title. The LDO model is attractive when private entities are not able to raise the full purchase price of the existing facility (e.g., as the BBO model requires). The LDO model is also very useful for public–private risk sharing when the project is currently losing money.

Wraparound Addition

A private firm expands an existing government-owned core facility. The private firm holds legal title to the addition only. The private firm might operate the entire facility under contract to the government, or only the portion it owns. The most important advantages of this model are that ownership is shared and the private firm is not responsible for repaying any debt incurred to build the core facility.

Temporary Privatization

A private firm takes over operation and maintenance of an existing government-owned facility, such as a bridge in need of repair. It then expands or repairs the facility, operates it, and collects user charges long enough to recover the cost of the expansion/repair (including a reasonable return on invested capital) or until its temporary franchise expires. The host government continues to hold legal title. From the standpoint of the host government, this model's biggest advantages are that the private firm bears the financial risk and provides to the host government a contractual agreement that the tolls are temporary.

Speculative Development

A private firm identifies an unmet public need. Then, with the consent of the host government, it embarks on the process of planning and obtaining permits at its own expense and risk. After the private firm demonstrates the project's financial feasibility and develops a workable design, the host government joins in the development process in some fashion, perhaps by contributing to the financing of the project. This model is being tested in various forms in several projects in the United States.

Value Capture

Improving transportation to an area usually increases commercial activity. Value capture seeks to convert a portion of the private benefits of increased commercial activity to public use. For example, property values and retail sales may increase. This added private value is taxed in order to help pay for the transportation project. Because private businesses are usually reluctant to have any of their new value captured, value capture is often referred to as an "involuntary" partnership method.

Value capture is usually achieved by creating special tax or assessment districts around the new transportation project. Existing businesses and new commercial developers may be assessed a one-time fixed charge ("impact fees"), annual fees ("special assessments" based on square feet developed), or a percentage tax rate applied to the increase in property value. The tax/fee collecting agency then transfers the resulting revenue to the project financing agency. In some cases, the revenue stream is sufficiently stable to support the issuance of bonds. The bond proceeds can be donated to the transportation project to cover a portion of its capital cost. Pennsylvania, Texas, Michigan, Virginia, and Iowa are among the states that have used value capture to pay for transportation improvements.

Use-Reimbursement Model

This model is distinguished by having the host government or a public authority enter into a utilization contract with the project company. The utilization contract would obligate the host government or public authority to make payments sufficient to service all project-related debt independent of the level of passenger traffic volume. The host government or public authority would be reimbursed out of passenger revenues.

The use-reimbursement model is often used in connection with large, privately financed public-use capital investment projects. The model exposes the public authority to the credit risks of the project; the utilization contract can be structured so as to represent a de facto financial guarantee of project debt.

LEGISLATIVE PROVISIONS THAT CAN AFFECT PUBLIC–PRIVATE PARTNERSHIPS

All but the final two public–private partnership models in the previous section involve the private partner in a leading role in the planning, financing, and operation of the project. Past experience suggests

strongly that the "wrong" legislative provisions can inhibit such public–private partnerships whereas the "right" legislation can provide a
meaningful impetus to their development.

Provisions That Discourage Public–Private Partnerships

Most legislative provisions that tend to discourage public–private partnerships share a common flaw: a misallocation of high costs and significant risks between the public and private partners, particularly in the
early stages of the project. Without an appropriate sharing of risks and
an opportunity for the private partner to earn a fair rate of return on
its investment, a partnership is likely to fail. Legislative provisions that
discourage private participation in infrastructure projects include:

- Requiring formal legislative approval of project agreements after
  they have been negotiated by the government agency. The need
  to obtain legislative approval creates a highly uncertain environment. The private project developer is put at risk (e.g., with delays, modifications, and/or rejection) for all the costs it incurs in
  negotiating the project agreements with the government agency.
- Requiring the developer to post excessive bonds or to acquire excessive amounts of private insurance. The private partner often
  has to invest substantial sums in planning, designing, and securing permits for a project. A bond or insurance adds to these costs.
  Bonds, especially those that may be forfeited for reasons not entirely within the private developer's control, may make the financial risk too great to bear. However, a modest bond—or, perhaps
  instead, the threat of forfeiture of the franchise—may be necessary to ensure that the franchisee acts with appropriate haste to
  build the facility.

  Very large amounts of insurance to protect against certain
  types of risks may not be commercially available at a reasonable
  cost. Nevertheless, appropriate insurance coverages must be
  arranged to ensure either that the facility can be rebuilt and returned to operation or that the project debt will be fully repaid
  soon after, in the event that a natural disaster, such as a fire or
  an earthquake, occurs.
- Allowing relatively uninhibited competition from future government-sponsored projects. Exposing a public–private facility to
  the risk of future policy changes, especially those that might create unanticipated competition with the facility, increases the

project's economic risk—specifically, the risk of inadequate future revenue. It may therefore render the project difficult, or even impossible, to finance.

- Allowing (or requiring) ad hoc regulation of toll rates or rate of return on investment. Toll-rate or rate-of-return guidelines should be agreed on in advance of construction.[10] Demand for a public-use transportation facility tends to be less predictable and more price-sensitive than demand for utilities, such as electricity and water. Therefore, prospective investors in transportation and similar infrastructure projects need assurances that their willingness to bear the risk of construction and initial operations will not be second-guessed by a future public utilities commission.[11]

- Prohibiting local government financial involvement in the project. Often, the ability of a project to obtain private financing will depend on the willingness and ability of local governments to provide some degree of financial support, as well as political support. Indeed, the financial community may be more impressed that the local government is involved at all, and less concerned about the amount of the dollar investment. *Any* amount of investment gives the local government a financial stake in the success of the project. Such involvement can help protect the project against unfavorable government policy changes in the future.

- Requiring private developers to use government procurement methods. With its own capital at risk, a private developer may insist on having the freedom to choose the most cost-effective subcontracting method. Government procurement procedures, which typically require competitive bidding, are designed for government purchases rather than private investment.

- Requiring government approval of detailed design specifications before construction can begin. Experience indicates that design–build techniques—in which construction begins before the final detailed plan is completed—can substantially reduce the cost of constructing a project. Requiring government approval of detailed plans before construction can begin eliminates most of these potential cost savings.

Provisions That Encourage Public–Private Partnerships

Several legislative provisions can help deal with the relatively high business and regulatory risks and thereby encourage public–private partnerships:

- Allowing a private entity to propose what it believes is a financially viable project (rather than requiring private entities to
  choose from a list of projects developed by the government). Because of their profit motivation, private entities tend to be better
  than government agencies at identifying attractive project development opportunities. One example is the Dulles Toll Road Extension, in Loudon County, Virginia.
- Providing government assistance in planning, obtaining permits,
  acquiring land, and resolving intergovernmental and interagency
  disputes. The host government's comparative advantage in this
  area can significantly speed the progress of a project.
- Having the government partially or fully fund environmental and
  land use studies. The high cost of environmental impact studies—
  and having to conduct them at a time when final project approval
  is still uncertain—serves as a powerful deterrent to private-sector
  participation in infrastructure projects.
- Providing loans to cover a portion of the project's capital costs.
  Such loans improve the financial feasibility of a project by reducing the amount of private financing that is needed. They also
  give the host government a financial stake in the success of the
  project.
- Providing law enforcement services for a private project. Airports and railroads often arrange for their own security personnel. Toll roads have special problems for which state highway
  patrols have a comparative advantage. The host government can
  provide these services on a contractual basis.[12]
- Deferring local property (or state) taxes. Tax deferral represents
  one method by which a host government can "invest" in a project
  without having to commit funds directly.
- Exempting partnership projects from sales tax on construction
  supplies. Many states do not collect sales tax on supplies procured
  to construct infrastructure owned by state or local governments.
  The same principle could be applied to assist public–private infrastructure projects.[13]
- Placing reasonable limitations on tort liability. In many states,
  the state, as part of its sovereign immunity, enjoys a higher level
  of tort liability protection than private entities do.[14]
- Providing free (or subsidized) use (via lease or sale) of government-owned land, or acquiring right-of-way through eminent domain. In general, land is the easiest contribution for the host

government to make to a project. It is also potentially the largest stumbling block for a private developer. The government's power of eminent domain can be particularly useful in this regard.

- Allowing commercial development on the project site. Commercial development is a natural accompaniment to infrastructure projects. Revenues from commercial activities can make projects that would otherwise be difficult to finance acceptable to investors.

CONCLUSION

Project financing offers a potentially useful means by which a country can promote the development of a valuable resource deposit or the establishment of a stand-alone production facility. Project financing has often been used for such purposes. Whether project financing *should* be used for such a purpose in any particular situation will depend, ultimately, on whether project financing affords the lowest-cost means of accomplishing the project when all social benefits and costs, as well as all private benefits and costs, are properly considered.

Public–private partnerships have the potential to help meet the transportation and other infrastructure needs of the United States. Various structures are available. Such partnerships will be viable only if the risks and returns are properly allocated between the public-sector and private-sector entities involved. In particular, the private entities must be able to expect to earn rates of return commensurate with the risks they are being asked to bear.

11

Case Study: The Indiantown Cogeneration Project

T he Indiantown Cogeneration Project (the "Project") furnishes an interesting case study in how a project can be financed in the public securities markets. On November 9, 1994, Indiantown Cogeneration, L.P. ("Indiantown" or the "Partnership") and Indiantown Cogeneration Funding Corporation (the "Funding Corporation") jointly sold $505 million of first mortgage bonds (the "First Mortgage Bonds") to investors in a registered public offering.[1] Contemporaneously with the $505 million offering, the Martin County Industrial Development Authority sold an additional $125 million of 31-year tax-exempt bonds (the "1994 Tax-Exempt Bonds"), the proceeds of which it had agreed to lend to Indiantown. The long maturity was useful to the Partnership for asset-liability management purposes.

The debt issues are noteworthy because Moody's Investors Service and Standard & Poor's both rated them investment grade (Baa 3/BBB−), even though the Project was still under construction. The quality of the Project's sponsors (Bechtel Enterprises, General Electric Capital, and Pacific Gas & Electric) and the strength of the Project's contractual arrangements were crucial in attaining the

---

This chapter is based on Anne Schwimmer, "Indiantown Project Financing Is the Largest Sold This Year," *Investment Dealers' Digest* (November 21, 1994), p. 14, and Indiantown Cogeneration, L.P./Indiantown Cogeneration Funding Corporation, *Prospectus for $505,000,000 First Mortgage Bonds* (November 9, 1994).

investment-grade rating, which in turn was critical in making a public market available for the First Mortgage Bonds.

PROJECT DESCRIPTION

The Project involves the construction and operation of a coal-fired cogeneration facility (the "Cogeneration Facility") in southwestern Martin County, Florida. The Cogeneration Facility, with an electric generating capacity (net) of 330 megawatts (MW) and a steam export capability of 175,000 pounds per hour, was certified as a "qualifying cogeneration facility" under the Public Utilities Regulatory Policy Act of 1978 (PURPA). The Partnership will sell the electric power to Florida Power & Light Company ("FPL") under a 30-year power purchase agreement, and will sell the steam to Caulkins Indiantown Citrus Company ("Caulkins") under a 15-year energy services agreement.[2] The expected capital cost of the Project at the time of the First Mortgage Bond offering was approximately $588.3 million. Financing costs would add $181.7 million, for a total cost of $770 million. Table 11.1 provides a statement of estimated sources and uses of funds. Note that the uses of funds include a $37 million owners' contingency, which allows for possible cost overruns. Even though the construction contract is a turnkey contract, any design changes will increase the turnkey cost. An independent engineering firm found the $37 million contingency reasonable.

The Purchasers

FPL is a public utility regulated by the Florida Public Service Commission (the "FPSC"). Its service area spans 35 Florida counties and contains approximately 27,650 square miles with a population of 6 million, or approximately half the population of Florida. FPL will take the electric power it purchases from the Cogeneration Facility into its electricity grid and sell it to its regular customers.

Caulkins was founded in 1972. It is an established wholesale citrus juice processor. Caulkins uses steam in an evaporation process to produce citrus concentrate and in a drying process to create cattle feed. Steam cost is a significant component in Caulkins's overall production costs. Substituting the relatively low-cost cogenerated steam for steam Caulkins currently produces using natural gas will result in production cost savings. The typical processing season for Caulkins begins in

TABLE 11.1   Estimated Sources and Uses of Funds for the Indiantown Cogeneration Project (Dollar Amounts in Thousands)

SOURCES OF FUNDS	
First Mortgage Bonds	$505,000
1994 Tax-Exempt Bonds	125,010
Equity Contribution of Partners	140,000
TOTAL SOURCES OF FUNDS	$770,010
USES OF FUNDS	
CAPITAL COSTS	
Engineering, Procurement, and Construction Costs	$438,730
Electrical, Potable Water and Sewer Interconnection	6,850
Property Acquisition Costs	8,811
Steam Host Modifications	14,500
Development Costs and Fees	30,442
Mobilization and Spare Parts	10,618
General & Administrative Costs and Fees	13,057
Taxes	8,827
Start-up Consumables	3,584
Initial Working Capital	3,450
Fuel Reserve	5,000
Title Insurance	3,187
Other Construction-Related Costs	4,223
Owners' Contingency	37,000
TOTAL CAPITAL COST	$588,279
FINANCING COSTS	
Initial Bank Financing Interest and Related Expenses	$ 58,441
Cost of Termination of Interest Rate Hedging Agreements	(7,046)[a]
First Mortgage Bonds and Tax-Exempt Bonds Interest and Related Expenses	84,311
Equity Loan Interest and Related Expenses	33,524
Tax-Exempt Bond Debt Service Reserve Account	12,501[b]
TOTAL FINANCING COSTS	$181,731
TOTAL USES OF FUNDS	$770,010

[a] The termination of the Partnership's interest rate hedging agreements will result in a net payment to the Partnership of $7,046,000.

[b] The Debt Service Reserve Letter of Credit will also be available on the Commercial Operation Date to serve as a debt service reserve for the holders of the First Mortgage Bonds and the 1994 Tax-Exempt Bonds.

Source: Indiantown Cogeneration, L.P./Indiantown Cogeneration Funding Corporation, *Prospectus for $505,000,000 First Mortgage Bonds* (November 9, 1994), p. 53.

November and continues into June of the following year. The Caulkins plant's operating schedule is advantageous to the Cogeneration Facility because approximately 70 percent of Caulkins's annual steam usage will occur in the first five months of the calendar year. Should an unexpected reduction in steam usage occur, Caulkins would have more than seven months to make the necessary adjustments to ensure that the minimum annual steam quantity is taken.

The Cogeneration Facility

Bechtel Power Corporation ("Bechtel Power") was responsible for constructing the Cogeneration Facility pursuant to a fixed-price turnkey construction contract (the "Construction Contract"). The Construction Contract specified a fixed price of $438.7 million. Bechtel Power's responsibilities included design, engineering, procurement, and construction services; plant start-up; training of personnel; and performance testing. Bechtel Power is a recognized leader in serving the needs of the power generation market. For more than 40 years, Bechtel Power had been involved in constructing or engineering more than 56,000 MW of electric generating capacity. Within the past 15 years, Bechtel Power had been involved in the engineering and construction of 20 cogeneration projects for nonutility generators, including two other projects that utilized technology similar to that employed in the Project.

Construction began on October 21, 1992. The guaranteed date for substantial completion of the Cogeneration Facility under the Construction Contract is January 21, 1996 (the "Guaranteed Completion Date"). *Mechanical completion* would occur when, except for minor items of work that would not affect the performance or operation of the Cogeneration Facility, (1) all materials and equipment had been installed substantially in accordance with the Construction Contract; (2) all required systems had been installed and tested; (3) the power plant had been cleaned out as necessary; (4) all the equipment and systems could be operated safely; (5) the Cogeneration Facility was ready to commence start-up, testing, and operations; and (6) a punchlist of the uncompleted items had been mutually agreed between the Partnership and Bechtel Power. Bechtel Power's obligation to achieve mechanical completion of the Cogeneration Facility was not subject to any cap on liquidated damages. *Substantial completion* would occur when the Cogeneration Facility completed performance tests demonstrating that (1) the emissions did not exceed the emission levels specified in the

Construction Contract and (2) the Cogeneration Facility had achieved a capacity output of at least 270 MW during the first 72 hours of a 100-hour test period and 88 percent of the guaranteed net electrical output during the 100-hour test. *Final completion* would occur when (1) mechanical completion had occurred and (2) either the Cogeneration Facility had met all its performance tests and the specified availability test, or Bechtel Power had paid all liquidated damages that were due.[3]

According to outside management consultants, at the time of the First Mortgage Bond offering, construction of the Cogeneration Facility was approximately three-quarters complete, and was within the project budget. Based on this construction status, the consultants concluded that the facility should achieve substantial completion on or before the Guaranteed Completion Date. If the facility failed to achieve substantial completion by the Guaranteed Completion Date, Bechtel Power would have to pay substantial liquidated damages.

Bechtel Power also guaranteed the Cogeneration Facility's net electrical output, plant heat rate, lime consumption, availability, and certain emission levels. If the Cogeneration Facility did not achieve guaranteed performance levels, Bechtel Power would have to pay liquidated damages. However, Bechtel Power's total liability for delay and performance liquidated damages was subject to a cap of $100 million (in addition to any delayed completion insurance payments).

Technology

The Cogeneration Facility would utilize conventional and commercially proven pulverized coal technology consisting of a single, pulverized coal reheat steam generator, an automatic extraction turbine-generator, and associated equipment. Coal would be crushed, ground, mixed with air, and delivered to the steam generator for combustion. This process would produce both superheated steam and reheat steam. Steam produced by the steam generator would first drive the turbine-generator. The "waste steam" would be extracted from the turbine-generator and supplied to Caulkins for process steam thermal use. The condensate would be returned to the Cogeneration Facility via a closed loop piping system.

The underwriters of the First Mortgage Bond offering engaged engineering consultants to review the plant design and equipment specifications to determine the reasonableness of the design. The consultants expressed the opinion that the overall design is in accordance with recognized utility engineering codes, standards, and practices. They also expressed the opinion that (1) the technology used in the Cogeneration Facility is a sound and proven method of electric and thermal generation and (2) if the Cogeneration Facility is designed, operated, and maintained as proposed, it should have a useful life extending beyond the final maturity of the First Mortgage Bonds.

Steam Generator and Auxiliary Equipment

Foster Wheeler, a leading international supplier of equipment, engineering, and construction services, contracted to supply the pulverized-coal-fired steam generator and auxiliary equipment. Foster Wheeler agreed to supply four coal pulverizers. They would be sized so that three of them, operating at 90 percent of rated capacity, could maintain full steam generator load. This would allow one pulverizer to be out of service for maintenance. General Electric Company ("GE") would supply the turbine-generator for the facility. GE is one of the leading manufacturers of turbine-generator sets in the world. Bechtel Power obtained, and agreed to provide the Partnership with the benefit of, 18-month limited warranties from the vendors of the steam generator, the turbine-generator, and the flue-gas cleanup system.

THE PARTNERSHIP AND THE SPONSORS OF THE PROJECT

The Partnership is a Delaware limited partnership that was formed in October 1991 to develop, acquire, own, engineer, construct, test, and operate a coal-fired cogeneration facility having a net design capacity of approximately 330 MW (net) then under construction in Martin County, Florida. The general partners are Toyan Enterprises ("Toyan"), a California corporation and an indirect wholly owned subsidiary of PG&E Enterprises, and Palm Power Corporation ("Palm"), a Delaware corporation and an indirect wholly owned subsidiary of Bechtel Enterprises, Inc. Figure 11.1 shows the ownership structure for the Project. PG&E Enterprises is a wholly owned subsidiary of Pacific Gas and Electric Company. Bechtel Enterprises is a developer and merchant banker in the engineering and construction industry. The limited partner is TIFD III-Y Inc. ("TIFD"), a Delaware corporation and an indirect wholly owned subsidiary of General Electric Capital Corporation ("GE Capital"). Toyan, Palm, and TIFD own 48 percent, 12 percent, and 40 percent, respectively, of the partnership interests.

FIGURE 11.1   Ownership Structure for the Indiantown Cogeneration Project

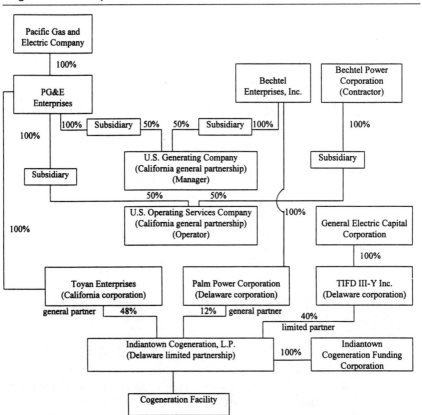

Source: Indiantown Cogeneration, L.P./Indiantown Cogeneration Funding Corporation, *Prospectus for $505,000,000 First Mortgage Bonds* (November 9, 1994), pp. 5, 69–71.

Project Development

The Cogeneration Facility has been developed on behalf of Indiantown by U.S. Generating Company, a California general partnership. The general partners are PG&E Generating Company, a subsidiary of PG&E Enterprises, and Bechtel Generating Company, a subsidiary of Bechtel Enterprises. PG&E Generating Company and Bechtel Generating Company each own 50 percent of U.S. Generating. U.S. Generating was formed, as of January 1989, to develop and manage the construction and operation of electric power generating facilities throughout the United States. At the time of the First Mortgage Bond offering, U.S.

Generating had under development or management 14 independent power projects having an aggregate generating capacity in excess of 2,500 MW. The Partnership and U.S. Generating entered into a management services agreement (the "Management Services Agreement") for the management and administration of the Cogeneration Facility. The term of the Management Services Agreement extends beyond the final maturity date of the First Mortgage Bonds.

Project Operation

U.S. Operating, a California general partnership between wholly owned subsidiaries of PG&E Enterprises and Bechtel Power, will provide operation and maintenance services for the Cogeneration Facility under an operation and maintenance services agreement (the "Operating Agreement"). U.S. Operating was formed to provide operating and maintenance services for electric power generating facilities. At the time of the First Mortgage Bond offering, U.S. Operating was providing technical services at five other independent power plants, three of which had been in commercial operation since mid-1988.

Management of the Partnership

The activities of the Partnership are governed by a partnership agreement (the "Partnership Agreement"). The Partnership Agreement establishes a Board of Control, which has full and exclusive power and authority, to the extent it does not delegate such authority, to take any actions in respect of the management and control of the Partnership. Palm, Toyan, and TIFD are defined as the Board of Control Partners. Each Board of Control Partner has the right to appoint two members of the Board of Control and one alternate. At each meeting of the Board of Control, at least one of the members (or a duly appointed alternate) appointed by each Board of Control Partner must be present (in person or by telephone) in order to have a quorum for the transaction of business. Actions by the Board of Control require the unanimous affirmative vote of the Board of Control members present at the meeting.

Equity Loan Agreement

The Partnership and TIFD entered into an Equity Loan Agreement pursuant to which TIFD agreed to lend $139 million to the Partnership for use in connection with the financing of completion of construction, testing, start-up, and initial operation of the Cogeneration Facility. By June 30, 1994, TIFD had advanced the entire $139 million to the Partnership.

Equity Contribution Agreement

The Partners agreed to contribute $140 million of equity to the Partnership either to repay amounts outstanding under the Equity Loan Agreement or to finance the completion of construction, testing, start-up, and initial operation of the Cogeneration Facility. TIFD was obligated to make the equity contribution to the Partnership of up to $140 million pursuant to an Equity Contribution Agreement. GE Capital guaranteed TIFD's obligations under the Equity Contribution Agreement. The Partners contributed the $140 million of equity on December 26, 1995.

Allocation of Profits and Losses and Distributions to Partners

Net profits and losses are allocated to the partners in accordance with their respective ownership percentages:

General Partners:	
Toyan	48%
Palm	12
Limited Partner:	
TIFD	40
Total	100%

All distributions, other than liquidating distributions, will be made in accordance with the partners' respective percentage interests as shown above.

PRINCIPAL PROJECT CONTRACTS

The financial integrity of a project financing depends on the strength of the credit support provided by the contractual arrangements that govern the sale of product, supply of raw materials, provision of management

FIGURE 11.2   Principal Contracts Supporting the Financing of the Indiantown Cogeneration Project

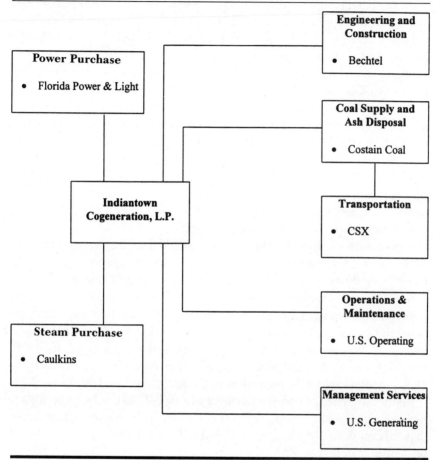

Source: Indiantown Cogeneration, L.P./Indiantown Cogeneration Funding Corporation, *Prospectus for $505,000,000 First Mortgage Bonds* (November 9, 1994), p. 31.

services, and so on. The principal contracts associated with the Project are typical of cogeneration projects that have been financed on a nonrecourse basis in recent years. Figure 11.2 shows the principal contracts supporting the financing for the Project.

Power Purchase Agreement

Indiantown, as seller, and FPL, as purchaser, entered into a 30-year Agreement for the Purchase of Firm Capacity and Energy, dated as of

March 31, 1990 (the "Power Purchase Agreement"). FPL's payments for electricity and capacity were expected to provide approximately 99 percent of Partnership revenues. The Power Purchase Agreement (as amended) was approved by the FPSC. The FPSC also issued a Determination of Need for the Cogeneration Facility, in which it found that the cost of electricity to be provided by the Cogeneration Facility is reasonable and that the Cogeneration Facility is the most cost-effective alternative available to meet FPL's 1996 need for firm capacity and energy. Under the terms of the Power Purchase Agreement, FPL is obligated to purchase electric generating capacity made available to it and electric power from the Partnership. This purchase obligation extends from the Commercial Operation Date (as defined) through the later of (1) December 1, 2025, and (2) 30 years from the Commercial Operation Date. Achievement of substantial completion of the Cogeneration Facility under the Construction Contract would be sufficient to declare that the Commercial Operation Date had occurred.

Payments by FPL to the Partnership under the Power Purchase Agreement will consist of (1) monthly capacity payments and (2) monthly energy payments. The capacity payments will have two components: (1) an unescalated fixed capacity payment and (2) an escalated fixed operation and maintenance payment. Together, these payments are expected by the Partnership to cover all of the Partnership's fixed costs, including debt service. FPL is required to make capacity payments to the Partnership for the electric generating capacity the Partnership makes available to FPL, regardless of the amount of electric energy FPL actually purchases. Capacity payments from FPL are subject to adjustment on the basis of a capacity billing factor. The capacity billing factor depends on both output produced and output available to be produced but not dispatched by FPL.

The energy payments FPL makes were expected to cover all of the Partnership's variable costs of energy production. A fuel price escalation provision in the Power Purchase Agreement is substantially the same as the one contained in the Coal Purchase Agreement described below. This contract feature is designed to mitigate any mismatches that might otherwise occur between the energy payments that FPL will make to the Partnership and the Partnership's cost of fuel.

The Power Purchase Agreement gives FPL broad control over power dispatch levels. FPL may suspend its receipt of energy for specified reasons, including safety reasons or system emergencies. This contract feature gives FPL the flexibility to adjust its energy purchases from the Cogeneration Facility based on FPL's relative costs of power from its alternative sources. FPL's energy payments are adjusted to compensate the Partnership for costs associated with inefficiencies resulting from energy dispatch at less than full load. Consequently, fluctuations in dispatch levels were not expected to have a significant impact on the Partnership's profitability.

The Partnership was required to provide FPL with either an unconditional, irrevocable, direct-pay letter of credit or earnest money, to ensure completion of the Cogeneration Facility by December 1, 1995:[4]

- $1 million within 15 business days after the FPSC approved the Power Purchase Agreement;
- An additional $2 million within 15 business days after certification of the power plant site pursuant to the Florida Electrical Power Plant Siting Act;
- An additional $6 million within 15 business days after the closing of the Partnership's construction loan for the Cogeneration Facility.

The Power Purchase Agreement requires the Partnership to pay FPL for each day beyond December 1, 1995, that the Commercial Operation Date does not occur. The Commercial Operation Date occurred December 22, 1995, and the Partnership paid FPL approximately $500,000 to compensate for the delay. The Power Purchase Agreement contains a number of restrictive covenants concerning Indiantown and the performance of the Cogeneration Facility. Certain obligations of the Partnership under the Power Purchase Agreement would have to be secured by letters of credit.

FPL has the right to terminate the Power Purchase Agreement upon the occurrence of certain specified events of default, such as performance failures or violations of law or permits. The Power Purchase Agreement also gives FPL a "regulatory out." If FPL at any time is denied authorization to recover from its customers any payments to be made under the Power Purchase Agreement, FPL can adjust those payments to the amount it is authorized to recover from its customers. Moreover, it can require the Partnership to give back payments subsequently disallowed by the FPSC. If FPL's obligations are materially altered as a result of the operation of the regulatory out clause, the Partnership may terminate the Power Purchase Agreement upon 60 days' notice. The Partnership and FPL would, in that event, be required to attempt in good faith to negotiate a new power purchase contract or an agreement for transmission of the Cogeneration Facility's capacity and energy to another purchaser. However, if the Partnership terminates the Power Purchase Agreement, a termination fee would be due.

Each party is excused from failure to perform under the Power Purchase Agreement if such failure is caused by an event of force majeure. *Force majeure* is defined in the Power Purchase Agreement as an event that is beyond the reasonable control of the party and is not caused by that party's negligence or lack of due diligence. Such events include actions or inactions of civil or military authority (including courts and governmental or administrative agencies), acts of God, war, riot or insurrection, blockades, embargoes, sabotage, epidemics, explosions and fires not originating in the Cogeneration Facility or caused by its operation, hurricanes, floods, strikes, lockouts, or other labor disputes or difficulties. Equipment breakdown resulting from deficiencies in design, construction, operation, maintenance, or otherwise that occur within the Cogeneration Facility do not qualify as events of force majeure.

Steam Purchase Agreement

The Partnership entered into a 15-year Energy Services Agreement, dated as of September 8, 1992 (the "Steam Purchase Agreement"), with Caulkins. The Steam Purchase Agreement provides for the Partnership to sell up to 745 million pounds of steam per year to Caulkins. It requires Caulkins to purchase a minimum equal to the lesser of (1) 525 million pounds of steam per year and (2) the minimum quantity of steam per year necessary for the Cogeneration Facility to maintain its status as a qualifying cogeneration facility under PURPA. The annual steam price is (1) $100,000 for quantities of steam up to and including 720 million pounds per operating year, and (2) $2.20 per thousand pounds of steam for quantities of steam in excess of 720 million pounds and less than or equal to 745 million pounds per operating year. An independent expert opined that the amount of steam necessary for the Cogeneration Facility to maintain qualifying facility status is less than 525 million pounds of steam per year.

The Steam Purchase Agreement has a term of 15 years from the January 1 following the Commercial Operation Date. Either party can renew the agreement for five additional years. The agreement can be extended for two additional terms of five years each, if Caulkins and the Partnership both agree.

If Caulkins fails to take the minimum steam quantity in any year (except in the event of force majeure), it will have to pay liquidated damages (up to $10 million) to the Partnership. This obligation is secured by a bank letter of credit. The Partnership is liable to Caulkins for liquidated damages (also up to $10 million) in the event the Partnership fails to supply Caulkins with steam or defaults under the Steam Purchase Agreement. This obligation is secured by a letter of credit. Caulkins must provide the Partnership with at least 18 months' notice if it intends to close the Caulkins facility. In that event, the Partnership has the right to purchase or lease the Caulkins facility based on its fair market value.

Construction Contract

Indiantown and Bechtel Power entered into a fixed-price Amended and Restated Turnkey Construction Contract, dated as of September 18, 1992 (the "Construction Contract"). The Construction Contract covered the design, engineering, procurement of equipment and materials for, construction, start-up, and testing of the Cogeneration Facility.

The fixed, base price for the Cogeneration Facility under the Construction Contract is $438.7 million. The $438.7 million contract price is subject to change only due to: (1) changes in the scope of work mutually agreed to by the parties; (2) changes requested by the Partnership; (3) the occurrence of certain force majeure events; (4) the Partnership's failure, delay, or error in providing information or other items required by the Construction Contract; (5) any change in the design criteria due to circumstances beyond Bechtel Power's or its subcontractors' reasonable control; (6) delay resulting from interference by the Partnership, its employees, or agents; or (7) any other event or circumstances defined as a Change in the Construction Contract.

The Construction Contract defines the requirements for mechanical completion, substantial completion, and final completion discussed earlier in the chapter. As noted there, Bechtel Power's obligation to achieve mechanical completion of the Cogeneration Facility is not subject to the overall limit on liquidated damages. Bechtel Power was obligated to achieve substantial completion by the Guaranteed Completion Date (January 21, 1996). Final completion had to occur within 365 days after the later to occur of (1) substantial completion or (2) the Date Certain (December 1, 1996). Bechtel Power would have to pay specified delay damages in an amount equal to the Project's debt service (less an amount equal to any net revenues earned by the Partnership from the operation of the Cogeneration Facility) for each day or part thereof that the Project is delayed beyond the Guaranteed Completion Date until the earliest to occur of substantial completion, the Date Certain, or final completion. Bechtel Power's liquidated damages are limited to $100 million.

Operating Agreement

The Partnership and U.S. Operating entered into the Operating Agreement, dated as of September 30, 1992. Under this agreement, U.S. Operating is responsible for operating and maintaining the Cogeneration Facility. The term of the Operating Agreement is 30 years with automatic renewal for successive 5-year periods, unless previously terminated by either party.

U.S. Operating is responsible for supplying operating personnel to observe, receive training from Bechtel Power, and participate in the testing and start-up of the Cogeneration Facility. After the earlier of substantial completion or final completion, U.S. Operating shall perform all operation and maintenance of the Cogeneration Facility. These responsibilities include providing qualified operating personnel, training such personnel (in conjunction with Bechtel), making all repairs, purchasing spare parts, and providing other services related to the operation of the Cogeneration Facility as needed, all according to industry standards. One hundred and fifty days prior to substantial completion, and prior to the beginning of each subsequent calendar year, U.S. Operating will prepare an annual budget and an annual operating plan which it will submit for approval to the Partnership.

Management Services Agreement

The Partnership and U.S. Generating entered into the Management Services Agreement, dated as of September 30, 1992. That agreement covers the management and administration of the Partnership's business. The term of the Management Services Agreement is 34 years. U.S. Generating is responsible for the day-to-day management and administration of the Partnership, including construction, start-up, testing, operation, and management of the Cogeneration Facility (but excluding any responsibilities delegated to U.S. Operating under the Operating Agreement) and administration and performance of the Partnership's obligations under each of the Project's contracts. U.S. Generating must monitor and maintain compliance with all required permits, licenses, and governmental approvals obtained by or for the Partnership. In addition, U.S. Generating will prepare all financial or other reports required pursuant to the Project's contracts.

Coal Purchase Agreement

The Partnership entered into a Coal Purchase Agreement, dated as of August 4, 1992 (the "Coal Purchase Agreement"), with Costain Coal Inc. ("Costain Coal"). The Coal Purchase Agreement provides for the purchase of bituminous coal for the Cogeneration Facility and the disposal of ash residue. The term of the Coal Purchase Agreement is 30 years. According to independent experts, Costain Coal had adequate coal reserves, production capacity, operating knowledge and experience, and coal preparation and loadout facilities to meet the tonnage and quality specifications set forth in the Coal Purchase Agreement.

Costain Coal is required to supply all of the Cogeneration Facility's coal requirements, including a 30-day stockpile. The Coal Purchase Agreement specifies maximum coal deliveries of 1.2 million tons of coal per year to the Cogeneration Facility. The Partnership does not have any obligation under the Coal Purchase Agreement to purchase any annual minimum quantity of coal. Indiantown can therefore adjust its coal purchases in line with the expected electric power dispatch from the Cogeneration Facility.

Costain Coal is required to supply coal that meets the criteria specified in the Coal Purchase Agreement. Deviations from certain of these specifications will trigger payments to adjust for savings or costs owing to variations in coal, lime, and ash qualities. The Coal Purchase Agreement also establishes minimum quality standards. Indiantown may reject coal deliveries that do not meet these standards.

Coal and Ash Waste Transportation Agreement

Costain Coal and CSX Transportation Inc., a wholly owned subsidiary of CSX Corporation, entered into a Coal and Ash Waste Transportation Agreement, dated as of August 8, 1992, for the transportation of coal to the Cogeneration Facility and the backhaul of ash waste from the Cogeneration Facility to the ash disposal sites. The term of this agreement is 30 years from the Commercial Operation Date.

PROJECTED OPERATING RESULTS

Stone & Webster prepared projections of the revenues and expenses of the Cogeneration Facility (the "Projected Operating Results"). The Projected Operating Results cover the calendar years ending December 31, between 1996 and 2025. They assumed commercial operation would commence January 21, 1996.

Assumptions

These are the basic assumptions on which the Projected Operating Results are based.

- *Annual Operating Revenues from the Sale of Electricity to FPL.* The Power Purchase Agreement provides for the sale of electric generating capacity and energy to FPL for a term of 30 years. The Power Purchase Agreement permits FPL to schedule power dispatch on a daily basis to meet its system needs. It also requires FPL to pay certain fixed charges whether or not the Cogeneration Facility is dispatched on-line, and to pay certain variable charges based on the amount of electricity delivered to FPL. The Base Case assumes the Cogeneration Facility to be dispatched at full load when dispatched at all. The Partnership's economics are relatively insensitive to dispatch levels because the energy payment is adjusted for operating inefficiencies resulting from dispatch at less than full load.

  The capacity payment rates are given in Table 11.2. The capacity revenue is based on 330 MW (net) generating capacity multiplied by the sum of the applicable capacity rate and the fixed operation and maintenance amount. The fixed operation and maintenance payment is $5,170 per MW-month as of January 1996. This figure is escalated annually based on the DRI/McGraw-Hill GDP Implicit Price Deflator. The fixed capacity payments are adjusted based on the "capacity billing factor," which Stone & Webster estimated would be 97.5 percent each year. This capacity billing factor results in a bonus that increases the capacity payment from FPL to the Partnership by 10 percent.

  The monthly energy payment equals the unit energy price ($.02153 per kWh in 1992) multiplied by the kilowatt-hours of energy produced and adjusted by the applicable hourly efficiency factor. This factor is designed to compensate the Partnership for

TABLE 11.2   Schedule of Capacity Rates

Year Ending December 31,	Capacity Rate ($/MW-month)
1996–2015	$23,000
2016	12,500
2017	12,220
2018	11,940
2019	11,670
2020	11,390
2021	11,110
2022	10,820
2023	10,560
2024	10,280
2025	10,000

Source: Indiantown Cogeneration, L.P./Indiantown Cogeneration Funding Corporation, *Prospectus for $505,000,000 First Mortgage Bonds* (November 9, 1994), p. B-28.

higher marginal fuel costs at dispatch levels below full load. The unit energy price is adjusted at the same weighted average escalation rate as the unit energy costs.

- *Annual Operating Revenues from the Sale of Thermal Energy.* Under the Steam Purchase Agreement, the Partnership agreed to sell steam to Caulkins at a base price of $100,000 for steam quantities up to 720 million pounds per year. Stone & Webster assumed that Caulkins would purchase 525 million pounds of steam per year. Beginning in the second full year of operations, the base fee is adjusted according to a formula based on one-half of the change in the consumer price index plus one-half of the change in the average price of wholesale natural gas from the previous year.

- *Interest Income.* Interest is earned on funds maintained in the Debt Service Reserve Account. These funds are assumed to earn 7.875 percent annually, which is the interest rate on the first series of 1994 Tax-Exempt Bonds. Interest is also earned on funds held in various disbursement accounts. The projections assume an interest rate 0.5 percent less than the annual inflation rate as projected by DRI/McGraw-Hill.

- *Annual Operating Expenses for Coal and Ash Disposal.* The Partnership agreed to purchase coal at a base price of $26.00 per ton in 1992, which would be adjusted annually according to indexes set forth in the Coal Purchase Agreement. The Base Case assumes annual adjustments in this price based on the DRI Producer Price Index for Coal, which was projected to increase 4.1 percent per year. The Base Case projections assume coal usage at the rate of 133.4 tons per hour based on 100 percent capacity utilization (330 MW (net)) when steam is produced and at the rate of 128.2 tons per hour when steam is not produced.

- *Annual Operations and Maintenance Expenses.* The Base Case assumes U.S. Operating meets all operating performance and target levels and therefore is entitled to the maximum earned fees and bonuses provided for under the Operating Agreement.
- *Annual Management Services Expenses.* The Partnership has agreed to pay U.S. Generating for the management and administration of the Partnership's business with respect to the Cogeneration Facility. The base annual fee is $650,000, which is adjusted annually based on changes in the DRI/McGraw-Hill GDP Implicit Price Deflator.
- *Financing Assumptions.* The projected debt service payments were provided by the underwriters of the First Mortgage Bonds based on (1) an aggregate principal amount of $505,000,000 of First Mortgage Bonds issued in series with 10 maturities (see Figure 11.3 on page 231) and (2) $125,010,000 aggregate principal amount of the two series of 1994 Tax-Exempt Bonds, consisting of $113,000,000 principal amount at 7.875 percent and $12,010,000 principal amount at 8.050 percent.

Base Case Results

The Base Case Projected Operating Results are shown in Table 11.3. For the Base Case, the projected revenues from the sale of electrical and thermal energy are adequate to pay annual operating and maintenance expenses, fuel expenses, and other operating expenses. Operating income falls significantly after 2015 because the capacity payment rate drops significantly beginning in 2016 (see Table 11.2). The minimum annual interest coverage of the First Mortgage Bonds is 1.75 times, and the weighted average annual interest coverage is 2.50 times over the life of the First Mortgage Bonds.[5] The minimum annual debt service coverage for the First Mortgage Bonds is 1.47 times, and the weighted average annual debt service coverage is 1.50 times over the life of the First Mortgage Bonds.[6]

Sensitivity Analyses

Stone & Webster performed a variety of sensitivity analyses. They are described and their results are summarized in Table 11.4. A 2 percent increase in the plant heat rate, a 1 percent greater inflation rate, and a 10 percent reduction in the average annual dispatch of electricity each has only a small impact on the Project's interest coverage and debt service coverage ratios. Reducing the availability factor to 84 percent has a greater impact; nevertheless, the Partnership can still service its debt with a large margin of safety. Even with 1 percent higher inflation *and* reduced availability (case S 5), the annual interest coverage ratio never falls below 1.64 times and the annual debt service coverage ratio never falls below 1.14 times. The sensitivity analyses suggest that the Partnership will be able to service its debt in a timely manner under reasonably adverse circumstances.

PROJECT FINANCING

The $505 million public offering of First Mortgage Bonds consisted of 10 tranches that were scheduled to mature between 2 years (series A-1) and 26 years (series A-10) from the date of issue. The sponsors considered offering the First Mortgage Bonds in a Rule 144A placement but opted instead for a registered public offering in order to appeal to "total return investors," who desire the greater liquidity that a registered public offering can typically achieve.[7]

Table 11.5 shows the capitalization of Indiantown at June 30, 1994. It also shows Indiantown's capitalization as of that date adjusted to reflect the effect of (1) issuing $505 million principal amount of First Mortgage Bonds, (2) issuing $125.01 million principal amount of the 1994 Tax-Exempt Bonds, and (3) the application of the net proceeds received from the sale of the two bond issues to repay the Partnership's existing indebtedness.

Initial Construction Financing

As illustrated in Table 11.5, the initial financing for the Project came from four sources: (1) commercial bank financing provided by a syndicate of banks led by Credit Suisse and Credit Lyonnais (which reached $202.6 million as of June 30, 1994); (2) a $113 million issue of

TABLE 11.3   Base Case Projected Operating Results

	1996	1997	1998	1999	2000
PERFORMANCE					
Max. Capacity (net)(Mw)	330	330	330	330	330
Average Annual Dispatch	76.8%	88.3%	88.3%	88.3%	88.3%
Electric Sales to Florida					
Power & Light (Mwh)	2,099,030	2,553,155	2,553,155	2,553,155	2,553,155
Steam Sales (Mlbs)	496,233	525,000	525,000	525,000	525,000
Coal Consumption (Tons)	834,719	1,012,269	1,012,269	1,012,269	1,012,269
PRICES					
Electric Capacity Payment ($/kw-yr)	$ 338.64	$ 340.14	$ 341.88	$ 343.85	$ 345.95
Electric Energy Payment ($/Mwh)	23.54	24.32	25.22	26.17	27.19
Steam Price ($/Mlbs)	0.19	0.20	0.21	0.23	0.24
Coal ($/Ton)	27.71	28.90	30.26	31.65	33.13
OPERATING REVENUES ($000)					
Electric Capacity	116,317	123,472	124,101	124,818	125,582
Electric Energy	49,404	61,844	63,834	66,094	68,575
Steam	95	104	110	118	127
Total Operating Revenues	165,816	185,419	188,046	191,031	194,284
OPERATING EXPENSES ($000)					
Costain Fuel & Ash Disposal Cost	48,491	60,502	62,716	65,082	67,607
Operations & Maintenance	11,546	12,922	13,271	13,669	14,093
Other Operating Expenses	14,589	15,605	16,007	17,795	16,757
Total Operating Expenses	74,626	89,029	91,994	96,546	98,457
OPERATING INCOME ($000)	91,190	96,390	96,051	94,485	95,828
Adjustments	3,357	4,395	4,160	4,385	4,103
CASH AVAILABLE FOR DEBT SERVICE ($000)	94,547	100,785	100,211	98,870	99,931
Total Annual Debt Service	64,317	67,934	67,812	66,860	67,624
ANNUAL INTEREST EXPENSE COVERAGE	1.75	1.78	1.79	1.80	1.85
ANNUAL DEBT SERVICE COVERAGE	1.47	1.48	1.48	1.48	1.48

Source: Indiantown Cogeneration, L.P./Indiantown Cogeneration Funding Corporation, *Prospectus for $505,000,000 First Mortgage Bonds* (November 9, 1994), pp. B-36, B-37, B-38.

tax-exempt bonds, which were supported by a letter of credit issued by Credit Suisse; (3) a $139 million loan from GE Capital, one of the equity investors in the Project; and (4) $100,000 of partners' capital. Such high leverage during the construction period is common, but lenders require that acceptable contracts be in place to ensure completion.

The Refinancing

Indiantown effected a refinancing in 1994 and 1995. As illustrated in Table 11.5, the proceeds from the $505 million of First Mortgage Bonds and $125.01 million of 1994 Tax-Exempt Bonds were used to repay the bank debt in full, refund the $113 million principal amount of 1992 Tax-Exempt Bonds in full, and repay the Original Equity Loan in full. The remaining funds were used to pay for a portion of the construction costs. Even though the Original Equity Loan was repaid,

2001	2002	2003	2004	2005	2010	2015	2020	2025
330	330	330	330	330	330	330	330	330
80.7%	88.3%	88.3%	88.3%	88.3%	88.3%	88.3%	88.3%	88.3%
2,331,719	2,553,155	2,553,155	2,553,155	2,553,155	2,553,155	2,553,155	2,553,155	2,553,155
525,000	525,000	525,000	525,000	525,000	525,000	525,000	525,000	525,000
926,237	1,012,269	1,012,269	1,012,269	1,012,269	1,012,269	1,012,269	1,012,269	1,012,269
$ 348.19	$ 350.58	$ 353.11	$ 355.73	$ 358.44	$ 373.45	$ 390.95	$ 272.55	$ 280.59
28.26	29.35	30.51	31.73	32.99	39.97	47.50	56.57	67.39
0.26	0.28	0.30	0.32	0.34	0.45	0.55	0.66	0.80
34.66	36.18	37.81	39.55	41.33	51.21	61.23	73.43	88.06
126,394	127,259	128,179	129,131	130,115	135,561	141,916	98,936	101,856
64,931	73,974	76,819	79,848	82,971	100,347	119,645	142,376	169,400
137	147	157	169	180	234	288	349	423
191,462	201,380	205,156	209,148	213,266	236,141	261,849	241,660	271,678
64,388	72,932	75,809	78,839	81,954	99,222	118,423	140,904	167,689
14,202	15,024	15,534	16,063	16,609	19,631	23,158	27,372	32,352
20,025	21,303	18,610	18,286	22,139	22,006	25,233	32,062	31,027
98,615	109,259	109,953	113,188	120,702	140,859	166,814	200,338	231,068
92,847	92,121	95,203	95,960	92,564	95,282	95,035	41,322	40,610
4,442	4,782	4,134	4,536	5,137	5,335	5,533	6,659	7,084
97,289	96,903	99,337	100,496	97,701	100,617	100,568	47,981	47,694
65,737	65,025	66,995	67,798	65,693	67,532	67,123	30,821	30,831
1.83	1.86	1.95	2.03	2.04	2.64	4.61	4.40	28.15
1.48	1.49	1.48	1.48	1.49	1.49	1.50	1.56	1.55

GE Capital remained committed to fund up to $140 million of the remaining construction cost of the Cogeneration Facility. Also, GE Capital was obligated to make an equity contribution to the Partnership not later than five days after its completion date in the amount of $140 million pursuant to the Equity Contribution Agreement. The general partners, Toyan and Palm, would reimburse GE Capital for their respective pro rata shares of the partners' equity commitment.

Financial Structure upon Completion of the Project

The estimated sources and uses of funds for the Project in Table 11.1 suggest the capital structure shown in Table 11.6 upon completion of the Project. Long-term debt would represent 81.8 percent of total capitalization. Roughly four-fifths of this debt would be taxable. The other one-fifth would be tax-exempt.

TABLE 11.4 Description and Results of Sensitivity Analyses (Dollar Amounts in Millions)

Sensitivity Case	Title	Description
S1	Increased Heat Rate	The heat rate increases by 2 percent. An increase in plant heat rate is an indication of decreasing plant efficiency. This results in a small increase in Costain Fuel & Ash Disposal Cost.
S2	Increased Inflation Rate	All escalation rates increase by 1 percent.
S3	Reduced Dispatch	The dispatch of electricity decreases by 10 percent in every year. At dispatch of less than full load, revenues are not negatively affected because the Power Purchase Agreement provides for full-capacity payment and for adjustment of the electric energy revenues to compensate for lower thermal efficiencies.
S4	Reduced Availability Factor	The availability factor decreases to 84.0 percent (versus 88.3 percent in the base case) beginning in 2001 and extending through 2025, except that in every major maintenance year between 2001 and 2025 the availability factor is 80.7 percent as in the base case.
S5	Combination of Cases 2 and 4	

Summary of Results of Sensitivity Analyses

	1996	1997	1998	1999	2000	2005	2010	2015	2020	2025	Minimum	Weighted Average
Operating Revenues:												
Base case	166	185	188	191	194	213	236	262	242	272		
S1	166	186	189	192	195	215	238	264	244	275		
S2	168	189	193	197	201	228	261	301	299	355		
S3	161	180	182	185	188	205	226	250	227	255		
S4	166	185	188	191	194	197	219	243	226	254		
S5	168	189	193	197	201	211	242	280	280	332		
Operating Income:												
Base case	91	96	96	94	96	93	95	95	41	41		
S1	90	96	96	94	96	92	95	95	41	40		
S2	90	95	95	93	95	91	94	93	38	38		
S3	92	97	97	95	96	93	96	96	42	42		
S4	91	96	96	94	96	81	83	82	33	32		
S5	90	95	95	93	95	79	81	80	28	28		
Cash Available for Debt Service:												
Base case	95	101	100	99	100	98	101	101	48	48		
S1	94	100	100	99	100	98	100	100	48	47		
S2	94	100	100	98	99	97	100	100	46	48		
S3	95	102	101	99	100	98	101	101	49	49		
S4	95	101	100	99	100	86	88	88	39	39		
S5	94	100	100	98	99	85	87	86	37	37		

(Continued)

227

TABLE 11.4 *(Continued)*

Summary of Results of Sensitivity Analyses

	1996	1997	1998	1999	2000	2005	2010	2015	2020	2025	Minimum	Weighted Average
Annual Interest Coverage:												
Base case	1.75	1.78	1.79	1.80	1.85	2.04	2.64	4.61	4.40	28.15	1.75	2.50
S1	1.73	1.76	1.78	1.79	1.84	2.03	2.64	4.61	4.38	28.01	1.73	2.49
S2	1.74	1.77	1.78	1.79	1.84	2.02	2.63	4.59	4.26	28.30	1.74	2.48
S3	1.76	1.79	1.80	1.81	1.85	2.05	2.66	4.65	4.48	28.75	1.76	2.52
S4	1.75	1.78	1.79	1.80	1.85	1.79	2.32	4.03	3.60	22.88	1.66	2.28
S5	1.74	1.77	1.78	1.79	1.84	1.77	2.30	3.97	3.36	22.08	1.64	2.25
Annual Debt Service Coverage:												
Base case	1.47	1.48	1.48	1.48	1.48	1.49	1.49	1.50	1.56	1.55	1.47	1.50
S1	1.46	1.47	1.47	1.47	1.47	1.49	1.49	1.50	1.55	1.54	1.46	1.49
S2	1.47	1.48	1.47	1.47	1.47	1.47	1.48	1.49	1.51	1.56	1.47	1.48
S3	1.48	1.49	1.49	1.49	1.48	1.50	1.50	1.51	1.58	1.58	1.48	1.51
S4	1.47	1.48	1.48	1.48	1.48	1.31	1.31	1.31	1.27	1.26	1.26	1.37
S5	1.47	1.48	1.47	1.47	1.47	1.29	1.30	1.29	1.19	2.21	1.14	1.35

Source: Indiantown Cogeneration, L.P./ Indiantown Cogeneration Funding Corporation, *Prospectus for $505,000,000 First Mortgage Bonds* (November 9, 1994), pp. B-32–B-53.

TABLE 11.5 Capitalization of Indiantown Cogeneration, L.P., at June 30, 1994

	As of June 30, 1994	As Adjusted
Long-Term Debt:		
Initial Bank Financing	$202,621,500	$ 0
First Mortgage Bonds	0	505,000,000
1992 Tax-Exempt Bonds	113,000,000	0
1994 Tax-Exempt Bonds	0	125,010,000
Original Equity Loan	139,000,000	0
New Equity Loan[a]	0	0
Total Long-Term Debt	454,621,500	630,010,000
Partners' Capital:		
Toyan Enterprises	48	48
Palm Power Corporation	12	12
TIFD III-Y, Inc.	40	40
Total Partners' Capital	100	100
Total Long-Term Debt and Partners' Capital	$454,621,600	$630,010,100

[a] Funds available under the New Equity Loan Agreement will be drawn from time to time after the Closing Date to fund construction of the Cogeneration Facility. Not later than five days after the completion date, the Partners will be obligated to make a $140,000,000 equity contribution to the Partnership pursuant to the Equity Contribution Agreement.

Source: Indiantown Cogeneration, L.P./Indiantown Cogeneration Funding Corporation, *Prospectus for $505,000,000 First Mortgage Bonds* (November 9, 1994), p. 54.

TABLE 11.6 Projected Capital Structure for Indiantown Cogeneration, L.P., Upon Project Completion (Dollar Amounts in Millions)

	Amount	Percent
Long-Term Debt:		
First Mortgage Bonds	$505.0	65.6%
1994 Tax-Exempt Bonds	125.0	16.2
Total Long-Term Debt	$630.0	81.8%
Equity:		
Partners' Equity	140.0	18.2
Total Capitalization	$770.0	100.0%

Source: Table 11.1.

Interest Rate Swap Agreements

Indiantown entered into six interest rate swap agreements in October 1992. The swap agreements accreted from an initial aggregate notional amount of $16,578,600, in November 1992, to a final aggregate notional principal amount of $535 million by December 29, 1995. Thereafter, the notional balance is fixed at $535 million through December 2010. The Partnership entered into the swap agreements in order to hedge its interest rate risk exposure associated with the construction period variable rate debt. It anticipated making a permanent placement of fixed-rate debt near the end of 1994. The 2010 swap expiration would protect the Project against interest rate risk exposure in the event the fixed-rate financing should be substantially delayed. Swap payments were based on the spread between 8.30 percent (weighted average fixed rate under the six agreements) and LIBOR.

The Public Offering of First Mortgage Bonds

Figure 11.3 furnishes a summary of terms for the issue of First Mortgage Bonds. The First Mortgage Bonds consisted of 10 tranches, which were sold in a registered public offering. The First Mortgage Bonds were issued in series at interest rates between 7.38 percent (for Series A-1, maturing June 15, 1996) and 9.77 percent (for Series A-10, maturing December 15, 2020). As illustrated in Figure 11.3, $197.8 million principal amount (39 percent of the issue) matures in 2010 (16 years from the date of issue) and $268.4 million principal amount (53 percent of the issue) matures in 2020 (26 years from the date of issue).

The First Mortgage Bonds contain a number of features designed to protect the bondholders' financial interests. There is a limitation on the incurrence of additional debt; this provision prevents, or at least limits, any dilution in the security backing the First Mortgage Bonds that might occur if additional debt could be issued without limit. There is also a limitation on partnership distributions. This feature limits the partners' ability to distribute cash out of the Partnership. Bondholders, of course, would prefer to keep as much cash as possible in the Partnership because it provides additional security for the First Mortgage Bonds.

The indenture for the First Mortgage Bonds also provides for the appointment of a Disbursement Agent and the establishment of several

---

**FIGURE 11.3   Summary of Terms for the Indiantown First
Mortgage Bonds**

Co-Issuers: Indiantown Cogeneration, L.P. and Indiantown Cogeneration Funding Corporation ("ICFC"). ICFC has nominal assets, and it will not conduct any operations. Certain institutional investors that might be limited in their ability to invest in securities issued by partnerships (by the legal investment laws of their states of organization or their charter documents) might be able to invest in the First Mortgage Bonds because ICFC is a corporate co-obligor.

Principal Amount Offered: An aggregate of $505,000,000 of First Mortgage Bonds offered in ten series:

Series	Principal Amount	Interest Rate	Final Maturity
A-1	$ 4,397,000	7.38%	June 15, 1996
A-2	4,398,000	7.56	December 15, 1996
A-3	4,850,000	7.80	June 15, 1997
A-4	4,851,000	7.97	December 15, 1997
A-5	5,132,000	8.19	June 15, 1998
A-6	5,133,000	8.19	December 15, 1998
A-7	4,998,000	8.39	June 15, 1999
A-8	4,999,000	8.43	December 15, 1999
A-9	197,839,000	9.26	December 15, 2010
A-10	268,403,000	9.77	December 15, 2020

Interest Payment Dates: Semiannually on June 15 and December 15, commencing June 15, 1995.

Mandatory Redemptions: (1) Principal of the Series A-1, A-2, A-3, A-4, A-5, A-6, A-7, and A-8 First Mortgage Bonds is payable only on their respective final maturity dates. Principal of the Series A-9 and A-10 First Mortgage Bonds is payable in installments semiannually on each Interest Payment Date commencing June 15, 2000, and June 15, 2011, respectively. The initial average life dates for the Series A-9 and A-10 First Mortgage Bonds are as follows:

Series	Initial Average Life Date
A-9	September 4, 2006
A-10	July 5, 2015

(2) The First Mortgage Bonds are also subject to mandatory redemption upon receipt by the Partnership of casualty proceeds or eminent domain proceeds in the event that all or a portion of the Cogeneration Facility is destroyed or taken and all or a portion of the Cogeneration Facility is not capable of being rebuilt, repaired, or replaced (except when the proceeds not used for repair or replacement do not exceed $5 million and certain other requirements are met).

Optional Redemption: The First Mortgage Bonds are not subject to optional redemption prior to final maturity.

(Continued)

FIGURE 11.3   *(Continued)*

Ratings: The First Mortgage Bonds are rated "BBB−" by Standard & Poor's Corp. ("S&P"), "Baa 3" by Moody's Investors Service, Inc. ("Moody's"), and "BBB" by Fitch Investors Service, Inc.

Ranking: The First Mortgage Bonds will rank (1) pari passu in right of payment with all future additional series of first mortgage bonds, if any, and with all other present and future Senior Debt (as defined) and (2) senior in right of payment to all Subordinated Debt (as defined).

Security: The First Mortgage Bonds will be secured ratably with all other senior secured indebtedness of the Partnership (subject to the priority of payment of Working Capital Loans) by a lien on and security interest in the Collateral. The Collateral will consist of: (1) real property owned or leased by the Partnership; (2) personal property owned by the Partnership, including equipment, receivables, insurance, and other tangible and intangible assets; (3) all of the Partnership's right, title, and interest in and to all Project Contracts (as defined); (4) all of the Partnership's right, title, and interest in and to the Equity Loan Agreement; (5) all revenues of the Partnership and all Accounts established pursuant to the Disbursement Agreement; (6) all permits and other governmental approvals to the extent permitted by law; and (7) the stock of ICFC.
   The other senior secured indebtedness of the Partnership initially will be comprised of (1) the Partnership's obligations in respect of $125,010,000 of 1994 Tax-Exempt Bonds, (2) a letter of credit facility not to exceed $65 million required to satisfy certain of the Partnership's obligations under the Project Contracts; (3) a $15 million Working Capital Facility; and (4) a Debt Service Reserve Letter of Credit in an amount up to $65 million.

Nonrecourse Obligations: The obligation to make payments of principal of, premium, if any, and interest on the First Mortgage Bonds will be obligations solely of the Partnership and ICFC. None of the partners of the Partnership has any obligation with respect to the payment of the First Mortgage Bonds.

Debt Service Reserve Account: A Debt Service Reserve Account for the benefit of the holders of the First Mortgage Bonds will be established under the Disbursement Agreement. The Partnership will provide the Disbursement Agent on the Closing Date with a letter of credit in an amount of up to $65 million from a financial institution rated at least "A" by S&P and "A2" by Moody's. Drawings on the Debt Service Reserve Letter of Credit will be available on and after the Commercial Operation Date to pay principal of and interest on the First Mortgage Bonds, interest on any loans created by drawings on such Debt Service Reserve Letter of Credit, and principal of and interest on the 1994 Tax-Exempt Bonds.

Limitation on Incurrence of Additional Senior Debt: The Partnership can issue additional first mortgage bonds and incur other debt which will rank on a parity with the First Mortgage Bonds ("Senior Debt") for various purposes, including to finance a major expansion of the Cogeneration Facility, provided that after giving effect to such issuance (1) the projected average annual senior debt service coverage ratio through the final maturity date of the First Mortgage Bonds and

---

FIGURE 11.3   *(Continued)*

---

the projected minimum annual senior debt service coverage ratio through the final maturity date of the First Mortgage Bonds are at least equal to the lesser of (x) such projected ratios without giving effect to the issuance of such Senior Debt and (y) 1.45 to 1 (or in the case of Senior Debt required to complete construction of the Cogeneration Facility, 1.40 to 1) and 1.30 to 1, respectively, and (2) as a result thereof a debt ratings downgrade by any two of the specified rating agencies does not occur. The Partnership may also issue additional Senior Debt for certain limited purposes, including the financing of required modifications to the Cogeneration Facility, if, after giving effect to such issuance, the projected average annual senior debt service coverage ratio is at least 1.25 to 1 through the final maturity date of the First Mortgage Bonds.

Limitation on Partnership Distributions: Distributions may be made by the Partnership only from moneys on deposit in the Partnership Distribution Account. No distributions may be made prior to the Final Completion Date or if there is an event of default continuing under the indenture for the First Mortgage Bonds. In addition, the Partnership may not make a distribution unless (1) the average total debt service coverage ratio for the two semiannual payment periods immediately preceding the distribution date is at least 1.20 to 1 and (2) the average total debt service coverage ratio for the current semiannual payment period and the next succeeding semiannual payment period is projected to be at least 1.20 to 1. However, the Partnership may make distributions to a partner in respect of such partner's income tax liabilities, so long as the Partnership certifies that (1) the average senior debt service coverage ratio for the two semiannual payment periods immediately prior to the distribution date is at least 1.10 to 1 and (2) the average senior debt service coverage ratio for the current semiannual payment period and the next succeeding semiannual payment period is projected to be at least 1.10 to 1.

Ownership and Control Requirements: Prior to Final Completion, PG&E Enterprises, Bechtel Enterprises, and GE Capital are required to maintain their current respective ownership interests in the Partnership. In addition, while any of the First Mortgage Bonds remain outstanding, PG&E Enterprises and Bechtel Enterprises are required to maintain control of the management and operation of the Partnership and to maintain general partnership interests in the Partnership. Finally, while any of the First Mortgage Bonds remain outstanding, PG&E Enterprises, Bechtel Enterprises, and GE Capital must own partnership interests representing at least 20 percent in the aggregate of the ownership interests in the Partnership.

Other Principal Covenants: The indenture contains additional limitations on, among other things, the extent to which the Partnership may incur secured and unsecured subordinated indebtedness; grant additional liens; amend the Project Contracts; and merge, consolidate, or sell assets.

Source: Indiantown Cogeneration, L.P./Indiantown Cogeneration Funding Corporation, *Prospectus for $505,000,000 First Mortgage Bonds* (November 9, 1994), pp. 13–20.

dedicated cash reserve accounts. The Disbursement Agent controls all disbursements out of these accounts. The Disbursement Agent is responsible for ensuring that funds are spent only for purposes for which such spending is authorized and that the Partnership's cash is spent in accordance with the hierarchy set out in the indenture.[8]

The Public Offering of the 1994 Tax-Exempt Bonds

The development and initial construction of the Cogeneration Facility were funded in part through the issuance of $113 million principal amount of 1992 Tax-Exempt Bonds. They were issued for the benefit of the Partnership by the Martin County Industrial Development Authority (the "Authority"). They were refunded by two new series of fixed-rate 1994 Tax-Exempt Bonds with an aggregate principal amount of $125,010,000. One series, comprised of $113 million of bonds, was issued concurrently with the offering of the First Mortgage Bonds. The second series was issued subsequently. The 1994 Tax-Exempt Bonds are not supported by a letter of credit but instead are secured by the collateral ratably with the First Mortgage Bonds. The 1994 Tax-Exempt Bonds were issued to finance certain expenditures that qualify for tax-exempt financing. Because the interest on these bonds is exempt from income taxation, they carry a lower interest rate than First Mortgage Bonds of the same maturity would require.

Equity Commitments

The three partners committed to contribute $140 million of equity to Indiantown. This funding obligation was originally satisfied through the equity loan TIFD provided. As discussed earlier in the chapter, the Partnership applied part of the proceeds from the First Mortgage Bond issue to repay the original equity loan. The Partnership then entered into a new loan agreement with TIFD on substantially the same terms as the original loan agreement. TIFD also entered into the Equity Contribution Agreement with the Disbursement Agent. That agreement obligated it to contribute up to $140 million of equity to the Partnership by the earlier of (1) five days after completion and (2) December 1, 1996. Under certain circumstances, the equity contribution could be accelerated by the Disbursement Agent.

The sponsors of a project generally prefer to loan funds to a project during the construction period because those loans earn interest.

Lenders want to ensure that the sponsors' loans will convert to equity upon completion. More importantly, they want assurances that the equity funds will be available to repay part of *their* loans if completion does not occur. The Equity Contribution Agreement provides those protections to the holders of the First Mortgage Bonds.

Working Capital Facility

Almost every project needs a working capital loan facility. Such a facility is available to meet the project's needs for temporary working capital. The Partnership arranged a $15 million working capital facility. Drawings under this facility have a 90-day maturity. Amounts payable under the facility are secured ratably with all other senior secured indebtedness of the Partnership (i.e., the First Mortgage Bonds). In addition, working capital loans have priority over the First Mortgage Bonds and the 1994 Tax-Exempt Bonds (1) with respect to the payment of principal, interest, and fees out of available cash, and (2) with respect to their right to receive payments out of the Partnership's receivables and proceeds from the sales of final inventory in the event the Partnership's collateral is foreclosed upon.

CONCLUSION

The project financing arranged for the Indiantown Cogeneration Project illustrates that the public debt market in the United States will provide funds to a project prior to completion in those cases where the sponsors have put in place sufficiently strong contractual arrangements to support the financing. Moreover, project debt can even qualify for investment-grade ratings. I expect that the public debt market will grow in importance as a funding source, at least for project financings involving relatively low technological risk.

12

Case Study: The Tribasa Toll Road Project

I n many developing countries, there is a tremendous need for new and improved infrastructure—transportation systems (e.g., roads, railways, and airports), telecommunications systems (e.g., modern telephone networks), and utility projects (e.g., power stations, water plants, and sewage facilities). Typically, the host country is unable, or unwilling, to provide all the necessary financing itself. Some projects, such as electric power generating plants and toll roads, lend themselves to project financing. Project financing for electric power generating plants is discussed in Chapters 8 and 11. This chapter discusses toll road financing.

THE MEXICAN GOVERNMENT'S TOLL ROAD PROGRAM

Mexico has an extensive system of toll roads. Generally, they have been constructed either with public-sector funds or pursuant to public programs designed to stimulate private-sector investment. Typically, a competitive bidding process takes place, and the winner is awarded a concession to construct or improve a highway. The government grants the winning bidder a concession to finance, build or improve, operate, and maintain a highway (subject to government regulation) for a specified period of time. In return, the concession holder obtains the right to receive the toll revenues generated by the highway during the concession period.

Toll roads are typically financed in stages. The concession holder arranges short-term borrowing and makes equity contributions to finance construction. It later arranges longer-term financing secured by an assignment of the toll revenues from the concession once the highway is in operation. Concession holders must receive government approval to assign their rights under the concessions.

The Mexican government furnishes the design for the toll roads. It also monitors their construction and regulates their operation. Each concession specifies its term, the construction requirements, the toll for each category of vehicle, operating standards, maintenance reserve requirements, and concession fees payable to the government. Concessions typically provide that their terms may be lengthened if highway use falls below specified levels. Some concessions state that if actual traffic exceeds certain specified levels, either the term of the concession will be reduced or the concession holder will have to pay a portion of the toll revenues to the government. The concession holder is required to properly maintain and operate the toll road during the concession. When the concession terminates, the right to operate the highway and collect toll revenues reverts to the government. The government owns the toll road throughout the term of the concession.

The government retains the right to terminate the concession without compensation upon the occurrence of certain events. Such events include failure to pay any amounts due the government, negligence in operating the highway, failure to maintain the highway properly, and charging tolls in excess of those approved.

Tribasa's Toll Road Concessions

Several years ago, two wholly owned subsidiaries of Grupo Tribasa, S.A. de C.V. ("Grupo Tribasa"), obtained toll road concessions in Mexico. One involved the 13.9-mile Ecatepec-Pirámides toll road located near Mexico City. The other involved the 29-mile Armería-Manzanillo toll road located on the west coast of Mexico. (The two toll roads are referred to collectively as the "Tribasa Toll Roads.") These concessions entitled Grupo Tribasa to construct, operate, and maintain the two toll roads. The Pirámides toll road opened in 1965. Grupo Tribasa had operated it since 1991; its concession was initially for approximately 4 years but was later extended to 20 years. It had also operated the Manzanillo toll road since 1991; that concession was initially for approximately 9 years but was later extended to 13 years. Both concessions could be extended further if traffic volumes failed to reach certain specified targets.

A combination of contractor financing and other local sources of financing funded the construction and initial operation of both toll roads. The initial funding was refinanced in 1993 after Grupo Tribasa had successfully operated the toll roads under the concessions for a few years.

INFRASTRUCTURE FINANCING ALTERNATIVES

Financing for infrastructure projects has traditionally been obtained from several different sources:

- Government funding (grants, loans, or loan guarantees);
- Suppliers (principally construction firms and equipment suppliers);
- Bilateral and multilateral agencies (grants and loans);
- Bank credit facilities (provided the corporate or sovereign sponsor provides acceptable credit support);
- Private placements of securities with institutional investors (provided the corporate or sovereign sponsor provides acceptable credit support).

The latter two categories tend to be very sensitive not only to capital market conditions generally but also to perceptions regarding the sponsor's creditworthiness. Unfortunately, the governments of most developing nations do not have either the financial resources or sufficient creditworthiness to finance all the infrastructure projects they regard as essential. They have therefore sought to attract private-sector financing. This often takes the form of granting concessions to private entities and permitting them to borrow on the strength of the cash flow the concessions are expected to generate.

RISK CONSIDERATIONS IN FOREIGN INFRASTRUCTURE PROJECTS

Structuring a cross-border financing for a foreign infrastructure project requires the sponsors to find ways to mitigate a variety of risks. Two of these risks, currency risk and political risk, are peculiar to cross-border projects.

Currency Risk

There are at least three important aspects to currency risk: (1) the risk that the local currency will depreciate in value—for example, as the result of the host government's formally devaluing it; (2) the risk that the revenue and cost streams are currency-mismatched—for example, when the revenues are generated in a weak currency while the debt is denominated in a strong currency; and (3) the risk of inconvertibility of the local currency into another currency that is needed to pay certain expenses, such as debt service.

Devaluation increases the amount of revenue that a project must generate in order to service its debt. A significant devaluation could seriously impair a project's ability to service its debt, perhaps even triggering a default. Even without a formal devaluation, exchange rate fluctuations can potentially harm the project if the local currency depreciates in value relative to the currency in which the project's debt is denominated. Finally, even if the local currency holds its relative value, the project's sponsors will have to be able to convert sufficient local currency into the currency in which the debt is denominated in order to meet the project's debt service obligations. Exchange controls or other restrictions on the repatriation of funds could seriously impair the project's ability to service its debt.

Political Risk

Foreign projects involve certain risks that are specific to the country in which the project is located. Recent events involving Enron's Dabhol Power Project in the state of Maharashtra, in India, illustrate this problem.[1] The projects face (1) the risk that the current government may be voted out of office (or removed in some other manner) and replaced by a new government that will not be supportive of the project (which happened in Maharashtra); (2) the risk that government policy could change to the detriment of the project (even when the government does not change)—for example, by imposing foreign exchange controls, reneging on a promised tax holiday, or expropriating the project's assets; or (3) the risk that unanticipated developments, such as civil unrest or a national strike, in the host country might adversely affect the project.

Infrastructure projects often require extensive government approvals. If the government's attitude toward a project changes, the remaining permits may prove very difficult, or even impossible, to secure. Outside providers of funds will generally be very reluctant to advance any moneys until the procurement of permits has been completed.

Tax factors can be particularly important. A significant change in the local tax regime that reduces the project's after-tax cash flow stream would reduce the amount of cash flow available to service project debt. For example, the host government might decide to introduce a new excise tax that applies to the project's output. Or, the cancellation of a favorable tax treaty could adversely affect a project, perhaps by eliminating the very low rate at which withholding tax had previously been levied on distributions of dividends and interest to foreign investors.

Two other types of risk, economic risk and completion risk, can be very important in connection with an infrastructure financing.

Economic Risk

An infrastructure project, by its very nature, involves the provision of basic goods and services to the public. A project that produces a single good (such as a power plant) or provides a single service (such as a toll road) is dependent on the demand for that particular good or service. That level of demand will in turn be affected by the state of the local economy.

Some infrastructure projects do not involve contractual undertakings (from creditworthy parties or anyone else) that guarantee demand for the project's good or service. Consider toll roads. The host government is unlikely to guarantee a minimal level of usage or a minimum of toll revenue. It may agree to adjust the concession period based on the level of usage. That factor reduces the economic risk to some degree, but it provides less economic risk protection than a sound take-or-pay contract would provide.[2]

Typically, there is little, if any, reliable data on which to base financial projections in the early stages of an infrastructure project. The sponsors can arrange for ridership (or usership) studies, but how reliable are they? Lenders may therefore view lending during the construction phase of an infrastructure project as involving an unacceptably high degree of risk. An infrastructure project with a satisfactory operating history is easier to refinance than it is to finance initially.

Infrastructure projects also tend to have long useful lives. Their financing thus requires a high proportion of very long-term debt in order to enable the project both to provide the good or service at a publicly acceptable price and to comfortably service its debt. If private-sector financing is to be arranged, the private-sector entities that arrange the financing will have to own the project, or a concession to operate it, over a period long enough to enable them to fully repay the debt.

Infrastructure financing does not always permit the traditional remedies that exist when a borrower defaults. In the case of a toll road, for example, the host government may own it, so there is no asset on which the lenders can foreclose. Also, as a practical matter, the toll road cannot be moved, and the concession rights are often nontransferable.

Completion Risk

Infrastructure projects tend to be large and complex. They typically require long construction lead times. Occasionally, they also embody either a new technology or some new application of an existing technology. An existing toll road that is being refinanced involves no completion risk, technological or otherwise.

To finance construction, it is usually desirable to tap into local sources of capital to the maximum extent possible. The local financing provides some comfort to the other providers of capital concerning the merits of the project. If local capital sources won't support it, why should they? Moreover, it is essential to engage independent experts to review the capital cost estimates, the demand forecasts (price and volume), and the financial projections, and to certify their reasonableness.

TRIBASA TOLL ROAD TRUST 1 FINANCING

In November 1993, Salomon Brothers placed $110 million of 10½ percent notes due 2011 (the "Notes"). Figure 12.1 contains a summary of terms for the Notes. The Notes were issued by a single-purpose Mexican trust (the "Trust"). The obligations of the Trust were secured by the collection rights under the two toll road concessions and the toll revenues generated by them. The funds were raised in order to refinance the Tribasa Toll Roads. This financing (the "Tribasa Toll Road Trust 1 Financing") illustrates how cross-border financing can be arranged for an infrastructure project.[3] It consisted of a Eurobond offering and a simultaneous Rule 144A private placement in the United States.

Several infrastructure projects in less-developed countries have been financed through the international capital markets. The SEC's

---

FIGURE 12.1   Summary of Terms for the Tribasa Toll Road Trust 1 Notes

---

Issuer: Tribasa Toll Road Trust 1 (the "Trust").

Amount: US$110 million aggregate principal amount of Notes.

Issue Price: The Notes will be issued at 100 percent of their principal amount.

Interest: The Notes will bear interest at the rate of 10 ½ percent per annum (the "Coupon Rate"). Interest will be payable semiannually in arrears on the first business day of June and December in each year, beginning June 1, 1994.

Scheduled Final Payment: December 1, 2005 (if all payments of principal are made in accordance with the Scheduled Amortization Schedule).

Scheduled Amortization: The amount of principal that must have been paid on a cumulative basis pursuant to the Scheduled Amortization Schedule, as set forth in Table 12.1.

Contractual Maturity Date: December 1, 2011 (the date by which all outstanding principal on the Notes must be repaid).

Contractual Amortization: The minimum amount of principal that must be paid (on a cumulative basis) on or prior to each Debt Payment Date, as set forth in Table 12.1. Failure so to pay principal will result in an Event of Default.

Late Payment Premiums: To the extent that all or a portion of the Scheduled Amortization Amount remains unpaid on any Debt Payment Date after giving effect to any principal payments on such date, a "late payment premium" will begin to accrue. The late payment premium will accrue on the amount of the payment deficiency at a rate of 1 percent per annum.

Additional Amounts: Under existing law, interest payments on the Notes paid to nonresidents of Mexico are generally subject to a 15 percent Mexican withholding tax. The Trust will, subject to specified exceptions and limitations, pay such additional amounts as will result in payment to the holders of the Notes of the amounts that would otherwise have been receivable by them in respect of principal, interest, and any other payments on the Notes in the absence of such withholding.

Debt Service Reserve Fund: The Debt Service Reserve Fund will be funded with an initial deposit to the fiscal agent of $7,361,000 from the proceeds of the offering. The balance credited to the Debt Service Reserve Fund will be required to equal $11,000,000 by December 1, 1995, and will be subject to certain minimum funding levels thereafter, so long as there are Notes outstanding. If, on any Debt Payment Date, funds on deposit in the General Account are insufficient to make payments of interest or to pay the Contractual Amortization Amount, funds shall be withdrawn from the Debt Service Reserve Fund for such purpose. Funds may also be withdrawn from the Debt Service Reserve Fund to pay Scheduled Amortization Amounts if other

FIGURE 12.1 *(Continued)*

available funds are insufficient to do so, but only to the extent that funds remaining on deposit in the Debt Service Reserve Fund (after paying any such Scheduled Amortization) are at least equal to the amount of the interest payable and the Contractual Amortization Amount due on the next Debt Payment Date.

Optional Redemption: The Notes are subject to redemption, in whole, at the option of Grupo Tribasa, beginning 5 years from the date of issuance at par plus a premium equal to the excess, if any, of (1) the then present value of all remaining principal and interest payments owing on the Notes (based on the Scheduled Amortization Schedule), discounted at a rate equal to the yield to maturity on the interpolated yield on U.S. Treasury notes with a maturity approximately equal to the then-remaining weighted average life of the Notes plus 150 basis points, over (2) the principal amount of the Notes to be redeemed and, if applicable, the amount of any withholding tax.

Mandatory Redemption: The Notes are subject to mandatory redemption in whole, at par together with accrued interest to the date of the redemption, in the event that (1) the Mexican government, through no fault of Grupo Tribasa, undertakes a "statutory redemption" of both of the Tribasa Toll Roads or (2) both of the Tribasa Toll Roads become inoperable or are the subject of a "temporary appropriation," in either case for a period in excess of six months, or are substantially or totally destroyed and the insurance proceeds are insufficient to repair, replace, or reconstruct them.

A taking of only one of the Tribasa Toll Roads would not trigger a mandatory redemption of the Notes in whole. Rather, amounts received as consideration would be paid as principal, without premium, to Noteholders on the next succeeding Debt Payment Date.

Tax Redemption: The Notes may be redeemed at the option of Grupo Tribasa in whole, upon not less than 30 nor more than 60 days' notice, at par together with accrued interest to the date fixed for redemption if, as a result of any change or amendment to any applicable Mexican tax laws (or regulations or rulings promulgated thereunder) or the application, administration, or official interpretation thereof, the Trust has or will be obligated to pay additional amounts on the Notes in respect of Mexican taxes imposed at a rate of deduction or withholding in excess of 15 percent.

Blockage Events: Upon the occurrence of certain "blockage events," (1) dividends may not be paid to Grupo Tribasa, (2) the Trust will not be permitted to incur subordinated indebtedness, and (3) payments will not be permitted on any outstanding subordinated indebtedness.

Source: Tribasa Toll Road Trust 1, *Rule 144A Placement Memorandum for US$110,000,000 10 ½% Notes due 2011* (November 15, 1993), pp. 4–8.

TABLE 12.1 Amortization Schedule for the Notes

Subject to the availability of funds, principal payments in accordance with the Scheduled Amortization Schedule will commence on June 1, 1996, and the principal of the Notes will be fully repaid on December 1, 2005. The Contractual Amortization Schedule requires principal amortization to commence not later than June 1, 1997, and requires that principal of the Notes be fully repaid by December 1, 2011.

Debt Payment Date	Scheduled Amortization Principal Payment	Contractual Amortization Principal Payment
June 1, 1994	US$ 0	US$ 0
December 1, 1994	0	0
June 1, 1995	0	0
December 1, 1995	0	0
June 1, 1996	1,284,630	0
December 1, 1996	1,384,650	0
June 1, 1997	2,210,660	1,585,860
December 1, 1997	2,333,560	1,669,120
June 1, 1998	3,282,140	1,756,750
December 1, 1998	3,436,150	1,848,980
June 1, 1999	4,344,160	1,946,050
December 1, 1999	4,365,730	2,048,220
June 1, 2000	5,259,840	2,155,750
December 1, 2000	5,278,220	2,268,930
June 1, 2001	6,192,170	2,388,040
December 1, 2001	6,248,590	2,513,420
June 1, 2002	7,237,370	2,645,370
December 1, 2002	7,355,510	2,784,250
June 1, 2003	8,739,840	2,930,430
December 1, 2003	8,949,340	3,084,270
June 1, 2004	10,260,630	3,246,200
December 1, 2004	10,647,280	3,416,620
June 1, 2005	8,590,560	3,596,000
December 1, 2005	2,598,970	3,784,790
June 1, 2006	0	3,983,490
December 1, 2006	0	4,192,620
June 1, 2007	0	4,412,730
December 1, 2007	0	4,644,400
June 1, 2008	0	4,888,230
December 1, 2008	0	5,144,870
June 1, 2009	0	5,414,970
December 1, 2009	0	5,699,260
June 1, 2010	0	5,998,470
December 1, 2010	0	6,313,390
June 1, 2011	0	6,644,840
December 1, 2011	0	6,993,680
	US$110,000,000	US$110,000,000

Source: Tribasa Toll Road Trust 1, *Rule 144A Placement Memorandum for US$110,000,000 10½% Notes due 2011* (November 15, 1993), p. 43.

adoption of Rule 144A under the Securities Act of 1933 (the "1933 Act"), which established an exemption from the registration requirements of the 1933 Act, has facilitated the direct placement of securities in the United States. As discussed in more detail in Chapter 9, Rule 144A permits qualified institutional buyers (QIBs) to resell unregistered securities to other QIBs with minimal restrictions. By permitting the resale of unregistered securities, Rule 144A has created liquidity in the secondary market for private placements. This in turn has made the U.S. institutional market more attractive to foreign issuers, including sponsors of foreign projects who would like to borrow U.S. dollars on a long-term basis.

The Trust

The Grupo Tribasa subsidiaries that held the concessions contributed to the Trust their rights to collect the tolls granted under their concessions. They agreed to contribute the toll revenues they actually collect in the future, investment income the Trust earns on its assets, and any insurance proceeds received under insurance policies arranged for the toll roads.

The Dedicated Accounts

The trustee established four accounts on behalf of the Trust: (1) a general account into which toll revenues (net of value added tax (VAT)) would be deposited and out of which funds would be dispersed to cover operating expenses, debt service payments, and other authorized expenditures; (2) a government concession fee account, which would collect amounts over time so as to enable the trustee to make the annual fee payments to the Mexican government, as specified in the concessions; (3) a major maintenance account, into which funds (in pesos) would be deposited so as to be available to cover the cost of major maintenance and repairs to the toll roads; and (4) a debt service reserve fund.

The debt service reserve fund was established in the United States (with a U.S. bank serving as the fiscal agent). The debt service reserve fund holds U.S. dollar balances, which are available to pay debt service on a timely basis should the general account lack sufficient funds to cover a scheduled debt service payment. A portion of the proceeds from the Tribasa Toll Road Trust 1 Financing was used to provide the initial funding for the debt service reserve fund. Thereafter, cash remaining after the payment of the toll roads' operating and adminis-trative expenses is deposited into the debt service reserve fund, as re-quired, to bring its balance up to the minimum specified level.

The Operating Agreement

At the closing for the Note issue, the trustee entered into an operating agreement with a subsidiary of Grupo Tribasa to serve as the toll road operator (the "Operator"). The Operator is responsible for operating and maintaining the toll roads, collecting the tolls, paying the value added tax to the Mexican government, making weekly deposits into the general account, and preparing various performance reports. The Operator is paid a monthly fee. Its performance is guaranteed by Grupo Tribasa.

Allocation of Project Cash Flow

The Operator collects the toll revenues and deposits them into a spe-cial segregated account. The Operator applies the balance in the fol-lowing manner:

1. Value-added tax (VAT) is deducted. The Operator holds the VAT in a segregated account from which it is paid directly to the Mexican government.
2. Each week, the Operator transfers the toll revenues net of VAT to the general account.
3. Each month, the Operator sets aside peso funds within the general account to cover withholding tax payments.[4] The Op-erator then applies the remaining funds in the general account to (a) make the monthly deposit into the government con-cession fee account; (b) pay the administrative and operating fees and the expenses of the toll roads and the Trust; (c) if re-quired, convert peso funds to U.S. dollars and contribute the U.S. dollars to the debt service reserve fund to restore its bal-ance to the specified minimum maintenance level; and (d) if required, transfer peso funds to the major maintenance ac-count to bring its balance up to the level that an independent engineer determines is adequate to cover foreseeable mainte-nance expenditures.
4. Semiannually, funds are withdrawn from the general account and used for the following purposes, in order of priority: (a) pay

withholding taxes; (b) convert funds to U.S. dollars and transfer them to the fiscal agent who will make distributions of interest and principal to the Noteholders; (c) transfer funds to the fiscal agent, to the extent required and to the extent funds are available, if Noteholders are entitled to a late payment premium (described below); and (d) provided no event of default or of blockage (described below) exists *and* certain specified financial tests are met, make dividend distributions to Grupo Tribasa.

CREDIT ANALYSIS

The profitability of the Tribasa Toll Roads and the creditworthiness of the Notes are sensitive to the volume of traffic using the toll roads. Table 12.2 provides the base case financial projections contained in the Rule 144A placement memorandum for the Notes. These projections are based on a traffic and revenue report prepared by URS Consultants and included in the placement memorandum.

Base Case Ratios

The selected financial ratios indicate that net cash flow covers total debt service each year at least 1.40 times. Revenues available for debt service cover total debt service each year at least 1.45 times. Base case coverages at these levels would be deemed adequate.

Sensitivity Analysis

The placement memorandum contained a second set of projections, called the *reduced economic activity (REA) case*. The REA case is more conservative than the base case. It assumes that employment grows more slowly than in the base case: 0.4 percent in 1994, 0.5 percent in 1995, 0.8 percent in 1996 and 1997, and 0.7 percent each year thereafter. Thus, for example, the annual rate of employment growth varies between 2.6 percent and 3.9 percent in the region of the Pirámides toll road during the life of the concession in the base case. The range is 2.0 percent to 3.0 percent per annum in the REA case. As a result, the annual rate of traffic growth is about 1 percent slower in the REA case.

Table 12.3 compares the revenues, cash flow, and financial ratio projections for the two cases. In the REA case, inflation in Mexico is

TABLE 12.2   Base Case Financial Projections (Peso Amounts in Millions)

	1994	1995	1996	1997
Sources and Uses of Funds				
Piramides-Net Revenues(1)	54.4	60.8	68.7	78.0
Manzanillo-Net Revenues(1)	16.8	18.8	21.1	24.4
Net Revenues	71.2	79.6	89.8	102.4
O&M(2)	(10.0)	(11.1)	(12.6)	(14.3)
Insurance & Administration	(2.4)	(2.6)	(2.9)	(3.1)
Operating Cash Flow	58.8	65.8	74.4	85.0
Investment Income(3)	2.8	5.1	8.0	9.1
Revenues Available for Debt Service ("RADS")	61.6	70.9	82.3	94.0
Deposit to Major Maintenance Account(4)	(4.6)	(3.6)	(2.6)	(2.6)
Net Cash Flow ("NCF")	57.0	67.3	79.7	91.4
Interest Payments(5)	(38.9)	(38.8)	(40.1)	(40.7)
Withholding Tax Payments(6)	(2.0)	(4.4)	(7.1)	(7.2)
Scheduled Amortization Payments(7)	(0.0)	(0.0)	(9.3)	(16.6)
Total Debt Service ("TDS")	(40.9)	(43.2)	(56.5)	(64.5)
Period Cash Flow	16.2	24.1	23.2	26.9
Distribution to Grupo Tribasa(8)	0.0	0.0	0.0	24.1
Selected Account Balances				
Ending General Account ("GA") Balance	10.3	28.3	52.4	56.9
Ending General Account Balance (US$MM)	$ 3.2	$ 8.3	$ 14.8	$ 15.4
Ending DSRF Balance (US$MM)	$ 9.2	$ 11.0	$ 10.7	$ 10.3
General Account + DSRF Balance (US$MM)	$ 12.3	$ 19.3	$ 25.6	$ 25.7
Contractual Amortization (US$MM)	$ 0.0	$ 0.0	$ 0.0	$ 3.3
Selected Financial Ratios				
RADS/TDS(9)	1.51x	1.65x	1.46x	1.46x
NCF/TDS(10)	1.40x	1.56x	1.41x	1.42x
(NCF + GA)/TDS(11)	1.55x	2.43x	2.72x	3.22x
(GA + DSRF)/Outstanding Principal(12)	11.2%	17.6%	23.8%	25.0%
Macroeconomic Assumptions				
Period Inflation	7.6%	8.1%	8.9%	8.7%
Ending Ps/US$ Exchange Rate	3.25	3.39	3.53	3.69

(1) Gross Toll Revenues less value added tax and payments to the Transportation Ministry. Based on the base case contained in the Independent Engineer's Traffic and Revenue Report.
(2) Operations and Maintenance. Pursuant to the terms and conditions of the Operating Agreement, a uniform rate of 14 percent of "Net Revenues."
(3) Consists of income on the General Account, the Debt Service Reserve Fund ("DSRF"), and the Major Maintenance Account ("MMA"). Interest on the DSRF is assumed to accrue at 4 percent per annum; interest on the General Account and the MMA is assumed to accrue at an annual rate equal to the Mexican inflation rate for the period plus 3 percent for 1994–1996 and at 1 percent over the Mexican inflation rate thereafter.
(4) Based on estimates provided by the Independent Engineer.
(5) Based on the Coupon Rate of 10½ percent per annum.
(6) Based on an assumed rate of 4.9 percent for the Debt Payment Dates through and including June 1, 1995, and 15 percent thereafter.
(7) Based on the Scheduled Amortization Schedule.
(8) Based on the Restricted Payments formula.
(9) Ratio of Revenues Available for Debt Service to Total Debt Service.
(10) Ratio of Net Cash Flow to Total Debt Service.
(11) Ratio of Net Cash Flow plus beginning General Account balance to Total Debt Service.
(12) Ratio of General Account balance plus Debt Service Reserve Fund balance to outstanding principal of Notes, assuming Scheduled Amortization payments are made.

Source: Tribasa Toll Road Trust 1, *Rule 144A Placement Memorandum for US$110,000,000 10½% Notes due 2011* (November 15, 1993), p. 26.

				Period Ended					
1998	**1999**	**2000**	**2001**	**2002**	**2003**	**2005**	**2007**	**2009**	**2011**
88.5	100.0	112.2	126.4	142.6	160.0	201.6	252.8	316.3	395.1
27.7	31.3	35.2	40.1	44.9	51.0	1.2	0.0	0.0	0.0
116.2	131.3	147.4	166.5	187.5	211.0	202.8	252.8	316.3	395.1
(16.3)	(18.4)	(20.6)	(23.3)	(26.3)	(29.5)	(28.4)	--	--	--
(3.4)	(3.7)	(4.0)	(4.3)	(4.7)	(5.1)	(6.0)	--	--	--
96.6	109.2	122.8	138.9	156.6	176.4	168.4	--	--	--
9.4	9.6	9.5	9.2	8.5	6.9	5.8	--	--	--
105.9	118.9	132.3	148.1	165.0	183.3	174.2	--	--	--
(2.8)	(3.1)	(4.2)	(4.5)	(4.9)	(3.9)	(2.5)	--	--	--
103.1	115.8	128.1	143.6	160.1	179.3	171.7	--	--	--
(40.5)	(39.3)	(37.0)	(33.6)	(28.8)	(22.5)	(3.7)	--	--	--
(7.1)	(6.9)	(6.5)	(5.9)	(5.1)	(4.0)	(0.7)	--	--	--
(25.6)	(34.7)	(43.8)	(54.0)	(66.0)	(83.5)	(57.2)	--	--	--
(73.3)	(80.9)	(87.3)	(93.4)	(100.0)	(110.0)	(61.5)	--	--	--
29.8	34.9	40.8	50.1	60.2	69.4	110.2	--	--	--
33.6	41.2	49.7	62.1	75.7	66.8	165.6	--	--	--
55.6	48.3	37.7	24.0	5.0	4.7	0.0	--	--	--
$ 14.4	$ 12.0	$ 9.0	$ 5.5	$ 1.1	$ 1.0	$ 0.0	--	--	--
$ 9.6	$ 9.8	$ 10.2	$ 10.6	$ 11.4	$ 11.9	$ 0.0	--	--	--
$ 24.0	$ 21.8	$ 19.2	$ 16.1	$ 12.4	$ 12.9	$ 0.0	--	--	--
$ 3.6	$ 4.0	$ 4.4	$ 4.9	$ 5.4	$ 6.0	$ 7.4	$ 9.1	$ 11.1	$ 13.6
1.45x	1.47x	1.51x	1.58x	1.65x	1.67x	4.01x	--	--	--
1.41x	1.43x	1.47x	1.54x	1.60x	1.63x	3.95x	--	--	--
3.05x	2.92x	2.71x	2.52x	2.24x	1.77x	4.28x	--	--	--
25.0%	25.0%	25.0%	25.0%	25.0%	40.3%	--	--	--	--
8.5%	8.5%	8.5%	8.5%	8.5%	8.5%	8.5%	8.5%	8.5%	8.5%
3.86	4.03	4.20	4.38	4.57	4.77	5.19	5.65	6.15	6.69

greater and the peso devalues more rapidly (relative to the dollar). Revenues are greater in the REA case because higher inflation more than offsets the lower traffic volumes. But the faster devaluation of the peso increases the amount of pesos that must be set aside to service the Notes. As a result, the coverages are somewhat lower in the REA case.

Prospective investors would undoubtedly perform additional sensitivity analyses. For example, they might want to "stress-test" the adequacy of the debt service reserve fund by testing how large a peso devaluation the credit support arrangements for the Notes could withstand. They would also carefully evaluate all the other risk minimization features that would help provide credit support for the Notes.

TABLE 12.3 Results of Sensitivity Analysis (Peso Amounts in Millions)

	Period Ended													
	1994	1995	1996	1997	1998	1999	2000	2001	2002	2003	2005	2007	2009	2011
Revenues														
Base Case	71.2	79.6	89.8	102.4	116.2	131.3	147.4	166.5	187.5	211.0	202.8	252.8	316.3	395.1
REA Case	71.2	82.1	95.3	109.7	126.6	145.1	164.4	185.1	208.3	235.2	224.9	281.6	352.2	440.4
Revenues Available for Debt Service (RADS)														
Base Case	61.6	70.9	82.3	94.0	105.9	118.9	132.3	148.1	165.0	183.3	174.2	--	--	--
REA Case	62.3	74.0	88.2	102.6	119.0	133.1	149.1	166.1	184.4	204.5	192.9	--	--	--
Net Cash Flow (NCF)														
Base Case	57.0	67.3	79.7	91.4	103.1	115.8	128.1	143.6	160.1	179.3	171.7	--	--	--
REA Case	57.6	70.2	85.3	99.7	115.7	129.4	144.1	160.6	178.3	199.6	189.6	--	--	--
Total Debt Service (TDS)														
Base Case	40.9	43.2	56.5	64.5	73.3	80.9	87.3	93.4	100.0	110.0	61.5	--	--	--
REA Case	42.7	47.3	63.9	75.1	87.8	98.5	107.7	116.9	126.8	141.4	81.1	--	--	--
RADS/TDS														
Base Case	1.51x	1.65x	1.46x	1.46x	1.45x	1.47x	1.51x	1.58x	1.65x	1.67x	4.01x	--	--	--
REA Case	1.46	1.57	1.38	1.37	1.36	1.35	1.38	1.42	1.45	1.45	3.36	--	--	--
NCF/TDS														
Base Case	1.40	1.56	1.41	1.42	1.41	1.43	1.47	1.54	1.60	1.63	3.95	--	--	--
REA Case	1.35	1.49	1.33	1.33	1.32	1.31	1.34	1.37	1.41	1.41	3.30	--	--	--
(NCF + GA)/TDS														
Base Case	1.55	2.43	2.72	3.22	3.05	2.92	2.71	2.52	2.24	1.77	4.28	--	--	--
REA Case	1.47	2.20	2.37	2.86	3.01	2.78	2.55	2.33	2.02	1.53	3.56	--	--	--
(GA + DSRF)/Outstanding Principal														
Base Case	11.2%	17.6%	23.8%	25.0%	25.0%	25.0%	25.0%	25.0%	25.0%	40.3%	--	--	--	--
REA Case	10.6	16.1	21.0	26.6	25.0	25.0	25.0	25.0	25.0	40.1	--	--	--	--

Source: Tribasa Toll Road Trust 1, *Rule 144A Placement Memorandum for US$110,000,000 10¹/₂% Notes due 2011* (November 15, 1993), pp. 26–27.

RISK MINIMIZATION FEATURES

The credit support structure crafted for the Tribasa Toll Road Trust 1 Financing included several features that were designed to limit the Noteholders' exposure to project risks.

Dual Debt Amortization Schedule

The debt amortization structure consisted of two separate debt repayment schedules. The Notes are scheduled to mature in 2011. A *contractual amortization schedule* specifies a series of debt repayments that would retire the entire issue of Notes by 2011. If the Trust fails to repay principal in accordance with this schedule, there is an event of default under the terms of the Notes. Such an event permits the Noteholders to accelerate the maturity of the Notes. They can also terminate the Operator. When the Trust is in default, dividend distributions to Grupo Tribasa are prohibited.

There is also a faster *contingent amortization schedule.* If the Trust is able to repay the Notes according to this more accelerated repayment schedule, the Notes will be fully repaid by 2005. Failure to repay principal in accordance with the contingent amortization schedule does not constitute an event of default. However, two remedies are required. Dividend distributions to Grupo Tribasa are prohibited, and the Trust must pay Noteholders a *late payment premium.* This premium is equal to 1 percent per annum on all unpaid contingent amortization amounts. Thus, failure to make the full contingent amortization payments both penalizes the equity investors and increases the amount of interest payable on the Notes, to compensate Noteholders for the slower return of their capital.

The dual debt amortization structure allows for the variability of the project's toll revenue stream. Suppose the project's cash flows fall below what is required to meet the contingent amortization schedule but are adequate to meet the contractual amortization schedule. There is no default, but lenders are compensated by the late payment premium until the repayment shortfall is eliminated. At the same time, the prohibition on dividend distributions to Grupo Tribasa traps within the Trust funds that might otherwise be paid out as dividends. This reduces the Noteholders' agency costs; it gives Grupo Tribasa, which serves as both Operator and equity investor, incentives to operate the toll roads as efficiently as possible so as to enable the Trust to meet the contingent amortization schedule.

Debt Service Reserve Fund

Devaluation is usually a concern when a project in a developing country borrows funds denominated in a major currency. The debt service reserve fund was designed to mitigate this risk. The reserve fund is maintained in the United States in U.S. dollars (rather than pesos) in order to eliminate the reserve fund's exposure to foreign exchange risk. To the extent the debt service reserve fund falls below the specified minimum in any month, pesos (to the extent available) from the general account must be converted to U.S. dollars and remitted to the debt service reserve fund. Moneys in the debt service reserve fund are available to pay debt service on the Notes in the event the funds available in the general account are inadequate—for example, as a result of a peso devaluation.

Limitations on Dividend Distributions

Dividend distributions are permitted (semiannually) only under the following circumstances: (1) all senior cash payment obligations have been met, as described above; (2) one month's operating and administrative expenses have been provided; (3) no event of default or of blockage (defined below) has occurred and is continuing; (4) the ratio of net cash flow to scheduled debt service for the immediately preceding four semiannual periods has satisfied specified tests; and (5) the amounts in the debt service reserve fund and the other accounts (taken collectively) exceed a specified minimum. If all these conditions are satisfied, the aforementioned excess aggregate account balance is available for distribution.

A limitation on dividend distributions is frequently found in corporate loan agreements in the United States. Dividends reduce liquidity and equity; thus, they reduce the protection that liquid assets and equity afford lenders. The limitation is designed to prevent dividend distributions that might jeopardize the Trust's liquidity or impair the Noteholders' senior position. The Trust is permitted to pay dividends only to the extent it truly has excess cash.

The financing structure also specifies certain *blockage events*. Such events include nonpayment of scheduled amortization, an insufficient debt service reserve fund amount, an inadequate major maintenance account balance, bankruptcy of a concession holder, a breach of either the trust agreement or the operating agreement, or impairment of either concession. The provision for blockage events gives the Noteholders four basic remedies (but not acceleration). So long as a blockage event occurs and is continuing: (1) dividend distributions are prohibited, (2) subordinated debt cannot be incurred, (3) payments to subordinated lenders are prohibited, and (4) the frequency with which certain deposits must be made to accounts maintained for the benefit of the Noteholders is increased.

Blockage events trigger remedies that are designed to protect the Noteholders without giving rise to an event of default and the drastic consequences that would result. This is sensible because, although an event of default would trigger acceleration of the Notes, the Noteholders' remedies are limited. The toll roads belong to the government, and the Noteholders (or their representative) cannot foreclose on the concessions and sell them. Also, the Notes are nonrecourse to Grupo Tribasa.

Construction and Technology Risk

Noteholders had no exposure to completion risk because both toll roads were operational. In addition, each toll road had a lengthy, well-documented operating history, which limited the Noteholders' economic risk exposure.

Detailed Traffic Report

Economic risk is a critically important consideration in connection with almost any project. It can be particularly vexing for an infrastructure project. What will be the number of users? What price will they be willing to pay for the good or service?

Mexican toll roads pose a special problem. Toll roads in Mexico are superior to other roadway alternatives. However, they are not exclusive routes. They are used primarily by commercial and tourist traffic. This feature makes them especially sensitive to economic factors (e.g., in contrast to water usage). Moreover, the granting of a toll road concession in Mexico is conditioned on the existence of a competing transportation route (i.e., a non-toll-road alternative).

Grupo Tribasa commissioned a detailed traffic report, which it included in the placement memorandum for the Notes. The traffic report enabled prospective purchasers of the Notes to quantify the economic risks of the toll roads, and therefore the credit risks of the Notes. The traffic report provided a detailed operating history of the toll roads. It also analyzed the business and financial prospects of the two toll roads. Such a report must be thorough, and it must be prepared by independent experts. The thoroughness and overall quality of such a report can significantly affect the willingness of outside investors and lenders to advance funds to a project. The quality of the detailed traffic report prepared in connection with the Tribasa Toll Road Trust 1 Financing seems to have been an important consideration to prospective purchasers of the Notes.[5]

Amendments to the Terms of the Concessions

The Mexican government has agreed to revise the terms of various concessions to improve their capacity to support outside financing. The terms of the Grupo Tribasa concessions were amended and supplemented to permit toll increases and to allow for transferability of revenues. Also, as noted above, the terms of both concessions were extended.

Tax Arrangements

First, the Operator transfers cash to the general account net of VAT. (The Operator is obligated to make the VAT payments to the Mexican government.) Second, a separate government concession fee account has been established. Funds are deposited monthly from the general account. Third, peso funds are set aside monthly in the general account, for the payment of withholding taxes due the Mexican government. The withholding tax is levied on interest payments on the Notes. However, the Trust is required under the terms of the Notes to "gross-up" the interest payments to the Noteholders to fully cover any withholding taxes. The Noteholders are therefore protected against increases in withholding taxes.[6]

Ability to Remove the Operator

The trustee of the Trust can remove the Operator, insist on toll increases, or demand operating changes if an event of default occurs. This power reduces the Noteholders' agency costs. If the Operator mismanages the toll roads, it can be removed. In that case, its flow of operating fees ceases.

Insurance

The Trust arranged suitable business interruption insurance and property and liability insurance. Provision was made to pay the insurance premiums out of operating cash flow, and the Operator guaranteed payment of the specified deductibles. An independent engineer was engaged to regularly examine each toll road and ensure that both toll roads are properly maintained. Proper maintenance reduces the likelihood that situations might occur that would give rise to an insurance liability (e.g., poor road conditions causing, or contributing to the severity of, a serious accident).

Trust Structure

The trust structure was employed to insulate the Noteholders from bankruptcy risk associated with Grupo Tribasa or its subsidiaries that hold the concessions.

CONCLUSION

The Tribasa Toll Road Trust 1 Financing illustrates the types of contractual and other credit support arrangements that must be put in place to enable an infrastructure project to obtain financing in the international capital market. More importantly, it demonstrates that capital is available for such projects. That fact is encouraging because of the enormous need for infrastructure development—but the very limited local financing capacity—that exists in so many developing countries.

13

Case Study: The Euro Disneyland Project

Project sponsors need to address two basic questions early in the planning stages for a project:

1. Should one or more separate legal entities be established to finance, construct, own, and operate the project, and if so, how should each be organized?
2. What credit support arrangements will have to be put in place in order to attract the required capital?

The Euro Disneyland Case Study illustrates how one major corporation addressed these issues, how financially restructuring a project can reallocate risk to other project participants and away from the original sponsor, and how the sponsor can derive benefits from this risk reallocation.

INTRODUCTION

Euro Disneyland would introduce to Europe a theme park and resort concept that The Walt Disney Company ("Disney") had developed—and seemingly perfected—in the United States and Japan over the

This case study is based on Bruner and Langohr (1994) and Euro Disney S.C.A. (1990, 1993, 1994a, 1994b).

preceding 35 years. The first phase of the project (the "Euro Disneyland Project") has been completed; other stages are scheduled to be completed through 2011.

The complex financing structure Disney devised for the Euro Disneyland Project ultimately proved to be too highly leveraged. The high leverage created significant financial risk for a company that turned out to have relatively high operating risk. The financial success of the project depended importantly on the project entity's being able to develop and sell substantial real estate holdings at a significant profit in order to generate cash to pay down debt to a sustainable level. However, the real estate boom in France ended abruptly— principally because of a severe recession in Europe and an increase in interest rates.

At the time the project financing was arranged, it was viewed very favorably. One article assessing Disney's arrangement with the French government concluded that the Euro Disneyland Project will be "profitable. And . . . the wealth will be shared."[1] A second article praised the structure and indicated that Disney had applied all the lessons it had learned from its other three theme parks in California, Florida, and Tokyo.[2] In 1989, it seemed that Disney was well on its way to a huge success.

PROJECT DESCRIPTION

Disney planned to build the theme park and resort on approximately 4,800 acres of land located 32 kilometers due east of Paris. Disney chose this site based on availability, communications, and proximity to potential customers, after considering more than 200 possible sites in France and Spain. Approximately 17 million people lived within a 2-hour drive. More than 100 million lived within a 6-hour drive. About half of the developable land, 2,115 acres, would be devoted to entertainment and resort facilities. Another 1,994 acres would be set aside for retail, commercial, industrial, and residential purposes. The balance of 691 acres would be used for regional and primary infrastructure, such as roads and railway tracks.

Upon completion, Euro Disneyland would be the largest theme park and resort development in Europe. It would be ideally situated at the hub of a vast transportation network. Euro Disneyland would be linked to Paris by the RER (regional express metro) suburban railroad system. It would be linked to the rest of France and Europe by the A4 motorway, and, in June 1994, by the high-speed *train à grande vitesse* (TGV) railroad network.

The project would feature two separate theme parks. It would be built in phases. Phase I would include the Magic Kingdom theme park, which would be modeled after similar theme parks in the United States and Japan; six hotels; an entertainment center; the Davy Crockett Campground; and related infrastructure and amenities. Phase IA would consist of the initial investment in the Magic Kingdom theme park, the Magic Kingdom Hotel, and peripheral development. Disney planned to complete Phase IA and open the Magic Kingdom in April 1992. Disney expected Phase IA to cost FF14 billion.[3] Phase II would include a second theme park, the Disney MGM Studios Europe, based on Disney's MGM Studios theme park in Florida; additional hotel development; a water recreation facility; offices; and industrial, retail, and residential developments.

Disney planned to build a comprehensive resort facility containing more than 20 hotels (with 18,200 rooms). It would have six hotels (with 5,200 rooms) ready by 1992 when the Magic Kingdom would open. The other hotels would be added over a 20-year period. The resort facility would eventually include two golf courses, a water recreation area, campgrounds with 2,100 sites, and a large retail and entertainment complex. Disney's plans also included commercial development consisting of single- and multifamily residences, time-share apartments, more than 7.5 million square feet of office space, more than 8 million square feet of industrial space, and more than 1 million square feet of retail space.

DISNEY

Disney is a diversified entertainment company with headquarters in Burbank, California. Disney's operations fall into three principal segments: (1) the theme parks and resorts segment generated roughly 40 percent of the $8.5 billion in total revenue and 43 percent of the $1.7 billion in total operating income in 1993; (2) the filmed entertainment segment accounted for 43 percent of revenues and 36 percent of operating income in 1993; and (3) the consumer products segment accounted for the remaining 17 percent of revenues and 21 percent of operating income. Disney is acknowledged as the world's leading theme park operator.

In the 1980s, Disney management had set a 20 percent growth target for the company. Expansion of theme park operations was an integral part of the strategy Disney had implemented to achieve that goal. With a well-penetrated American market, Disney realized that international expansion was necessary to achieve the growth target. The first international expansion took place in Asia; the Tokyo Disneyland theme park opened in 1983. The project was successful from the outset. This success prompted Disney to investigate other opportunities for international expansion. With the European Union taking shape, Europe seemed like an ideal site.

PROJECT OWNERSHIP STRUCTURE

The original plan called for Disney to build, own, and operate the Euro Disneyland Project in a manner similar to its operation of Walt Disney World (Disney's Florida theme park) and Disneyland in Southern California. This ownership arrangement would ensure Disney 100 percent of the future earnings potential of the park. Disney management was determined not to repeat two mistakes of years past: (1) letting others build the lucrative hotels near the park, as happened at Disneyland in Southern California, and (2) allowing another company to own a Disney theme park, as occurred in Tokyo (where Disney only collects royalties from the immensely profitable attraction). Although the ownership structure would enable Disney to retain 100 percent of the upside potential, it would also leave Disney with 100 percent of the risks inherent in such a tremendous financial undertaking. Disney's then-current management had transformed Disney from a company with $1 billion of revenues into one with annual revenues of $3.4 billion (in 1988), mainly through internal growth. The corporate managers felt they could find a more advantageous way to structure the project.

Financial projections indicated expected profitability from the first year of operations (1992) amounting to approximately FF204 million on theme park revenues of FF4.25 billion and total revenues of FF5.48 billion.[4] Net income was expected to reach FF972 million on total revenues of FF10.93 billion in 1995. For the year 2001, Disney projected total revenues of FF22.43 billion and net profit of FF1.76 billion. With such impressive profit expectations, it seemed inconceivable that Disney would want to bring additional participants into the project. However, under the agreement Disney negotiated with the French government—the Agreement on the Creation and the Operation of Euro Disneyland en France (the "Master Agreement")—Disney was required to sell a majority stake in the project entity to European investors in order to "share the wealth."

In the spring of 1989, Disney set in motion a series of transactions that altered the ownership, management, financing, and control of the Euro Disneyland Project. Figure 13.1 illustrates the resulting ownership structure. Disney reduced its 100 percent equity interest in the project to 49 percent. The transactions initiated in the spring of 1989 would also reimburse Disney for FF1.9 billion of project development costs, increase the project's leverage substantially, and result in the public offering of common stock by a company that had never earned any revenues. The change in project structure was made in part in response to the French government's request, but limiting the risk exposure of Disney's shareholders was undoubtedly another important consideration.

Project Entities

The primary participants alongside Disney included a bank consortium (consisting of about 60 banks), the French government, other creditors, and public shareholders. Ownership, however, was limited to two French "owner companies" provided for in the Master Agreement.

1. *Euro Disneyland S.C.A.* (EDSCA), one of the two owner companies, is organized as a *société en commandité par actions* (S.C.A.), which is very similar to a limited partnership. Disney would own 49 percent of EDSCA. The remaining 51 percent would be held by European investors after the public offering. EDSCA's principal corporate purpose would be to develop and operate the Euro Disneyland Project complex. EDSCA would be managed by its *gérant*.
2. *Euro Disney S.A.* (EDSA), a *gérant* or management company, was established as a wholly owned subsidiary of Disney. EDSA manages, but has no ownership interest in, EDSCA. Its sole responsibility is to manage EDSCA in that company's "best interest." EDSA would have, for the most part, broad discretion in managing the day-to-day affairs of the Euro Disneyland Project. EDSA would initially receive a base fee

FIGURE 13.1   Ownership Structure for the Euro Disneyland Project

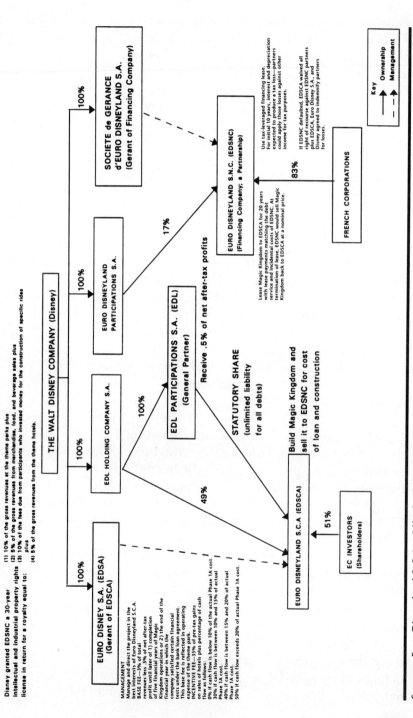

Disney granted EDSNC a 30-year intellectual and industrial property rights license in return for a royalty equal to:

(1) 10% of the gross revenues at the theme parks plus
(2) 5% of the gross revenues from merchandise, food, and beverage sales plus
(3) 10% of the fees due from participants who invested money for the construction of specific rides plus
(4) 5% of the gross revenues from the theme hotels.

THE WALT DISNEY COMPANY (Disney)

100%

EURO DISNEY S.A. (EDSA)
(Gerant of EDSCA)

100%

EDL HOLDING COMPANY S.A.

100%

EURO DISNEYLAND PARTICIPATIONS S.A.

100%

SOCIETE de GERANCE d'EURO DISNEYLAND S.A.
(Gerant of Financing Company)

MANAGEMENT
Manage and direct the project in the best interests of Euro Disneyland S.C.A.
BASE FEE—3% of total revenues less .5% of net after-tax profit until later of 1) completion of five financial years of Magic Kingdom operations or 2) the end of the financial year in which the company satisfied certain financial tests under the bank loan agreement. This base fee is reflected in operating expense of the theme park.
INCENTIVE FEE—35% of pre-tax gains on sales of hotels plus percentage of cash flow as follows:
0% if cash flow is below 10% of the actual Phase 1A cost.
30% if cash flow is between 10% and 15% of actual Phase 1A cost.
40% if cash flow is between 15% and 20% of actual Phase 1A cost.
50% if cash flow exceeds 20% of actual Phase 1A cost.

EDL PARTICIPATIONS S.A. (EDL)
(General Partner)

100%

Receive .5% of net after-tax profits

17%

STATUTORY SHARE
(unlimited liability for all debts)

EURO DISNEYLAND S.N.C. (EDSNC)
(Financing Company; a Partnership)

Build Magic Kingdom and sell it to EDSNC for cost of loan and construction

49%

Lease Magic Kingdom to EDSCA for 20 years with lease payments matching the debt service and incidental costs of EDSNC. At termination of lease, EDSNC would sell Magic Kingdom back to EDSCA at a nominal price.

Use tax-leveraged financing lease. For initial 10 years, interest and depreciation expected to produce a tax loss—partners could apply those losses against other income for tax purposes.

83%

FRENCH CORPORATIONS

If EDSNC defaulted, EDSCA waived all right of recourse against EDSNC partners plus EDSCA, Euro Disney S.A., and Disney agreed to indemnify partners for losses.

EURO DISNEYLAND S.C.A (EDSCA)

51%

EC INVESTORS
(Shareholders)

Key
——▶ Ownership
- - -▶ Management

Sources: Euro Disneyland S.C.A., *Offer for Sale of 10,691,000 Shares* (October 5, 1989), p. 53, and Bruner and Langohr (1994), p. 742.

261

equal to 3 percent of EDSCA's total annual revenues, less 0.5 percent of EDSCA's net after-tax profits. This arrangement would continue until the later of (1) the Magic Kingdom's completion of its fifth year of operation or (2) the end of the fiscal year in which EDSCA satisfied certain financial tests specified in its bank loan agreement. Thereafter, the base fee would increase to 6 percent of annual revenues less 0.5 percent of EDSCA's net after-tax profits. EDSA would also receive a management incentive fee equal to 35 percent of any pretax gains realized on the sale of hotels, and a varying percentage of EDSCA's pretax cash flow.[5]

    3.   *Euro Disneyland S.N.C.* (EDSNC), a *société en nom collectif,* was to serve essentially as a financing company. It would finance the cost of the Magic Kingdom through a tax-advantaged leveraged lease. Structured as a specialized limited-purpose partnership, it would own the Euro Disneyland theme park. EDSCA would build the park and then sell it to EDSNC at the cost of the land and construction. EDSNC would borrow the funds to pay the purchase price. It would then lease the Magic Kingdom back to EDSCA for 20 years. The lease payments would be designed to cover EDSNC's debt service payment obligations and other expenses. After 20 years, assuming EDSNC had fully repaid its debt obligations, EDSNC would sell the park back to EDSCA at a predetermined nominal price. EDSNC would then dissolve.

    EDSNC is the second owner company, managed by its *gérant,* which is also a wholly owned subsidiary of Disney. Disney would initially own 17 percent of EDSNC, with the remaining 83 percent owned by certain French corporations. The structure chosen for EDSNC would enable the tax losses anticipated during the early years of Euro Disneyland's operation (resulting principally from the interest and depreciation tax deductions) to be channeled to the French corporations, which would be able to utilize them to shelter other taxable income. Disney expected EDSNC to realize losses for income tax purposes for roughly the first 10 years of its existence.

    The partners of EDSNC are legally liable for EDSNC's debt. However, EDSCA waived any right of recourse against the partners should EDSNC default. Moreover, Disney, EDSCA, and Euro Disneyland Participations agreed to indemnify the partners for any liabilities they might incur if EDSNC defaulted.

    4.   In addition to European shareholders, other participants include the supervisory board, or *conseil de surveillance,* and *EDL Participations S.A.* (EDL). The *conseil de surveillance* is assigned to monitor the general affairs and management of EDSCA, report on

the performance of its *gérant,* approve contracts between the *gérant* and EDSCA, and prepare an annual report. The shareholders of EDSCA, or *associés commanditaires,* can elect the members of the supervisory board and approve the annual accounts and dividend payments. They have no liability for the debts of EDSCA. Interestingly, the supervisory board was not given the power to remove the *gérant* or to force it to act on any particular matter in any particular way. By design, the outside shareholders would hold a majority stake but lack control.

EDL, an indirect wholly owned subsidiary of Disney, would serve as the general partner of EDSCA. As general partner, it would have unlimited liability for all of EDSCA's debt and other liabilities. EDL's immediate parent, *EDL Holding Company S.A.* (EDL Holding), a French *société anonyme* and a wholly owned subsidiary of Disney, would own the 49 percent of the shares of EDSCA not held by the public. EDL would receive 0.5 percent of EDSCA's net after-tax profits each year. It could not be removed as general partner of EDSCA without its consent. It could not dispose of its general partnership interest in EDSCA without the approval of holders of a majority of EDSCA's shares.

MASTER AGREEMENT WITH THE FRENCH GOVERNMENT

The French government played a significant role in Euro Disneyland's development. Disney and the French government signed the Master Agreement in February 1988. The French government agreed to:

- Provide 1,665 hectares of land for the theme park resort and for commercial and residential development. The land would be sold to Euro Disneyland at a fixed price based on (1) the price of raw agricultural land in 1971, or approximately FF111,000 per hectare, plus (2) the cost of direct and indirect infrastructure (other than roads and railways) and (3) certain overhead charges.[6] At the time, raw land zoned for commercial uses in the Île-de-France region was selling at prices ranging from FF170,000 to FF210,000 per hectare (see Bruner and Langohr, 1994, p. 737). EDSCA would have 20 years to complete the land purchases at the quoted fixed price.
- Finance, construct, and operate a 20-km extension of the Paris suburban railroad. The extension would provide direct access to the gates of the Magic Kingdom from central Paris. As part of

the extension, the French government would build two railroad stations, a car park, and a bus station.

- Finance and construct two junctions to link a major highway, the A4 motorway, with Euro Disneyland.
- Contribute FF200 million, which would cover part of the cost of constructing secondary roads.
- Provide up to FF4.8 billion in loans at a fixed annual rate of 7.85 percent.[7] The loans would mature in 20 years with amortization beginning in the sixth year.
- Apply the lowest rate of value added tax (VAT), 5.5 percent, to all consumer products sold at Euro Disneyland.[8]

In addition to the undertakings contained in the Master Agreement, the French government agreed to:

- Provide high-speed TGV train service to Euro Disneyland starting in June 1994.
- Allow EDSNC to depreciate Magic Kingdom assets over a 10-year period, rather than the usual 20-year period.

Analysts estimated that the entire package of concessions from the French government was worth between FF3.3 billion and FF6 billion, or roughly the equivalent of $54,000 to $98,000 for each new job the project would create (see Bruner and Langohr, 1994, p. 737).

In signing the Master Agreement, Disney agreed on behalf of EDSCA and EDSNC to:

- Open the Magic Kingdom by April 1992.
- Guarantee a minimum of 9.13 million one-way journeys each year on the suburban rail system, for a period of 5 years after opening.[9]
- Pay FF45 million for utility and electrical networks.
- Guarantee a minimum amount of tax revenue to Seine-et-Marne.[10]
- Encourage share ownership in EDSCA by European Economic Community nationals.
- Use French and other European Economic Community contractors and suppliers.
- Include at least one attraction in the Magic Kingdom depicting French and European civilization.

- Refrain from opening or licensing another theme park within 800 km of Euro Disneyland for 5 years after opening the Magic Kingdom.
- Hold at least 17 percent of the shares of EDSCA and EDSNC until the fifth anniversary of opening day.

PROJECT FINANCING

The project financing transactions initiated in the spring of 1989 transformed the Euro Disneyland Project from an internally financed and privately owned project to a highly leveraged and publicly owned entity in which Disney would hold a minority interest. However, although Disney would hold only a minority interest in the equity of the project, it would still control the construction and operation of the theme park and would have the right to own and control the development of the hotels and other real estate.

The project financing would introduce many additional stakeholders into the Euro Disneyland Project through a two-stage process. The first stage would involve a private placement of common shares and debt securities called *Obligations Remboursables en Actions* (ORAs) to four investor banks and EDL Holding. EDL Holding would serve as the shareholder of record for Disney's 49 percent stake in the new company. The second stage of this process involved EDSCA's initial public offering (IPO). The IPO would result in 50.5 percent of the shares being sold to the investing public. (The remaining 0.5 percent would be retained by the original four investor banks, as discussed below.)

Phase IA of the Euro Disneyland Project initially had a projected capital cost of FF14 billion. The projected sources of these funds, in millions of French francs, are shown in the following summary:

	EDSNC	EDSCA	Total
Bank loans	FF 4,300	FF 200	FF 4,500
Government loans	3,000	1,800	4,800
EDSNC equity	2,000	—	2,000
EDSCA equity	1,000*	1,700	2,700
Total	FF10,300	FF3,700	FF14,000

*EDSCA invested this amount in EDSNC.

The equity portion of the project financing would take place in two stages, as reflected in Table 13.1:

1. *Sale of Shares and ORAs in March 1989.* EDSCA arranged for four banks—Banque Indosuez, Banque Nationale de Paris, S.G. Warburg & Company, and Caisse Nationale de Crédit Agricole—to purchase a total of 510,000 shares of stock at FF15 per share. At the same time, EDL Holding bought 465,000 shares at FF10 per share. The four banks and EDL Holding also purchased ORAs issued by EDSCA; the banks' ORAs would be repaid from the proceeds of EDSCA's IPO, and EDL Holding's ORAs would be converted into shares of EDSCA.
2. *IPO by EDSCA in October 1989.* The IPO was expected to raise net proceeds of FF5.73billion. Following the IPO, EDSCA would have 170 million shares outstanding.

Disney's net cash investment in EDSCA would be approximately FF833 million, consisting of: (1) FF250,000 for 25,000 shares in 1985; (2) FF4,650,000 for 465,000 shares in March 1989; and (3) FF828.1 million for the ORAs, also in March 1989. After the IPO, EDSCA's total assets would be FF9.3 billion.

Leverage

Based on the pro forma financial statements presented in Table 13.1, the expected total assets of EDSCA at September 30, 1989, would amount to FF4,832,596,000. Liabilities and shareholders' equity would consist of FF2,691,762,000 of liabilities and FF2,140,834,000 of equity. This debt–equity mix would imply a debt-to-equity ratio of 126 percent. Assuming the exercise of the outstanding options and warrants and a successful IPO by EDSCA, equity would increase to FF6,577,984,000. This increase in equity would reduce the debt-to-equity ratio to approximately 41 percent. However, Disney projected that the debt-to-equity ratio would subsequently increase to approximately 200 percent by 1994, just prior to completion of Phase 1A of the Euro Disneyland Project. EDSCA felt it could justify this level of debt based on its expectation that it would be able to develop the hotel real estate, sell it at a substantial profit, and use the proceeds to pay down debt. However, as we now know, this strategy was not successful because of the collapse in the real estate market, and the degree of leverage proved to be excessive.

TABLE 13.1 Pro Forma Balance Sheet of EDSCA as of September 30, 1989 (Thousands of French Francs)

	Actual (Dec. 31, 1988)	Pro Forma Adjustments	Expected (Sept. 30, 1989)	Pro Forma Adjustments	Pro Forma (Sept. 30, 1989)
Assets					
Intangible assets	0	8,644[a]	8,644		8,644
Tangible assets	0	475,630[a]	475,630		475,630
Deposits	0	4,232[a]	4,232		4,232
Total fixed assets	0		488,506		488,506
Construction in progress	0	1,748,653[a]	1,748,653		1,748,653
Current assets:					
Accounts receivable	0	761,994[a]	761,994		761,994
Cash and investments	251	(1,010,518)[a] 2,133,250[b]	1,122,983	(1,292,850)[c] 5,730,000[e]	5,560,133
Total current assets	251		1,884,977		6,322,127
Deferred charges	0	710,460[a]	710,460		710,460
Total Assets	251	4,832,345[ab]	4,832,596	4,437,150[ce]	9,269,746
Equity and Liabilities					
Share capital	250	9,750[b]	10,000	828,100[c] 3,100[d] 858,800[e] 1,550[e]	1,700,000
Share premium	25	2,550[b]	2,575	4,866,550[e]	4,870,675
Accumulated losses	(24)		(24)		(24)
Current period net income	0	7,333[a]	7,333		7,333
Subtotal	251		19,884		6,577,984
ORAs and warrants	0	2,120,950[b]	2,120,950	(2,120,950)[c]	0
Deferred taxes	0	4,688[a]	4,688		4,688
Current liabilities:					
Payable to Euro Disney S.A.	0	1,908,567[a]	1,908,567		1,908,567
Other accounts payable	0	537,124[a]	537,124		537,124
Total current liabilities	0		2,445,691		2,445,691
Deferred revenues	0	241,383[a]	241,383		241,383
Total Equity and Liabilities	251	4,832,345[ab]	4,832,596	4,437,150[cde]	9,269,74

[a] Change resulting from project development activities.
[b] Change resulting from the sale of ORAs and EDSCA shares.
[c] Change resulting from the repayment and conversion of ORAs.
[d] Change resulting from the exercise of warrants.
[e] Change resulting from the initial public offering by EDSCA.
Source: Bruner and Langohr (1994), p. 748.

The Initial Public Offering

In the fall of 1989, EDSCA went public in one of the largest IPOs of common stock by a company that had no operating history. The shares were offered at FF72 each (£7.07 each in the United Kingdom). The expected net proceeds of FF5.73 billion were to be used to repay debt—including the ORAs held by the investor banks and FF1.9 billion of project development loans extended by Disney prior to the offering—as well as to fund construction costs. The offering was successful. Approximately 85.9 million shares were offered. Within three days, total demand reached 10 times that amount. Shares were listed for public trading on the Brussels, London, and Paris stock exchanges.

Projected Returns to Disney

In spite of Disney's giving up 51 percent of the equity ownership in the project, the net present value (NPV) of the project with respect to Disney would remain essentially the same. Tables 13.2 and 13.3 indicate, respectively, the expected cash flows to Disney under two alternative assumptions: (1) the Euro Disneyland Project is financed on a stand-alone basis, and (2) it is financed as a fully integrated internal project. These projections are based on the information contained in the October 5, 1989, offering circular for EDSCA's IPO.

The net present value of the project to Disney, at a 12 percent discount rate, would be FF25,923.1 million if the project was a fully integrated internal project. It would be FF24,169.7 million if the project was financed as proposed. The difference is only FF1,753.4 million, or roughly 6.8 percent of the net present value if the project were fully integrated. Consequently, by adopting the project financing structure, Disney decreased its equity ownership by 51 percent but reduced its expected net present value by only approximately 6.8 percent. Disney substantially reduced its risk exposure without giving up much profit potential. Disney would obtain significant financial benefits in the form of management fees, incentive fees, and royalties. These payments would seemingly guarantee Disney a significant return even if the project was only marginally successful.

INTERESTS OF THE PARTICIPANTS IN THE PROJECT

A project financing will be successful only if it satisfies a community of interests. All the parties must determine that the benefits from participating outweigh the costs. To be successful, a project financing must allocate the rewards from the project in a manner that is commensurate with the allocation of project risks.

Disney Considerations

Disney significantly reduced its financial risk exposure while preserving the opportunity to earn an attractive rate of return. Disney negotiated extremely favorable management, licensing, incentive, and merchandising fees. EDSCA paid Disney approximately FF330 million in fiscal 1992 and approximately FF482 million in 1993. Without these costs, EDSCA would have made a small profit in 1992.

The French government offered Disney various concessions worth roughly FF6.0 billion. Disney recovered FF1.9 billion of the development costs of the Euro Disneyland Project and monetized its remaining ownership interest through the public offering. After the IPO, Disney owned 49 percent of EDSCA, for which it had contributed only 13 percent of EDSCA's book value. Moreover, it controlled the management of the project through its 100 percent ownership of the project *gérant*.

French Government Considerations

Several factors motivated the French government. Unemployment in the region near the park was high. Construction of the park would create approximately 30,000 jobs. The French government also stood to benefit from a new source of tax revenue. In the first year alone, if the expected 11 million visitors spent only the $40 entrance fee, the government would realize $440 million of tax revenue. Increased revenues would also be generated from utility and electric networks, as well as from suburban rail systems. The French government estimated that foreign tourists would spend $1 billion in the local economy, and it hoped that France would become the capital of the European tourist industry.

Thus, Euro Disneyland would (1) provide a substantial number of jobs to local residents, (2) inject a substantial amount of money into the local economy during construction of the facility, (3) attract to the area a large number of visitors whose spending would stimulate the local economy, (4) have a favorable effect on land values in the area, and (5) allow French and other European investors to share in the wealth the Euro Disneyland Project was expected to create.

TABLE 13.2   Projected Cash Flows to Disney, Assuming the Euro Disneyland Project Is Financed on a Project Basis (Millions of French Francs)

	Base Fees	Incentive Fees	Royalties[a]	Profit Participations	Dividends
1989					
1990					
1991					
1992	197.4	55.0	302.0	1.0	137.0
1993	244.8	171.0	333.0	1.9	281.0
1994	320.5	477.0	387.0	2.5	419.0
1995	393.5	963.0	422.0	4.8	606.0
1996	573.4	1,820.0	717.0	5.6	775.0
1997	614.1	1,976.2	778.9	6.1	850.1
1998	657.6	2,145.8	846.2	6.7	932.6
1999	704.1	2,329.9	919.3	7.3	1,023.0
2000	754.0	2,529.9	998.7	8.0	1,122.2
2001	807.4	2,747.0	1,085.0	8.8	1,231.0
2002	851.2	2,948.9	1,159.0	9.6	1,306.9
2003	897.4	3,165.6	1,238.0	10.4	1,387.4
2004	946.1	3,398.2	1,322.5	11.4	1,472.9
2005	997.4	3,647.9	1,412.7	12.4	1,563.6
2006	1,051.5	3,916.0	1,509.0	13.5	1,660.0
2007	1,099.3	4,204.9	1,615.2	14.5	1,843.6
2008	1,149.2	4,515.1	1,728.8	15.5	2,047.6
2009	1,201.4	4,848.2	1,850.4	16.6	2,274.1
2010	1,256.0	5,205.9	1,980.6	17.7	2,525.6
2011	1,313.0	5,590.0	2,120.0	19.0	2,805.0
2012	1,356.9	5,986.7	2,241.6	20.7	2,989.8
2013	1,402.3	6,411.6	2,370.2	22.5	3,186.8
2014	1,449.2	6,866.7	2,506.2	24.5	3,396.7
2015	1,497.7	7,354.1	2,650.0	26.6	3,620.5
2016	1,547.8	7,876.0	2,802.0	29.0	3,859.0

[a] These royalties consist of (1) 10 percent of the gross revenues at the theme parks plus (2) 5 percent of the gross revenues from merchandise, food, and beverage sales plus (3) 10 percent of the fees due from participants who invested money for the construction of specific rides plus (4) 5 percent of the gross revenues from the theme hotels.
[b] This calculation assumes *all* cash inflows other than terminal value are taxed at the rate of 35 percent.

EDSNC Return	Reimbursement Payments	Investment Outlay	Pre-Tax Terminal Value	Cash Flow to Disney	
				Untaxed	*Taxed*[b]
		(833.0)		(833.0)	(833.0)
(340.0)	1,909.0			1,569.0	900.0
	360.0			360.0	234.0
61.3	493.0			1,246.6	810.3
61.3				1,093.0	710.5
61.3				1,667.3	1,083.8
61.3				2,450.6	1,592.9
61.3				3,952.3	2,569.0
61.3				4,286.7	2,786.4
61.3				4,650.1	3,022.6
61.3				5,045.0	3,279.3
61.3				5,474.1	3,558.2
61.3				5,940.5	3,861.3
				6,275.5	4,079.1
				6,698.8	4,354.2
				7,151.0	4,648.2
				7,634.0	4,962.1
				8,150.0	5,297.5
				8,777.4	5,705.3
				9,456.2	6,146.5
				10,190.7	6,624.0
				10,985.9	7,140.8
				11,847.0	7,700.6
				12,595.8	8,187.3
				13,393.5	8,705.8
				14,243.3	9,258.2
				15,148.9	9,846.8
			134,281.7[c]	150,395.5	110,462.9
			NPV @ 12%		24,169.7

[c] The pre-tax terminal value is estimated by capitalizing the sum of base fees, incentive fees, royalties, profit participations, and dividends at 12 percent, S.G. Warburg's estimated discount rate. The estimated terminal value assumes no growth after the investment horizon. The after-tax terminal value is calculated assuming a tax basis of 1,173 (EDSNC Return in 1990 plus Investment Outlay) and a 30 percent capital gain tax rate.

Sources: Euro Disneyland S.C.A., *Offer for Sale of 10,691,000 Shares* (October 5, 1989), and Bruner and Langohr (1994), p. 749.

TABLE 13.3   Projected Cash Flows to Disney, Assuming the Euro Disneyland Project Is Financed as a Fully Integrated Internal Project (Millions of French Francs)

	Operating Income	Amortization and Depreciation	Net Interest Expense (Income)	Taxes[a]
1989				
1990				
1991				
1992	2,043.0	700.0	(219.0)	791.7
1993	2,464.0	684.6	(213.0)	937.0
1994	3,312.0	680.9	(11.0)	1,163.1
1995	4,590.0	817.2	(70.0)	1,631.0
1996	6,800.0	949.4	376.0	2,248.4
1997	7,203.3	946.2	360.6	2,394.9
1998	7,630.4	940.5	345.8	2,549.6
1999	8,082.9	932.4	331.6	2,713.0
2000	8,562.2	922.2	318.0	2,885.5
2001	9,070.0	910.3	305.0	3,067.8
2002	9,553.8	896.8	314.8	3,233.7
2003	10,063.3	886.6	324.8	3,408.5
2004	10,600.1	879.7	335.2	3,592.7
2005	11,165.5	876.2	345.9	3,786.9
2006	11,761.0	876.0	357.0	3,991.4
2007	12,432.6	879.4	356.0	4,226.8
2008	13,142.5	881.6	355.0	4,475.6
2009	13,893.0	882.6	354.0	4,738.7
2010	14,686.4	882.5	353.0	5,016.7
2011	15,525.0	881.4	352.0	5,310.6
2012	16,469.3	879.4	43.4	5,749.1
2013	17,471.1	869.8	5.3	6,113.0
2014	18,533.8	854.6	0.7	6,486.6
2015	19,661.1	834.9	0.1	6,881.4
2016	20,857.0	812.1	0.0	7,300.0

[a] Pre-tax income is taxed at the rate of 35 percent. Pre-tax income equals operating income minus net interest expense.

[b] The pre-tax terminal value is estimated by capitalizing the free cash flow of the project at 12 percent, S.G. Warburg's estimated discount rate. The estimated terminal value assumes no growth after the investment horizon. The after-tax terminal value is calculated

Capital Expenditures	Debt Incurred (Repaid)	Terminal Value	Cash Flow to Disney
3,800.0	2,767.5		(1,032.5)
5,100.0	2,767.5		(2,332.5)
5,100.0	2,767.5		(2,332.5)
392.0	990.0		2,768.3
610.0	669.0		2,483.6
3,408.0	2,410.0		1,842.9
3,461.0	2,169.0		2,554.2
886.0	(1,600.0)		2,639.0
830.5	(1,498.6)		3,064.8
778.4	(1,397.2)		3,499.9
729.6	(1,295.8)		3,945.3
683.9	(1,194.4)		4,402.6
641.0	(1,093.0)		4,873.6
692.6	(962.0)		5,247.6
748.3	(831.0)		5,637.3
808.6	(700.0)		6,043.3
873.7	(569.0)		6,466.2
944.0	(438.0)		6,906.6
922.4	(438.4)		7,368.4
901.4	(438.8)		7,853.3
880.8	(439.2)		8,363.0
860.7	(439.6)		8,898.9
841.0	(440.0)		9,462.9
688.8	(352.0)		10,515.4
564.2	(264.0)		11,394.4
462.1	(176.0)		12,263.0
378.5	(88.0)		13,148.1
310.0	0.0	86,733.5[b]	100,792.6
		NPV @ 12%	25,923.1

assuming a tax basis of 15,740.2 (aggregate capital expenditures of 37,297.5 minus aggregate amortization and depreciation of 21,557.3) and a 30 percent capital gain tax rate.

Sources: Euro Disneyland S.C.A., *Offer for Sale of 10,691,000 Shares* (October 5, 1989), and Bruner and Langohr (1994), p. 750.

European Creditor Bank Considerations

A consortium of about 60 banks eagerly agreed to provide the construction loans. These loans were all nonrecourse to Disney. Motivated by an opportunity to earn fees and interest income *and* hold an equity stake, and perhaps charmed by the Disney name, the banks were quite willing to extend credit. The banks, however, had much at risk. In the event of default, the assets that served as collateral might prove difficult to liquidate. The assets of the park consisted of the land, exhibits, and rides, none of which could be disposed of easily. Other lenders had hotels collateralizing their loans. Soon after the loans were extended, real estate values became severely depressed, making liquidation difficult. Also, what value would the hotels have if the theme park were forced to close?

The banks undoubtedly took comfort from Disney's overall management of the Euro Disneyland Project. Disney would have enormous reputational capital at stake. A failure of the project could have serious implications for future Disney theme park and resort projects.

European Equity Investors' Considerations

The European equity investors contributed a substantial amount of cash in exchange for a 51 percent equity interest. Of the total equity of FF6,570,675,000 as of September 30, 1989, Disney contributed approximately FF833,000,000, or approximately 12.67 percent of the capital, for 49 percent of the equity. The European investors invested approximately FF5,737,675,000, or approximately 87.33 percent of the capital, for 51 percent of the equity. Accordingly, the European investors were substantially diluted from the outset. It appears that the European equity investors were enticed by the prior success of Disney; they anticipated that this success would easily transfer to the Euro Disneyland Project. As evidenced by the heavy demand for the shares of EDSCA at the initial offering price of FF72, European investors welcomed the opportunity to invest alongside Disney.

FINANCIAL PROJECTIONS

EDSCA published detailed financial projections in the offering circular for its initial public offering. Table 13.4 presents income projections and

TABLE 13.4 Profit Projections for EDSCA (Millions of French Francs)

	1992	1993	1994	1995	1996	2001	2006	2011	2016
Revenues:									
Magic Kingdom[a]	FF4,246	FF4,657	FF5,384	FF5,853	FF6,415	FF9,730	FF13,055	FF18,181	FF24,118
Second theme park	0	0	0	0	3,128	4,565	6,656	9,313	12,954
Resort and property development	1,236	2,144	3,520	5,077	6,386	8,133	9,498	8,979	5,923
Total revenues	5,482	6,801	8,904	10,930	15,929	22,428	29,209	36,473	42,995
Operating expenses:									
Magic Kingdom	2,643	2,836	3,161	3,370	3,641	5,504	7,384	10,175	13,097
Second theme park	0	0	0	0	1,794	2,644	3,695	5,020	6,830
Resort and property development	796	1,501	2,431	2,970	3,694	5,210	6,369	5,753	2,211
Total operating expenses	3,439	4,337	5,592	6,340	9,129	13,358	17,448	20,948	22,138
Operating income	2,043	2,464	3,312	4,590	6,800	9,070	11,761	15,525	20,857
Operating expenses (income):									
Royalties	302	333	387	422	717	1,085	1,509	2,120	2,802
Pre-opening amortization	341	341	341	341	341	0	0	0	0
Depreciation	255	263	290	296	625	658	723	842	228
Interest expense	567	575	757	708	1,166	920	623	352	0
Interest and other income	(786)	(788)	(768)	(778)	(790)	(615)	(266)	0	0
Lease expense	958	950	958	962	975	1,242	882	83	0
Management incentive fees	55	171	477	963	1,820	2,747	3,916	5,590	7,876
Total other expenses (income)	1,692	1,845	2,442	2,914	4,854	6,037	7,387	8,987	10,906
Profit before taxation	351	619	870	1,676	1,946	3,033	4,374	6,538	9,951
Taxation	147	260	366	704	818	1,274	1,837	2,746	4,180
Net profit	FF204	FF359	FF504	FF972	FF1,128	FF1,759	FF2,537	FF3,792	FF5,771
Dividends payable	FF275	FF425	FF625	FF900	FF1,100	FF1,750	FF2,524	FF3,379	FF5,719
Tax credit or payment	0	138	213	313	450	536	865	1,908	2,373
Total return	FF275	FF563	FF838	FF1,213	FF1,550	FF2,286	FF3,389	FF5,287	FF8,092

[a] Includes the Magic Kingdom Hotel.

Source: Euro Disneyland S.C.A., *Offer for Sale of 10,691,000 Shares* (October 5, 1989), p. 36.

projected total returns to the equity investors, by year, for the period 1992–1996 and at 5-year intervals thereafter through 2016. Table 13.5 provides cash flow projections for EDSCA for the same years.

VALUATION

In a traditional spin-off, equity carve-out, or IPO of a previously privately held company, the investment banker usually has the luxury of having historical operating results on which to base future projections and prepare a valuation. Historical industry patterns can be evaluated, and the company being valued can be compared to comparable companies. In addition, the company's management team may be staying on, adding an important intangible value. The company's business plan can then be realistically evaluated. However, even with an abundance of historical information, assessing the value of an IPO entails making an educated guess. The valuation of EDSCA posed an even greater challenge: It was not a going concern at the time of its IPO. Nevertheless, based on its analysis of Disney's projections, the British investment bank S.G. Warburg concluded that EDSCA's shares were worth approximately FF70 each.

Discount Rate

The first challenge Warburg faced was estimation of the appropriate discount rate to use in its discounted cash flow analysis. Warburg concluded that there were no publicly traded companies that were directly comparable to EDSCA. However, it identified two French companies that had somewhat similar risk profiles (albeit significant differences).

The first company was Club Mediteranée, which had a globally diversified destination resort portfolio. In contrast, Euro Disneyland had only one theme park. Club Med diversified its risk through its global portfolio; if weather or political problems persist at any one resort, tourists can be accommodated at other locations. Additionally, Club Med's destination options encourage repeat visits, whereas one may not be inclined to visit the same resort twice.

The second company was Accor, the leading French hotel operator. Again, similarities existed but the differences were great. Accor's hotels were dispersed over a large geographic area, thus limiting the company's exposure to difficulty in any one area. Also, the value of

TABLE 13.5 Cash Flow Projections for EDSCA (Millions of French Francs)

	1992	1993	1994	1995	1996	2001	2006	2011	2016
Sources of Funds:									
Profit before tax and incentive fees	FF 406	FF 790	FF1,347	FF2,639	FF3,766	FF5,780	FF8,290	FF12,128	FF17,827
Incentive fees	(55)	(171)	(477)	(963)	(1,820)	(2,747)	(3,916)	(5,590)	(7,876)
Depreciation and amortization	597	604	631	638	967	658	723	842	228
Issuance of long-term debt	990	693	2,950	2,950	0	779	1,146	0	0
Total	1,938	1,916	4,451	5,264	2,913	4,470	6,243	7,380	10,179
Uses of Funds:									
Capital expenditures:									
Magic Kingdom	(310)	(326)	(293)	(313)	(334)	(335)	(471)	(658)	(114)
Second theme park	0	0	(2,950)	(2,950)	(102)	(101)	(134)	(178)	(196)
Resort and property development	(31)	(139)	(62)	(198)	(450)	(205)	0	(5)	0
Acquisition of land	(51)	(145)	(103)				(339)		
Repayment of long-term debt	0	(24)	(540)	(781)	(1,600)	(1,872)	(1,584)	(440)	0
Loan to financing company	0	24	47	71	94	259	0	0	0
Taxes paid	(139)	(414)	(519)	(858)	(971)	(1,280)	(1,843)	(2,746)	(4,180)
Dividends payable	(275)	(425)	(625)	(900)	(1,100)	(1,750)	(2,524)	(3,379)	(5,719)
Total	(806)	(1,449)	(5,045)	(5,929)	(4,463)	(5,284)	(6,895)	(7,406)	(10,209)
Changes in Working Capital:									
(Increase) decrease in resort and property development inventories due to funding of projects and sales	(979)	(678)	507	785	1,527	656	65	0	0
Increase in current liabilities	200	10	9	212	21	27	35	45	57
Total	(779)	(668)	516	997	1,548	683	100	45	57
Change in Net Liquid Funds[a]	FF353	FF(201)	FF(78)	FF332	FF(2)	FF(131)	FF(552)	FF19	FF27

[a] Consists primarily of cash and cash equivalents.

Source: Euro Disneyland S.C.A., *Offer for Sale of 10,691,000 Shares* (October 5, 1989), p. 37.

Euro Disneyland's hotels would undoubtedly fall significantly if the theme park performed poorly.

Warburg believed that equity investors would require a 20 percent rate of return prior to opening (October 1989 to April 1992), to reflect the riskiness of the project (in particular, the fact that it was not a going concern), and a 12 percent rate of return after opening. The 12 percent discount rate was derived by analyzing the cost of capital for Disney, Accor, and Club Med. These companies had costs of capital of 9 percent, 11.3 percent, and 11.9 percent, respectively. The 12 percent discount rate was only marginally higher than the required rates of return for Accor and Club Med. Consequently, this discount rate did not seem to give adequate consideration to the risk differential between the established operations of the comparable companies and the start-up nature of EDSCA. It would seem appropriate to have included a higher risk premium in valuing the shares of EDSCA, in order to take into consideration that the theme park had not been constructed and would not be in operation for several more years. Also, Warburg evaluated the dependence on the sale of real estate as a low-risk proposition. A more appropriate discount rate would have been several percentage points higher to compensate for the added risk.

In addition, it is not clear that Warburg adequately considered the proposed capital structure in determining the discount rate of 12 percent. The debt-to-equity ratio of EDSCA at the time of the offering was only 40 percent. However, it was expected to increase to over 200 percent by 1995. This high degree of leverage would substantially increase the financial risk associated with EDSCA's shares, as compared to the other companies. It does not seem that this level of financial risk was appropriately reflected in the 12 percent discount rate Warburg used.

Estimated Attendance at Euro Disneyland

It was generally assumed in 1989 that two factors would be critical to the success of the Euro Disneyland Project: (1) attendance at the theme park and its related facilities and (2) the development of the real estate. It was felt that attendance at the theme park would be an important factor in its success, but that the number of guests visiting the park each year would exceed expectations. The projections Disney prepared assumed 11 million visitors in the first year. This figure was generally considered conservative. An analysis prepared by Arthur D. Little, a consulting firm, projected a minimum attendance of 11.7 million in the first year and suggested a possibility of up to 17.8 million admissions.[11] One article noted that Disney conservatively estimated first-year attendance at 11 million and remarked that Disney was notorious for understating attendance estimates.[12]

Forecasted Prices

Disney also assumed that certain revenue-generating items, such as ticket prices, hotel and campsite rates, and lease rates, would increase at a rate 1.5 percent greater than the rate of general price inflation in France. In the United States, Disney's ticket prices had grown at a real rate of 2.6 percent per annum over the preceding 17 years. Therefore, it did not seem unrealistic to expect that prices could rise faster than inflation without causing a dramatic decrease in park attendance, hotel reservations, or commercial leasing within the complex.

Results

Investors seemed to believe that if the theme park could meet its target of 11 million visitors the first year, EDSCA would be profitable. The target was met, but Euro Disneyland's performance fell well short of expectations. Disney and its advisers failed to see the signs of the approaching European recession, which resulted in lower per-capita spending. Hotel occupancy rates were below expectations. Moreover, guests were not staying as long or spending as much as expected on the high-priced food and merchandise. The depressed real estate market also made hotel sales unlikely; the capital gains from hotel sales were projected to be an important source of returns from the Euro Disneyland Project.

Seasonality

Both Disneyland (California) and Walt Disney World (Florida) are in locations with warm climates, where year-round operation of all rides and attractions is feasible. Thus, fairly strong year-round attendance is a realistic expectation. This was unlikely to be the case in France, where the weather is not warm and pleasant year-round. (In the sensitivity analysis discussed below, Warburg tested the attendance assumption by using a reduced attendance forecast of 10 million the first year. This reduction begins to affect dividends adversely in 2001.)

Other Shortcomings

Additional assumptions regarding European habits proved to be inaccurate. For example, EDSCA assumed that Europeans do not eat breakfast. Much to EDSCA's surprise, more than 2,000 visitors began showing up for breakfast in a hotel restaurant designed to accommodate 300. EDSCA executives also believed that they could change European habits, such as a reluctance to pull their children from school in midsession as American parents do, or a preference for longer holidays rather than short breaks. Additional errors made things worse. An insufficient number of rest rooms for bus drivers and a policy of serving no alcohol in the theme park, in a country where a glass of wine with lunch is standard, are just two examples.

Real Estate Ownership and Development

Based on its experience in California and Florida, Disney believed it was essential to control the land and hotels around the Euro Disneyland Project. In California, the original Disney park had been enormously successful. However, Disney did not own any land. It therefore could not expand the facility or offer ancillary services, such as hotels. The restricted acreage was quickly surrounded by hoteliers and fast-food outlets that took advantage of the millions of visitors each year. In Florida, however, Disney owned sufficient land but did not build enough of its own hotel rooms. Disney built hotels with 7,000 rooms and then watched the total number of hotel rooms in the area grow from 4,000 in 1971 to over 70,000 in 1989. These Florida hotels had averaged 92 percent occupancy with an average room rate of $166 per night.[13] In addition, it was estimated that visitors tended to stay an extra day at the Disney hotels, which resulted in more hotel revenue and an additional estimated $90 per day spent on food and merchandise per person.

The value of property around the theme parks also increased significantly. In California, land values had increased by 20 percent per year for 25 years.[14] In Florida, they had increased by 30 percent per year.[15] In establishing the Euro Disneyland Project, Disney wanted to ensure that it would have control over land and real estate development in order to capture these economic benefits. But the financial success of the Euro Disneyland Project would depend on the ability of EDSCA to develop the resort property and sell the developed properties quickly at substantial profits.

Real Estate Projections

The projections Disney prepared were based on very favorable assumptions regarding the development and sale of real estate. For example, through 1995, over 74 percent of each year's projected pre-tax income would result from real estate development activities (see Table 13.4).[16] If the real estate development activities in the years 1992 through 1995 did not perform as planned, EDSCA could suffer a substantial cash shortage. This is indeed what happened.

Dividend Projections

EDSCA's dividend policy required a payout that was substantially equal to net income each year through 1995. This dividend policy increased EDSCA's borrowing requirements. (The net change in debt in each of those years exceeded the dividend amount.) Consequently, EDSCA's dividend policy would be funded through borrowing, with the expectation that future cash flows would be sufficient both to maintain that dividend policy and to pay off the debt.

Sensitivity Analysis

Warburg conducted a sensitivity analysis on returns to investors, based on key assumptions provided by Disney. Table 13.6 contains the results of the sensitivity analysis. Although the analysis demonstrated the effect on the internal rate of return of 10 percent swings in key value drivers through 2017, the base assumptions appear to have been overly optimistic to begin with. Warburg could have taken this into account by increasing the sensitivity ranges for the key value drivers from the 10 percent level to 15 percent or even 20 percent. The most sensitive value driver was reduced per-capita spending. In addition, Warburg varied only one variable at a time. Sensitivity analyses often include a "worst case scenario" in which several variables experience a 10 percent (or greater) change.

TABLE 13.6 Sensitivity Analysis

Case	Assumptions	Net Dividend per Share for Years Beginning April 1						Net Value in April 1993[a]	Internal Rate of Return over Period to 2017[b] Issue Price (FF72)
		1992	1995	2001	2006	2011	2016		
Company's base case projections		1.6	5.3	10.3	14.8	19.9	33.6	131	13.3%
Reduced attendance	10 million visits in the first year of operation of the Magic Kingdom.	1.6	5.3	9.4	13.8	18.4	31.7	119	12.7
Increased attendance	12 million visits in the first year of operation of the Magic Kingdom.	1.6	5.3	11.1	15.9	21.3	35.6	141	13.8
Reduced per-capita spending	Per-capita spending at both theme parks is lower by 10 percent.	1.6	4.8	8.9	12.9	17.4	30.3	112	12.3
Increased per-capita spending	Per-capita spending at both theme parks is higher by 10 percent.	1.6	5.3	11.6	16.6	22.3	37.0	147	14.1

Delay	A six-month delay in the opening of the Magic Kingdom.	1.6	4.5	9.7	12.6	21.8	33.6	122	12.8
Increased construction costs	Costs of construction of Phase IA are higher by 10 percent.	1.6	5.3	10.2	15.1	20.4	34.0	129	13.2
Reduced resort and property development income	Income from all resort and property development is lower by 10 percent.	1.6	5.3	9.8	14.3	19.3	33.0	126	13.0
Increased resort and property development income	Income from all resort and property development is higher by 10 percent.	1.6	5.3	10.8	15.4	20.4	34.3	135	13.5

[a] Net value in April 1993 equals the present value of the stream of gross dividends per share and the assumed residual value in 2017, using a discount rate of 12 percent.

[b] EDSCA is assumed to be capitalized at 12.5 times net profit available for distribution in the year ending March 31, 2017, for the purpose of determining EDSCA's terminal value in 2017.

Source: Euro Disneyland S.C.A., Offer for Sale of 10,691,000 Shares (October 5, 1989), p. 38.

Overoptimism?

The valuation of EDSCA at FF72 per share now appears to have been overly generous. It was subsequently revealed that "Several European financial institutions, including Lazard Frères—Disney's own advisor—worried that the plan was too clever. . . . The company was overleveraged. The public offering price seemed high, and the proposed financing appeared risky because it relied on capital gains from future real estate transactions."[17] As noted, the project encountered difficulty for several reasons: (1) interest rates started to rise by the time EDSCA began to borrow heavily; (2) a prolonged recession began in Europe; (3) the real estate market in France became severely depressed; and (4) EDSCA's operating results were disappointing, particularly for the hotels.

It is easy to look back with the benefit of hindsight and criticize Warburg's valuation of the EDSCA shares. European investors, however, perceived the shares as fairly valued. Following the offering in 1989, and continuing through the opening of the park in 1992, EDSCA's shares traded at a premium; some investors paid as much as FF160 a share. It was not until losses started to accumulate that the market value of EDSCA's shares began to decline.

CORPORATE GOVERNANCE ISSUES

The organizational structure of EDSCA further complicated the situation. Disney placed its top management at EDSA, the management company, and not at EDSCA. Their incentive bonuses, through stock options, were issued in shares of Disney stock. However, the interests of EDSCA's shareholders and Disney's shareholders could be diametrically opposed. Options should have been based on the EDSCA share price, for a better alignment of management incentives and shareholder interests. Additionally, there was the potential for managerial gridlock to develop. The Disney-controlled management companies were responsible for the operation of the theme park. The supervisory board oversaw and approved all contracts entered into by the *gérant*. However, the supervisory board lacked the authority to make the *gérant* take action and the power to remove the *gérant*. The supervisory board could refuse to approve contracts if it objected to the *gérant's* actions. That response could potentially immobilize the company.

OPERATING RESULTS

Euro Disneyland opened on schedule on April 15, 1992. However, it became apparent within two months of the opening that the Magic Kingdom was not attracting visitors at the rate initially expected. Farmers and truckers blocked roads leading to the park in the summer of 1992, to express grievances unrelated to Euro Disneyland. Attendance suffered.

In its first year of operations, EDSCA reported revenues of $738 million and a net loss of $135 million. Fiscal 1993's performance was worse. EDSCA reported revenues of $873 million and a net loss of $1.1 billion (or $528 million before the cumulative effect of accounting changes). For the fiscal year ended September 30, 1993, EDSCA reported a loss of FF5.337 billion (equivalent to approximately $920 million), one of the largest losses in French corporate history.

The development and operation of the hotels and other resort property produced results significantly below projections. The cash flow realized from the sale of real estate was also well below projections. Because the success of the Euro Disneyland Project depended strongly on the cash flows from the real estate activity to pay down EDSCA's debt, a severe cash shortage developed. Until a restructuring was completed, it was unclear whether EDSCA could continue as a going concern.

In comparing the actual results with the projected results, the real estate activity appears to be the most disappointing. At the time of the IPO, EDSCA estimated that the occupancy of the hotels would run between 80 percent and 85 percent, as compared to 90 percent+ occupancy rates for the Disney hotels in Florida.[18] However, Disney did not anticipate that visitors to Euro Disneyland would rather stay in Paris, just 35 miles from the theme park, either forsaking the park's hotels altogether or minimizing their stay. Compared to the original expectations, the actual occupancy rates were extremely disappointing, reportedly as low as 55 percent.[19] The disappointing results for the hotels also contributed to Disney's inability to sell them at an acceptable price.

A second problem concerned the hotel room rates: They were too high for the market. For example, a room at the flagship Disneyland Hotel originally cost about FF2,000 (or $340) per night. This rate was approximately the same as the cost of a room at a top hotel in Paris. In an attempt to increase hotel occupancy, Disney substantially reduced room rates. For example, at the low-end hotels, such as the Sante Fe, rates were reduced from the equivalent of $76 per night to $51 per night, a reduction of over 32 percent.[20] Similar reductions were made at the other hotels, including those at the high end. These rate reductions increased occupancy but resulted in hotel revenue falling well below projected amounts.

The Magic Kingdom was generally successful when considered by itself. The attendance estimates of 11 million were essentially reached in the first year. However, in order to reach this attendance level, EDSCA had to reduce ticket prices significantly.[21] Cutting ticket prices for French citizens boosted attendance but took a big bite out of projected revenues. As many as 70 percent of winter visitors have been estimated to have taken the discount offered French citizens.[22]

In addition to problems with the real estate and resort property development, the estimated cost of the Euro Disneyland Project substantially exceeded estimates. Phase IA was expected to cost FF14 billion. It actually cost more than FF18 billion. As these additional costs were financed through added borrowing, EDSCA's financial problems were exacerbated. Eventually, EDSCA's total debt stood at nearly FF21 billion, or the equivalent of approximately $3.75 billion.[23]

RECENT DEVELOPMENTS

Today, Disney is in the process of trying to turn around the Euro Disneyland Project. At one point, it was on the verge of bankruptcy. On March 14, 1994, Disney, EDSCA, and a steering committee representing EDSCA's creditors announced a massive financial restructuring of EDSCA. Disney agreed to invest an additional $750 million as part of the restructuring plan. The plan, which was accepted by 61 of EDSCA's 63 banks, reduced EDSCA's debt from the equivalent of approximately $3.52 billion to approximately $1.73 billion. As part of the plan, Disney agreed to forfeit for 5 years the management fees and royalties from ticket and merchandise sales. These fees could not be collected at all if the theme park were forced to close. The plan also called for the bank consortium to forgive 18 months' interest payments, defer principal repayments for three years, and provide approximately $500 million of additional loans. The plan provided for a FF6 billion (equivalent to $1.07 billion) rights offering, in which Disney would subscribe for its 49 percent share at a cost of approximately $508 million. The creditor banks would underwrite the remaining 51 percent of the rights offering to the other shareholders.

The plan represented a mixed blessing for EDSCA's shareholders. The restructuring and rights offering would increase the likelihood of EDSCA's survival as a going concern. However, the offering would more than quadruple the number of shares outstanding, severely diluting nonsubscribing shareholders. Nevertheless, their shares might have become worthless if EDSCA had been forced into bankruptcy.

The rights offering was successful. Shareholders were allowed to subscribe for 7 new shares for every 2 shares held, creating 600 million new shares, at 10 francs per share. The offering was 80 percent subscribed by existing shareholders (including Disney, at 49 percent). The underwriting syndicate, led by Banque Nationale de Paris, Banque Indosuez, and Caisse de Dépôts et Consignations, took up the unsubscribed shares. In conjunction with the rights offering, a wealthy Saudi investor agreed to invest up to $500 million for as much as 24 percent of EDSCA by purchasing any unsubscribed shares.[24] This commitment sent a favorable signal to investors, which contributed to the success of the rights offering.

In spite of the poor performance of EDSCA to date, Disney may nevertheless realize a sizable return on its investment in the Euro Disneyland Project. In the early 1970s, Walt Disney World in Orlando got off to a slow start. But it has turned out to be one of the most profitable resorts in the world. It appears that Disney is turning Euro Disneyland around by making changes in its operating policies to better suit European tastes. These changes seem to be having a positive effect on the park's operating results. EDSCA reported that its loss for the fiscal first half ended March 31, 1996, narrowed to FF169 million ($33 million) from FF241 million a year earlier. Attendance at Euro Disneyland and occupancy at the Euro Disney hotels both grew on a year-to-year basis.

CONCLUSION

Euro Disneyland's performance would seem to suggest that Disney was very wise to structure the Euro Disneyland Project in the manner it did. Disney understood the risks involved in the project. By forming a separate company and arranging for outside equity investors, Disney limited its risk exposure in the project while sacrificing only a relatively small percentage of its potential returns from the project.

14

Case Study: The Eurotunnel Project

The first recorded plans for a cross-English Channel link between the United Kingdom and France date back to 1753.[1] Since the early nineteenth century, other plans for linking Britain with the mainland have periodically been drafted and then shelved. In 1882, tunneling actually started on the British side. But it was abandoned soon after. The mouth of the unfinished tunnel still yawns from the chalk bedrock near Dover.

The Eurotunnel Project was initiated in 1984. The construction was planned as a twin-bore rail tunnel with associated infrastructure, rolling stock, and terminals. Upon completion, scheduled for 1993, it would join the rail systems of the United Kingdom, France, and the rest of mainland Europe. Its comfortable, fast, frequent, and reliable service would furnish a valuable link between the United Kingdom and France, beneath the English Channel. The construction was technically straightforward from an engineering standpoint. However, the enormity of the undertaking would require close logistical coordination.

The project had symbolic value. It was initiated at about the time members of the European Economic Community (EEC) were ratifying the Single European Act to create, by 1992, a single integrated European economic system. The project was also innovative. The method of financing, which provided for private capital to bear the long-term

This chapter is based on Eurotunnel P.L.C./Eurotunnel S.A. (1987, 1990, 1994) and the following case materials: Roy C. Smith and Ingo Walter, "Eurotunnel—Background," Case Study, New York University, undated; Roy C. Smith and Ingo Walter, "Eurotunnel—Debt," Case Study, New York University, undated; and Roy C. Smith and Ingo Walter, "Eurotunnel—Equity," Case Study, New York University, undated.

infrastructure development risk, had not been tested in the world capital markets for decades.

HISTORICAL BACKGROUND

In 1973, French President Georges Pompidou and British Prime Minister Edward Heath signed a treaty to construct a twin-bore rail tunnel under the English Channel. Tunneling began in 1974. But when Heath's Conservative government was defeated, the treaty lapsed without ratification by the British Parliament, and tunneling was again abandoned.

In the early 1980s, investigations probed the possibility of constructing a fixed link across the English Channel (i.e., a bridge or tunnel), financed purely by private capital. Studies commissioned by the British and French governments culminated in the publication of a report by the Anglo-French Study Group in 1982. The report recommended construction of a rail link. However, it was widely believed at the time that the report would never be implemented.

In May 1984, Banque Indosuez, Banque Nationale de Paris, Credit Lyonnais, Midland Bank, and National Westminster Bank (together, the "Arranging Banks") presented to the governments of the United Kingdom and France a report detailing how a fixed link across the Channel, consisting of a twin-bore rail tunnel, might be project financed entirely with private capital. The Arranging Banks subsequently teamed up with some of the largest construction companies in the United Kingdom and France to form The Channel Tunnel Group Limited in the United Kingdom and France Manche S.A. in France (CTG and FM, respectively). CTG-FM was organized as a general partnership to develop what would become the Eurotunnel System. With its prior experience, CTG-FM was the consortium most advanced in its plans when the British and French governments issued a joint "Invitation to Promoters" in April 1985. Interested parties were invited to submit bids, before the end of October 1985, for the financing, construction, and operation of a fixed link across the Channel without recourse to government funds or guarantees.

Ten proposals were submitted in October 1985. Four principal contenders were identified:

1. EuroRoute: a £4.8 billion part-bridge, part-tunnel road and rail link.

2. CTG-FM Eurotunnel System: a £2.6 billion twin-bore rail tunnel.
3. Eurobridge: a £5 billion 23-mile composite fiber suspension bridge.
4. Channel Expressway: a £2.5 billion twin-bore road tunnel with separate rail tunnel.

In January 1986, the Eurotunnel System was selected as the winning project. In February 1986, the British and French governments signed a treaty by which they authorized construction of the Eurotunnel System and agreed to grant the concession to operate the Eurotunnel System (the "Concession") to the winning bidders, CTG in the United Kingdom and FM in France. CTG-FM then provided £50 million in seed capital (referred to as "Equity Offering I").

The Concession gave CTG-FM the right to build and operate the Eurotunnel System for a period of 55 years from the date the treaty was ratified. CTG-FM would have the discretion to establish tariffs and to determine its own operating policies for the Eurotunnel System. The British and French governments committed that no competing fixed link could be built before the end of 2020 without CTG-FM's approval. At the end of the Concession, in 2042, ownership of the Eurotunnel System would revert to the British and French governments.

The Eurotunnel Project encountered early opposition. A group of ferry owners, port interests, and environmentalists established Flexilink to oppose construction of a fixed link between England and France. Flexilink predicted a severe price war between the fixed link and ferry operators if the fixed link were built. Flexilink subsequently accused CTG-FM of misestimating the capital cost of the Eurotunnel System, tariffs, and traffic. It argued that the growth in cross-Channel traffic would slow down and that the tunnel would prove to be unprofitable and end up as a drain on British taxpayers.

THE EUROTUNNEL SYSTEM

The Eurotunnel System would comprise:

- Twin rail tunnels and a service tunnel under the English Channel;
- Two terminals, one at Folkestone near Dover in the United Kingdom and the other at Coquelles near Calais in France;
- Specially built shuttles to carry passenger and freight vehicles between the terminals;

- Inland clearance depots for freight at the French terminal and at Ashford (near Folkestone) in the United Kingdom;
- Connections to nearby roads and rail facilities.

Each of the two main tunnels would have an internal diameter of 7.6 meters and a total length of approximately 50 km. In addition, there would be a service tunnel of 4.8 meters internal diameter. Cross-passages would link it to the main tunnels. The service tunnel would provide ventilation to the main tunnels. It would also facilitate routine safety and maintenance work and provide a safe refuge in case of emergency. Two crossovers were planned between the rail tunnels. These would allow trains to continue to operate during periods of tunnel maintenance, albeit at a reduced frequency on a single track.

PROJECT OWNERSHIP STRUCTURE

The ownership structure for the Eurotunnel Project, illustrated in Figure 14.1, could be described as a dual-bodied transnational

FIGURE 14.1 Ownership Structure for the Eurotunnel Project

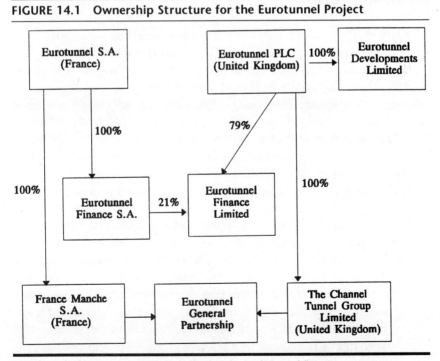

Source: R. C. Smith and I. Walter, "Eurotunnel—Background," p. 4.

hybrid. It involves parallel groups of companies with common shareholders. The two groups are separately registered; Eurotunnel PLC is located in the United Kingdom and Eurotunnel S.A. is located in France. They are joined together in a general partnership (hereafter referred to as "Eurotunnel").

CTG and FM had previously entered into an association constituting a partnership under English law and a *société en participation* under French law, for the purpose of constructing and operating the Eurotunnel System. Profits and losses (after financing and other costs but before depreciation and taxes) would be divided equally between CTG and FM.

Eurotunnel Finance Limited and Eurotunnel Finance S.A. would manage Eurotunnel's finances. Eurotunnel Developments Limited would enter into joint venture arrangements with third parties to develop property in the United Kingdom not required for the Eurotunnel System, business opportunities brought about as a result of the Eurotunnel System, and Eurotunnel System traffic.

CONSTRUCTION

Construction was to be carried out by a consortium of construction firms known as Transmanche Link. The consortium entered into a single general-obligation contract to design, construct, test, and commission a fully operational rail system within seven years of signing the construction contract. The construction contract was signed in August 1986. Transmanche Link was a joint venture of Translink of the United Kingdom, which consisted of five leading British construction firms, and Transmanche Construction of France, which consisted of five leading French construction firms.

The construction contract was divided into three principal parts:

1. *Target works.* The tunnels and underground structures would comprise the target works. They would account for about 50 percent of the contract price. The contractors would be paid for the target works on a cost-plus basis providing for a 12 percent profit margin. The construction contract contained an incentive structure: If the actual cost were less than the target cost, Transmanche Link would receive 50 percent of the savings; if it were more, Transmanche Link would pay 30 percent of the cost overrun, up to a ceiling equal to 6 percent of the target cost.

2. *The lump-sum works.* The terminals, the fixed equipment, and the mechanical and electrical elements of the Eurotunnel System would comprise the lump-sum works. They would be paid for on a lump-sum basis. Transmanche Link would realize all the savings if the lump-sum works were delivered under budget, but would have to pay the full cost of any cost overrun.

3. *The procurement items.* These items consisted of the locomotives and the shuttles. Transmanche Link would subcontract for these items. Eurotunnel would pay the subcontracted bid price directly to the subcontractors. Transmanche Link would oversee the bidding and supervise the subcontractors. It would be reimbursed for its direct costs and paid a profit margin equal to about 12 percent of the value of the procurement items.

Transmanche Link would be held liable for damages of about £350,000 per day for delays up to 6 months, and £500,000 per day thereafter if the Eurotunnel Project was delayed beyond the final completion deadline. The obligations of Transmanche Link would be secured by a performance bond equal to 10 percent of the total value of the contract, which would be released upon completion of the Eurotunnel Project. In addition, 5 percent of the amount due to Transmanche Link as progress payments would be withheld or covered by a performance bond during the construction period. The payments or the bond would be released in two installments, 12 months and 24 months following completion of the Eurotunnel Project. The five French and five British parent companies of Transmanche Link would also give general guarantees covering 100 percent of the contractual obligations of Transmanche Link. The joint liability of each of the French parents and the several liability of each of the British parents was limited to 50 percent and 10 percent, respectively.

Transmanche Link would not be entitled to any release from obligations due to strikes by its own labor force; however, general strikes interrupting the required flow of goods or materials would be an event of force majeure and would lead to extension of the completion deadline. Similarly, Transmanche Link would be liable for delays and cost overruns caused by accidents or flooding. However, it would not be liable for delays or cost overruns caused by (1) changes in specifications made by Eurotunnel, (2) actions taken by the British or French governments, or (3) bedrock conditions that turned out to be different from those Eurotunnel had determined to be reasonably expected.

It was widely believed that construction of the Eurotunnel System would not be a difficult technical exercise. Conditions for construction of the Eurotunnel System were excellent. Moreover, the simplicity of the design—which had been a key factor in its selection by the British and French governments—increased the chances that the Eurotunnel Project would be completed on time and within budget.

The risk of interruption of service following completion was deemed to be low. Eurotunnel and Transmanche Link believed that once the three tunnels were completed, only a major earthquake could cause the tunnel to flood and collapse.

PROJECT FINANCING

Eurotunnel estimated that it would cost approximately £4.8 billion to build the Eurotunnel System:

Construction costs	£2.8 billion
Corporate and other costs	0.5
Provision for inflation	0.5
Net financing costs	1.0
Total	£4.8 billion

Table 14.1 provides a detailed cost breakdown. To meet these costs and cover possible cost overruns, Eurotunnel planned to raise £6.0 billion:

Equity	£1.0 billion
Loans	5.0
Total	£6.0 billion

To cope with the tricky problem of raising this amount of funds for a greenfield venture without third-party guarantees, Eurotunnel planned to raise the funds in stages:

1. Prior to the Eurotunnel Project's selection by the British and French governments, the Arranging Banks obtained strongly worded letters of intent from 33 banks to underwrite loans of approximately £4.3 billion.
2. Following the Eurotunnel Project's selection, in January 1986, the founding shareholders contributed equity of £50 million to CTG-FM (which constituted Equity Offering I).
3. The Arranging Banks then worked to increase the size of the underwriting syndicate to 40 banks in the spring of 1986 and

TABLE 14.1   Expected Cost of the Eurotunnel Project (Millions of Pounds Sterling)

	1986	1987	1988	1989	1990	1991	1992	1993	Total
Construction[a]	£14	£168	£504	£575	£671	£507	£300	£22	£2,761
Owning group costs[b]	37	103	81	74	70	66	73	61	565
Inflation[c]	0	3	30	68	118	130	110	30	489
Net financing costs[d]	8	49	29	95	160	245	327	111	1,024
Total expected cost	£59	£323	£644	£812	£1,019	£948	£810	£224	£4,839

[a] Up to the opening of the Eurotunnel System. The cost is expressed in April 1987 prices.
[b] Owning group costs consist of (in millions of pounds sterling): Management £146.8, Operations 38.1, Office 20.6, Finance 51.6, Insurance 65.0, Land and property 29.1, Parliamentary 15.1, Maitre d'Oeuvre 72.7, and Provisional sums 126.3.
[c] Up to June 30, 1993, at current prices.
[d] Net financing costs are based on an assumed base borrowing rate (before margin) of 9 percent and an assumed interest rate on invested cash balances of 8.5 percent.
Source: R. C. Smith and I. Walter, "Eurotunnel—Background," p. 23.

to formalize their lending obligations in a collective binding commitment to underwrite a £5 billion syndicated loan. The Arranging Banks planned to complete syndication after the construction contract had been signed and a further equity offering (Equity Offering II) had been completed.

4. Eurotunnel planned a second issue of shares (Equity Offering II) in June 1986. Eurotunnel hoped the issue would raise an additional £150–£250 million.

5. The Arranging Banks would then syndicate the £5 billion project loan and enter into the underwriting agreement. Drawdowns would not be permitted until a total of £1 billion of equity had been raised and at least £700 million of it had been invested in the Eurotunnel Project.

6. A third equity offering, Equity Offering III, would raise the balance of the £1 billion of equity. It was planned for the first half of 1987.

It was anticipated that during the Eurotunnel System's first full year of operation, 79 percent of its total costs would consist of capital charges (i.e., interest and depreciation). Capital charges as a proportion of total costs would decline steadily thereafter. Eurotunnel expected that, after completion risk had been eliminated, it would be able to refinance much of the project debt with cheaper financing, which would further reduce the debt service burden.

ECONOMIC RISK

The two national-government-owned railway companies, British Rail (BR) and Société Nationale des Chemins de Fer Francais (SNCF), would be the two largest direct customers of the Eurotunnel System. Their relationship with the Eurotunnel System would be defined by contract. Eurotunnel expected that half of the Eurotunnel System's revenues would come from these two railways; the other half would come from road vehicles. The vehicles, together with their drivers and passengers, would be transported in specially designed shuttles running at speeds of up to 160 kph between the terminals.

Eurotunnel expected to have a competitive advantage over existing cross-Channel transportation—via ferry, hovercraft, and airline services. Eurotunnel's services would be less vulnerable to the adverse weather conditions in the Channel that can seriously disrupt ferry and hovercraft crossings. Eurotunnel could operate all year, and it planned to offer a higher frequency of service than the existing ferry and hovercraft operators. Figure 14.2 compares the shuttle's cross-Channel travel time to those of the ferry and hovercraft services, outside the periods of exceptional demand and under good weather conditions.

In France, SNCF proposed to build a new high-speed rail line between Paris and Brussels and to construct a branch that would link the new rail line to the French terminal of the Eurotunnel System. The proposed lines would enable the new passenger trains to travel at speeds of up to 300 kph in France and Belgium. With planned improvements to traditional tracks in the United Kingdom, direct rail service between London and Paris would take approximately 3 hours, and direct service between London and Brussels would take approximately 2 hours and 30 minutes. Figure 14.3 compares the expected travel times between London and Paris before and after the introduction of high-speed train service. The Eurotunnel System and the high-speed train would be competitive with the air travel time.

To assess the likely future demand for the Eurotunnel System and the resultant revenue prospects for the concession period, Eurotunnel commissioned various marketing studies. The marketing consultants (1) reviewed past trends in passenger and freight traffic by sea and passenger traffic by air between the United Kingdom and mainland Europe; (2) assessed the likely total traffic flows in 1993 and thereafter; (3) estimated the Eurotunnel System's share of this future market ("diverted traffic"); (4) prepared a forecast of the incremental traffic to

FIGURE 14.2 Comparison of Cross-Channel Travel Times for Three Modes of Travel

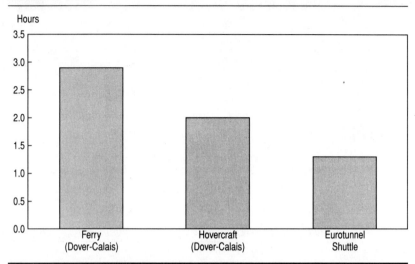

Source: Eurotunnel P.L.C./Eurotunnel S.A., *Offer for Sale of 220,000,000 Units with New Warrants* (November 16, 1987), p. 28; and R. C. Smith and I. Walter, "Eurotunnel—Background," p. 11.

FIGURE 14.3 Comparison of Travel Times between London and Paris for Various Modes of Travel

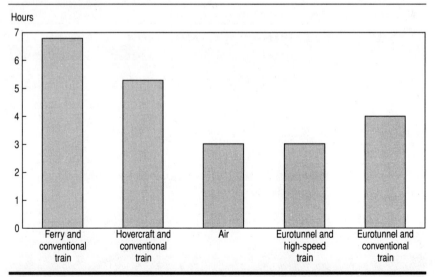

Source: Eurotunnel P.L.C./Eurotunnel S.A., *Offer for Sale of 220,000,000 Units with New Warrants* (November 16, 1987), p. 29; and R. C. Smith and I. Walter, "Eurotunnel—Background," p. 12.

297

TABLE 14.2 Projected Demand for the Eurotunnel System

A. Historical and Projected Cross-Channel Traffic Growth Rate

	1975–1985 Annual Growth Rate (%)	Actual 1985	1985–1993 Annual Growth Rate (%)	Forecast 1993	1993–2003 Annual Growth Rate (%)	Forecast 2003	2003–2013 Annual Growth Rate (%)	Forecast 2013
Type of traffic:								
Passengers (millions of trips per annum)	6.5	48.1	3.7	64.3	3.2	88.1	2.4	111.9
Freight (millions of gross tonnes per annum)	5.0	60.4	4.3	84.4	3.8	122.1	3.4	169.8

B. The Eurotunnel System's Estimated Market Share

	1993 Tunnel Traffic	Share of Global Market to Tunnel (%)	2003 Tunnel Traffic	Share of Global Market to Tunnel (%)	2013 Tunnel Traffic	Share of Global Market to Tunnel (%)
Type of traffic:						
Passengers (millions of trips per annum):						
Shuttles	12.4		16.1		18.2	
Railways	14.5		17.9		21.6	
Total	26.9	42	34.0	39	39.8	36
Freight (millions of gross tonnes per annum):						
Shuttles	7.5		10.3		13.0	
Railways	7.3		10.3		14.2	
Total	14.8	17	20.6	17	27.2	16

C. Forecast of Created Traffic

	1993[a] Price Induced	Other	2003 Price Induced	Other	2013 Price Induced	Other
Category:						
Passengers (millions of trips per annum)	2.8	—	3.6	1.9	4.3	2.5
Freight (millions of gross tonnes per annum)		—		0.5		0.6

D. Forecast of Total Revenues (Millions of Pounds Sterling at 1987 Prices)

	1993[a] Diverted	Created	Total	2003 Diverted	Created	Total	2013 Diverted	Created	Total
Category:									
Shuttle	241.2	9.7	250.9	314.7	24.0	338.7	367.7	31.2	398.9
Rail	192.0	15.4	207.4	221.2	26.2	247.4	243.6	25.0	268.6
Ancillary	40.3	2.1	42.4	50.9	5.0	55.9	57.2	6.5	63.7
Total	473.5	27.2	500.7	586.8	55.2	642.0	668.5	62.7	731.2

Source: R. C. Smith and I. Walter, "Eurotunnel—Background," pp. 24–25.
[a] Stated as for a full year of operation.

which the Eurotunnel System was likely to give rise ("created traffic"); and (5) estimated the revenues the Eurotunnel System could expect to realize from providing transportation services and related ancillary services.

Table 14.2 summarizes the consultants' assessments. These assessments were based on the assumptions that (1) high-speed rail service would be available between London and both Paris and Brussels at the start of the Eurotunnel System's operations and (2) Eurotunnel would be permitted to operate its facilities duty-free throughout the concession period.

The marketing studies concluded that the Eurotunnel System was economically feasible. They projected that the total cross-Channel traffic market would grow from 48.1 million passenger trips and 60.4 million tonnes of freight in 1985 to 88.1 million passenger trips and 122.1 million tonnes of freight by 2003. They concluded that the Eurotunnel System would be able to capture a large proportion of this growing market. The Eurotunnel System would not require prebooking, and it would be substantially faster and more convenient and reliable than existing ferry services. It would also be competitive with air services in terms of both cost and time. The studies projected that the Eurotunnel System would capture roughly 42 percent of the cross-Channel passenger market in 1993. Concerning rail freight, the Eurotunnel System would provide a through service for the first time. Because the service would avoid transshipment, rail freight would become competitive with road freight to and from the United Kingdom. In 1993, roughly 17 percent of cross-Channel freight traffic would go through the Eurotunnel System, according to the studies. The passenger and freight market shares were projected to decline to 36 percent of passenger traffic and 16 percent of freight traffic by 2013.

The marketing studies also concluded that the Eurotunnel System's existence would lower the cost of travel and thereby generate a certain amount of new traffic. According to the marketing forecasts, the Eurotunnel System would carry a total of 30 million passengers and 15 million tonnes of freight in its first full year of operations.

Revenue would come from three sources: (1) shuttle fares (assumed at opening to match the then-prevailing fares for Dover–Calais ferries), (2) railway charges and tolls, and (3) ancillary revenues, consisting principally of catering and duty-free sales to passengers, and charges levied on the use of the tunnel as a conduit for cables.

As Table 14.2 indicates, the marketing studies projected that total revenue in 1993, stated for a full year of operations, would approximate

£500 million in April 1987 prices and would rise to £642 million in 2003. The revenue breakdown was expected to be: shuttle revenue 50 percent, rail revenue 41 percent, and ancillary revenue 9 percent.

The base case projections were predicated on a United Kingdom GDP growth rate of 2.15 percent per annum (p.a.) from 1985 to 2003, and 2.0 percent p.a. thereafter; a French GDP growth rate of 2.25 percent p.a.; and a Belgian GDP growth rate of 1.9 percent p.a. Table 14.3 illustrates the effect on revenues of variation in growth rates of 0.5 percent p.a. and the effect of varying ferry tariffs and tunnel tolls by 10 percent.

After reviewing the marketing studies, Prognos AG of Switzerland concurred with the marketing studies' conclusion that the ferry operators had a very limited ability to reduce their tariffs in response to

TABLE 14.3 Sensitivity of Projected Eurotunnel Revenues to Changes in GDP Growth Rate, Ferry Tariffs, and Tunnel Tolls

A. Effect on Revenues of Varying GDP Growth Rate

	1993		2003	
	Increase by 0.5% p.a.	Decrease by 0.5% p.a.	Increase by 0.5% p.a.	Decrease by 0.5% p.a.
Passengers	+4.9%	−4.9%	+7.0%	−7.0%
Freight	+6.2	−6.2	+12.4	−12.4
Total	+5.1%	−5.1%	+8.5%	−8.5%

B. Effect on Revenues of Varying Ferry Tariffs and Tunnel Tolls

	Both Charges Reduced	Ferry Charge Reduced	Tunnel Charge Reduced	Tunnel Charge Increased	Ferry Charge Increased	Both Charges Increased
Changes relative to the base case:						
Ferry tariffs	−10.0%	−10.0%	—	—	+10.0%	+10.0%
Tunnel tolls	−10.0%	—	−10.0%	+10.0%	—	+10.0%
Revenue change:						
Car passengers	−10.5%	−19.6%	+11.3%	+10.7%	+22.0%	−9.2%
Coach passengers	−10.5	−8.7	−2.0	+10.7	+8.7	+1.9
Lorries (RoRo)	−9.7	−10.5	+0.9	+9.7	+10.5	−0.8
Container/wagons	−11.2	−8.0	−3.4	+11.3	+7.9	+3.1
Total traffic revenue	−6.4%	−9.0%	+3.3%	+6.5%	+9.8%	−2.6%

Source: R. C. Smith and I. Walter, "Eurotunnel—Background," p. 14.

the opening of the Eurotunnel System. Prognos stated that a price war would be to the disadvantage of the ferry operators in the long term.

Eurotunnel signed agreements with BR and SNCF guaranteeing, for the first 12 years of the Eurotunnel System's operation, the payment of 60 percent of forecast tolls. These agreements would be critical to the success of the Eurotunnel Project.

PROJECTED FINANCIAL RESULTS

Table 14.4 shows the projected income for the Eurotunnel Project. It was assumed that the Eurotunnel System would open in May 1993, at which time it would be fully operational for all forms of shuttle and train traffic. The projections also made these key assumptions:

- United Kingdom gross domestic product would grow at 2.15 percent p.a. between 1985 and 2003 and at 2.00 percent p.a. between 2003 and 2013. The growth rate in traffic was assumed to decrease each year after 2013, reaching zero in 2042.
- No alternative fixed link across the English Channel would become operational before the concession period ends in 2042.
- The tariffs the Eurotunnel System charges would, on average, equal the ferry tariffs on the Dover–Calais route and would remain constant in real terms.
- Rail usage charges would conform to the specifications of the railway usage contract, and the high-speed railway linking Brussels, Paris, and the Eurotunnel System terminal in France would be operational by the time the Eurotunnel System opened.
- Eurotunnel would be permitted to make duty-free and tax-free sales to shuttle passengers (the principal source of the ancillary revenues reported in Table 14.4).
- Traffic and revenues would conform to the traffic and revenue projections prepared by Eurotunnel's traffic and revenue consultants.
- Subject to restrictions contained in Eurotunnel's loan agreement, all profits available for distribution each year would be distributed as dividends to shareholders.
- The sterling–franc exchange rate would remain constant at £1:FF10 throughout the entire concession period.
- The rates of inflation in revenues, overhead, operating costs, and capital expenditures would be identical each year. The specific annual inflation rates assumed in preparing the projections were:

4.0 percent in 1987; 4.5 percent in 1988; 5.0 percent in 1989; 5.5 percent in 1990; and 6.0 percent in 1991 and thereafter.

- The interest rate on cash balances would be a constant 8.5 percent p.a. throughout the concession period.
- CTG and FM would share all revenues and costs (other than depreciation and taxes) equally throughout the concession period.
- The travel privileges granted subscribers to Equity Offering III (discussed below) would not materially affect the Eurotunnel System's revenues, operating costs, or tax liabilities.

PROJECT DEBT FINANCING

In February 1986, National Westminster Bank, Midland Bank, Banque Indosuez, Banque Nationale de Paris, and Credit Lyonnais were attempting to syndicate the £5.0 billion project loan (the "Project Loan Facility") for the Eurotunnel Project among approximately 40 second-tier

TABLE 14.4 Profit Projections for the Eurotunnel Project (Millions of Pounds Sterling)

	1993[a]	1994	1995	1996	1997	1998	1999
Turnover:							
Shuttle	£251	£384	£423	£463	£505	£551	£599
Rail	194	314	341	368	396	430	459
Ancillary	43	64	71	77	85	91	100
Total Turnover	488	762	835	908	986	1,072	1,158
Operating Costs:							
Fixed expenses	(53)	(88)	(92)	(99)	(107)	(117)	(126)
Variable expenses	(33)	(57)	(63)	(69)	(76)	(89)	(90)
Total Operating Costs	(86)	(145)	(155)	(168)	(183)	(206)	(216)
Depreciation	(103)	(158)	(159)	(160)	(162)	(167)	(169)
Interest, net	(229)	(351)	(322)	(307)	(291)	(277)	(265)
Profit before taxation	70	108	199	273	350	422	508
Taxation	(7)	(18)	(38)	(53)	(69)	(88)	(198)
Profit after taxation	63	90	161	220	281	334	310
Transfer to reserves	(1)	(2)	(3)	(3)	(4)	(6)	(7)
Profit for the year aviliable for distribution	62	88	158	217	277	328	303
Dividends payable	—	149	169	217	277	328	303
Per Unit	—	£0.39	£0.44	£0.56	£0.71	£0.85	£0.78

[a] The figures for 1993 are for the period from the opening date in May through the end of December.

underwriting banks. These banks were asked to give pre-underwriting commitments that would be conditional on several key events, specified below. Owing to the size and complexity of the Eurotunnel Project and the length of time anticipated between commitment and syndication, the Arranging Banks asked the underwriting banks to furnish letters of commitment. They expected to convert these commitments into a full underwriting agreement, which would underpin the loan syndication. In February 1986, however, the borrower had not yet been formed, the construction contract had not yet been drafted, and the governments of the United Kingdom and France had not yet granted the Concession to CTG and FM. Therefore, it would have been premature to sign a formal underwriting agreement.

The Arranging Banks had good reason to approach the market in this slightly unorthodox manner. They felt it was essential for them to augment their underwriting commitments—rumored to be approximately £4.3 billion—in order to secure commitments for the full £5.0

2000	2001	2002	2003	2013	2023	2033	2041
£652	£709	£770	£836	£1,763	£3,527	£6,682	£10,650
493	530	569	612	1,191	2,105	3,641	5,526
109	117	127	138	282	552	1,033	1,648
1,254	1,356	1,466	1,586	3,236	6,184	11,356	17,824
(137)	(148)	(161)	(174)	(314)	(562)	(1,006)	(1,604)
(98)	(107)	(116)	(130)	(317)	(645)	(1,240)	(2,000)
(235)	(255)	(277)	(304)	(631)	(1,207)	(2,246)	(3,604)
(171)	(173)	(176)	(184)	(234)	(271)	(328)	(383)
(234)	(212)	(190)	(171)	39	173	370	616
614	716	823	927	2,410	4,879	9,152	14,453
(240)	(279)	(321)	(361)	(934)	(1,893)	(3,547)	(5,573)
374	437	502	566	1,476	2,986	5,605	8,880
(9)	(5)	—	—	—	—	—	—
365	432	502	566	1,476	2,986	5,605	8,880
365	432	502	566	1,476	2,986	5,605	8,880
£0.94	£1.11	£1.29	£1.46	£3.80	£7.70	£14.44	£22.88

Source: Eurotunnel P.L.C./Eurotunnel S.A., *Offer for Sale of 220,000,000 Units with New Warrants* (November 16, 1987), pp. 54–55.

billion budgeted for total credit facilities. They believed that arranging these additional commitments would preserve political momentum and demonstrate to the equity market that the Eurotunnel Project's entire debt financing was "locked up." Only then could Eurotunnel hope to tap the equity market successfully.

Conditions Precedent to Signing the Underwriting Agreement

The following events would have to occur before the underwriting banks would formally enter into the underwriting agreement:

1. The British and French governments would have to grant the Concession.
2. Eurotunnel S.A. and Eurotunnel PLC would have to be incorporated, and their general partnership would have to be formed.
3. The construction contract would have to be negotiated and signed.
4. The United Kingdom Parliament would have to pass the Channel Tunnel Bill in order to ratify the treaty and the Concession.
5. The French National Assembly would have to pass parallel legislation.
6. An order authorizing the acquisition of the land for the French terminal would have to be issued.
7. A site suitable for dumping the earth and rock excavated during tunnel construction would have to be obtained.
8. An equity issue (Equity Offering II) in the amount of £150 million would have to be completed.

Terms and Conditions of the Project Loan Facility

The Arranging Banks proposed the following terms and conditions for the Project Loan Facility.

1. *Amount.* The total loan amount would be denominated in three currencies:

Amount	Sterling Equivalent
£2,600 million	£2,600 million
FF21,000 million	£2,100 million
US$450 million	£300 million

The sterling equivalent was: £1.00 = FF10.00 = US$1.50.

2. *Use of Proceeds.* It was anticipated that 80 percent of the funds would be used to pay for budgeted capital costs and the other 20 percent would be available in the form of a stand-by cost overrun facility.

3. *Conditions Precedent to Drawdowns.* In addition to the customary conditions precedent in Euromarket syndicated loans, the following conditions would have to be fulfilled:

- A third equity offering (Equity Offering III) would have to be completed to increase total paid-in equity capital to £1.0 billion.
- Capital expenditures representing at least £700 million would have to be funded out of equity capital.
- Satisfactory construction progress (as specified in the Credit Agreement) would have to be made.
- The banks would have to continue to be reasonably satisfied with the validity of the capital cost estimate.

4. *Availability, Repayment, and Refinancing.* The Project Loan Facility would be available for a period of 7 years. Drawdowns could be made in the form of either cash or letters of credit (to secure third-party loans).

Repayments would be made out of cash flow, and final repayment would occur no later than 18 years after signing the loan agreement. The cash flow statement in Table 14.5 shows anticipated repayments during the first 11 years of operation. Eurotunnel planned to refinance the Project Loan Facility before maturity.

Eurotunnel would be allowed to prepay in full the outstanding loan balance at any time after the opening of the Eurotunnel System to regular traffic. Prepayment could be made without fee after two complete summers of operation, at the rate of 20 percent per year of the total principal amount, subject to Eurotunnel maintaining certain ratios. Assuming that the Eurotunnel System proved profitable, early refinancing was likely.

5. *Fees.* Eurotunnel would pay the syndicating banks the following fees:

- To the Arranging Banks: ⅛ percent of the total amount of funds raised.
- To the Underwriting Banks: ⅞ percent of the underwritten amount, payable to each bank pro rata to its underwriting commitment.

TABLE 14.5   Base Case Sources and Uses of Funds (Millions of Pounds Sterling)

	1993	1994	1995	1996	1997	1998	1999	2000	2001	2002	2003
Sources of Funds:											
Profit before tax	£70	£108	£199	£273	£350	£422	£508	£614	£716	£823	£927
Depreciation	103	158	159	160	162	167	169	171	173	176	184
Issue of long-term debt	321	0	776	352	361	452	0	0	0	0	0
Issue of capital	0	52	25	0	0	0	0	0	0	0	0
Total	494	318	1,159	785	873	1,041	677	785	889	999	1,111
Uses of Funds:											
Asset purchases	£262	£37	—	—	—	£39	—	—	—	£9	£108
Debt repayment	0	0	£799	£493	£478	561	£111	£102	£111	122	133
Dividends paid	0	0	181	173	229	290	318	308	377	442	513
Taxes paid	0	15	84	103	128	158	175	192	251	290	331
Subtotal	262	52	1,064	769	835	1,048	604	602	739	863	1,085
Change in Nonliquid Working Capital	(3)	(7)	(11)	(11)	(10)	(12)	(7)	(14)	(10)	(12)	(20)
Change in Cash and Cash Equivalents	£229	£259	£84	£5	£28	£(19)	£66	£169	£140	£124	£6

Source: Eurotunnel P.L.C./Eurotunnel S.A., *Offer for Sale of 220,000,000 Units with New Warrants* (November 16, 1987), pp. 54–55.

- Pre-Loan Commitment Fee: ¼ percent p.a. on committed amounts, payable from March 14, 1986, until the signing of the Credit Agreement.
- Regular Commitment Fee: ⅛ percent p.a. on the undrawn amount. Amounts covered by the additional commitment fee would be excluded. The regular commitment fee would be payable from the date of signing the Credit Agreement until the end of the availability period.
- Additional Commitment Fee: ¼ percent p.a. on the undrawn amount budgeted to be used in the current half year; ⁵⁄₁₆ percent p.a. on any amounts drawn over the budgeted amount.

6. *Interest.* For drawdowns of up to 80 percent of the Project Loan Facility, the interest rate would be bank cost of funds in the relevant currency plus a margin of 1¼ percent p.a. before completion; the margin would decrease to 1 percent p.a. after completion. If, three years after the opening of the Eurotunnel System to regular traffic, conditions do not permit refinancing, the margin would increase to 1¼ percent p.a.

For drawdowns in excess of 80 percent of the Project Loan Facility (i.e., use of the stand-by facility), the interest rate would be bank cost of funds in the relevant currency plus a margin of 1¾ percent p.a. prior to completion; the margin would decrease to 1¼ percent p.a. after completion. If, three years after completion, conditions do not permit refinancing, the margin would increase to 1½ percent p.a.

For drawdowns in excess of 90 percent of the Project Loan Facility, the stand-by margins would increase by a further ⅛ percent p.a.

7. *Security.* All the assets of Eurotunnel, including the Eurotunnel System, the Concession, and the contractors' performance bonds, would be pledged to the lending banks to secure the Project Loan Facility.

8. *Negative Pledges.* Eurotunnel would not be able to conduct any business other than the Eurotunnel Project without bank permission. Eurotunnel would not be able to borrow except under the Project Loan Facility.

9. *Events of Default.* Eurotunnel would be in default under the Project Loan Facility if any of the following events occurred: (1) one of the default cover ratio tests is not met; (2) Eurotunnel System opening is delayed for more than one year; (3) an unremedied breach of Eurotunnel's obligations occurs; or (4) once repayments start, the amounts

outstanding under the Project Loan Facility exceed certain specified amounts.

10. *Default Cover Ratios.* Eurotunnel would not be allowed (1) to make any drawdowns if the ratio of (a) the present value of the projected net cash flow to (b) the bank outstandings is below 1.2; (2) to partially refinance if the ratio is below 1.3; or (3) to pay dividends if the ratio is below 1.25. A decline of the ratio to below 1.00 for 90 days (or more) would constitute an event of default.

11. *Third-Party Loans.* Eurotunnel believed that the European Investment Bank (EIB), an international lending agency of the EEC, would make funds of up to £1 billion available to the Eurotunnel Project on a fixed-rate long-term basis at concessional rates of interest. However, EIB was not prepared to take completion risk. It was therefore anticipated that EIB's advances would be guaranteed by letters of credit drawn under the Project Loan Facility during the construction period and that, following project completion, the letters of credit would be allowed to lapse. In May 1987, EIB committed in principle to lend £1.0 billion to the Eurotunnel Project. It signed the loan agreement in July 1987.

12. *Multicurrency Option.* Although the obligations under the commitments were to be denominated in pounds sterling, French francs, and U.S. dollars (in the amounts indicated above), it was anticipated that the Project Loan Facility would permit borrowings denominated in other currencies at the option of Eurotunnel.

The treaty between the United Kingdom and France was ratified, and the Concession came into force in July 1987. Later that month, the underwriting of the £5.0 billion Project Loan Facility was finalized. The Project Loan Facility was syndicated in September 1987 among 130 banks worldwide.

PROJECT EQUITY FINANCING

The prospectus for Equity Offering III, dated November 16, 1987, outlined the terms under which the international syndicate of underwriters were offering 45.9 percent of the equity of Eurotunnel PLC (EPLC) and Eurotunnel S.A. (ESA) to investors through the issuance of 220 million paired shares with warrants attached (Units). Equity Offering III was intended to raise £770 million of equity to bring the total equity raised for the Eurotunnel Project to £1.023 billion.

Equity Offering II, a private placement consisting of £200 million worth of Eurotunnel paired shares, was launched in October 1986. It had been undersubscribed in the United Kingdom, and demand in the United States had been disappointing. Political and organizational uncertainties, which had led to doubts about whether the Eurotunnel Project would ever be built, were largely responsible. The British subunderwriters had avoided significant losses due to (1) oversubscription in France, Japan, and Germany and (2) the Bank of England's pressuring investment houses in the City of London to subscribe.

Eurotunnel in November 1987

By November 1987, all the significant political and legal impediments to constructing the Eurotunnel System had been removed. The syndication of the £5.0 billion Project Loan Facility was completed in September 1987. But the stock market crash of October 1987 had introduced a new element of uncertainty.

Equity Offering III

Equity Offering III consisted of an initial public offering of the Units. Each Unit included a single share of EPLC (the U.K. company), a single share of ESA (the French company), and one detachable warrant. A holder could exchange 10 warrants plus 230 pence plus 23 French francs at any time between November 15, 1990, and November 15, 1992, to obtain one additional share each in EPLC and ESA. The Units would trade in the public equity markets in London and Paris. Under the articles of association of both companies, the shares of EPLC and ESA were paired and could not be separated.

The Underwriting

Equity Offering III was a fully underwritten offering divided into three tranches: (1) a French tranche, (2) a British tranche, and (3) an international tranche. In December 1986, Eurotunnel awarded jointly to Banque Indosuez and Robert Fleming & Co. the mandate to be lead managers and underwriters of Equity Offering III. The lead managers subsequently expanded the underwriting syndicate to include other leading issuing houses from France and the United Kingdom. In April 1987, the underwriters decided to postpone Equity Offering III until October 1987. In the interim, Eurotunnel signed a £73.5 million equivalent bridge loan (denominated in pounds sterling and French francs), which would be repaid out of the proceeds from Equity Offering III. In November 1987, the underwriters decided that the French tranche should consist of 101 million Units, underwritten at a price of FF35 per Unit; the British tranche should comprise 101 million Units, underwritten at a price of 350p per Unit; and the international tranche should amount to 18 million Units at a price of 175p plus FF17.50 per Unit.

Equity Placements

Both the British tranche and the French tranche were to be placed in accordance with standard equity issuance practices in those countries. In the United Kingdom, the underwriters had preplaced 42 million Units with certain institutional investors, leaving only 59 million Units to be subunderwritten and allocated to bidders. In France, Units would be distributed largely through the banking system on a first-come, first-served basis.

Projected Returns to Equity Investors

Equity investors in Eurotunnel would look primarily to the stream of dividends their shares would provide for the return of and a return on their Eurotunnel equity investments. The life of the Eurotunnel System, from the investors' perspective, would have three distinct phases:[2] (1) the construction period (1987–1992), when equity funds would be invested; (2) the start-up period (1993-1995), when final testing would be conducted, operations would commence, and dividend payments would commence; and (3) the main operating period (from 1995 to the end of the concession period in 2042), when dividends would be paid. Beginning with this latter period, dividends were projected to grow as project debt was amortized and as revenues increased with inflation. Table 14.6 reproduces the dividend projections in the prospectus for Equity Offering III.

In addition to dividends, Eurotunnel offered travel privileges to individual subscribers[3] to Equity Offering III, on the following basis:

Number of Units Purchased	Travel Privileges
100	One round trip to be taken within one year of the opening of the Eurotunnel System.
500	One round trip per year during the first 10 years of operation of the Eurotunnel System.
1,000	Two round trips per year until the end of the concession period.
1,500	An unlimited number of shuttle trips until the end of the concession period.

Market Response to the Offering

In Paris, confidence in Equity Offering III was strong. The mood in London, however, was cautious. Managers of performance-related funds, such as unit trusts and investment trusts, were not enthusiastic because of the 7-year gap between the investment and the initial

TABLE 14.6   Projected Dividends to Eurotunnel Shareholders[a] (Millions of Pounds Sterling Except for Per-Share Amounts)

1993–1998	1993	1994	1995	1996	1997	1998
Turnover	£488	£762	£835	£908	£986	£1,072
Profit before taxation	70	108	199	273	350	422
Profit for the year available for distribution	62	88	158	217	277	328
Dividends: Total	—	149	169	217	277	328
Per paired share	—	£0.39	£0.44	£0.56	£0.71	£0.85

Later Years	2003	2013	2023	2033	2041
Turnover	£1,586	£3,236	£6,184	£11,356	£17,824
Profit before taxation	927	2,410	4,879	9,152	14,453
Profit for the year available for distribution	566	1,476	2,986	5,605	8,880
Dividends: Total	566	1,476	2,986	5,605	8,880
Per paired share	£1.46	£3.80	£7.70	£14.44	£22.88

[a] Assumes the rate of inflation is 4 percent p. a. in 1987, rises to 6 percent p. a. by 1991, and remains at 6 percent p. a. thereafter.

Source: Eurotunnel P.L.C./Eurotunnel S.A., *Offer for Sale of 220,000,000 Units with New Warrants* (November 16, 1987), pp. 54–55.

receipt of dividends. Pension funds were concerned about whether the degree of risk made the investment inappropriate (or worse, illegal) for them.[4] Nevertheless, Equity Offering III was successfully completed.

SENSITIVITY ANALYSIS

Eurotunnel prepared a number of sensitivity analyses in addition to its "best guess" cash flow projections (the "Base Case"). The sensitivity analyses tested the effects on project performance of changes in key variables:

Case	Change in Variable
1	Increasing construction costs and related expenses by 10 percent.
2	Delaying tunnel opening by 6 months and encountering construction and operating cost overruns of £270 million.
3	Reducing revenues by 15 percent each year throughout the concession period.
4	Assuming high-speed Brussels–Paris Eurotunnel railway service is never available.
5	Increasing real interest rates by 2 percent p.a. (i.e., from 8.5 percent to 10.5 percent p.a.).
6	Increasing the rate of inflation, in 1 percent increments, from 5 percent in 1987 to 9 percent in 1991; decreasing it, in 1 percent decrements, to 6 percent in 1994; and keeping it constant at 6 percent p.a. thereafter.
7	Combining cases 2, 3, and 5 into a severe downside case.

Table 14.7 summarizes the results of these sensitivity analyses and compares them with the Base Case.

RECENT DEVELOPMENTS

The Eurotunnel System was originally scheduled to open in May 1993. After a number of delays, due principally to construction cost, equipment delivery, and testing problems, the tunnel was formally opened to freight service May 6, 1994. Regular passenger service began November 14, 1994. It was originally expected to cost £4.8 billion but wound up costing approximately £10.5 billion (equivalent to $16 billion), more than double the original £4.8 billion cost estimate.[5] The

TABLE 14.7 Sensitivity Analysis

Case	Banks' Maximum Exposure (£ billion)	Earliest Final Repayment	First Year's Debt Cover Ratio	Earliest Permitted Refinancing	First Dividends Permitted
Base Case	£4.068	2005	1.29	1996	1995
1	4.654	2005	1.15	2002	1998
2	4.646	2005	1.14	2002	1999
3	4.116	2005	1.10	2004	2001
4	4.058	2005	1.25	1996	1995
5	4.347	2005	1.15	2000	1999
6	4.709	2005	1.26	1996	1996
7	5.193	2008	0.85	none permitted	2008

Source: Eurotunnel P.L.C./Eurotunnel S.A., Offer for Sale of 220,000,000 Units with New Warrants (November 16, 1987), pp. 56–57; and R. C. Smith and I. Walter, "Eurotunnel— Debt," p. 7.

cost overruns led to a protracted dispute between Transmanche Link and Eurotunnel, which delayed construction. It also necessitated a rights issue in 1990 that raised the equivalent of £532 million (net of expenses).[6] The rights issue was underwritten by ten leading issuing houses in France and the United Kingdom.

Compounding Eurotunnel's problems, competition from ferry operators, who cut fares, reduced Eurotunnel's anticipated future revenues, creating a projected cash bind.[7] As the opening day neared, Eurotunnel projected, as of October 1993, that it would not break even until 1998 and that it would soon run out of cash.[8] At the same time, Eurotunnel announced that it would raise an additional £1 billion, half by borrowing from its international consortium of 220 banks and the other half through a second rights offering.[9] The estimated cash need was subsequently raised to between £1.6 billion and £1.8 billion.[10]

Eurotunnel conducted an underwritten rights offering to raise the equivalent of £816 million (net of expenses) in May and June 1994.[11] It was underwritten by Robert Fleming Securities, Banque Indosuez, Banque Nationale de Paris, and Caisse de Dépôts et Consignations. Shareholders could subscribe for three new shares for every five held. At the same time, Eurotunnel arranged a £647 million credit facility.

By summer 1994, a fare war was threatening to erupt.[12] Ferry operators were expected to cut fares sharply. This situation raised concerns that Eurotunnel might have to cut fares as well. Also, further delays in initiating passenger service meant that Eurotunnel would fail to meet the profit projections it had issued at the time of its May 1994 rights issue.[13] The profit shortfalls also threatened to put Eurotunnel in violation of certain covenants in its bank loan agreements.[14] Such violations could preclude Eurotunnel from making any drawdowns under its new line of credit, which could in turn precipitate another cash crisis.

Eurotunnel's situation worsened in 1995. A combination of aggressive airline advertising to promote competition on the London–Paris route, a strike by French train operators just prior to the start of the busy August travel period, and a bruising price war with English ferry operators worsened Eurotunnel's already precarious financial situation. Finally, in September 1995, Eurotunnel unilaterally suspended interest payments on more than £8 billion in bank loans.[15] It recently announced that it hoped to negotiate, by summer 1996, a debt-restructuring agreement that would satisfy both its 225 creditor banks and its 760,000 shareholders.[16]

CONCLUSION

The Eurotunnel Project illustrates the cost overrun risk and economic risk that accompany large, ambitious transportation projects. This is particularly so when there are competing modes of transportation—in this case, ferries—whose operators may reduce fares in order to compete. Like the Euro Disneyland Project discussed in Chapter 13, the Eurotunnel Project's experience highlights the financial problems that high leverage can bring.

In spite of its financial difficulties, as of the date regular passenger service began, the European financial community generally felt that the Eurotunnel Project would continue to operate. However, it recognized that Eurotunnel would require a financial restructuring to reduce its debt burden.[17] Recent events would appear to validate these concerns. Ultimately, the two governments and the creditor banks have so much at stake that the Eurotunnel Project is probably too big—and too visible—to be allowed to fail.

15

Conclusion

Project financing differs, in important respects, from financing a project as an integral part of a firm's asset portfolio. Project financing may be an attractive strategy when (1) the project is large and capable of standing alone as an independent economic unit, (2) the sponsoring company (or companies) is sensitive to the use of its debt capacity to support the project, (3) the sponsoring company (or companies) is sensitive to its risk exposure to the project, and (4) the sponsoring company (or companies) wishes to maintain operating control of the project and is willing to accept the complex contractual arrangements, tight covenants, and close monitoring that project financing entails.

REAPING THE BENEFITS OF PROJECT FINANCING

Under the right circumstances, project financing offers a number of advantages over directly financing a project on a conventional basis. The benefits that are available can be realized only after careful analysis and skillful financial engineering. The organization of the project, its legal structure, and its financing plan must reflect the nature of the project, identifiable project risks, the project's expected profitability, the creditworthiness of the various participants, the requirements for supplemental credit support to backstop the project's debt financing, the availability of project-related tax benefits, the financial positions of the project's sponsors, the needs of the host government, and any other factors that might affect the willingness of prospective lenders or equity investors to provide funds to the project. Project financing arrangements involve a community of interests among several parties. In the final analysis, the prospective economic rewards to each party must be commensurate with the risks each party will have to bear if the project moves forward. Only on that basis can each party's commitment to participate in the project be secured.

Project financing allocates returns and risks more efficiently than conventional financing. Project financing arrangements can be designed to allocate the project-related risks among the parties to the project who are in the best position to bear them (i.e., at lowest cost). Thus, engineering firms can bear the construction risk, raw material suppliers can bear the supply risk, the purchasers of the output can bear the product price risk, and so on.

Project financing can minimize the credit impact on the project sponsor(s). The contractual arrangements that support the project borrowings can be designed to minimize the direct financial commitments from the project's sponsor(s). (The direct financial commitments would be the sole source of credit support if the sponsor(s) financed the project internally.) As the rating agencies have become more sophisticated in their credit assessments, they have come to appreciate the manner in which project financing can draw on the credit support provided by other parties and thereby limit the credit exposure of the project's sponsor(s).

As a result of the credit support provided by other parties, project financing facilitates greater leverage than the project sponsor(s) could prudently manage if the project was financed internally. The higher leverage entails greater financial risk but it leads to greater returns if the project is successful. The higher leverage involves greater interest tax shields, which can enhance the project's value. Alternatively, limited partnership structures and/or leasing can be used to channel these tax benefits to other parties (in return for reduced financing costs).

Most recently, through the financing of hundreds of independent power projects, it has become evident that project financing is suitable for relatively low-risk projects that involve standardized nonproprietary technology. Financing such projects on a project basis can preserve a firm's internally generated cash flow to pursue projects that do involve a proprietary technology or are otherwise information-sensitive. Thus, informational asymmetry costs associated with other growth opportunities available to a firm can enhance the usefulness of project financing. Firms with attractive growth opportunities in areas where proprietary information is being kept secret from competitors will find project financing particularly attractive for their more routine activities, such as electric power cogeneration. Projects based on a proprietary technology are more likely than other projects to lead to supernormal rates of return. Thus, its choice of project financing for routine projects should send a positive signal to the capital market that a firm has valuable growth opportunities.

Project financing involves two other potential benefits. First, it can be used to avoid, or at least minimize, the impact of existing covenant restrictions in the sponsors' current debt agreements. However, the project borrowing arrangements will contain their own set of covenant restrictions. Second, project financing can achieve off-balance-sheet treatment of project debt. However, the accounting profession's expansion of disclosure requirements in recent years is making this particular benefit less and less tangible.

Project financing involves higher transactions costs than conventional financing. Principally, the higher costs are associated with tailoring the project financing arrangements. Monitoring costs are also significantly higher. Consequently, only comparatively large projects will be financed on a project basis; their size permits them to generate sufficient benefits to offset the necessary expenditures.

Despite the higher transactions costs, project financing can reduce the overall cost of capital in the right circumstances. As a result, project financing has attracted growing interest as a means of obtaining capital. Its potential is perhaps greatest for the many large infrastructure capital investment projects that are on the drawing boards in both the less developed and more developed countries. The projects are large and expensive, and the risks are great. But the potential benefits are enormous. Project financing could be the answer.

RECOGNIZING WHEN PROJECT FINANCING CAN BE BENEFICIAL

Given the complex decisions that have to be made in planning the financing of a major project, it is essential that the project sponsor(s) develop a thorough understanding of the proposed project—its risks, estimated investment requirements, and projected returns. Most importantly, the project sponsor(s) need to determine at the outset whether project financing is the most cost-effective method of financing the project.

Project financing has long been used to finance large natural resource projects involving several parties, such as the Trans Alaska Pipeline System (TAPS) Project, a joint venture among ten of the world's largest oil companies. A more recent joint venture, Hibernia Oil Field Partners, was recently announced to finance and develop a major oil field off the coast of Newfoundland.

A large project financing can, by facilitating a large-scale capital project, bring significant public benefits. For example, the Hibernia Oil Field Project will create jobs and provide economic stimulus to a severely depressed region. Its public benefits will begin years before the first drop of oil flows. Furthermore, it can create an environment suitable for development of other nearby oil fields. Because of these public benefits, both the Canadian Federal Government and the Newfoundland Provincial Government are becoming major players as the project moves forward. I expect that project financing will continue to be a pivotal factor, as in the TAPS Project and the Hibernia Oil Field Project, in the development of the world's natural resources.

POTENTIAL FUTURE APPLICATIONS OF PROJECT FINANCING

The number of opportunities to reap the benefits of project financing is likely to increase. Project financing would seem to be well-suited for financing flexible regional industrial facilities (for example, the Bev-Pak beverage container plant) that can make a variety of goods for the local market. Such facilities can achieve significant economies of scale, but only if they can serve the needs of multiple sponsors and operate on a scale that permits these economies to be realized. A significant risk is associated with whether a plant will be able to operate at full capacity. Independent ownership enables entering into arm's-length agreements with multiple firms so that a plant can operate at a profitable level of output and not have to depend on any single firm's success.

Infrastructure projects are, potentially, an even more fruitful area for project financing. Rebuilding the infrastructure in the more developed parts of the world, and building an adequate initial system of infrastructure in the less developed parts of the world, will require hundreds of billions of dollars. Infrastructure has typically been the responsibility of the public sector. But, even in the United States, it has been well-documented that public spending on infrastructure has fallen far short of what is needed to meet the country's infrastructure requirements. Some financial economists have proposed developing public–private partnerships to raise the funds needed to build, own, and operate these projects. Some initial efforts to structure project financings on this basis have been successful. But, in view of the magnitude of the funds needed and the complex risk–return structures, these projects pose a daunting challenge for both public officials and private financiers.

ORGANIZATIONAL (RE)FORM

Project financing involves the choice of an alternative organizational form. It differs significantly from the indefinite-life corporate form. The typical corporation has a portfolio of assets whose returns are not perfectly correlated; its managers enjoy wide discretion over the allocation of free cash flow; and it tends to perpetuate itself by reinvesting free cash flow in new assets and new businesses. A project financing is tied to a specific asset or pool of assets. It can be organized as a corporation, as a partnership, or as a limited liability company. The project entity is finite because it is tied to a finite-life project. Free cash flow is distributed to the equity investors rather than reinvested at the discretion of management. Some financial economists have even argued that project financing has the potential to alter fundamentally the structure of corporate governance. Finite-life organizational forms would be linked to specific facilities. They would pay out their free cash flow to their equity investors. Equity investors, rather than managers, would control the reinvestment of free cash flows generated by these finite-life enterprises. Finite-life organizations are perfectly appropriate for certain types of activities. Project financing, as described in this book, is a useful special form of financing, not a revolution in corporate organization and governance.

FINANCIAL ENGINEERING

Project financing can best be thought of as a form of asset-based financial engineering. It is asset-based because each financing is tailored around a specific asset or a related pool of assets. It involves financial engineering because, in so many cases, the financing structure cannot simply be copied from some other project. Rather, it must be crafted specifically for the project at hand.

This book has noted the many advantages (as well as the disadvantages) of project financing. It has described the circumstances in which project financing might be beneficial to a firm's shareholders, and has emphasized that a project financing must be designed to serve a community of interests among several parties to a project. Consequently, no single rationale can completely explain why firms employ project financing. Clever corporate financial engineers will continue to find new applications of project financing. As the financial environment continues to evolve, project financing will enjoy a prominent place among leading successful financing techniques.

Appendix A

Comparative Terms of
Selected Projects

Summary of Terms of Selected Completion Agreements

	Stingray Pipeline Company	New Zealand Aluminum Smelters Limited	Colonial Pipeline Company
Description of Project	Stingray Pipeline Company ("Stingray") was formed to construct and operate, in the Gulf of Mexico, a pipeline network that would gather and transport natural gas from offshore Louisiana to existing onshore facilities.	New Zealand Aluminum Smelters Limited ("NZAS") was organized to construct, own, and operate a 70,000-tons-per-year aluminum smelter and related casting facilities on the South Island of New Zealand.	Colonial Pipeline Company ("Colonial") was organized to construct and operate a common carrier pipeline with an initial capacity of 800,000 barrels per day. The pipeline would transport petroleum products from Houston, Texas, to Linden, New Jersey.
Obligors under Completion Agreement	Trunkline and Natural are each severally liable for 50% of the obligations under the completion agreement.	Comalco Limited, Showa Denko K.K., and Sumitomo Chemical Company Limited are severally liable for 50%, 25%, and 25%, respectively, of the obligations under the completion agreement.	The stockholders of Colonial (Texaco, Cities Service, Gulf Oil, American Oil, Phillips Petroleum, Sinclair Pipeline, Socony Mobil Oil, Pure Oil, and Continental Oil) are severally liable in their respective ownership percentages for the obligations under the completion agreement.

Definition of Obligation with Respect to:			
Completion	Trunkline and Natural will individually and collectively use their best efforts to ensure that Stingray completes the pipeline network. The facilities must be completed reasonably within the time schedule, and substantially in the same form, as described in Stingray's application to the Federal Power Commission, provided that, in any event, such facilities must be completed and in operation on or before December 31, 1976.	Each obligor will contribute to NZAS its pro rata share of the funds necessary to enable NZAS to complete the construction of the aluminum plant, which must have an annual capacity of not less than 70,000 tons of aluminum.	Colonial agrees to use its best efforts to complete the construction of the pipeline by no later than November 30, 1964.
Cost Overruns	In case Stingray does not have sufficient funds available to cover the full cost of constructing and completing the facilities, Trunkline and Natural will make cash advances or otherwise arrange to provide Stingray with funds sufficient to complete construction. The sponsors may contribute such funds in the form of equity subscriptions or subordinated loans.	See "Completion."	In the event that the funds Colonial raises through the sale of stock and notes are not sufficient to enable Colonial to complete the pipeline, each stockholder is obligated to contribute to Colonial its pro rata share of the funds Colonial requires to complete the pipeline. The sponsors may contribute such funds in the form of subscriptions for additional shares of common stock or subordinated loans.

(Continued)

Summary of Terms of Selected Completion Agreements *(Continued)*

	Stingray Pipeline Company	New Zealand Aluminum Smelters Limited	Colonial Pipeline Company
Debt Repayment	If at any time prior to completion both Trunkline and Natural determine that it is not desirable to complete construction of the pipeline network, then, in lieu of providing funds to Stingray, Trunkline and Natural may retire the project debt in full by purchasing from the bank lenders all notes then outstanding. Trunkline and Natural must repurchase all such notes if: (1) the facilities are not completed and in operation by December 31, 1976, or (2) all governmental approvals necessary to operate the facilities have not been received by December 31, 1976.	None.	None.

Definition of Completion	Completion is defined to occur when Stingray has constructed and placed into operation a pipeline network that will enable it to transport the volumes of gas sufficient to cause Trunkline and Natural to become obligated to pay the charges specified in their transportation contracts with Stingray.	Completion is not defined.	Completion is defined to occur when (1) substantially all segments of the pipeline have been placed in operation and (2) Colonial has been provided with $1,000,000 of working capital.
Circumstances under Which Completion Obligation Is Void	None.	Showa Denko and Sumitomo are relieved of their obligations to contribute funds to NZAS if, after using their best efforts, they fail to obtain any authorizations from Japanese governmental bodies that may be necessary before they can make such contributions. Comalco will, to the extent that Showa Denko or Sumitomo is so relieved, contribute to NZAS all the additional funds needed to complete the project.	None.

325

Summary of Terms of Selected Purchase and Sale Contracts

	Colonial Pipeline Company	Queensland Alumina Limited	Churchill Falls Power Project
Description of Project	Colonial Pipeline Company ("Colonial") was organized to construct and operate a common carrier pipeline with an initial capacity of 800,000 barrels per day. The pipeline would transport petroleum products from Houston, Texas, to Linden, New Jersey.	Queensland Alumina Limited ("QAL") was formed in Queensland, Australia, in 1963, to construct, own, and operate a plant to convert bauxite into alumina. Its initial capacity was 600,000 long tons of alumina per year.	The Churchill Falls Power Project is a large hydroelectric facility developed on the Churchill River in Labrador, Canada, by Churchill Falls Labrador Corporation Limited ("CFLCo"). It has an installed rated capacity of 5,225,000 kilowatts.
Type of Contract	THROUGHPUT AGREEMENT	TOLLING AGREEMENT	TAKE-OR-PAY CONTRACT
Summary of Contract	The "Shippers" (Texaco, Cities Service, Gulf Oil, Phillips Petroleum, Standard Oil of Indiana, Phillips Petroleum, Sinclair Refining, Socony Mobil Oil, Pure Oil, and Continental Oil) are severally obligated over a 30-year period to provide Colonial with sufficient cash to meet all of its obligations either (1) by shipping petroleum products through the pipeline or (2) by making advance cash payments for transportation.	The sponsors (Kaiser Aluminum and Chemical Corporation, Conzinc Riotinto of Australia Ltd., Alcan Aluminum Ltd., and Pechiney Compagnie de Produits Chimiques et Electrometallurgiques) severally agree (1) to have QAL process bauxite into alumina, each according to a fixed percentage of capacity, and (2) to pay, regardless of QAL's inability to deliver alumina, (a) a tolling charge that includes all expenses and charges of any nature incurred by QAL, and (b) if necessary, a standby charge in the event any participant fails to take its designated output. The participants must pay a portion of these charges, in an amount sufficient to cover debt service, directly to the trustee.	Hydro-Quebec agrees (1) to purchase substantially all of the energy generated by CFLCo for an initial period of 40 years with a renewal period of 25 years, (2) to provide, subject to certain restrictions, any additional funds necessary to complete the hydroelectric facility once CFLCo had raised $700 million from investors, (3) to advance sufficient cash to enable CFLCo to meet all its debt service obligations, and (4) to make cash advances as may be required to enable CFLCo to repair or replace physical plant.

Contract Quantity	Each Shipper agrees to ship its percentage of the amount of petroleum products that will be sufficient to enable Colonial, at its published tariff rates, to realize sufficient cash revenue to pay all its cash obligations. Cash obligations are defined to include all expenses (excluding depreciation), obligations, and liabilities, including interest payments, principal repayments, taxes, operating expenses, and expenditures for additions or betterments.	Each participant agrees to take its assigned percentage of the capacity output of the plant, which the project was intended to reach after one year's operation at 75% of capacity. In addition, any participant could request expansion of the plant to a maximum capacity of 1,800,000 long tons per year, subject to an expansion agreement.	Power generation was scheduled to increase during the construction period from slightly over 8 billion kwh per year initially to over 31 billion kwh per year at completion (both quantities measured at the point of delivery to Hydro-Quebec).
Contract Price	The contract price was established by the published tariff rate Colonial filed with the Interstate Commerce Commission.	A tolling charge of $45.92 per long ton, applicable until early in the seventh year of operations, was designed to provide a profit sufficient to permit full utilization of a special Australian investment allowance of approximately $18 million available to QAL. Thereafter, the tolling charge would have to be sufficient to cover the actual costs of QAL. The tolling charges were projected, at time of financing, to average $36.45 per long ton over the first 25 years of operation.	The base rate for power was set equal to 2.7734 mills per kwh for the first 20 years of operation. Thereafter, the base rate would decline according to a fixed schedule over the remaining 20 years. The base rate was subject to adjustment based on the final completion cost of the facility and certain other factors.

(Continued)

327

Summary of Terms of Selected Purchase and Sale Contracts *(Continued)*

	Colonial Pipeline Company	Queensland Alumina Limited	Churchill Falls Power
Term of Contract	30 years from the date of Completion (as defined).	25 years from the December 31 immediately following the Plant Commencement Date (as defined).	The term of the power contract extends to the later of (1) 44 years from the date of initial delivery and (2) 40 years from the expected completion date. The contract is subject to renewal for an additional 25 years.
Buyers' Obligations	The Shippers are required to ship quantities of petroleum products through the pipeline as described above under "Contract Quantity." If for any reason (including Shippers' failure to ship their contract quantities, Colonial's inability to provide transportation, or an event of force majeure) Colonial has insufficient cash available to meet all of its obligations, then each Shipper agrees to advance to Colonial its share of such cash deficiency (as an advance payment for transportation).	Each participant is obligated (1) to take at least 95% of its share of the alumina scheduled to be delivered in each period and (2) to supply its share of the bauxite QAL needs to meet such delivery schedule. QAL will charge each participant the tolling charge for every ton of alumina the participant commits to take in a period and a standby charge for every ton of a participant's share of capacity output the participant does not commit to take in a period. The standby charge for each period is equal to QAL's total cost of production that period less any variable costs that period (primarily, the cost of materials). In every period, each participant must pay directly to the trustee an amount sufficient to cover the interest,	Subject to certain recapture rights granted to CFLCo, Hydro-Quebec is obligated to purchase a specified minimum amount of available power at all times, once CFLCo has completed a fixed period of proven deliveries. This obligation is subject to certain penalties to be awarded Hydro-Quebec against CFLCo in the event of deficiencies in the amount of power CFLCo generates. The purchase obligation does not apply during periods when Hydro-Quebec cannot take power because of an event of force majeure. In addition, Hydro-Quebec is obligated to advance funds, if necessary, for completion, for debt service requirements, or for restoration of plant.

Buyers' Obligations (continued)	principal, trustee's fees, and any other charges QAL owes to the lenders for that period ("Tolling Charge Prepayments"). These payments are netted against the tolling and standby charges the participant owes for that period. Under separate agreements, the participants agreed (1) to complete the project, (2) to supply additional amounts of working capital not otherwise available to QAL, and (3) to supply funds to QAL for capital improvements necessary to maintain the project.	
Effect of Force Majeure on Parties' Obligations	Obligations of Shippers and Colonial remain in effect in all events.	The participants are obligated to pay tolling and standby charges regardless of QAL's inability to deliver alumina, even when such inability is the result of an event of force majeure.	An event of force majeure cannot terminate the power contract. Force majeure is defined to include acts of government, wars, civil disturbances, strikes, floods, fires, sabotages of labor or materials or transport, and other events that are beyond the reasonable control of the parties and that prevent the parties from performing their obligations. The failure of equipment or the improper operation of equipment does not constitute force majeure. Furthermore, the obligations of Hydro-Quebec with respect to completion, debt service, and plant restoration are not relieved by force majeure.

(Continued)

Summary of Terms of Selected Purchase and Sale Contracts *(Continued)*

	Colonial Pipeline Company	Queensland Alumina Limited	Churchill Falls Power
Buyers' Rights upon Seller's Failure to Deliver	Shippers' obligations remain in effect regardless of any failure by Colonial to accept shipments or provide transportation.	Any reduction in QAL's actual deliveries below the committed deliveries in a period correspondingly reduces each participant's tonnage that is subject to tolling charges. However, the difference in tonnage between capacity output and actual deliveries is still subject to standby charges. These standby charges and the Tolling Charge Prepayments are unconditional obligations of the participants that remain in effect in all events.	Hydro-Quebec is entitled to penalties in the event of certain defined deficiencies in power delivery by CFLCo. The penalty is $10 per megawatt of deficiency if the period of deficiency lasts between 30 minutes and 4 hours. It increases according to a specified schedule as the period of deficiency lengthens. If CFLCo, other than in an event of force majeure, is unwilling to operate the plant but the plant is operable, Hydro-Quebec can cause the plant to be operated for the account of CFLCo until CFLCo resumes operating it.
Impact of Buyers' Default	Each Shipper's obligation to advance its share of any cash deficiency to Colonial, as described above under "Buyers' Obligations," also covers cash deficiencies that result from a Shipper's failure to perform its obligations under the throughput agreement.	The obligations of the participants are several. No participant is required to assume the obligations of a defaulting participant. However, if a participant defaults, the remaining participants have the option of assuming the defaulting participant's obligations in order to prevent project default.	No deficiency penalty will be applied to CFLCo if CFLCo is unable to deliver power due to disruptions in the Hydro-Quebec system. In that event, CFLCo will not be assessed any deficiency penalty for the period it takes CFLCo to restore service.

Limitations on Substitution for Buyer	No amendment to the purchase contract can increase or decrease any Shipper's percentage share of obligations under the contract by more than 1½% of the total of such percentages.	A participant cannot assign or transfer its rights and obligations to any other party without the consent of all the other participants, except (1) among subsidiaries of the participant, (2) through a merger into or acquisition by a corporation that assumes all of the obligations of the participant being merged or acquired, or (3) through certain transfers to Comalco Industries Pty Limited (owner of the bauxite reserves supplying QAL).	Hydro-Quebec may assign its rights and obligations to any successor corporation with which it has merged or become amalgamated, or to which it has transferred substantially all its assets as part of a corporate reorganization.
Conditions Governing Contract Effectiveness	The contract is effective when it has been duly executed by all parties.	The contract is effective upon the date of signature by all parties.	The contract is effective when it has been duly executed by both parties.

Appendix B

Other Examples of Project Financings

The projects listed below have been analyzed using a basic set of descriptive characteristics. They illustrate the rich variety of project financing. The projects described are:

- Coso Geothermal Project
- Hamersley Iron Ore Project
- Hibernia Oil Field Project
- Lornex Mining Project
- Paiton Energy Project
- Pembroke Cracking Project
- Pittsburgh Coal Seam Project
- Queensland Alumina Project
- Reserve Mining Project
- Trans Alaska Pipeline System (TAPS) Project

Readers interested in other examples might consult *Directory of Innovative Financing* (1995), which summarizes approximately 50 other recent projects.

Coso Geothermal Project

Sponsors	Caithness Corporation
	California Energy Company, Inc. ("California Energy")
Project Description	The Coso Geothermal Project consists of three geothermal facilities located at the Naval Weapons Center at China Lake, California. Geothermal

energy is extracted from the earth's interior in the form of steam by drilling geothermal wells. The steam is used to generate electricity. All three facilities are "qualified independent power producers" under PURPA. They have an aggregate generating capacity of approximately 240 megawatts. California Energy serves as the managing general partner and operator; it owns a 50 percent interest (approximate) in the project. Electricity deliveries commenced in 1987.

Structure

Each of the three geothermal facilities is owned by a separate partnership. California Energy, the managing general partner of each, is 37-percent-owned by Peter Kiewit Sons, Inc.

Contracts

In December 1979, California Energy entered into a 30-year contract with the United States Navy to explore for, develop, and use the geothermal resource at the China Lake site in return for specified royalty payments. Electricity generated by the Coso facilities is sold to Southern California Edison Company ("SCE") pursuant to three long-term "Standard Offer No. 4" contracts that expire in 24, 30, and 20 years from the date of signing. Under PURPA provisions, SCE is required to purchase electricity from qualifying facilities. The three contracts require SCE to pay for both capacity and energy. Energy payments are fixed under each contract for the first 10 years, except for specified increases. Thereafter, electric power purchase prices are based on SCE's "avoided cost" of generating electricity. Capacity payments are fixed over the life of each contract.

Financing

The three geothermal facilities were financed initially through the sponsors' equity contributions and bank borrowings. In December 1992, the three partnerships refinanced the bank debt with the proceeds from the sale of $560 million of senior secured notes (the "Coso Notes") in a private placement under Rule 144A. The Coso Notes were issued by Funding Corp., a special-purpose corporation owned by the three partnerships and formed for the exclusive purpose of issuing the

Coso Notes. Funding Corp. lent the entire proceeds of the Coso Note issues to the partnerships. The obligations of the partnerships under the Coso Notes are nonrecourse to the project sponsors, although the three loans are cross-collateralized.

Significant Features (1) In December 1992, the three Coso partnerships refinanced their existing bank debt with the proceeds from the sale of the Coso Notes. The Coso Notes were rated investment-grade by both Moody's Investors Service and Standard & Poor's, the first project-related financings to achieve that status.

(2) The December 1992 refinancing was the first pooled project debt financing sold outside the private placement market.

(3) The December 1992 refinancing was also the first project financing arranged in the quasi-public Rule 144A market.

(4) The Coso Notes contain covenants specific to geothermal projects, which are otherwise very similar to the covenants contained in debt issued publicly to finance independent power projects.

Hamersley Iron Ore Project

Sponsors Conzinc Riotinto of Australia Limited ("CRA")

Kaiser Steel Corporation ("Kaiser")

Project Description Hamersley Iron Pty. Limited ("Hamersley") was formed to finance the development of extensive iron ore deposits located in the Hamersley Range in Western Australia. Hamersley secured the mining rights pursuant to an agreement with the State of Western Australia. Hamersley entered into contracts to sell iron ore to seven Japanese steel companies.

History Hamersley was organized in 1965. It is 60-percent-owned by CRA and 40-percent-owned by Kaiser.

Financing A bank loan agreement with nine U.S. banks and three Canadian banks provided up to US$120 million of funds, and the two sponsors provided total equity of US$60 million to finance the development of the mine. A special-purpose finance subsidiary, Hamersley Iron Finance, subsequently funded out this short-term debt in the Australian, International, and U.S. capital markets.

Security

CRA and Kaiser agreed to cause Hamersley to complete the project by a specified date, which entailed the commitment to cause Hamersley by that specified date to be in a position to perform all its obligations under the iron ore agreements in full and in a timely manner. The sponsors also agreed to contribute funds to Hamersley to the extent required to enable Hamersley (1) to pay all additional costs required to complete the project and (2) to pay any penalties specified in the iron ore agreements if Hamersley is unable to commence timely deliveries. Hamersley Holdings Pty. Limited, Hamersley's parent, had to pledge all the common stock of Hamersley to secure the bank loan.

Significant Features

1. The bank loan agreement required the sponsors collectively to contribute US$27.5 million before any borrowings could be made and limited cumulative borrowings to no more than two times the cumulative total of shareholders' investments as of any drawdown date. This restriction, coupled with the other covenants in the loan agreement, protected lenders.

2. Credit support took the form of tight completion undertakings and substantial sponsor equity investments (rather than contractual undertakings by the iron ore purchasers). Economic analysis suggested that Hamersley could support a 2:1 debt-to-equity ratio following project completion.

Hibernia Oil Field Project

Sponsors

Chevron Oil ("Chevron")

Columbia Gas System ("Columbia")

Gulf Canada Resources ("Gulf")
Mobil Oil of Canada ("Mobil")
Petro-Canada

Project Description   Hibernia Oil Field Partners ("Hibernia") was formed in 1988 to develop a major oil field off the coast of Newfoundland, 195 miles southeast of St. John's. Mobil, with a 33 percent share, serves as managing general partner and project operator. The field will cost approximately US$4.1 billion to develop. It is expected to begin production in 1997 and to reach peak production of 135,000 barrels of oil per day before 2000. Reserves total roughly 615 million barrels, enough to support 16 to 20 years of production.

Financing   The Canadian Federal Government will provide C$2.7 billion (equivalent to roughly US$2.23 billion) in grants and loan guarantees. It will pay 25 percent of the construction cost up to a maximum of C$1.04 billion and guarantee up to C$1.66 billion of nonrecourse project loans. In return, it will get 10 percent of the project's profits after all project loans have been repaid. The Newfoundland Provincial Government will forgo most of the sales tax that would otherwise be payable on the purchase of the project's output and will also accept royalty payments at a reduced rate.

Significant Features   1. The project is too large and too risky for any of the partners to undertake prudently on its own.

2. The financial support provided by the Canadian Federal Government and Newfoundland Provincial Government was crucial to launching the project.

Lornex Mining Project

Sponsors   Rio Algom Limited ("Rio Algom")
The Yukon Consolidated Gold Corporation Ltd. ("Yukon")

9 Japanese Smelting and Trading Companies (the "Purchasers")

Project Description

Lornex Mining Corporation Ltd. ("Lornex") was organized to develop and operate a copper-molybdenum mine in British Columbia, Canada. Rio Algom received 53 percent of project equity in return for providing equity financing. Yukon and certain individual investors received approximately 20 percent of project equity in return for providing nominal financing and the mineral properties to be mined by Lornex. Other equity investors purchased 25 percent of project equity for cash, and 2 percent of the equity was conveyed to the Purchasers for entering into purchase contracts. Rio Algom assumed responsibility for construction of the project and also agreed to manage operations following completion.

Financing

A total of US$123.6 million was raised to fund development: $21.2 million from Rio Algom in return for income debentures and equity, $2.4 million from Yukon in return for income debentures and equity, $28.6 million from the Purchasers in return for notes (the "Purchaser Notes") and equity, $7.4 million from the other investors in return for equity, $60.0 million from three Canadian banks in return for a mortgage loan secured by the Lornex mining property, and $4.0 million from the sale of mortgage bonds to finance the construction of employee housing. The repayment of the Purchaser Notes will be made in-kind through deductions from their copper concentrate purchase cash payment obligations.

Security

In addition to the mortgage interest in the Lornex mining property granted in favor of lenders to support the bank loan, security was provided by pledging the purchase contracts with the Purchasers covering Lornex's entire production of copper concentrates through 1984 with the price based primarily on the London Metal Exchange's ("LME") seller's price for wire bars.

Significant Features   1. Lornex was able to achieve greater leverage
than would have otherwise been possible as a
result of financing based on the credit provided by
the contracts with the Purchasers. Accordingly,
Rio Algom, Yukon, and the other equity investors
had to put up less equity than would otherwise
have been required.

2. By indexing the price to be received by Lornex
to the LME seller's price for wirebar copper, the
equity owners would have the benefit of always
knowing that the copper concentrates would be
sold while still achieving the cyclical returns
associated with commodity-based pricing.

Paiton Energy Project

Sponsors   General Electric Power Funding Corporation
("GE")

Mitsui & Company ("Mitsui")

PT Batu Hitam Perkasa ("Batu")

Southern California Edison Company ("SCE")

Project Description   PT Paiton Energy Company ("Paiton") was organized to finance, construct, and own Indonesia's
first large private power project at a cost of
roughly $2.5 billion. The project will be located on
a site 100 kilometers southeast of Surabaya in East
Java. Mission Energy BV, a subsidiary of SCE, led
the project and owned 32.5 percent of it. Mitsui
owned 32.5 percent; GE, 20 percent; and Batu,
the remaining 15 percent. Paiton plans to build
two 660-megawatt coal-fired generators by early
1999. Each will provide 615 megawatts of electricity to PT Perusahaan Listrik Negara ("PLN"),
the state-owned power utility, under a 30-year
electricity purchase agreement. The project's
generating capacity is equivalent to roughly 10
percent of PLN's 1995 generating capacity.

Purchase Agreement   PLN and Paiton entered into a 30-year electricity
purchase agreement in February 1994. The
Indonesian government refused to guarantee

PLN's payment obligations, which delayed the financing.

Financing

Paiton provided $680 million of equity for the project and borrowed $1.62 billion from an international syndicate consisting of eight banks led by the Chase Manhattan Bank and Industrial Bank of Japan. The Export–Import Bank of Japan guaranteed $900 million of the loans. The U.S. Export–Import Bank guaranteed $540 million of loans. The remaining $180 million is not covered by loan guarantees. In addition, the Overseas Private Investment Corporation agreed to directly lend $200 million for construction purposes. The loans were structured to cover four years of construction and 12 years of operation.

Security

The electricity purchase agreement is the primary source of credit support. It was pledged to the lenders, who will also have a mortgage on substantially all the assets of Paiton. The sponsors also provided a completion undertaking.

Significant Features

1. The substantial loan guarantees provided by the export credit agencies were crucial to arranging the financing. To complete the financing, they increased their guarantees above the amounts they had originally planned. Because of the absence of an Indonesian government guarantee, the export credit agencies had to become comfortable with the project's economics before they would enter into their loan guarantee commitments.

2. This was the first independent power project to be financed in Indonesia.

Pembroke Cracking Project

Sponsors

Gulf Oil Corporation ("Gulf")
Texaco Inc. ("Texaco")

Project Description

Pembroke Cracking Company ("Pembroke") was formed to construct, own, and operate a fluid catalytic cracking unit and related facilities in the Pembroke Milford Haven area of Wales, where wholly owned British subsidiaries of Gulf and Texaco had existing refineries.

History

Pembroke was formed as a partnership under the laws of England in 1977. Wholly owned subsidiaries of Gulf and Texaco each owned 50 percent of Pembroke. The subsidiaries' performances were severally guaranteed by Gulf and Texaco.

Financing

Pembroke Capital Company Inc. ("Pembroke Capital"), 50 percent owned by Gulf and 50 percent owned by Texaco, was formed to raise funds secured by Pembroke notes. Pembroke was financed by just $1,000 of partner equity contributions and approximately $900 million of long-term debt issues, including $200 million of 14 percent 10-year notes that Pembroke Capital sold in the U.S. debt market in 1981.

Security

Gulf and Texaco are severally obligated (35 percent Gulf/65 percent Texaco) to advance funds to Pembroke in the form of subordinated loans to the extent required to enable Pembroke to complete construction, or in the event of abandonment, to enable Pembroke to repay fully all project-related borrowings. A throughput agreement severally obligated Gulf and Texaco (35 percent Gulf/ 65 percent Texaco) (1) to process sufficient petroleum feedstocks to enable Pembroke to meet all its expenses and (2) in the event Pembroke has a cash deficiency for any reason, to pay sufficient cash to Pembroke on demand to eliminate the cash deficiency. All such payments would be treated as advance processing payments.

Significant Features

1. The joint venture approach allowed the development of a larger facility (offering economies of scale).

2. A throughput agreement supported by a cash deficiency agreement provided the security for the project financing. As a result of the expected profitability of the project and the strength of the security arrangements, the project was able to be financed with virtually 100 percent debt.

Pittsburgh Coal Seam Project

Sponsors

Hydro-Electric Power Commission of Ontario ("HEPCO")

United States Steel Corporation ("Steel")

Project Description

Steel agreed to develop a coal property, on which it owned the mineral rights, and to deliver 90 million tons of coal to HEPCO. HEPCO agreed to make advance payments for capital facilities and development work, to purchase 90 million tons of coal, and to guarantee unconditionally a leveraged lease for mine machinery, washing facilities, and a loading site.

Purchase Agreement

HEPCO and Steel entered into a coal purchase-and-sale agreement under which HEPCO is obligated to purchase all the coal from the mine (subject to certain limits). The sales price of the coal is calculated to be the sum of (1) the actual costs of production, including amortization of HEPCO's advances and Steel's investments; (2) transportation costs to point of delivery; (3) a "basic price component" of $1.70 per ton, which is indexed to the Consumer Price Index but may never be less than $1.45 per ton; and (4) an incentive fee for improving on estimated costs of production. HEPCO bears the risk of a sales price lower than the contracted price, and also reaps any profits should the actual price received exceed the contracted price.

Financing

HEPCO agreed to advance up to $38 million for capital facilities and development work on the mine. Steel agreed to invest any funds required beyond this amount. HEPCO recovers its advances as an offset against its coal payment obligations. Steel recovers its investments as they are amortized through the coal price.

Leveraged lease financing was arranged for the mine machinery and equipment; total cost was not to exceed $70 million. Morgan Guaranty Trust

("MGT") served as the equity owner, and Prudential, Travelers, and Connecticut General served as lenders. Steel was the lessee.

Security

If the total of HEPCO's advances, Steel's investments, and the value of the leased properties exceeds $118 million, Steel is obligated to furnish all other funds necessary to complete the mine as equity, for which no amortization would be available.

As security for its advances and Steel's coal delivery obligations, HEPCO received a mortgage on the mine properties.

Security for the lease consisted of liens on the equipment and the minerals and the pledge of HEPCO's "absolute and unconditional" guarantee of all amounts due under the lease, regardless of mine completion or delivery. Loans were also secured by pledge of payments under lease. The lessor and the leveraged lease lenders had no recourse to Steel under the lease.

Significant Features

1. The project financing arrangement may be viewed as a form of production payment in which Steel supplied the mineral assets and HEPCO provided the credit support for the financing. This financing structure permitted Steel to realize a significant return on its assets while limiting its financial exposure.

2. Utilization of a leveraged lease effectively reallocated the tax benefits of ownership to a U.S. taxpayer able to utilize them (MGT), thereby significantly reducing overall cost; as a Canadian governmental authority, HEPCO could not have used them.

Queensland Alumina Project

Sponsors

Alcan Aluminum Limited ("Alcan")

Comalco Limited ("Comalco")

Conzinc Riotinto of Australia Limited ("CRA")

Kaiser Aluminum & Chemical Corporation ("Kaiser")

Pechiney Ugine Kuhlmann ("Pechiney")

Project Description   Queensland Alumina Limited ("QAL"), a joint venture, was organized to develop a 500-million-ton bauxite deposit in Australia, and, in connection therewith, to build and operate a plant for the processing of the bauxite into alumina. The alumina plant had a rated capacity of 2 million tons per year, following its third expansion. The alumina was turned over to the various participants for processing in their respective aluminum reduction facilities.

History   Alcan, CRA, Kaiser, and Pechiney organized QAL in 1963 to process bauxite purchased from a Comalco subsidiary. Comalco became a full-fledged member in the QAL project in the late 1960s.

Financing   QAL was financed by sponsor equity contributions, a $133 million private placement, and a series of public offerings of Eurobonds denominated in both U.S. dollars and Deutsche marks aggregating $200 million. Project sold 16 debt issues, some public and the others private, in the Australian, European, and U.S. debt markets.

Security   Tolling contracts between QAL and the sponsors severally and unconditionally obligated the sponsors to pay their proportional share of QAL's debt service obligations. Tolling charge prepayments were made (quarterly) directly to the trustees for the respective debt issues. The lenders also received a mortgage on substantially all of the assets of QAL, and the sponsors provided a completion undertaking.

Significant Features   1. The participation of, and credit support provided by, five project sponsors permitted the development and subsequent expansion of QAL with lower respective capital commitments than would have been required if each sponsor had proceeded alone. The joint venture approach also allowed the development of a larger facility (offering economies of scale).

2. A "hell-or-high-water" tolling contract provided the security for the project financing. As a result of the expected profitability of the project and the strength of the security arrangements, the project was able to be financed with virtually 100 percent debt.

Reserve Mining Project

Sponsors

Armco Inc. ("Armco")

Republic Steel ("Republic")

Project Description

Reserve Mining Company ("Reserve") was formed as a so-called "cost company" to mine taconite, a low-grade iron-bearing material, from the Mesabi Iron Ore Range in Minnesota, and to process the taconite into high-grade iron ore pellets for use as feedstock in steel mills owned by Armco and Republic.

Structure

Reserve was owned equally by Armco and Republic. The two owners received equal amounts of output from Reserve. Reserve transferred iron ore pellets at "cost" to Armco and Republic. In 1977, the IRS revoked Reserve's cost company status. Reserve at that point became taxable as an association. Consequently, in 1979, Reserve commenced selling its pellet production at fair market value to Armco and Republic.

Reserve entered into several long-term leases pursuant to which it paid royalties to the owners of the property, in accordance with the amount of taconite ore removed. The royalties were subject to escalation clauses based on the wholesale price index.

Financing

Since the organization of Reserve in 1939, Armco and Republic have contributed over $50 million to Reserve in the form of subordinated loans and a nominal amount of common equity. The sponsors can recover the subordinated debt solely from the delivery of iron ore, unless Reserve is liquidated.

Security   The senior long-term debt of Reserve was secured by mortgages on the leased mining properties, the mining equipment, the processing facilities, the railroad, and the power plant. In addition, Armco and Republic entered into a cash deficiency agreement and a supplemental cash deficiency agreement pursuant to which each was severally obligated to pay to Reserve (or, in case of an event of default under the senior long-term debt obligations, to the mortgage trustee) 50 percent of any deficiency in the amount of funds Reserve has available to meet its obligations under the senior long-term debt obligations.

Significant Features   1. The joint venture structure enabled the two sponsors to participate in a larger and more efficient operation (due to economies of scale) than either sponsor alone would have been able to develop without significantly increasing its investment.

2. The use of the "cost company" structure permitted the sponsors to avoid intercorporate taxation of dividends.

Trans Alaska Pipeline System (TAPS) Project

Sponsors   Amerada Hess Corporation ("Hess")

Atlantic Richfield Company ("Arco")

British Petroleum Company ("BP")

Chevron Oil ("Chevron")

Exxon Corporation ("Exxon")

Getty Oil Company ("Getty")

Mobil Oil Corporation ("Mobil")

Phillips Petroleum Company ("Phillips")

Standard Oil Company (Ohio)("Sohio")

Union Oil Company ("Unocal")

Project Description	Trans Alaska Pipeline System (TAPS) project involved the construction of an 800-mile pipeline, at a cost of US$7.7 billion, to transport crude oil and natural gas liquids from the North Slope of Alaska to the port of Valdez in southern Alaska. The project commenced in 1969, and the first Alaskan crude oil was shipped via TAPS in the summer of 1977. TAPS involved a greater capital commitment than all the other pipelines previously built in the continental United States combined.
Structure	Hess, Arco, BP, Chevron, Exxon, Getty, Mobil, Phillips, Sohio (now wholly owned by BP), and Unocal owned undivided joint interests in TAPS.
Financing	BP, Exxon, Mobil, and Sohio sold over US$5.6 billion of debt securities to fund their respective portions of project capital cost, including a U.S. private placement in 1975 for Sohio/BP Trans Alaska Pipeline Capital, Inc. that raised US$1.75 billion from 76 lenders, representing the largest public or private financing ever accomplished for a corporate entity up to that point in time.*
Security	Sohio/BP Trans Alaska Pipeline Capital, Inc., pledged, as security for its TAPS-related borrowings, a combination of (1) a portion of BP's and Sohio's oil reserves in the North Slope and (2) a portion of future revenues to be received from the sale of crude oil produced from the North Slope.
Significant Features	1. The joint venture structure permitted the sponsors to finance their respective ownership interests separately, which enabled certain sponsors to achieve the lowest possible cost of debt for their investments in TAPS because of their triple-A credit ratings.
	2. The project is noteworthy because of its huge capital cost and the technical challenges that were caused by the hostile terrain and climate.

---

* Phillips, Groth, and Richards (1979) describe how Sohio financed its share of the project cost.

Appendix C

Legal Investment Requirements Governing New York Life Insurance Companies

To raise long-term debt funds from life insurance companies, it is essential to qualify the project's senior long-term debt as a permitted investment for life insurance companies that are subject to the New York Insurance Law. Section 1405 of Article 14—Investments of the New York Insurance Law sets forth the defining standards for investments that qualify as permitted investments for life insurance companies that are organized under New York law. Insurance companies that are organized under the laws of other states and that conduct an insurance business in New York generally are guided in their investments by the restrictions set forth in Section 1405.

Section 1405 of the New York Insurance Law specifies the following investment restrictions for life insurance companies that are organized under New York law:

> 1. *Governmental obligations.* Debt obligations, not in default, issued, assumed, guaranteed, or insured by (i) the United States of America or by any agency or instrumentality thereof, (ii) any state of the United States of America, (iii) the District of Columbia, (iv) any territory or possession of the United States of America or any other governmental unit in the United States, or (v) any agency or instrumentality of any governmental unit referred to in items (ii), (iii) and (iv) above, provided that, in the case of obligations issued, assumed, guaranteed or insured by any governmental unit referred to in item (iv) above or any agency or instrumentality referred to in item (v) above, such obligations are by law (statutory or otherwise) payable, as to both principal and interest, from taxes levied or by law required to be levied or from adequate special revenues pledged or otherwise appropriated or by law required to be provided for the purpose of such payment, but in no event shall obligations be eligible for investment under this paragraph if payable solely out of special assessments on properties benefitted by local improvements.

2. *Debt obligations and preferred shares of American corporations (or joint-stock associations or business trusts)* (i) Debt obligations, not in default, whether or not secured and with or without recourse, issued, assumed, guaranteed, insured or accepted by such American institutions (or trustees or receivers therefor) and (ii) preferred shares of any such American institution, provided, however, that after giving effect to any such investment in preferred shares of any institution, the aggregate amount of investments in preferred shares of such institution made under this section shall not exceed 2% of the insurer's total admitted assets.

3. *Debt obligations secured by real property or interests therein.* Debt obligations, or participations therein, secured by liens on real property or interests therein located within the United States and not eligible under paragraphs (1) or (2), provided that no insurer making investments under the authority of this section shall invest in or loan upon the security of any one property, under the authority of this paragraph, more than 2% of its total admitted assets.

4. *Real property or interests therein.* Investments in real property or interests therein located in the United States, held directly or evidenced by partnership interests, stock of corporations (including, without limitation, subsidiaries engaged or organized to engage exclusively in the ownership and management of real property or interests therein), trust certificates or other instruments, and acquired (i) as an investment for the production of income or to be improved or developed for such investment purpose, or (ii) for the convenient accommodation of the insurer's business; provided that, after giving effect to any such investment, (I) the aggregate amount of such investments made under this paragraph and then held by such insurer shall not exceed 25% of the insurer's total admitted assets, (II) the aggregate amount of investments made under item (i) of this paragraph and then held by such insurer shall not exceed 20% of the insurer's total admitted assets, and (III) investments held under item (i) above in each property constituting such investment (including improvements thereon) shall not in the aggregate exceed 2% of the insurer's total admitted assets.

5. *Personal property or interests therein.* Investments in personal property or interests therein located or used wholly or in part within the United States, held directly or evidenced by partnership interests, stock of corporations (including, without limitation, subsidiaries engaged or organized to engage exclusively in the ownership and management of personal property or interests therein), trust certificates or other instruments, provided that, after giving effect to any such investment, (i) the aggregate amount of such investments made under this paragraph and then held by such insurer shall not exceed 10% of the insurer's total admitted assets and (ii) investments held under this paragraph in the item of personal property constituting such investment shall not in the aggregate exceed 1% of the insurer's total admitted assets.

6. *Common equity interests.* Investments in common shares, partnership interests, trust certificates or other equity interests (other than preferred shares or equity investments made under paragraphs (4) or (5)) of American corporations (or joint-stock associations or business trusts), provided that, after giving effect to any investment made under this paragraph, (i) the aggregate

amount of investments made under this paragraph in the institution in which such investment is then being made and then held by such insurer shall not exceed 2% of the insurer's total admitted assets and (ii) the aggregate amount of all investments made under this paragraph and then held by such insurer shall not exceed 20% of the insurer's total admitted assets.

Some New York life insurers are willing to purchase unsecured debt obligations of industrial corporations only if they qualify as "legal reserve investments" according to the "earnings test" that previously existed under Section 81(2)(b) of the former New York Insurance Law. That earnings test required that the obligor's ratio of earnings before fixed charges and interest to fixed charges (1) average at least 1.5 times for the preceding five years and (2) amount to at least 1.5 times in either of the two preceding years. In addition, virtually all life insurance companies have a strong aversion to purchasing debt securities from issuers whose debt is not rated NAIC-1 or NAIC-2 by the National Association of Insurance Commissioners ("NAIC"). A debt rating of NAIC-2 corresponds to a debt rating in the lowest investment-grade category (Baa range for Moody's Investors Service, BBB range for Standard & Poor's Corporation, BBB range for Fitch Investors Service, and BBB range for Duff & Phelps Corporation). The NAIC-1 rating corresponds to the higher investment-grade categories of the major debt rating services (AAA through A). As a general rule, an NAIC-2 rating would require a fixed charge coverage ratio greater than the 1.5 times requirement that existed under the earnings test of Section 81(2)(b).

The debt of a project still in its start-up phase normally cannot meet either the earnings test or the debt rating standard. The project's bonds would therefore have to qualify on some other basis. Fixed-income obligations can usually qualify, provided they are adequately secured and have investment qualities and characteristics wherein the speculative elements are not predominant. If the security for the debt instrument consists of contractual obligations in the form of take-or-pay contracts or similar agreements, which are pledged to lenders, and if such assigned obligations are themselves unsecured, then the parties to such agreements must satisfy the standards of an obligor on an unsecured permitted investment in order for project debt to qualify as a permitted investment. For project debt to qualify under Section 1405, the source(s) of credit support must, at all times—from the issuance of the debt until its retirement—be in place and therefore available to satisfy all the project's debt service obligations. When contractual obligations furnish the principal means of credit support, the following requirements must normally be satisfied:

1. Each key contract must be noncancelable by either party, except under specific contractual conditions, with the cancellation provisions designed so as to provide adequate protection for project lenders.

2. The noncancelable contracts require payments sufficient to cover all operating expenses of the project, including debt service, throughout the life of the project's debt obligation(s).
3. The unsecured debt obligations of each obligor under the project contracts must qualify under Section 1405.

Certain requirements of project financings—such as the requirements that the contract securing the debt obligation be payable in all events, including force majeure, and that it produce revenues sufficient to pay all the operating expenses of the project and cover debt service requirements—follow logically from the statutory requirements concerning permitted investments. Similarly, unless creditworthy parties are contractually obligated to repay project debt in the event the sponsors fail to complete the project, the project debt is not adequately secured.

Any requirements to complete the project or to restore it in the event of a serious disruption, on the other hand, probably go beyond the strict legal requirements. Requiring such undertakings may reflect a business judgment by the insurance companies that a revenue-producing facility furnishes stronger security than recourse to the general credit of the contracting parties without the credit support the commitment of project revenue provides. Whether lenders insist on receiving an undertaking to complete the project will depend, to a great extent, on the size of the project debt in relation to the financial strength of the ultimate obligors. In any case, there is no reason to believe that lenders must insist, on purely legal grounds, on completion of a project if it is clear that, pursuant to contractual obligations assigned as security for their investment, creditworthy parties will have to repay project debt in the event the sponsors fail to complete the project.

With regard to projects located outside the United States, with the borrower also located outside the United States, Section 1405 imposes certain limitations on Canadian, foreign (non-Canadian), and otherwise nonqualifying investments. "Qualifying" Canadian investments are limited to 10 percent of total admitted assets. "Qualifying" foreign (other than Canadian) investments are limited to 1 percent of total admitted assets. To qualify, Canadian and other foreign investments must be of substantially the same kinds and grades as qualifying United States investments. Finally, a New York life insurer may invest (1) up to 3 percent of its total admitted assets in foreign securities that fail to qualify under any other provision of Section 1405, provided the investment is guaranteed by an obligor whose debt is rated in one of the two highest rating categories by one of the major United States debt rating services *and* any foreign currency risk is fully hedged; and (2) up to 2 percent of its total admitted assets in other foreign investments. However, Section 1405 also requires that such foreign investments be diversified appropriately.

Bibliography

Beidleman, Carl R., Donna Fletcher, and David Vesbosky, "On Allocating Risk: The Essence of Project Finance," *Sloan Management Review* (Spring 1990), pp. 47–55.

Berger, Allen N., and Gregory F. Udell, "Collateral, Loan Quality, and Bank Risk," *Journal of Monetary Economics*, vol. 25 (January 1990), pp. 21–42.

Berlin, Mitchell, and Jan Loeys, "Bond Covenants and Delegated Monitoring," *Journal of Finance*, vol. 43 (June 1988), pp. 397–412.

Berlin, Mitchell, and Loretta J. Mester, "Debt Covenants and Renegotiation," *Journal of Financial Intermediation*, vol. 2 (June 1992), pp. 95–133.

Blackwell, David W., and David S. Kidwell, "An Investigation of Cost Differences Between Public Sales and Private Placements of Debt," *Journal of Financial Economics*, vol. 22 (December 1988), pp. 253–278.

Boot, Arnoud W. A., Anjan V. Thakor, and Gregory F. Udell, "Secured Lending and Default Risk: Equilibrium Analysis, Policy Implications and Empirical Results," *Economic Journal*, vol. 101 (May 1991), pp. 458–472.

Brickley, James A., Ronald C. Lease, and Clifford W. Smith, Jr., "Ownership Structure and Voting on Antitakeover Amendments," *Journal of Financial Economics*, vol. 20 (January/March 1988), pp. 267–291.

Bruner, Robert F., and Herwig Langohr, "Euro Disneyland S.C.A.: The Project Financing," in Robert F. Bruner, *Case Studies in Finance*, 2nd ed., Burr Ridge, IL: Irwin, 1994, ch. 49.

Carey, Mark S., Stephen D. Prowse, and John D. Rea, "Recent Developments in the Market for Privately Placed Debt," *Federal Reserve Bulletin*, vol. 79 (February 1993), pp. 77–92.

Carey, Mark S., Stephen D. Prowse, John D. Rea, and Gregory Udell, "The Economics of Private Placements: A New Look," *Financial Markets, Institutions & Instruments,* vol. 2 (August 1993a), pp. 1–67.

Carey, Mark S., Stephen D. Prowse, John D. Rea, and Gregory Udell, *The Economics of the Private Placement Market,* Washington, DC: Board of Governors of the Federal Reserve System, December 1993b.

Carr, Josephine, Robert Clow, and Christina Morton, "Weaving the Disney Spell," *International Financial Law Review,* vol. 19 (January 1990), pp. 9–11.

Castle, Grover R., "Project Financing—Guidelines for the Commercial Banker," *Journal of Commercial Bank Lending,* vol. 57 (April 1975), pp. 14–30.

Chan, Yuk-Shee, and George Kanatas, "Asymmetric Valuations and the Role of Collateral in Loan Agreements," *Journal of Money, Credit and Banking,* vol. 17 (February 1985), pp. 84–95.

Chemmanur, Thomas J., and Kose John, "Optimal Incorporation, Structure of Debt Contracts, and Limited-Recourse Project Financing," New York University Working Paper FD-92-60, 1992.

Chen, Andrew H., John W. Kensinger, and John D. Martin, "Project Financing as a Means of Preserving Financial Flexibility," University of Texas Working Paper, 1989.

Chrisney, Martin D., "Innovations in Infrastructure Financing in Latin America," Innovative Financing for Infrastructure Roundtable, Washington, DC: Inter-American Development Bank, October 23, 1995.

Cooper, Kerry, and R. Malcolm Richards, "Investing the Alaskan Project Cash Flows: The Sohio Experience," *Financial Management,* vol. 17 (Summer 1988), pp. 58–70.

Darrow, Peter V., Nicole V.F. Bergman Fong, and J. Paul Forrester, "Financing Infrastructure Projects in the International Capital Markets: The Tribasa Toll Road Trust," *The Financier,* vol. 1 (August 1994), pp. 9–19.

Davis Polk & Wardwell, "Adoption of Rule 144A and Amendments to Rule 144A," in Edward F. Greene et al., eds., *Rule 144A: The Expanded Private Placement Market,* Englewood Cliffs, NJ: Prentice-Hall, 1990.

Diamond, Douglas W., "Monitoring and Reputation: The Choice between Bank Loans and Directly Placed Debt," *Journal of Political Economy,* vol. 99 (August 1991), pp. 689–721.

Directory of Innovative Financing, Washington, DC: Inter-American Development Bank, October 1995.

Duddy, John, "Managing the Risks Inherent in Infrastructure Projects," Innovative Financing for Infrastructure Roundtable, Washington, DC: Inter-American Development Bank, October 23, 1995.

Easterwood, John C., and Palani-Rajan Kadapakkam, "The Role of Private and Public Debt in Corporate Capital Structures," *Financial Management*, vol. 20 (Autumn 1991), pp. 49–57.

El-Gazzar, Samir, Steven Lilien, and Victor Pastena, "The Use of Off-Balance Sheet Financing to Circumvent Financial Covenant Restrictions," *Journal of Accounting, Auditing and Finance*, vol. 4 (Spring 1989), pp. 217–231.

Emery, Douglas R., and John D. Finnerty, *Principles of Finance with Corporate Applications*, St. Paul, MN: West, 1991.

Enron Global Power & Pipelines L.L.C., *Prospectus for 8,700,000 Common Shares* (November 15, 1994).

Euro Disney S.C.A., *Annual Report 1990.*

Euro Disney S.C.A., *Annual Report 1993.*

Euro Disney S.C.A., *Prospectus for Rights Offering of 595,028,994 Shares of Common Stock* (June 17, 1994b).

Euro Disney S.C.A., *Proxy Statement for Extraordinary General Meeting* (June 8, 1994a).

Euro Disneyland S.C.A., *Offer for Sale of 10,691,000 Shares* (October 5, 1989).

Eurotunnel P.L.C./Eurotunnel S.A., *Offer for Sale of 220,000,000 Units with New Warrants* (November 16, 1987).

Eurotunnel P.L.C./Eurotunnel S.A., *Rights Issue of 199,435,068 New Units* (November 1990).

Eurotunnel P.L.C./Eurotunnel S.A., *Rights Issue of 323,884,308 New Units* (May 1994).

Fama, Eugene F., and Michael C. Jensen, "Agency Problems and Residual Claims," *Journal of Law and Economics*, vol. 26 (June 1983), pp. 327–349.

Ferreira, David, "The Public Sector as a Facilitator of Private Infrastructure Investment," Innovative Financing for Infrastructure Roundtable, Washington, DC: Inter-American Development Bank, October 24, 1995.

Figlewski, Stephen, *Hedging with Financial Futures for Institutional Investors*, Cambridge, MA: Ballinger, 1986.

Financing the Future, Report of The Commission to Promote Investment in America's Infrastructure, Washington, DC: U.S. Department of Transportation, February 1993.

Fitch Investors Service, Inc., "Covenants Enhance Private Placements," Corporate Finance Industrials: Special Report, New York: FIS, October 28, 1991.

Forrester, J. Paul, "Terms & Structure of Debt Instruments Issued to Finance Infrastructure Projects," Innovative Financing for Infrastructure Roundtable, Washington, DC: Inter-American Development Bank, October 23, 1995.

Forrester, J. Paul, Jason H. P. Kravitt, and Richard M. Rosenberg, "Securitization of Project Finance Loans and Other Private Sector Infrastructure Loans," *The Financier*, vol. 1 (February 1994), pp. 7–19.

Gimpel, Jean, *The Medieval Machine: The Industrial Revolution of the Middle Ages*, New York: Holt, Rinehart, and Winston, 1976.

Global Project Finance, New York: Standard & Poor's, March 1995.

Hadley, Joseph, "Structuring Equity Investments for Infrastructure Projects," Innovative Financing for Infrastructure Roundtable, Washington, DC: Inter-American Development Bank, October 23, 1995.

Indiantown Cogeneration, L.P./Indiantown Cogeneration Funding Corporation, *Prospectus for $505,000,000 First Mortgage Bonds* (November 9, 1994).

James, Christopher, "Some Evidence on the Uniqueness of Bank Loans," *Journal of Financial Economics*, vol. 19 (December 1987), pp. 217–235.

Jensen, Michael C., "Agency Costs of Free Cash Flow, Corporate Finance and Takeovers," *American Economic Review*, vol. 76 (May 1986a), pp. 323–339.

Jensen, Michael C., "The Takeover Controversy: Analysis and Evidence," *Midland Corporate Finance Journal*, vol. 4 (Summer 1986b), pp. 6–32.

Jensen, Michael C., and William H. Meckling, "Theory of the Firm: Managerial Behavior, Agency Costs and Ownership Structure," *Journal of Financial Economics*, vol. 3 (October 1976), pp. 305–360.

Jensen, Michael C., and Richard S. Ruback, "The Market for Corporate Control: The Scientific Evidence," *Journal of Financial Economics*, vol. 11 (April 1983), pp. 5–50.

John, Teresa A., and Kose John, "Optimality of Project Financing: Theory and Empirical Implications in Finance and Accounting," *Review of Quantitative Finance and Accounting*, vol. 1 (January 1991), pp. 51–74.

Johnston, Russell, and Paul R. Lawrence, "Beyond Vertical Integration—The Rise of the Value-Adding Partnership," *Harvard Business Review*, vol. 88 (July/August 1988), pp. 94–101.

Kapner, Kenneth R., and John F. Marshall, *The Swaps Handbook*, New York: New York Institute of Finance, 1990.

Kensinger, John, and John Martin, "Project Finance: Raising Money the Old-Fashioned Way," *Journal of Applied Corporate Finance,* vol. 3 (Fall 1988), pp. 69–81.

Kwan, Simon, and Willard T. Carleton, "The Structure and Pricing of Private Placement Corporate Loans," University of Arizona Working Paper, February 1993.

Leland, Hayne E., and David H. Pyle, "Informational Asymmetries, Financial Structure, and Financial Intermediation," *Journal of Finance,* vol. 32 (May 1977), pp. 371–387.

Maher, Philip, "Adapt or Die," *Investment Dealers' Digest* (January 3, 1994), pp. 16–20.

Mao, James C. T., "Project Financing: Funding the Future," *Financial Executive* (April 1982), pp. 23–28.

Millman, Gregory J., "Financing the Uncreditworthy: New Financial Structures for LDCs," *Journal of Applied Corporate Finance,* vol. 5 (Winter 1991), pp. 83–89.

Myers, Stewart C., "Determinants of Corporate Borrowing," *Journal of Financial Economics,* vol. 5 (November 1977), pp. 147–175.

Myers, Stewart C., and Nicholas S. Majluf, "Corporate Financing and Investment Decisions When Firms Have Information That Investors Do Not Have," *Journal of Financial Economics,* vol. 13 (June 1984), pp. 187–221.

Nevitt, Peter K., *Project Financing,* London: Euromoney Publications, 5th edition, 1989.

Phillips, Paul D., John C. Groth, and R. Malcolm Richards, "Financing the Alaskan Project: The Experience at Sohio," *Financial Management,* vol. 8 (Autumn 1979), pp. 7–16.

Press, Eric G., and Joseph B. Weintrop, "Accounting-Based Constraints in Public and Private Debt Agreements," *Journal of Accounting and Economics,* vol. 12 (January 1990), pp. 65–95.

Public–Private Partnerships in Transportation Infrastructure, Washington, DC: Price Waterhouse, January 1993.

Ronen, Joshua, and Ashwinpaul C. Sondhi, "Debt Capacity and Financial Contracting: Finance Subsidiaries," *Journal of Accounting, Auditing and Finance,* vol. 4 (Spring 1989), pp. 237–265.

Sandler, Linda, "The Surge in Nonrecourse Financing," *Institutional Investor*, vol. 16 (April 1982), pp. 149–161.

Schipper, Katherine, and Abbie Smith, "A Comparison of Equity Carve-Outs and Seasoned Equity Offerings; Share Price Effects and Corporate Restructuring," *Journal of Financial Economics*, vol. 15 (January/February 1986), pp. 153–186.

Segars, Douglas, and Osman Qureshi, "Infrastructure Finance and Financial Guarantee Insurance," Innovative Financing for Infrastructure Roundtable, Washington, DC: Inter-American Development Bank, October 24, 1995.

Shah, Salman, and Anjan V. Thakor, "Optimal Capital Structure and Project Financing," *Journal of Economic Theory*, vol. 42 (June 1987), pp. 209–243.

Shapiro, Eli, and Charles Wolf, "The Role of Private Placements in Corporate Finance," Cambridge, MA: Harvard University, School of Business Administration, Division of Research, 1972.

Smith, Clifford W., Jr., "Investment Banking and the Capital Acquisition Process," *Journal of Financial Economics*, vol. 15 (January/February 1986), pp. 3–29.

Smith, Clifford W., Jr., and Jerold B. Warner, "On Financial Contracting: An Analysis of Bond Covenants," *Journal of Financial Economics,* vol. 7 (June 1979), pp. 117–161.

Smith, Roy C., and Ingo Walter, "Eurotunnel—Background." Case Study C03/04. New York: New York University, undated.

Smith, Roy C., and Ingo Walter, "Eurotunnel—Debt." Case Study C03. New York: New York University, undated.

Smith, Roy C., and Ingo Walter, "Eurotunnel—Equity." Case Study C04. New York: New York University, undated.

Smith, Roy C., and Ingo Walter, "Project Financing," *Global Financial Services*, New York: Harper & Row, 1990, pp. 191–238.

Smithson, Charles W., Clifford W. Smith, Jr., and D. Sykes Wilford, *Managing Financial Risk*, Burr Ridge, IL: Irwin, 1995.

Stulz, René M., "Managerial Control of Voting Rights; Financing Policies and the Market for Corporate Control," *Journal of Financial Economics*, vol. 20 (January/March 1988), pp. 25–54.

Stulz, René M., and Herb Johnson, "An Analysis of Secured Debt," *Journal of Financial Economics*, vol. 14 (December 1985), pp. 501–521.

Szewczyk, Samuel H., and Raj Varma, "Raising Capital with Private Placements of Debt," *Journal of Financial Research,* vol. 14 (Spring 1991), pp. 1–13.

Tribasa Toll Road Trust 1, *Rule 144A Placement Memorandum for $110,000,000 10½% Notes Due 2011* (November 15, 1993).

Tucker, Alan L., *Financial Futures, Options, & Swaps,* St. Paul, MN: West, 1991.

U.S. Securities and Exchange Commission, "Staff Report on Rule 144A," September 30, 1991.

U.S. Securities and Exchange Commission, "Staff Report on Rule 144A," January 23, 1993.

The Walt Disney Company, *1993 Annual Report.*

Webb, David C., "Long-Term Financial Contracts Can Mitigate the Adverse Selection Problem in Project Financing," *International Economic Review,* vol. 32 (May 1991), pp. 305–320.

Williamson, Oliver E., "Corporate Finance and Corporate Governance," *Journal of Finance,* vol. 43 (July 1988), pp. 567–591.

Wolf, Charles R., "The Demand for Funds in the Public and Private Corporate Bond Markets," *Review of Economics and Statistics,* vol. 56 (February 1974), pp. 23–29.

Worenklein, Jacob J., "Project Financing of Joint Ventures," *Public Utilities Fortnightly,* vol. 108 (December 3, 1981), pp. 39–46.

Wynant, Larry, "Essential Elements of Project Financing," *Harvard Business Review,* vol. 58 (May/June 1980), pp. 165–173.

Zanoni, Ronald A., and Louis A. Martarano, "Project Financing—A Case Study," in Dennis E. Logue, ed., *Handbook of Modern Finance: 1988 Update,* Boston: Warren, Gorham & Lamont, 1988, ch. 27A.

Zinbarg, Edward D., "The Private Placement Loan Agreement," *Financial Analysts Journal,* vol. 31 (July/August 1975), pp. 33–35, 52.

Zwick, Burton, "Yields on Privately Placed Corporate Bonds," *Journal of Finance,* vol. 35 (March 1980), pp. 23–29.

Notes

Chapter 1

1. In some cases, the securities and other borrowings are designed to be serviced and redeemed exclusively out of project cash flow. The project debt is then said to be *nonrecourse* to the project's sponsors. More often, project sponsors provide undertakings that obligate them to supplement the project's cash flow under certain (limited) circumstances. The project debt in that case is said to be *limited recourse*.

2. This example is cited in Gimpel (1976, p. 73). Kensinger and Martin (1988) discuss this example and provide an interesting summary of the history of project financing.

3. Charging interest was strictly prohibited throughout the Christian world around the time of the financing. Because the Frescobaldi was at risk, the loan arrangement did not violate canon law. To this day, financial engineering often involves designing financing mechanisms to cope with "troublesome" regulations.

4. A production payment loan is serviced from the cash flow generated as a particular mineral property (most often, certain specified oil and gas reserves) is developed. The amount of the loan and its amortization schedule are based on the size of the resource deposit and the planned production schedule, respectively.

5. Chen, Kensinger, and Martin (1989) and Kensinger and Martin (1988) discuss this example.

6. There is another important competitive advantage. PepsiCo, for example, would prefer to contract with an independent can manufacturer rather than depend on the excess capacity of a plant that Coca-Cola owns—and vice versa.

7. PURPA requires a specified minimum amount of steam usage apart from electricity generation in order to qualify as a "cogeneration" facility.

8. Such a contract is called a *take-if-offered contract*. Chapter 4 describes the different types of contractual arrangements for project financing.

Chapter 2

1. See Chemmanur and John (1992), Chen, Kensinger, and Martin (1989), John and John (1991), Kensinger and Martin (1988), Nevitt (1989), Shah and Thakor (1987), Wynant (1980), and Zanoni and Martarano (1988).

2. Researchers often say this question involves the issue of "optimal incorporation." However, other legal forms of organization, such as a general partnership or a limited partnership, may prove to be more advantageous in certain circumstances. Chapter 5 discusses the alternative legal structures and the relative advantages and disadvantages of each.

3. One of the projects they considered is the Eurotunnel Project, which I discuss in Chapter 14.

4. Infrastructure projects pose a challenge. For example, a government entity may grant a private company a *concession* to operate a toll road. But the government entity is unlikely to be willing to guarantee a minimum level of road traffic. As discussed in Chapter 12, the terms of the concession—the concession contract—can provide that the concession will be extended if traffic falls below projections. To protect its economic interest, the concessionholder must make sure that any such arrangement is carefully spelled out in the concession contract.

5. In a *spin off*, a firm either sells the shares of a subsidiary to outside investors or distributes the shares as a dividend to its current shareholders.

6. Management's discretion is limited, however. The market for corporate control imposes some discipline. However, large corporations may not be subject to the same degree of discipline as smaller corporations. See Jensen (1986a, b), and Jensen and Ruback (1983).

7. Shareholders can benefit from giving managers discretion when managers are better informed about the project than investors. However, when the assets under management control consist of natural resources, generic production facilities, or some other category that does not require intensive management, the benefits of any added discretion are likely to be outweighed by the increased uncertainty shareholders face as the result of management discretion over reinvestment decisions.

8. Williamson (1988) argues that project financing should enhance the value of ventures that lend themselves to governance by contracts. If the project's operating environment is stable, management discretion just adds to uncertainty. However, in an unstable operating environment, granting managers discretion can avoid the cost of recontracting. Hence, the nature of the project's future operating environment will affect the value of financing on a project basis.

9. Consider an oil and gas exploration project. Project financing can reduce the cost of acquiring and processing information for investors. Geotechnical data concerning oil and gas reserves are difficult to obtain and expensive to analyze. If the project were undertaken within a corporation, investors in all of the company's outstanding securities would find it very difficult to get this information. By isolating the project, however, project sponsors can provide these data to a limited set of investors, sparing all the other security holders the cost of acquiring and processing the information.

10. Hayne Leland and David Pyle first addressed this problem. See Leland and Pyle (1977).

11. There is an important difference in perspective. Shah and Thakor focus on the project being funded. Chen, Kensinger, and Martin focus on the other projects that the project sponsor(s) have under consideration (or might consider in the future).

12. The *asset substitution problem* concerns the incentive shareholders have to pursue high-risk projects—including even some projects that have a negative net present value. This problem is most serious when the firm is very highly leveraged. When debtholders will bear the brunt of the loss if the project fails but shareholders will reap most of the gains if it succeeds, shareholders will have an incentive to pursue high-risk projects. Such projects have the greatest potential for a "good" outcome, which will benefit the shareholders. They also entail the greatest risk of a "bad" outcome (because of the trade-off between risk and return), but when debtholders will bear most of the loss, shareholders will concern themselves primarily with the possibility of the "good" outcome. See Emery and Finnerty (1991, pp. 226–229).

13. The risk that free cash flow, if retained, might be invested in assets not to the equity investors' liking is referred to in finance as the "agency cost of free cash flow."

14. There is an important exception to this statement. If the sponsor is providing a significant degree of credit support for project borrowings, its bankruptcy could impair the project company's ability to service its debt.

15. Cogeneration involves the simultaneous production of two forms of energy, most often electricity and thermal energy (typically in the form of steam or hot water), from the combustion of a fuel, such as natural gas or fuel oil. The traditional form of cogeneration project is designed to meet all the thermal energy requirements of a facility, such as a manufacturing plant, and some portion of the facility's electric power requirements. Any excess electricity is sold to a regulated electric utility company.

Chapter 3

1. "Conversion Is Considered for Faulty Lead Smelter," *Wall Street Journal* (April 30, 1993), p. A2.

2. A detailed discussion of the various risk management vehicles is beyond the scope of this book. Interested readers are referred to Smithson, Smith, and Wilford (1995).

3. *Id.*

4. The holder of a cap contract *does* get the benefit of any decline in interest rates (unless the contract also specifies a floor rate of interest).

5. Forwards, futures, and swaps are available in all major currencies. Contract maturities of several years or longer are possible. Futures do not exist for most other currencies. Forwards or swaps can sometimes be arranged—for example, for emerging market currencies—although even when such contracts are available, maturities seldom can exceed a few months.

6. Duddy (1995) describes other methods for hedging currency risk and explains how they were applied to the Guacolda Power Project in Chile.

7. "Enron Project Is Scrapped by India State," *Wall Street Journal* (August 4, 1995), p. A3, and "Enron Pursues Arbitration in Dispute over Project Canceled by Indian State," *Wall Street Journal* (August 7, 1995), p. A9B.

8. "Enron Project Is Scrapped," *op. cit.*, p. A3. As of October 1995, it appeared hopeful that the project might be revived. However, Enron had to agree to renegotiate the power contract. Enron said that it was willing to match the power tariffs of comparable projects in Maharashtra that were awarded through competitive bidding. "Enron Project Is Reconsidered in India," *New York Times* (October 6, 1995).

9. BPA asserted that it had the legal right to do so under the doctrine of *frustration of purpose*. See Anne Schwimmer, "Project Financings Unravel Despite 'Ironclad' Contracts," *Investment Dealers' Digest* (September 4, 1995), pp. 12–13.

10. Sometimes, the requirements seem extreme. Lenders to the Kilroot Power Project in Northern Ireland insisted on the following covenant. If the power plant workers go on strike, Kilroot's owners must send in new operating personnel—by parachute!

Chapter 4

1. As a second example, a liquefied natural gas (LNG) project might involve (1) a take-or-pay contract for the LNG between the exporting entity and the U.S. buyer; (2) transportation contracts (various forms of charters, possibly of a hell-or-high-water nature) between the shippers and the U.S. buyer; (3) a cost-of-service contract between the LNG receiving terminal and regasification plant and the U.S. buyer; and (4) a cost-of-service contract between the U.S. buyer and its customers (i.e., one or more gas transmission and distribution companies).

2. Recall from Chapter 1 that Local Utility will include the cogeneration facility's electricity output in its base load generating capability. In

addition, Local Utility is an equity investor in the Cogeneration Project. Both factors serve to reduce the perceived risk of interruption.

Chapter 5

1. Fama and Jensen (1983) discuss how agency cost considerations can affect the choice of legal structure.

2. The facility must produce some form of output that can be divided among the sponsors.

3. An unaffiliated corporation can deduct 70% of the dividends it receives from another corporation. Thus, for example, if the corporate income tax rate is 35%, intercorporate dividends are taxed at a 10.5% rate (i.e., 0.3 × 35%). The deduction percentage increases to 80% when the ownership percentage is at least 20% (but is less than the 80% ownership that permits full tax consolidation and a 100% dividends received deduction).

4. Indiantown Cogeneration, L.P./Indiantown Cogeneration Funding Corporation, *Prospectus for $505,000,000 First Mortgage Bonds* (November 9, 1994), p. 13.

5. Individuals and certain closely held corporations are subject to further limitations under the passive activity and at-risk rules.

6. The general partner(s) cannot be "shell corporations," which have little or no assets. What constitutes "adequate capitalization" is not specified in the Internal Revenue Code. Tax counsel often advise that the general partners own in the aggregate at least 5 percent of the partnership's capital.

7. The list of activities that qualify for true partnership taxation includes exploration, development, production, mining, processing, refining, transporting, or marketing any mineral or natural resource. Minerals and natural resources are defined to include fertilizer, timber, and geothermal energy. To be taxed as a partnership, the MLP must derive at least 90 percent of its gross income *every* tax year from these qualifying activities.

8. For a recent example of an MLP that raised funds through a public offering of limited partner interests, see Kaneb Pipe Line Partners, L.P., *Prospectus for 3,500,000 Units* (September 18, 1995). Kaneb Pipe Line Partners owns and operates pipelines that transport refined petroleum products and terminals that store petroleum products and specialty liquids.

9. As of year-end 1995, 48 of the 50 states in the United States and the District of Columbia had enacted some form of limited liability company statute. Legislation was pending in the other two states.

10. Limited partners who participate in the management of the limited partnership, however, bear unlimited liability.

Chapter 6

1. The short-term promissory notes can be structured so as to qualify for one of the exemptions under the Securities Act of 1933. To obtain the

best prevailing rates, these notes must be rated P-1 (Moody's Investors Service) and A-1 (Standard & Poor's Corporation). In order to ensure these ratings, back-up bank credit lines would be required, in addition to the other project security arrangements discussed in this book.

Chapter 7

1. Nonquantified items can be a very important component of a capital investment project. However, such items should be introduced into the evaluation only *after* the direct cash flows have been identified and incorporated. The nonquantified items will then get proper consideration, and potential principal–agent conflicts will be minimized.

2. The gain is taxed at ordinary income tax rates until all prior depreciation deductions have been fully "recaptured." If, as a result of inflation, the asset is sold for more than was initially paid for it, all prior depreciation deductions are recaptured, and the excess above the original purchase price is taxed as a capital gain.

3. Compute the crossover point by finding the discount rate that makes the present value of the cash flow *differences* equal zero. Thus, for this example, the yearly differences are:

Year	0	1	2	3	4	5	6
Cash flow difference	0	50	50	0	−25	−50	−100

Verify that 15.3985 percent will make the present value of this cash flow stream equal zero.

Chapter 8

1. Figure 5.4 illustrates the ownership structure for the Cogeneration Project.

2. Lenders usually require a phase-in of equity investment during the construction period. It is supposed here that the lenders are prepared to fund the full construction cost of the project because they have received an acceptable take-out undertaking by long-term investors.

3. This event is often termed a *reversion*.

4. The reader could interpret the 10 percent rate of interest in Table 8.4 as a fixed rate of interest that had been achieved by entering into a deferred swap agreement. The cost of the agreement would then represent part of the $2 million cost of arranging long-term financing for the Cogeneration Project.

5. Ordinary income is assumed to be taxed at a 40 percent rate in order to allow for both federal and state taxation. For the same reason, capital gain is assumed to be taxed at a 33 percent rate.

6. The after-tax cash flow stream is identical to the cash flow stream in the final-most column of Table 8.5 except that the ($14.19) million would occur at the beginning of construction year − 2 to coincide with the timing of the passive equity investors' investment commitments.

7. Table 8.1 indicates that $16.719 million is spent in construction year − 2 for construction and financing. (Add the amounts for months 1 through 12 in the Total Construction and Financing column in Table 8.1.) Adding $6.2 million of preconstruction costs gives $22.919 million, 12.5 percent of which is $2.865 million. Table 8.1 also indicates that $90.589 million (add the Total Construction and Financing amounts for months 13 through 24) is spent in construction year − 1, 12.5 percent of which is $11.324 million.

Chapter 9

1. Hadley (1995) discusses these issues from a legal perspective.

2. See also *id.*, p. 11.

3. Scudder, Stevens & Clark, Inc., "Scudder Latin American Power," descriptive memorandum, undated. Latin Power also has the authority to invest in senior secured debt, convertible debt, or preferred stock. But the descriptive memorandum states that the fund will invest primarily in common equity. At least one mutual fund has recently raised funds in the public securities market that it will invest in debt and equity securities in the emerging economies. Templeton Emerging Markets Appreciation Fund, Inc., *Prospectus for 4,000,000 Common Shares* (April 29, 1994). The offering raised $60 million.

4. Enron Global Power & Pipelines L.L.C., *Prospectus for 8,700,000 Common Shares* (November 15, 1994), and Tom Pratt, "Warburg Structures Novel LLC for Enron's Foreign Projects," *Investment Dealers' Digest* (November 21, 1994), p. 13. EGP&P actually sold 10 million common shares because the underwriters exercised their *green* shoe option to purchase an additional 1.3 million shares from the company. Another example of a pooled equity vehicle is AES China Generating Company, which raised $200 million to make equity investments in energy projects in China. AES China Generating is approximately 44 percent owned by The AES Corporation, which develops, owns, and operates independent electric power generation facilities.

5. The limited liability company structure is discussed in Chapter 5.

6. A debt rating of no less than Baa 3 (Moody's Investors Service (Moody's)) or BBB− (Standard & Poor's (S&P)).

7. Maturities exceeding 20 years are not unprecedented, although they are rare.

8. The loan syndication process works much like the securities syndication process that investment banks conduct. The loan syndicator *underwrites* the loan by committing to lend the full amount. It then *sells down*

portions of this commitment to other banks. It earns a syndication fee for bearing the risk and cost of syndication.

9. NAIC-2 corresponds to a Duff & Phelps rating of BBB, a Fitch rating of BBB, a Moody's rating of Baa, and a Standard & Poor's rating of BBB.

10. The Standard & Poor's rating system is described in *Global Project Finance* (March 1995), pp. 140–141. S&P has six rating categories: PPR1 is highest and PPR6 lowest. PPR ratings may be modified by a plus or minus sign to indicate relative standing within a particular category.

11. A qualified institutional buyer is a financial institution (e.g., an insurance company or a bank) that invests for its own account (or for the account of other QIBs) and invests on a discretionary basis at least $100 million ($10 million in the case of registered securities dealers) in qualifying securities (generally consisting of money market instruments and publicly traded stocks and bonds). Individuals are not eligible as QIBs. There are roughly 150 reasonably active QIBs in the United States. In 1992, they purchased more than $30 billion of unregistered debt securities, in over 600 transactions.

12. A sale in compliance with Rule 144A must satisfy four basic criteria (Forrester, 1995). Most importantly, the securities can only be *offered for sale to QIBs*.

13. The Sithe/Independence Funding Corporation transaction is of interest because Sithe Energies had worked for several months on structuring the borrowing as a traditional private placement. Sithe Energies turned to the Rule 144A market because it afforded a lower cost of funds. See Maher (1994) for a discussion of the implications of Rule 144A for the traditional private placement market.

14. IFC's debt is rated triple-A, the highest debt rating obtainable.

15. The World Bank, *Annual Report 1992*, p. 60.

16. This investment is described in *IDB Projects*. Washington, DC: Inter-American Development Bank (October 1995), p. iii.

17. *Id.*, p. vii.

Chapter 10

1. *Wall Street Journal* (July 19, 1988), p. 17.

2. See *Financing the Future*, Report of The Commission to Promote Investment in America's Infrastructure, Washington, DC: U.S. Department of Transportation, February 1993.

3. The creation of public–private partnerships usually requires new legislation to eliminate various barriers that exist under prevailing law. Such barriers typically include federal, state, and local laws and regulations, such as those governing procurement procedures, that were not designed to

accommodate private investment in "public" projects. These laws and regulations tend to treat private firms simply as contractors. Consequently, they are not well suited to projects in which the financial and operating responsibilities are shared between the government and private sector or in which these responsibilities are borne solely by the private sector.

4. See *Public–Private Partnerships in Transportation Infrastructure,* Washington, DC: Price Waterhouse, January 1993, p. 4.

5. The AB 680 private toll road projects in California must pay "excess" profits into the State Highway Account. *Id.,* p. 4.

6. *Public–Private Partnerships in Transportation Infrastructure, op. cit.,* pp. 13–18, describes these financing structures in greater detail.

7. *Id.,* p. 13.

8. The previously mentioned toll road in Loudon County, Virginia, is an example. *Id.,* p. 14. The Tribasa Toll Road Project, discussed in Chapter 12, also fits the BOT model. The BOT model has been used to finance independent power projects in the Philippines (Ferreira, 1995) and the M5 motorway in Hungary, among many other projects (*Directory of Innovative Financing,* 1995).

9. The California AB 680 private toll road projects are examples. *Public–Private Partnerships in Transportation Infrastructure, op. cit.,* p. 14. The host government retains legal title in order to ensure government control.

10. This has generally been the case for private toll road projects in the United States. *Id.,* p. 20.

11. Nevertheless, economic regulation may be necessary to prevent the private partner from earning an excessive rate of return. However, the traditional methods of rate-of-return regulation may not be appropriate for certain types of infrastructure projects. Traditional rate-of-return regulation involves regular rate reviews and is best suited for businesses that experience stable and predictable demand for their services. Many public–private partnerships require a different approach because of the tendency for demand to be low in the early years and to pick up in the later years (investors must be allowed to earn higher rates of return in later years, to make up for low returns in earlier years); the higher price elasticity of demand for toll roads and other transportation services (monopoly pricing is less likely and revenues are less certain); the higher required rate of return (equity investors expect a rate of return commensurate with the riskiness of the project, and infrastructure projects tend to be riskier than traditional utility businesses); the uncertainty concerning what is the appropriate rate base (the rate base, which is the sum of the costs on which a rate of return may be earned, may require a new definition because of the mix of public and private funds); and the higher degree of regulatory risk (private investors in relatively high-risk infrastructure projects are unlikely to accept the political risk associated with regular rate reviews). *Id.,* p. 40.

12. The California toll road agreements give the private developers the option (which they plan to exercise) of contracting with the State of California to have the California Highway Patrol police the toll roads just as they would roads that are wholly owned by the state.

13. Alternatively, if sales tax is levied, collection could be deferred until the project is operational.

14. In California, the state will take legal title to the private toll roads once they are completed, in order to convey the state's higher level of tort liability protection to these projects. *Id.*, p. 24.

Chapter 11

1. The corporate co-issuer was used to qualify the issue for investment by financial institutions that are not permitted to invest in debt securities issued by partnerships.

2. Caulkins had effectively committed to purchase sufficient steam to enable the Cogeneration Facility to continue to qualify under PURPA. Specifically, Caulkins committed to a minimum purchase quantity equal to the lesser of (1) 525 million pounds of steam per year and (2) the minimum quantity of steam per year necessary for the Cogeneration Facility to continue to qualify under PURPA.

3. Final completion occurred on December 22, 1995, when the Cogeneration Facility commenced commercial operation.

4. This date could be extended (for not more than five months) because of force majeure.

5. The *weighted average annual interest coverage* was calculated as the total annual cash flow available for debt service divided by the total annual interest expense on the First Mortgage Bonds.

6. The *weighted average annual debt service coverage* was calculated as the total annual cash flow available for debt service divided by the total annual debt service on the First Mortgage Bonds.

7. *Indiantown Project Financing, op. cit.*, p. 14.

8. *Prospectus, op. cit.*, pp. 105–115.

Chapter 12

1. The Dabhol Power Project is discussed in Chapter 3.

2. Chapter 14 discusses the Eurotunnel Project, a high-profile transportation project that turned out to have considerably greater economic risk (as well as completion risk) than its sponsors originally envisioned.

3. Certain features of these financings and the credit support arrangements are summarized in Darrow, Bergman Fong, and Forrester (1994).

4. The terms of the Notes provide that the interest payments the Noteholders receive must be free of withholding taxes. Withholding taxes are not

deducted from the interest payments. Instead, they are paid out of the general account.

5. Darrow, Bergman Fong, and Forrester, *op. cit.,* p. 18.

6. They are protected except to the extent the higher withholding taxes might reduce the cash flow available for debt service.

Chapter 13

1. "Mickey Goes to the Bank," *The Economist* (September 16, 1989), p. 78.

2. "Le Defi Mickey Mouse," *Financial World* (October 17, 1989), pp. 18, 21.

3. Currency is stated in French francs (FF) throughout the study.

4. The profit projections are presented below in Table 13.4.

5. The percentage varies: (1) zero if the cash flow is below 10 percent of the actual cost of Phase IA; (2) 30 percent if the cash flow is between 10 and 15 percent of the cost of Phase IA; (3) 40 percent if the cash flow is between 15 and 20 percent of the cost of Phase IA; and (4) 50 percent if the cash flow is more than 20 percent of the cost of Phase IA. These thresholds increase proportionately if inflation is more than 5 percent per year, and they decrease proportionately if inflation is less than 4 percent per year.

6. Bruner and Langohr (1994, p. 737) estimate that these additional costs raised the price per hectare to approximately FF140,000.

7. At the time, the 20-year French government bond was priced to yield 9.1 percent.

8. By comparison, the VAT rate was 18.6 percent for consumer durables and 33 percent for luxury goods.

9. EDSCA would have to pay between 4 and 7 French francs (measured in 1986 francs) per journey to the extent actual traffic falls below 75 percent of the agreed minimum.

10. The aggregate taxes paid would have to reach FF200 million by 1999 (measured in 1986 francs). This guarantee was designed to compensate Seine-et-Marne for the FF200 million cost of primary and secondary infrastructure it built on account of the project.

11. "Maximising the Mouse," *Management Today* (September 1989), p. 56.

12. *Le Defi Mickey Mouse, op.cit.,* p. 21.

13. *Id.,* p. 21.

14. *Id.,* p. 18.

15. *Id.*

16. This figure was estimated by calculating the difference between revenues from real estate development and expenses from real estate development, and subtracting the incentive fee. The incentive fee is based on

gains from real estate sales and a percentage of cash flow. To be conservative, it was assumed that the entire incentive fee related to real estate activities. Total profit before taxation for the years 1992–1995 combined was projected to be FF3,516 million. Resort and property development revenues net of resort and property development operating expenses and management incentive fees for those four years combined were projected to be FF2,613 million.

17. "Fans Like Euro Disney But Its Parent's Goofs Weigh the Park Down," *The Wall Street Journal* (March 10, 1994), p. A12.

18. *Maximising the Mouse, op. cit.,* p. 56.

19. "Mickey N'est Pas Fini," *Forbes* (February 14, 1994), p. 42.

20. *Id.*

21. Off-season admission prices were cut to the equivalent of $30 (from $38) for adults. *Id.*

22. "Waiting for Dumbo," *The Economist* (May 1, 1993), p. 74.

23. "Montgomery Quits Top Financial Post at Euro Disney," *Wall Street Journal* (August 19, 1994), p. A6.

24. The commitment was limited so as to prevent the investor from owning more than 24 percent of EDSCA's shares. "Saudi to Buy as Much as 24% of Euro Disney," *Wall Street Journal* (June 2, 1994), p. A3, and "Two Big Issues Likely to Face Major Hurdles," *Wall Street Journal*, European edition (June 8, 1994), pp. 9–10.

Chapter 14

1. A French engineer, Albert Mathieu, prepared the plans. See "Eurotunnel Dig is Done," *Wall Street Journal* (December 10, 1993), p. A8.

2. In all three periods, Unit holders would be subject to capital gains or losses upon the sale of their Units.

3. The travel privileges were intended to attract retail investors, especially British residents.

4. An article in the *Financial Times,* on November 7, 1987, remarked that Equity Offering III would be a "remarkable coup" because of the adverse stock market conditions, the huge size of the offering, the uncertainties regarding the construction cost and schedule, the difficulties in projecting future traffic levels, and the time lag between the equity investment and the initial receipt of dividends.

5. "Eurotunnel Passenger Runs Begin," *Wall Street Journal* (November 15, 1994), p. A18.

6. See Eurotunnel Rights Issue, offering circular (November 1990), p. 36.

7. "Eurotunnel Lowers Revenue Forecast, Needs More Funds," *Wall Street Journal* (October 12, 1993), p. A17.

8. *Id.*

9. See Eurotunnel Rights Issue, offering circular (May 1994).

10. "Eurotunnel Shares Fall Further Amid Worries Over Fund-Raising," *Wall Street Journal* (May 24, 1994), p. 7.

11. Eurotunnel Rights Issue (May 1994), *op. cit.,* p. 8. See also "Two Big Issues Likely to Face Major Hurdles," *Wall Street Journal,* European edition (June 8, 1994), p. 9.

12. "Eurotunnel Rejects Report of Imminent Fare Cuts," *Wall Street Journal* (August 22, 1994), p. A5B.

13. "Eurotunnel, Citing Start-Up Delays, Says Revenue to Fall Short of Forecasts," *Wall Street Journal* (October 18, 1994), p. A14. Eurotunnel missed the peak summer season. As a result, revenues for 1994 were expected to be only a quarter of what had been projected.

14. *Id.*

15. "Eurotunnel Suspends Interest Payments," *Wall Street Journal* (September 15, 1995), p. A11.

16. "Eurotunnel Posts Wider Loss for 1995, Says Debt Accord Is Possible by Summer," *Wall Street Journal* (April 23, 1996), p. A18.

17. "Eurotunnel, Citing Start-Up Delays," *op. cit.,* p. A14.

Index